Why

Do

Men

Barbecue?

RICHARD A. SHWEDER

Why
Do
Men
Barbecue?

RECIPES

FOR

CULTURAL

PSYCHOLOGY

Harvard University Press
Cambridge, Massachusetts, and London, England
2003

PRINTED IN THE UNITED STATES OF AMERICA

Library of Congress Cataloging-in-Publication Data
Shweder, Richard A.
    Why do men barbecue? : recipes for cultural psychology / Richard A. Shweder.
      p. cm.
    Includes bibliographical references (p.) and index.
    ISBN 0-674-01057-4 (cloth : alk. paper) — ISBN 0-674-01135-X (paper : alk. paper)
      1. Ethnopsychology. 2. Pluralism (Social sciences). 3. Multiculturalism. I. Title.
GN502 .S59 2003
155.82—dc21   2002038818

I dedicate this book to the many powerful and articulate women of the Hindu temple town of Bhubaneswar in Orissa, India, who showed me that normal family practices and gender relations need not be the same wherever you go, and taught me to be slow to judge others.

I dedicate the book as well to the many powerful and articulate women in my own family—Bonnie Shweder, Elinor Walter, Candy Shweder, Lauren Shweder, Ronni Davir, Robin Shweder, Sylvia Shweder, and others. From all of you I have learned so much—about love, courage, travel, adventure, imaginative and analytic thinking, political critique and, of course, the pleasure of good arguments.

Finally, I offer these essays to all men and women who are romantic pluralists at heart and seek the view from manywheres. This book is for you, who believe that whether you are a girl or a boy one of the really good places to be raised is any place where you learn that there is no single best place to be raised, whether you are a girl or a boy.

Contents

Why

Do

Men

Barbecue?

The knowable world is incomplete if seen from any one point of view, incoherent if seen from all points of view at once, and empty if seen from nowhere in particular. The essays in this book are meant to illustrate and give character to that universal and fundamental truth.

Introduction: Anti-Postculturalism
(Or, The View from Manywheres)

I once had lunch with Margaret Mead at an American Anthropological Association round-table event. The year was 1971. Someone asked her, "Which society is the best place to raise children?" "Not so fast," Mead replied. "It depends if it is a boy or a girl. If a boy I would raise him in England, and send him off to one of those public schools and get him away from his mother. If a girl I would raise her in America, right here, right now in the thick of the women's liberation movement. This is the best time ever for a girl to be alive."

I do not know how Margaret Mead would reply to that same question today, thirty years later. As we enter the twenty-first century, the pictures of reality and ideals for flourishing drawn by the women's movement are neither homogeneous nor unitary, and the very idea of what it means to grow up as an American is hotly contested along religious, racial, and ethnic lines. But I think I know how I would reply: There is no single best place to be raised, whether you are a girl or a boy. But one of the really good places to be raised is any place where you learn that there is no single best place to be raised, whether you are a girl or a boy. I call that place postmodern humanism, or the view from manywheres, and in this collection of essays I try to take you there.

Postmodern humanism is postmodern in at least two ways. First, it is willing to set aside the triumphal modernist's narrative about the ascendancy of the West (the dark ages to enlightenment story) and reconsider the value of premodern and non-Western practices and understandings about the connections among person, society, nature, and divinity. Second, postmodern humanism is suspicious of all totalizing or unitary worldviews and appreciative of variety, diversity, and difference. It is a philosophy of life and a way of thinking based on a single maxim: The knowable world is incomplete if seen from any one point of view, incoherent if seen from all points of view at once, and empty if seen from nowhere in particular. Per this maxim, one should stay on the move, seeking out and engaging alternative points of view. The essays in this book can be read as just so many attempts to give character to that maxim and to the mindset that it is meant to encourage.

For example, one of the greatest divides in cultural sensibilities is over the nature and significance of gender relationships and their implications for family life and the rearing of children. Across that divide—a divergence in tastes and preferences that, given the flow of immigrants from Asia, Africa, and Latin America into Western or Northern liberal democracies in recent decades, has been replicated within the United States and various European nations—we confront each other as alien beings, lacking integrity and value. In the essays in this volume, I try to restore some value and integrity to the alien voices on both sides of the fault line by staying on the move between different cultural realities. Given the nature of things in a postmodern humanistic world, any success I achieve can be only partial.

Nevertheless, in these essays I seek the view from manywheres. I seek to understand the value and integrity of my own cultural world. This is a world in which adolescent boys and girls are strongly encouraged to affiliate (and sometimes even pushed together), and along with puberty come such practices as dating and dancing and kissing games. Later it is humankind instead of mankind, parenting instead of mothering, grownups holding hands in public, and adults, who now come in couples, sleeping together exclusively in the same room and preferably in the same bed. Most especially I seek to understand the value and integrity of those cultural worlds (so alien at first blush to the sensibilities of many First World men and women) that elaborate or develop the symbolism latent in the contrast between male and female. Such cultural worlds take special pride in the difference and separateness of the male and female realms. Along with puberty may come gender initiation and genital modification, gendered secrets, gendered cults, gendered space, purdah, veiling, as well as gendered ways of being ethical, civilized, or dignified. In such cultural worlds the ground on which you walk may be a goddess or an earth mother. Men and women may avoid each other in public spaces. Husband and wife may each have a separate bed or room. Women do not barbecue in such worlds, and men stay out of the kitchen.

After Culture

I am both a cultural anthropologist and a cultural psychologist, so the idea of culture plays a central part in the book. The idea of culture is quite popular these days across the social and public policy sciences—with the possible exception of anthropology, where debates about the viability and usefulness of the concept have been lively and various anticulture or postcultural positions have been quite visible. In this introduction I locate the intellectual posture and heritage of the essays in this book, all of which assume a decidedly procultural stance. I hazard an overview of contemporary views of culture in anthropology. Then I trace the outlines of the revived field called cultural psychology, which focuses on the study of difference and hence is no stranger to controversy.

Within anthropology some critiques of the idea of culture are associated with a fear of "the ethnography of difference" (which is often equated with the ethnography of disparagement) and with the worry that any description of cultural difference sows the seeds of invidious comparison and ethnic conflict, and thus should be disavowed. Other critiques are associated with doubts about the grounds and authority of ethnographic representation. They are linked to a point of view, radically skeptical and self-nullifying at its core, that the idea of culture is a fiction, the goal of objective representation is misguided, and the products of ethnography are largely fabricated in the service of domination. Still other critiques of the idea of culture can be traced to concern about the hubris of "West is Best" thinking and about First World or Northern World claims to cultural superiority. They are best understood as anticolonial acts of resistance to neocolonial or imperial attitudes, as counters to an increasingly popular civilizing project in which the "developed" peoples of the world instruct the "undeveloped" peoples of the world about how to live their lives.

Finally, some critiques are associated with claims about the emergence of a cosmopolitan capitalist economy. Some anticultural or postcultural critics imagine that we already live in a world of individuals without groups in which meanings are detached or abstracted from communities and traded on a free market of ideas. These critics believe that globalization has rendered the very notion of discrete cultures, or of a commitment to one's own culture, obsolete.

Are these reasons for doubting the usefulness of the culture concept persuasive? I think not. The essays collected in this volume are all about cultural psychology and the ethnography of difference. They are about the distinctive mentalities and modes of psychological functioning of members of different communities in Asia, Africa, Europe, and the United States. They are about community-based differences in who sleeps by whom at night. They are about differences in ideals of femininity and masculinity. They are about differences in the life of the emotions. They are about differences in cultural conceptions of mature adulthood and the stages of life. They are about differences in the moral concepts that are brought to bear in decisions about what is right and wrong. They are about differences in the way illness and suffering are explained and alleviated. They are about differences in human conceptions of a "normal" or "abnormal" body.

Some of the essays are provocative. They ask us to re-examine and broaden our own conceptions of what is natural, good, true, beautiful, useful, or real. In some instances they invite us to have a second and closer look at specific cultural practices—for example, parent/child cosleeping, arranged marriage, male and female circumcision—that we may have found curious, puzzling, or even highly distressing. They ask us to be slow to judge others and to be more fully informed before we take a moral stance. They invite us to reject radical relativism and to engage in informed cultural critique, but only after we have achieved a nonethnocentric conception of the moral domain and some knowledge of local ethnographic realities.

Each essay in this book is dedicated to the proposition that the recognition and appreciation of cultural differences is one of the noble, even if hazardous, aims of ethnography in particular and cultural anthropology in general. The idea of culture indeed remains viable in the face of recent postcultural critiques, does not necessarily lead to radical relativism, and is in fact essential for any genuine understanding of the human condition.

The essays are all "anti-postcultural"—they presuppose and illustrate the usefulness and viability of the idea of culture as a tool for social science research. They are dedicated to the proposition that anthropology has a special part to play in the community of disciplines, and that one of its primary roles is to test the limits of pluralism. Pluralism is the idea that things can be different but equal; anthropology contributes to the pluralism project through the close ethnographic examination (and cross-examination) of multiple cultural realities and alternative ways of life. As mentioned above, the foundational truth for such an intellectual enterprise is the maxim that "the knowable world is incomplete if seen from any one point of view, incoherent if seen from all points of view at once, and empty if seen from nowhere in particular." Given the choice between incompleteness, incoherence, and emptiness, this kind of anthropological approach to the study of cultures attempts to overcome incompleteness by staying on the move between different points of view or frames of reference. Its aim is to achieve that view from manywheres.

The substantive and pluralistic vision implicit in the very idea of a view from manywheres can be contrasted with the single-mindedness of the view from only here (the ethnocentric perspective). It can be contrasted with the emptiness and abstractness of the "view from nowhere in particular" (Thomas Nagel's visual metaphor for the ideal of perfect objectivity). It can be contrasted as well with the incoherence, intellectual chaos, and nihilism that arises when one holds firmly to no view at all (the perspective of the radical skeptic). In pursuit of the view from manywheres, anthropologists dedicated to the pluralism project want to know, are there other viable and self-perpetuating cultural realities that might be represented as truly alternative ways of life? Are the understandings and desires cultivated and made manifest in some other way of life the types of understandings and desires that might appeal to rational and morally decent human beings everywhere? Hence, the humanism in postmodern humanism. A common humanity made possible by giving permission to difference and by the recognition that people are not necessarily the same wherever you go.

Kroeber and Kluckholn's Risky Allegation

For an anthropological pluralist, the very best place to look for a viable concept of culture is in the seminal work of the American anthropologists A. L. Kroeber and Clyde Kluckholn. In the introduction to their monumental book *Culture: A Critical Review of Concepts and Definitions,* they declared in 1952: ". . . few intellectuals will challenge the statement that the idea of culture, in the technical anthropological sense, is one of the key notions in contemporary American thought." In that time period, scholars and intellectuals in the United States were confident that the concept of culture was deeply entrenched in the human sciences. Kroeber and Kluckholn even began their famous treatise proclaiming that the idea of culture was comparable in explanatory importance to the idea of gravity in physics, disease in medicine, and evolution in biology. They ended by adducing a unified (albeit ponderous) definition that became the mantra for cultural anthropologists who came of scholarly age in midcentury. "Culture," they wrote:

> consists of patterns, explicit and implicit, of and for behavior acquired and transmitted by symbols, constituting the distinctive achievement of human groups, including their embodiments in artifacts; the essential core of culture consists of traditional (i.e., historically derived

and selected) ideas and especially their attached values; culture systems may, on the one hand, be considered as products of action, on the other hand as conditioning elements of further action. (1952: 357)

Kroeber and Kluckholn were students of intellectual history and brilliant culture theorists, but they were not prophets. Little did they know that during the fifty years following the publication of their book, the idea of culture in its midcentury anthropological sense would be frequently debated, doubted, distrusted, and scorned and that the discipline of cultural anthropology itself would be rethought, remade, recaptured, and reinvented time and time again. They did not foretell the many types of humanists and social scientists (cognitive revolutionaries, structuralists, poststructuralists, sociobiologists, feminists, skeptical postmodernists, postcolonialists, subaltern theorists, globalization theorists) who would associate the concept of culture with a variety of supposed sins, including "essentialism," "primordialism," "representationalism," "monumentalism," "reification," "idealism," "positivism," "functionalism," "determinism," "relativism," "sexism," "racism," "nationalism," "colonialism," "Orientalism," and just plain old-fashioned "stereotyping." (See, for example, Abu-Lughod, 1991; Asad, 1973; Clifford and Marcus, 1986; Denzin, 1996; Fox, 1991; Freeman, 1983; Hymes, 1972; Kuper, 1999; Marcus and Fisher, 1986; Rabinow, 1983; Reyna, 1994; Rosaldo, 1989; Said, 1978; Sangren, 1988; Scheper-Hughes, 1995; Spiro, 1986; Wikan, n.d.).

Nor did Kroeber and Kluckholn anticipate the ironic fate of the concept of culture at the beginning of the twenty-first century. Today culture is once again a key concept in many of the social science and policy disciplines (including law), yet it is viewed with great suspicion in some quarters of cultural anthropology. After being reviled, pummeled, and rejected by one new wave intellectual movement after another, an idea of culture very much like the one recommended by Kroeber and Kluckholn in 1952 remains useful and defensible in social science research and public policy debates. The concept not only survives; it thrives (see, for example, Harrison and Huntington, 2000; Huntington, 1996a; Landes, 1998; Markus and Kitayama, 1991; Minow, 1990; Prentiss and Miller, 1999; Roland, 1996; Shapiro and Kymlicka, 1997; Wierzbicka, 1997). The contemporary discipline of anthropology continues to be a scene for various kinds of anticultural or postcultural critiques. Nevertheless, many anthropologists rehearse and recite some definition of culture and make good use of it in their scholarship (see, for example, D'Andrade, 1996; Dumont, 1970; Geertz, 1973; Hammel, 1990; LeVine et al., 1994; Sahlins, 1995, 1999; Shore, 1996; Shweder, 1991; Shweder and LeVine, 1984). It remains to be seen whether and just how soon the concept regains its former popularity in anthropology. That discipline has been historically identified with studies of culture. Tripling the irony, in recent years some anthropologists have abandoned the idea of culture and subjected it to intense critique under the banner of an intellectual movement known as cultural studies (Denzen, 1996).

The Standard View of Culture in North American Anthropology

Kroeber and Kluckholn's seminal definition of culture—which I shall refer to as the standard view from the perspective of North American cultural anthropology—was cumbersome, in part because it was so inclusive. It called on anthropologists to study not just other people's beliefs (their ideas of what the world is like) but also other people's normative standards (their ideas of what is good and what is right). It called on anthropologists to study not just the explicit "ethnosciences" and doctrinal moral and religious codes of the members of a community but their tacit, implicit, or intuitive understandings as well. It sought a middle course between the Scylla of a purely behavioral definition of culture and the Charybdis of a purely ideational one.

According to the standard view, culture should be defined in such a way as to avoid the hazards of both behaviorism and idealism. On the one hand, Kroeber and Kluckholn suggest, culture is more than just social habits or patterns of behavior that are learned and passed on from generation to generation. On the other hand, it is not just a system of categories, doctrines, propositions, or symbols per se. Thus in the 1952 definition, culture is defined as the ideational side of social action or social practice, and anthropologists are called upon to view cultural analysis as the interpretative study of behavior, although little is said about what particular theory of interpretation should guide the analysis.

Useful definitions deserve to be expressed in elegant terms, and Kroeber and Kluckholn's definition of culture is cumbersome, to say the least. But it is not the only expression of the standard view. The most exquisite and straightforward formulation is Robert Redfield's 1941 definition: "shared understandings made manifest in act and artifact." Another variation, perhaps the most famous definition of culture since the 1950s, is the one proposed by Clifford Geertz (1973: 89). He puts it this way: "the culture concept . . . denotes an historically transmitted pattern of meanings embodied in symbols, a system of inherited conceptions expressed in symbolic form by means of which men communicate, perpetuate, and develop their knowledge about and attitudes towards life." In 1984 Roy D'Andrade, writing very much within the North American anthropological tradition, defined culture this way, as "learned systems of meanings, communicated by means of natural language and other symbol systems, having representational, directive, and affective functions, and capable of creating cultural entities and particular senses of reality" (1984: 116).

The definitions proposed by Kroeber and Kluckhohn, Redfield, Geertz, and D'Andrade call out for specification and clarification. Nevertheless, those definitions are a good reference point for understanding current debates about the values and dangers associated with the very idea of culture. One can summarize the standard view by saying that culture refers to community-specific ideas about what is true, good, beautiful, and efficient. To be cultural, those ideas about truth, goodness, beauty, and efficiency must be socially inherited and customary. To be cultural, those socially inherited and customary ideas must be embodied or enacted meanings; they must be constitutive of (and thereby revealed in) a way of life. Alternatively stated, the standard North American anthropological view of culture refers to what the British philosopher Isaiah Berlin (1976) called "goals, values and pictures of the world" that are made manifest in the speech, laws, and routine practices of some self-monitoring and self-perpetuating group. A cultural account spells out those goals, values, and pictures of the world. A cultural account thus assists us in explaining why the members of a particular cultural community say the things they say and do the things they do to each other with their words and other actions. These goals, values, and pictures of the world or ideas about what is true, good, beautiful, and efficient are sometimes referred to as cultural models (D'Andrade, 1995; Holland and Quinn, 1987; Shore, 1996).

Fault Lines in Contemporary Anthropology

The standard North American anthropological view of culture was synthesized and defined by Kroeber and Kluckhohn before the discipline went through a series of revolutions and movements that fractured the field on the basis of different visions of its mission. Although proposing a map of the current intellectual camps within cultural anthropology may be hazardous, such a map is helpful in understanding the various types of anticultural, postcultural, and procultural positions that have emerged within anthropology over the past fifty years. I see four such camps in the field: identity politics, skeptical postmodernism, neopositivism, and romantic pluralism.

IDENTITY POLITICS

In this camp, anthropology is a platform for moral activism in the battles against racism, sexism, homophobia, and neocolonialism and a forum for identity politics in the fight against exploitation, discrimination, and oppression. Advocates of this conception of anthropology have several concerns about the idea of culture. They argue that culture is an excuse for the maintenance of authoritarian power structures and permits despots and patriarchs around the world to deflect criticism of their practices by saying "that is our custom" or "that is the way we do things" (see Abu-Lughod, 1991; Said, 1978; Scheper-Hughes, 1995; Wikan, n.d.). The claim by liberal First World feminists that "multiculturalism is bad for women" (Okin, 1999) is an expression of this view, which tends to associate culture with the idea of patriarchal domination (Haynes and Prakash, 1991; Raheja and Gold, 1991). This conception of the mission of anthropology is closely allied with a global human rights movement that has a firm sense of what is objectively and universally right and wrong.

However, not all moral activists in anthropology want to dump the idea of culture and some have found ways to put this idea to work in the service of their own political aims. Some who are active in the identity politics movement find the idea of culture politically and strategically convenient in their egalitarian battles on behalf of minority populations who do not live up to the achievement standards of majority populations. They use the idea to mitigate invidious comparisons between groups (for example, in terms of wealth, occupational success, or school performance) by denying that any real differences exist, attributing all differences to a history of oppression or discrimination, or celebrating the differences as "cultural." In the identity politics movement, the term "culture" is displacing the term "race," and it may not be too long before the expression "people of color" is superceded by a new shibboleth, "people of culture."

SKEPTICAL POSTMODERNISM

The second camp conceives of anthropology as a deconstructive discipline and as an arena for skeptical postmodern critiques of all ethnographic representations and so-called objective knowledge (see, for example, Clifford and Markus, 1986; Latour and Woolgar, 1979; Rabinow, 1983; also Culler, 1982; Foucault, 1973; Rosenau, 1992). Advocates of this conception of anthropology call for a deeply skeptical reading of all anthropological representations of others, especially of those accounts that make claims about some primordial, essential, or core cultural identity that members of some group are supposed to share. The skeptical postmodernists raise doubts about the reality and existence of groups. They are critical of all attempts to draw a portrait of others that represents them with any characteristic face. They are suspicious of the very idea of boundaries and borders and loyalties to a tribe or nation. They view the idea of a culture as a fiction, the goal of objective representation as misguided, and the products of ethnography as largely made up, or constructed in the service of domination.

One of the many ironies of contemporary anthropology is that for a while members of these first two camps of anthropology thought they were allies with a common enemy—hegemonic heterosexual First World white males, such as Kroeber, Kluckholn, Redfield, Geertz, and D'Andrade who historically had defined the mission of cultural anthropology. The camps' alliance, however, was short-lived. Identity politics requires a robust notion of identity and group membership. Moral activism requires a strong conviction that some things are objectively wrong. Skeptical postmodernism is intellectually incapable of lending support to either of those metaphysical notions and is readily put to use deconstructing the woman of Women's Studies, the imagined common identity of the ethnic group, and all supposed objective moral foundations for any political cause. If groups and collective identities are so easily dissolved, so too are claims about group rights and affirmative action.

NEOPOSITIVISM

The third camp thinks of anthropology as a pure positive science (see, for example, D'Andrade, 1995; Romney, Weller, and Batchelder, 1986; Sperber, 1985). In this view, anthropology is a value-neutral and nonmoralizing discipline. Positive scientists aim to represent, reliably and validly, the law-like patterns in the world and to develop universal explanatory theories and test specific hypotheses about objectively observable regularities in social and mental life. They want to protect anthropology from the other camps by describing or recording rather than judging, justifying, or condemning other peoples' practices, and by developing scientific standards for evaluating ethnographic evidence. This is a laudable aim, although one that has been contested by skeptical postmodernists. There has been much useful work in neopositivist fields such as cognitive anthropology representing the content, structure, and degree of sharing of cultural models (see, for example, D'Andrade, 1995; Holland and Quinn, 1987; Romney, Weller, and Batchelder, 1986). Nevertheless, the positive scientists in anthropology tend to duck a critical question close to the heart of all great social theorists. Is this particular social order really a moral order? Is this particular social order a way of living that might appeal to a rational and morally decent person; and if not, how can we make it become so?

When it comes to justifying social practices and beliefs or evaluating what is truly desirable or really "good" in social life, the neopositivists are very much like the skeptical postmodernists—both turn radically subjective or relativistic and believe there is no scientific or objective foundation for value judgments. The neopositivists, unlike the skeptical postmodernists, are willing to objectively document what people want and to make claims about the most efficient or adaptive way to get from here to there. Nevertheless, much like the skeptical postmodernists, they do not think it is possible to say whether getting "there" is desirable. Beyond questions of efficiency (no small matter, however), their positive science offers them no intellectual basis for evaluating cultural practices.

ROMANTIC PLURALISM

A fourth camp sees anthropology as a romantic discipline designed to test the limits of pluralism. Here we engage the intellectual agenda lending shape to the essays in this book. Pluralism is the idea that things can be different but equal, and that diversity can be good. It is a measure of some of the tensions within contemporary anthropology that, while the ethnography of difference is viewed with suspicion by some of the anticulturalists, "difference" is the main topic of investigation and interest for romantic pluralists. In contrast to anticulturalists, who worry that describing cultural differences prepares the way for invidious stereotyping, romantic pluralists see the recognition and appreciation of cultural differences as one of the principal goals of ethnography in particular and cultural anthropology in general. Romantic pluralists are quick to distinguish the ethnography of difference from the ethnography of disparagement.

The intellectual inheritance of the romantic tradition most relevant to this camp of anthropology is a conception of culture as an extension of the creative imagination, which is itself imagined to be a distinctive intellectual capacity of human beings (see Geertz, 1973; Sapir, 1963; Sahlins, 1995; Shweder, 1984, 1991). According to romantic pluralists, a genuine culture is a reality-binding product of the human mind that is not dictated by either logic or direct (meaning-free) experience. There is thus plenty of room within the limits of logic and experience for cultural variety, and for the historical creation of different lived conceptions of what it means to be a rational and morally decent human being. According to this view, social and cultural realities are not fully deducible by relying on logic alone. Nor are they simply found by combining direct experience with good logical reasoning. Instead, social and cultural realities are constructed by and for more or less rational agents, with a large assist from the human imagination when logic and direct experience do not suffice to answer fundamental questions about the meaning of things. In other words, most of the time.

According to romantic pluralists, the human creative imagination has the capacity to fill in, and give definition to, a vast discretionary space that stretches in between the necessary truths of formal logic and the uninterpreted evidence of the senses. Advocates of this conception of anthropology are dedicated not only to the project of accurate ethnographic representation, but also to the cognitive and moral defense of different ways of life, frames of reference, and points of view. They write about witchcraft, oracles, and magic (Evans-Pritchard, 1937; Luhrmann, 1989) and about conceptions of the person (Geertz, 1973), of family life, and of gender relations around the world (Menon and Shweder, 1998). They write about the local cultural meaning of rituals of initiation (Kratz 1994) or about non-Western religious traditions, while portraying the ideas and practices of others with respect, as different but equal to our own. This camp thinks of "different but equal" in the sense that the ideas and practices of others are represented as meaningful and imaginative, yet supportable within the broad limits of scientific, practical, and moral reason.

A FIFTH CAMP WITHIN ANTHROPOLOGY? THE RETURN OF CULTURAL DEVELOPMENTALISM AND THE FIRST WORLD'S BURDEN

Increasingly these days, as the world globalizes, the concept of culture (or "cultural capital") is used to explain differences in the economic, social, political, educational, scientific, and moral accomplishments of nations, groups, or peoples. An evolutionary or developmental view of culture has returned to the intellectual scene. Along with it comes the claim that some groups have the wrong goals, the wrong values, the wrong pictures of the world, and the wrong patterns of behavior. As a result, their economies are poor, their governments corrupt, and their people unhealthy, unhappy, and oppressed.

The cultural developmental view was popular at the very beginning of the twentieth century and is associated with the "civilizing project" or the "white man's burden" to uplift those who are ignorant, primitive, pagan, and poor. Quite remarkably, this view is becoming increasingly popular at the beginning of the twenty-first century as well, especially outside anthropology—for example, in economics and political science (Harrison, 1992; Harrison and Huntington, 2000; Landes, 1998). In development economics (for example, at the World Bank), the view that "culture counts" or that "culture matters" is now popular in part because it is a discrete way of telling "underdeveloped" nations (either rightly or wrongly) that the westernization of their cultures is a necessary condition for economic growth. Cultural developmentalists want to convert others to some preferred superior way of living. Their aim is to eliminate or at least minimize the differences between peoples rather than to tolerate or appreciate them as products of the creative imagination.

Relatively few anthropologists would describe themselves as cultural developmentalists. Nevertheless, that stance is more common in anthropology than many admit, especially when the topic concerns gender relations and family life practices, for example, polygamy, purdah, arranged marriage, bride price, female circumcision, and the association of femininity with domesticity and the production of children. Along with the international human rights movement and other groups promoting Western-style globalization, there are anthropologists who now take an interest in other cultures mainly as objects of moral scorn. The up-from-barbarism theme of certain versions of Western liberalism has once again become fashionable on the anthropological scene.

Culture Theory: Some Classic Problems

A detailed description of the core assumptions of each of the camps within cultural anthropology is well worth undertaking but is not possible here. Nevertheless, any introduction to or review of this topic should include at least brief reference to some classic questions that are always addressed (although answered somewhat differently) by the scholars in each of the camps.

THE PROBLEM OF DIFFERENCE OR THE PROBLEM OF THE "OTHER"

The problem of difference—what to make of it and what to do about it—is also called the "problem of the other," although the term "other" is used variously in the anthropological literature. It is sometimes used to connote difference per se, without any initial judgment of relative worth. It is also sometimes used to connote unbridgeable differences or a solipsistic gap between self-knowledge and a mysterious or spectral other whose identity can never be truly inscribed. Finally, it can connote the representation of others as less than or other than human, or as different in ways that condemn them to inferior status or justify their domination. Here I use the term to connote difference per se.

The problem of difference is not just a problem for anthropology. It arises whenever members of different groups (for example, Jesuit missionaries and Native North American Indians; British traders and Hindu Brahmans; Western feminist human rights activists and Islamic fundamentalist women) or members of different social categories (for example, gay men and heterosexual men) encounter each other. These individuals may find the encounter disturbing, strange, or astonishing because of a difference between self and other, and want to know what to make of it and (if they have the power) what to do about it.

In the history of anthropology, the problem of difference mostly concerned differences in the ideas and practices of members of different groups. What should one make of, and what should one do about, such ideas as witchcraft, ancestral spirit attack, reincarnation, or menstrual pollution? How about practices such as animal sacrifice, infanticide, purdah, child betrothal, suttee, or adolescent circumcision? Such encounters between anthropologists and the groups they study are obviously hazardous and fraught with dangers of many kinds, intellectual, ethical, and political. Who represents the other and to which audience and to what end? Who has voice and authority in such encounters? Who ought to have voice?

Confronted with apparent differences between other people's ideas and practices and their own, anthropologists have historically reacted in one of three ways, which are instructive to keep in mind when surveying the fault lines in cultural anthropology today. Some, known as universalists, have sought ways to minimize or erase the appearance of difference or to deny that any significant differences exist, and to treat otherness as an illusion. Some, known as developmentalists, have perceived in the encounter between cultures a story about a civilizing process. They have argued that the more evolved and progressive cultures (those that are enlightened, scientific, ethical, and rational) bear the white man's burden of lifting others up out of ignorance and superstition. Developed cultures, they suggest, have an obligation to intervene if necessary to bring a halt to the monstrous or barbaric practices of other lands. Still other anthropologists, known as pluralists, have argued that cultures can be different but equal, and they have cautioned against cultural imperialism, suggesting that one's own local cultural evaluations should not be confused with Universal Scientific, Practical, or Moral Reason.

GLOBALIZATION

The narrowest definition of globalization refers to the linking of the world's economies (for example, free trade across borders) with the aim of promoting aggregate wealth and economic growth. Yet the definition readily expands to include the free flow of capital and labor. A new cosmopolitan economic order is imagined, which consists entirely of global economic organizations such as the International Monetary Fund and the World Bank, multinational corporations, and multicultural states with open borders. According to this rather utopian vision of a borderless capitalism, goods, capital, and labor ought to be freely marketed on a worldwide scale for the sake of global prosperity. For those who adopt such a perspective, any desire for a homeland or an identity based on religion, ethnicity, race, or tribe with associated restrictions on residence and trade is viewed as illiberal and disparaged as a form of retrograde or irrational apartheid or ethnonationalism.

There is an even more expansive idea of globalization. Here the concept is extended to reach beyond just the removal of all barriers to trade, foreign investment, and the opening of borders to migrant labor. The idea is linked to demands for "structural adjustments" of lagging economies and for moral adjustments of lagging cultural traditions as well. The structural adjustments usually begin with the firing of an overemployed civil service and the reorganization of economic life to reduce imports and increase exports (in many countries this means cultural tourism, because there is little else to export)—all with the aim of accumulating foreign exchange. There may also be structural adjustments in the direction of Western ways of running banks, enforcing contracts, paying off debts, and settling disputes. "Transparency" and the elimination of "corruption" are key objectives in this structural adjustment process. Ultimately the idea is to model a political economy (including legal institutions) on the example of the United States. Such adjustments may be entered into voluntarily to encourage foreign investment or they may be mandated (such as by the World Bank) as necessary conditions for securing low-interest loans.

The most expansive idea of globalization equates the term with

Westernization (which is, in turn, equated with being modern). In this fully expanded form, the idea of globalization becomes an hypothesis about human nature and an imperial call for enlightened moral interventions into other ways of life in order to free them of their supposed barbarisms, superstitions, and irrationalities. This globalization hypothesis makes three related claims: (1) that Western-like aspirations, tastes, and ideas are objectively the best in the world; (2) that Western-like aspirations, tastes, and ideas will be fired up or freed up by economic globalization; and (3) that the world ought to become Westernized. Western-like aspirations include the desire for liberal democracy, free enterprise, private property, autonomy, individualism, equality, and the protection of natural or universal rights (the contemporary human rights movement is in many ways an extension of an expansive globalization movement). Another such aspiration is the notion that all social distinctions based on collective identities (such as ethnicity, religion, and gender) should be viewed as invidious. Yet another is the notion that individuals should transcend their tradition-bound commitments and experience the quality of their lives solely in secular and ecumenical terms, for example, as measured by wealth, health, or years of life.

The true connection between globalization narrowly conceived (free trade) and globalization expansively conceived (Western values, culture, and institutions taking over the world) has yet to be firmly established. Nevertheless, the picture of a cosmopolitan world of individuals without groups, in which meanings are detached or abstracted from communities and traded on a free market of ideas, has influenced the thinking of some anticulture and postcultural theorists. Whether that picture is realistic remains to be seen.

It is quite possible that other cultures do not need to become just like the United States to benefit from participation in an emergent global economy. Modern technologies (for example, television, cell phones, computers, weapons) and economic institutions such as private property seem to have effectively served many interests, including the interests of communitarians and religious fundamentalists all over the world. It is quite possible that a genuinely successful global political economy will not emerge, or will fail to sustain itself, or that efforts to globalize values and culture will be effectively resisted (in some cases, for very good reasons), or that the world will go to war. That is how the last big push to globalize the world came to an end, with World War I. Nevertheless, the idea that the rich nations of North America and Northern Europe have an obligation to use their economic and military power to civilize and develop the world is no less popular today than it was 100 years ago when the empire was British rather than American.

CULTURE: POPULAR OBJECTIONS AND COMMON MISATTRIBUTIONS

There have been many critiques of the idea of culture since the publication of Kroeber and Kluckhorn's *Culture: A Critical Review of Concepts and Definitions* in 1952. Some of these critiques are associated with a fear of the ethnography of difference, some with doubts about the grounds and authority of ethnographic representation, some with nervousness about the return of a universal civilizing project controlled by the First World, and some with exuberant or even utopian claims about the emergence of a cosmopolitan capitalist economy. Many reasons have been advanced for doubting the usefulness of the culture concept. But are they persuasive or decisive reasons? Those who continue to embrace some version of the Kroeber and Kluckhorn definition of culture tend to believe that their idea of culture does not carry the implications that are the supposed grounds for various anticultural or postcultural critiques.

For example, the Kroeber and Kluckholn definition of culture does not really imply that whatever is, is okay. Valid social criticism and questions of moral justification are not ruled out by the standard view of culture. Nothing in the Kroeber and Kluckhohn formulation suggests that the things that other peoples desire are in fact truly desirable or that the things that other peoples think are of value are actually of value. Consensus does not add up to moral truth. In other words, a definition of culture per se is not a theory of the good. From a moral point of view, one need not throw out the idea of culture just because a tyrant puts the word "culture" to some misuse or because some ethnic groups enter into geopolitical conflict.

The idea of culture also does not imply passive acceptance of received practice or a lack of agency, a common claim among anticulture theorists. Indeed, many proculture theorists find it astonishing to see the idea of agency or intentionality used as a synonym for resistance to culture in the discourse of anticulture theorists. Even fully rational, fully empowered, fully agentic human beings discover that membership in some particular tradition of meanings and values is an essential condition for personal identity and individual happiness. Human beings who are liberationists are no more agentic than fundamentalists, and neither stands outside some tradition of meaning and value.

The idea of culture also does not imply the absence of debate, contestation, or dispute among members of a group. Nor does it imply the existence of within-group homogeneity in knowledge, belief, or practice. "Natives are not all of the same opinion any more than we are; and some are better informed than others," wrote E. E.

Evans-Pritchard in his classic ethnography on *Witchcraft, Oracles and Magic among the Azande,* first published in the 1930s (Evans-Pritchard 1976: 247). Every cultural system has experts and novices; one does not stop being a member of a common culture just because cultural knowledge is distributed and someone knows much more than you do about how to conduct a funeral, apply for a mortgage, or consult an oracle. One does not stop being a member of a common culture just because there are factions in the community. The claim that there are between-group cultural differences never has implied the absence of within-group differentiation or that there is no variation around the mean. The idea of culture does not imply that every item of culture is in the possession or consciousness of every member of that culture.

The idea of culture merely directs our attention to those ideas about what is true, good, beautiful, and efficient that are acquired by virtue of membership in some group. Members of a cultural community take an interest in each other's ideas about what is true, good, beautiful, and efficient because those ideas (and related practices) have a bearing on the perpetuation of their way of life, and what they share is that collective inheritance. Because the standard view does not assume that a culture is a well bounded, fixed, and homogeneous block, the critique of the concept of culture that starts with the observation of internal variation and ends "therefore there is no cultural system" should have been a nonstarter.

Nor does the idea of culture imply that other kinds of peoples are "other," in the sense of being less than human or possessing qualities that entitle us to intervene in their way of life. We live in a multicultural world consisting (as Joseph Raz has put it) "of groups and communities with diverse practices and beliefs, including groups whose beliefs are inconsistent with one another." There are many new and creative cultural forms that emerge in multicultural contexts and the study of cultural hybridity has re-emerged as a significant area of research globally and locally.

Nevertheless, the aspirations (1) not to lose your cultural identity, (2) not to assimilate to mainstream pressures, (3) not to be scattered throughout the city, country, or world, (4) not to glorify the Diaspora, and (5) not to join the highly individualistic and migratory multinational, multiracial but (in many ways) monocultural cosmopolitan elite are real and legitimate aspirations, and those aspirations cannot be properly understood by treating them as illusions. They are certainly not the only legitimate aspirations in a multicultural world; there is much that can be said in favor of a liberal cosmopolitan life. But they are legitimate aspirations. Even in a "global world," cultural communities and ethnic groups are not going to disappear. We cannot avoid the question, what form does and should multiculturalism take in our emerging postmodern society (see Daedalus, 2000)? Perhaps that is one reason that so many social scientists and public policy analysts look to anthropology for a useful concept of culture, not for no concept of culture at all.

CULTURE AND PSYCHE MAKING EACH OTHER UP

The essays in this book not only presuppose the viability of the idea of culture but also put a pluralistic conception of culture to work to understand variations in human mentalities across social groups. Much of the psychological nature of human beings is neither homogeneous nor fixed across time and space. Therefore the tenet of *psychological* pluralism as well as cultural pluralism lies at the heart of cultural psychology. This tenet states that the study of normal psychology is the study of multiple psychologies and not the study of a uniform psychology for all peoples of the world. Research findings in cultural psychology thus raise provocative questions about the integrity and value of alternative forms of subjectivity across cultural communities.

Cultural Psychology: What Is It?

To adequately locate the essays in this book in their proper intellectual contexts, I must say more about cultural psychology, as a subject matter and as an academic enterprise. A major aim of the discipline is to document variations in modes of (and ideals for) normal psychological functioning across cultural communities. Cultural psychology assumes nonuniformity of mentalities across time and space. The discipline seeks to document the protean cultural aspects of human psychological nature. It can be defined as the study of the distinctive mentalities of particular peoples such as Balinese Hindus, Satmar Hasidim, Chinese Mandarins (see Geertz, 1973; Greenfield and Cocking, 1994; Markus, Kitayama, and Heiman, 1996; Miller, 1997; Shweder, 1991; Shweder and LeVine, 1984; Shweder et al., 1998).

Cultural psychology can thus be distinguished from general psychology, which is the study of mental structures and processes that are so widely distributed as to characterize the normal psychological functioning of all human beings (and perhaps even nonhuman primates as well). Research in cultural psychology has, for example, systematically corroborated the special status accorded to the defense of female honor in the mentality of many southern American white males (Nisbett and Cohen, 1995). Research in cultural psychology has recognized the sense of empowerment and feeling of virtue associated with modesty and the attitude of respectful restraint in the psychology of women in some regions of the contemporary non-Western world (Menon and Shweder, 1998). Such feelings of power and goodness associated with modesty contrast with ideas about (and ideals for) psychological functioning constructed in the contemporary Anglo-American cultural region.

Cultural psychology also assumes that many mental states (and some mental processes) are best understood as by-products of the never-ending attempt of particular groups of people to understand themselves and to make manifest their self-understandings through social practices (Bruner, 1990, Geertz, 1973; Wierzbicka, 1993, 1999). That might be called the premise of self-reflexive social construction. Whether studying Inuit Eskimos or Anglo-American middle-class urban liberals, cultural psychologists try to spell out the implicit meanings (the goals, values, and pictures of the world) that give shape to psychological processes (Briggs, 1970; White and Kirkpatrick, 1985). They examine the patchy or uneven distribution of those meanings on a global scale and investigate the manner of their social acquisition—for example, by means of participation in the symbolic practices, including linguistic practices, of a tradition-sensitive cultural group. Hence comes the need for a concept of culture not unlike the one defined by Kroeber and Kluckhohn, Redfield, Geertz, and D'Andrade.

OTHERS' MENTAL STATES

Cultural psychology attempts to develop a language for the comparative study of mental states that makes it possible to understand and appreciate the mental life of others. "Others" refers to members of a different cultural community who by virtue of lifelong membership in that group ascribe meaning to their lives in the light of wants, feelings, values, and beliefs that are not necessarily the same as one's own.

Cultural psychologists are interested, for example, in cultural variations in the degree to which feelings are constructed as emotions. Anna Wierzbicka (1999) has suggested that, while all human

beings have "feelings" such as pleasure and pain, arousal and serenity, many of the "emotions" lexicalized in the English language are
not universally available in the mental life of people around the
world. Researchers have delved into the character of the particular
emotions (Ifaluk "fago," American "happiness," Oriya "lajja") that
are important in different social worlds (Lutz, 1988; Kitayama and
Markus, 1994; Shweder and Haidt, 2000; see Chapter 3).

Cultural psychologists explore population-based variations in
social cognition, moral judgment, and the sources of personal
fulfillment or life satisfaction. For example, they have studied the
origin, significance, and place of filial piety and the social motivation to achieve in some East Asian populations (Yang, 1997). They
have investigated the self-empowering aspects of ascetic denial and
other forms of sacrifice among high caste women in South Asia
(Menon, 2000). They have documented the divergent meanings and
distinctive somatic and affective vicissitudes of such experiences as
loss or success for members of different cultural communities. It is
in the pursuit of such research questions that they have discovered
replicable cultural differences in reports about the quality of the
experience. In comparison to majority populations in Northern
Europe or the United States, majority populations in Samoa and
China are more likely to react to apparent loss with feelings such as
headaches, backaches, and other types of physical pain than with
feelings such as sadness or dysphoria (Levy, 1973, Kleinman, 1986).

Cultural psychologists also seek to document differences in
modes of thought (analytic versus holistic; Nisbett et al., 2001), in
self-organization (interdependent versus independent; Markus and
Kitayama, 1991), and in moral judgment (reliance on an ethics of
autonomy, community, or divinity across different types of groups;
Shweder et al., 1997 and Chapter 2).

Most research in cultural psychology has been pluralistic in its conception of normal psychological functioning and interdisciplinary in its conception of how to go about studying the origin, meaning, and social role of particular mental states on a worldwide scale. The field draws together anthropologists, psychologists, linguists, biologists, and philosophers in its study of the diverse modes of psychological functioning that have been produced, and socially endorsed, in different cultural traditions and that have made those traditions possible. Indeed, cultural psychology is sometimes described as the study of how culture and psyche make each other up.

PSYCHIC PLURALISM

Taken together, the premises of nonuniformity and of self-reflexive social construction sum up to the tenet of psychological pluralism. Cultural psychology is thus the study of the way the human mind (understood to consist of an inherently complex, heterogeneous collection of abstract or latent schemata) can be transformed, and made functional, in ways that are not equally distributed across time or space. I once coined the phrase, "one mind, many mentalities: universalism without the uniformity," which is meant to give expression to goals of a discipline aimed at developing a credible theory of psychological pluralism.

Cultural psychology can also be understood as a project designed to critically assess the limitations and incompleteness of all uniformitarian versions of the idea of psychic unity. Alternatively put, cultural psychology is the study of ethnic and cultural sources of diversity in emotional and somatic functioning, self-organization, moral evaluation, social cognition, and human development. It is the study of population differences in the things people know, think, want, feel, and value, and hence are customarily motivated to do, by virtue of membership in a group that has a history and a conception of its own destiny. "To be a member of a group," the eighteenth-century German romantic philosopher Johann Herder argued, "is to think and act in a certain way in the light of particular goals, values and pictures of the world; and to think and act so is to belong to a group" (Berlin, 1976, summarizing Herder).

Although the field of cultural psychology has many ancestral spirits (Giambattista Vico, Wilhelm Wundt, Wilhelm Dilthey, Edward Sapir, Ruth Benedict) and some very prominent contemporary advocates (Jerome Bruner, Michael Cole, Clifford Geertz, Jacqueline Goodnow, Patricia Greenfield, John Haidt, Giyoo Hatano, Shinobu Kitayama, Robert LeVine, John Lucy, Tanya Luhrmann, Hazel Markus, Joan Miller, Peggy Miller, Richard Nisbett, Barbara Rogoff, Paul Rozin, Anna Wierzbicka), Johann Herder is justly claimed as one of the original cultural psychologists, although he was probably not the first. For an account of the historical development of the field, see Jahoda (1991) and Cole (1996).

CULTURE AND THE CUSTOM COMPLEX

One of the contributions of cultural psychology is to revive a conception of culture, traceable to Kroeber and Kluckholn, that is both symbolic and behavioral. In the history of twentieth-century anthropological thought, the idea of culture has been variously defined, either behaviorally (as patterns of behavior that are learned and passed on from generation to generation) or symbolically (as the categories, beliefs, and doctrines that organize, rationalize and justify a way of life). In research on the cultural psychology of a particular cultural community, the notion of culture usually refers to community-specific ideas about what is true, good, beautiful, and efficient that are made manifest in behavior. In accord with Kroeber and Kluckholn's approach to culture, cultural psychologists thus engage in the interpretive, symbolic, or cognitive analysis of behavior. They assume that actions speak louder than words and that practices are a central unit for cultural analysis. Thus, what John Whiting and Irvin Child (1953) once referred to as the "custom complex" is a natural unit of analysis or starting point for a study in cultural psychology.

John Whiting was one of my teachers in the late 1960s and early 1970s in the Department of Social Relations at Harvard University. He was one of anthropology's great positivists. His career was dedicated to the rational assessment of testable hypotheses about the prevalence, distribution, and function of cultural practices around the world (for example, male and female initiation ceremonies). He was a free thinker who embraced within his intellectual circle a variety of anthropologists and psychologists spanning all the camps in contemporary anthropology. I think the members of that circle, including graduate students and senior scholars, hung together in part because they loved John Whiting's many intellectual and personal virtues. They loved his curiosity, his egalitarianism, his argumentative spirit, his passion for gathering new evidence, the grand scale of his research projects, and his optimism about the future of the social sciences. Whiting had more bright ideas in a day than most people have in a lifetime. It was fun to watch him smile and spin a theory. Not all of his concepts, hypotheses, and bright ideas panned out (nor did he expect them to), but some, such as the notion of the custom complex, were so good they deserved to be rediscovered.

Whiting and Child introduced the idea of a custom complex in 1953, but the basic idea was not carried forward until the rebirth of cultural psychology in the 1980s and 1990s. According to Whiting and Child, a custom complex "consists of a customary practice [for example, a family meal, arranged marriage, animal sacrifice, household sleeping arrangement, or a gender identity ceremony involving genital surgery] and of beliefs, values, sanctions, rules, motives and satisfactions associated with it" (see Chapters 1 and 4). Many labels can be placed on this type of unit of analysis, such as a life space or a habitus. Whatever the label, this unit of analysis makes it possible to conceptualize cultural psychology as the study of the way culture and psyche (what people know, think, feel, want, value and hence choose to do) afford each other's realization, and thus "make each other up."

Example of a Custom Complex: Genital Surgeries in Africa

A highly illuminating example of a custom complex is the circumcision ceremony or genital surgery that is customary for both boys and girls in many East and West African ethnic groups. In Sierra Leone, Mali, the Gambia, Ethiopia, Somalia, the Sudan, and Egypt, genital surgeries are culturally endorsed and receive high approval ratings from both men and women. Although many questions remain to be answered about the prevalence, distribution, function, and consequences of the practice, the global discourse about genital surgeries has in the past twenty years become an ethical discourse that goes well beyond any positivistic approach.

Human rights advocacy groups in Europe and in the United States have aggressively criticized the practice. The most comprehensive and rigorous review of the medical and demographic literature on African genital surgeries, however, suggests that widely publicized claims about the severe consequences of the custom for health, sexuality, and childbirth are inaccurate (Obermeyer, 1999; Morison et al., 2001). Nevertheless, these days one cannot avoid the stance of rational justification (what are the reasons for engaging in this practice?) and the process of moral evaluation (is this practice "good"?) when representing the socially endorsed practices of others.

For example, in a recent manuscript on the cultural psychology of male and female circumcision among the Kono people of Sierra Leone, Fuambai Ahmadu, who is both a native and an anthropologist, has written as follows (Ahmadu, 2000:301). "It is difficult for me—considering the number of these ceremonies I have observed, including my own—to accept that what appear to be expressions of joy and ecstatic celebrations of womanhood in actuality disguise hidden experiences of coercion and subjugation. Indeed, I offer that most Kono women who uphold these rituals do so because they want to—they relish the supernatural powers of their ritual leaders over against men in society, and they embrace the legitimacy of female authority and, particularly, the authority of their mothers and grandmothers."

As Ahmadu and other ethnographers who study genital surgeries in Africa have pointed out, among the goals, values, and pictures of the world (the cultural psychology) that make this practice meaningful and satisfying for the men and women for whom it is a custom complex are the following:

1. A culturally shared belief that the body (especially the genitals) is sexually ambiguous until modified through surgical intervention. According to this picture of the world, the foreskin of a boy is viewed as a feminine element and masculinity is enhanced by its removal. Similarly, the clitoris is viewed as an unwelcome vestige of the male organ. Kono females, as described by Ahmadu, seek to feminize and hence empower themselves by getting rid of it.

2. A culturally shared aesthetic standard in terms of which the genitals are viewed as ugly, misshapen, and unappealing if left in their natural state. For many African men

and women, the ideal of beauty is associated with a sexual anatomy that is smooth, cleansed, and cleaned (shaved) and free of all "fleshy encumbrances."

There is of course much more to be said about the beliefs, values, sanctions, motives, and satisfactions associated with genital surgeries in Africa. Nevertheless, in the light of these and other culturally endorsed reasons, a genital surgery is experienced as an improvement of the body in many East and West African ethnic groups (Ahmadu 2000; see Chapter 4 for a more complete discussion of the topic).

The cultural psychology of a different community's practices is likely to result in a depiction of other minds that is unsettling or at least surprising. Radical divergences in the moral evaluation of particular custom complexes, such as circumcision, are themselves an important topic for research in cultural psychology. Indeed, the cultural psychology of moral evaluation is currently an active research area (see Chapters 1–2, 4–5).

Cultural Psychology of Morality

The cultural psychology of morality is the study of judgments about actions and practices that are classified as loathsome, outrageous, shameful, evil, or wrong. On the basis of the ethnographic record, we now know at least five things about these judgments.

1. Moral judgments are ubiquitous. Members of every cultural community assume that they are parties to an agreement to uphold a certain way of life, praise or permit certain kinds of actions and practices, and condemn and prohibit others. In this regard, Emile Durkheim was right. The social order is a moral order vigilantly and inces-

santly sustained by small and large judgments about right and wrong, good and bad, virtue and vice.

2. Moral judgments do not spontaneously converge over time. Actions and practices that are a source of moral approbation in one community are frequently the source of moral opprobrium in another, and moral disagreements can persist over generations, if not centuries. For example, the current Western alarm over the practice of female circumcision in Africa is nothing new. Indeed, it is very much a replay of the moral indignation expressed in the 1920s by Christian missionaries and British colonial administrators as they embraced what they took to be their white man's burden to uplift the peoples of the "dark continent" from error, ignorance, barbarism, and confusion. Then, as now, majority populations in numerous African ethnic groups held the practice in high regard and resented the implication that they are either monsters or ignoramuses for engaging in what they think of as an honorable and morally motivated custom.

3. Moral judgments are experienced as cognitive judgments and not solely as aesthetic or emotive judgments. This truth about the cultural psychology of moral judgments has been noted by the philosopher Arthur Lovejoy. He points out that when someone says "it is wrong to oppress the helpless" or "the conduct of Adolph Hitler was wicked," they "do not in fact conceive of themselves merely to be reporting on the state of their own emotions" and mean to be saying something more than "I am very unpleasantly affected when I think of it" (Lovejoy, 1961: 253,255). On a worldwide scale, it appears that when folk make a moral judgment (for example, "circumcision

is an outrage," "abortion is evil," "it is wrong to put elderly parents in a nursing home"), they themselves believe there are matters of objective fact to which their judgment refers and that they are making a claim about some domain of moral truth. That is what makes their judgment "cognitive."

4. Moral judgments are experienced as aesthetic and emotive judgments and not solely as cognitive judgments. Despite the fact that moral judgments ("that's good," "that's wrong") are experienced as judgments about some domain of moral truth, such judgments resemble aesthetic and emotive judgments ("that's ugly," "that's disgusting"). They occur rapidly and without the assistance of deliberative reason, indeed without much need for conscious reflection at all. Moreover, moral judgments motivate action largely because they produce powerful feelings of ugliness, repugnance, guilt, indignation, or shame.

5. The imagined truths or goods asserted in deliberative moral judgments around the world are many, not one. The moral character of an action or practice such as voluntarily ending a pregnancy is typically established by connecting that action through a chain of factual, means-ends and causal reasoning to some argument-ending terminal good—for example, personal freedom, family privacy, or the avoidance of physical or psychological harm. On a worldwide scale, the argument-ending terminal goods of deliberative moral judgments privileged in a cultural community are rich and diverse, and they include such noble ends as autonomy, justice, harm avoidance, loyalty, benevolence, piety, duty, respect, gratitude, sympathy, chastity, purity, sanctity, and others. Several proposals

have been advanced in the social sciences for classifying these goods into a smaller set, such as the three ethics of autonomy, community, and divinity (see Chapter 2).

Thus we know from research in cultural psychology that moral judgments around the world are ubiquitous, passionate, motivating, truth-asserting, and divergent.

Notice in this regard that a stance of moral pluralism is not opposed to universalism. Culture theorists do not divide into only two types: those who believe that anything goes (the radical relativists) and those who believe that only one thing goes (the uniformitarian universalists). I am a universalist, but the type of universalism to which I subscribe is universalism without the uniformity, which is what makes me a pluralist. In other words, there are universally binding values, just too many of them. Those objectively valuable ends of life are diverse, heterogeneous, irreducible to some common denominator such as "utility" or "pleasure," and inherently in conflict with each other. All the good things in life cannot be simultaneously maximized. When it comes to implementing true values, there are always trade-offs, which is why there are different traditions of values (cultures) and why no one cultural tradition has ever been able to honor everything that is good.

Thus, one can be a pluralist and still grant that there are true and universally binding values and undeniable moral principles—for example, "cruelty is evil," "you should treat like cases alike and different cases differently," "highly vulnerable members of a society are entitled to protection from harm." One of the claims of pluralism, however, is that values and principles are objective only to the extent they are kept abstract and devoid of content. A related claim is that no abstract value or principle, in and of itself, can provide definitive guidance in concrete cases of moral dispute. In other words, it is possible for morally decent and rational people to look at each other's practices, emote, and say, "Yuck!"

There is plenty of "mutual yucking" going on in the world today. Circumcising and noncircumcising peoples, for example, almost always respond in that way to each other. The mutual yuck response is possible because objective values cannot in and of themselves determine whether it is right or wrong to arrange a marriage. Whether it is good or bad to sacrifice or butcher mammals such as goats or sheep. Whether it is savory or unsavory to put parents in an old age home. Whether it is vicious or virtuous to have a large family. Whether it is moral or immoral to abort a fetus. Whether it is commendable or contemptible to encourage girls as well as boys to enter into a Covenant with God (or to become full members of their society) by means of a ritual initiation involving genital modifications or circumcision. Morally decent and rational people can disagree about such things, even in the face of a plentitude of shared objective values.

It is tempting to suggest that it is precisely because moral reactions are ubiquitous, passionate, motivating, truth-asserting, and divergent that secrecy, separation, and local control have been characteristic adaptations. When two or more communities passionately disagree about the virtue of a practice or action, it makes sense to live and let live and keep out of each other's way. In our technologically wired, cosmopolitan world, which prizes the free flow of everything, it has become increasingly difficult for communities with divergent moral judgments to maintain distance or retain sufficient power to keep their judgments local.

The "immoral" or "barbaric" other is now in your home on a regular basis, made readily available by CNN or the *New York Times*. Even as you rest in your living room, you may be incited by words and images to react emotionally against someone or some practice on the other side of the globe. Postmodern humanists and the discipline of cultural psychology have a duty under such conditions of diminished understanding to urge caution in arriving at moral judgments and to supply a fuller exegesis of local meanings. As impossible as it may seem, one aim of postmodern humanism and cultural psychology is to develop a hard-nosed and critical capacity to see validity and virtue in the different beliefs and practices of others.

Cultural Psychology: What It Is Not

The tenet of psychic pluralism and the emphasis on goals, values, and pictures of the world as a source of psychological differences between cultural communities distinguish cultural psychology from other fields of study such as cross-cultural psychology and national character studies, with which it should not be confused.

IT IS NOT CROSS-CULTURAL PSYCHOLOGY

Research in cultural psychology proceeds on the assumption that psychological diversity is inherent in the human condition, and that culture and psyche are interdependent and make each other up. It should be noted, indeed emphasized, that any theory of psychological pluralism would lack credibility if it denied the existence of any and all universals. Indeed, cultural psychology presupposes many psychological universals, including feelings; wants; goals; and ideas of good and bad, of cause and effect, of part-whole relationships (see Shweder et al., 1998). However, the search for and the privileging of things that are uniform across all peoples is a project that goes under other names—for example, general psychology or perhaps even cross-cultural psychology.

Segall, Lonner, and Berry (1998) have described some of the goals of cross-cultural psychology. One goal is "to generate more nearly universal psychology, one that has pan-human validity" and to attain "a universally applicable psychological theory." A second, closely related goal it to "keep peeling away at the onion skin of culture so as to reveal the psychic unity of mankind at its core." It is for that reason that cross-cultural psychology (not to be confused with cultural psychology) can be viewed as a vigilant cousin of general psychology; they both share the same uniformitarian goals. Such goals give a special character to cross-cultural psychology. And they help explain why the following kinds of activities are typical of research by cross-cultural psychologists and distinguish that field from cultural psychology.

Cross-cultural psychologists study the boundary conditions for generalizations created in Western labs with Western (mostly college student) subjects—generalizations that, prior to critical examination by cross-cultural psychologists, have been presumptively interpreted as fundamental and universal. They do not try to represent the distinctive cultural psychology of particular peoples nor pursue research focused on differences in the way members of communities perceive, categorize, feel, want, choose, evaluate, and communicate that can be traced to differences in community-based goals, values, and pictures of the world. Rather cross-cultural psychologists seek to make sure that the hoped-for universal psychology is truly universal and to throw out any claim that only holds in the Anglo-American world. This is an extremely useful corrective for the tendency of Western psychologists to overgeneralize their findings, but it is not the same as undertaking a project in cultural psychology.

A second goal of cross-cultural psychology is to establish comparability or equivalence for measuring instruments across different populations. Often the point here is to show that people in different cultures really are alike, and that any reported differences in performance were due to noise, inappropriate measuring instruments, bad translations, or misunderstandings about the way to ask and answer questions. The instincts of a cultural psychologist run in quite a different direction. For a cultural psychologist, the "noise" is interpreted as a signal about true differences in cultural meanings and not as something to eliminate or overcome. Indeed, cultural psychologists are likely to worry if measuring instruments travel easily and well from university classroom to university classroom around the world and display the same psychometric properties. They may suspect that they are not in a truly different culture. This is because "peeling away the onion skin of culture so as to reveal the psychic unity of mankind at its core" is not what cultural psychology is about.

A third major goal of cross-cultural psychology is to focus on "independent variables" of the cultural environment, for example, nucleation of the family, literacy versus nonliteracy, that are thought to either promote or retard psychological development. In such research, development is almost always defined in terms of universal norms for cognitive, emotional, or social functioning (for example, Piaget's notion of formal operational thinking or Ainsworth's notion of healthy attachment). Cultural psychology, in contrast, is primarily concerned with the elaboration and discovery of alternative or plural norms for successful psychological development (LeVine, 1990; see Chapters 1 and 5).

It Is Not National Character Studies

Attempts to characterize whole populations in terms of generalized dispositions such as authoritarianism, Apollonianisn, or high need for achievement went out of fashion in anthropology in the late 1950s and early 1960s. Looking for variations in types of personality traits to explain differences in cultural practices or custom complexes (and vice versa) turned out to be a dead end. In efforts to describe individuals within and across cultural communities in terms of general dispositions or traits of character, within-group variations typically exceeded between-group variations. National character researchers discovered that "individuals within cultures vary much more among themselves than they do from individuals in other cultures" (Kaplan 1954) and hypothesized modal personality types typically characterize no more than a third of the population in any particular cultural group. Psychological anthropologists and cultural psychologists have long recognized that (quoting Melford Spiro, 1961): "it is possible for different modal personality systems to be associated with similar social systems, and for similar modal personality systems to be associated with different social systems."

A major insight, although a fragile one, of recent work in cultural psychology is that it is better to represent and interpret human behavior the way sensible economists do rather than the way personality trait theorists do. That is to say, it is better to think about behavior as emanating from agency, and to analyze it as the joint product of preferences (including goals, values, and ends of various sorts) and constraints (including beliefs, information, skills, material and social resources, and means of various sorts). This approach avoids the hazards of dispositional approaches in which behavior is interpreted as the by-product of mechanical forces pushing both from inside (in the form of personality traits) and outside (in the form of situational pressures). Ultimately, a fully successful piece of research in cultural psychology must avoid nominal dispositional categories such as holistic versus analytic and render behavior intelligible in terms of the particular goals, values, and pictures of the world that motivate and inform the domain-specific behaviors and routine practices of specific intentional agents. To do otherwise is to reify cultural stereotypes and fall into some of the traps of the past.

The Future: Going Indigenous

The field of cultural psychology that has re-emerged on the North American and European scene during the past twenty years is quite similar to an intellectual movement that has grown up in the non-Western world and is increasingly known as "indigenous psychology." One of the most eminent theoreticians of this movement, Kuo-shu Yang, the Taiwanese psychologist, lists several ways to indigenize psychological research. Here are four of Professor Yang's virtues for the aspiring indigenous psychologist of China (Yang, 1997):

1. "Give priority to the study of culturally unique psychological and behavioral phenomena or characteristics of the Chinese people."
2. "Investigate both the specific content and the involved process of the phenomenon."
3. Make it a rule to begin any research with a thorough immersion into the natural, concrete details of the phenomenon to be studied.
4. Let research be based upon the Chinese intellectual tradition rather than the Western intellectual tradition.

These virtues define cultural psychology as well, although it remains to be seen how many of us can live up to such demanding standards. Even today, with the rebirth of cultural psychology, not all research actually begins with fieldwork or with a thorough immersion into the natural concrete details of the phenomenon to be studied. All too often, research still starts with a published finding from some Western lab, which is then subjected to critical examination by means of various attempts at replication with populations from other societies. But things are changing. Given the increasingly international and interdisciplinary character of collaborative scholarship in cultural psychology, I look forward to more research that keeps faith with Kuo-shu Yang's high ideals.

One looks forward as well to deep and lively debates about the questions most central to this book. What stance should one take toward multiculturalism in our contemporary liberal democratic society? How is it possible to be a pluralist who values difference without saying that anything goes? What is the role of a liberal education in promoting the ideals of a postmodern humanism?

That last topic is most directly treated in the essay "Fundamentalism for Highbrows," which was originally an address on the aims of education delivered to the incoming class at the University of Chicago. In the context of this particular collection of essays, it is my hope that "Fundamentalism for Highbrows" might be lifted out of its original academic setting and viewed as the continuation of a lifelong conversation about the meaning and value of life in contemporary liberal democratic societies. These days, however, post-September 11, the question looms large, what is and what ought to be the role of postmodern liberal educational institutions in developing the moral life of the mind in a multicultural world? Can they, should they, help us achieve the view from many-wheres?

This collection of essays seeks to give character and definition to the proposition that the knowable world is incomplete if seen from any one point of view, incoherent if seen from all points of view at once, and empty if seen from nowhere in particular. Could it be that the recognition or revelation of that universal and fundamental truth is one of the more momentous experiences one might have at school, and is one of the noblest of ends toward which a genuinely liberal education might be aimed?

1

Who Sleeps by Whom Revisited

with Lene Balle-Jensen and William Goldstein

This chapter focuses on sleeping arrangements among high-caste families in a Hindu temple town in Orissa, India, and among Anglo-American middle-class families. Determining who sleeps by whom in a family household is a symbolic action or nonverbal vehicle of meaning that simultaneously expresses and realizes the moral ideals of a cultural community. This chapter discusses methods for extracting the moral "goods" implicit in where family members sleep at night. It also traces interconnections between cultural practices, morality, ethnopsychological knowledge, and personality development.

We begin with a discussion of a recent commentary by the renowned pediatrician Dr. T. Berry Brazelton on parent-child co-sleeping arrangements (Brazelton 1990). Dr. Brazelton's self-conscious rumination ponders the question, "Who *ought* to sleep by whom in the human family?" His reflections, although brief, are deep and revealing. They provide students of cultural psychology and Anglo-American cultural studies with a glimpse of the way ethnopediatric "wisdom," local moral sensibilities, culture-specific character traits, and historically evolved family practices reinforce each other, and perhaps even make each other up.

Co-sleeping: Re-evaluating the Anglo-American Stance

Dr. Brazelton poses a fascinating and complex moral question: Should children be allowed (encouraged, required) to routinely sleep in the same bed with their parent(s)? For most Anglo-American middle-class readers, the answer to that question will seem obvious: "No! Children should not routinely sleep in the same bed with their parent(s). They should be taught to sleep alone."

In the past that was the answer Dr. Brazelton gave to parents. Yet more recently he has had some cross-cultural conversations with pediatricians in Japan, where children typically co-sleep with their parents and continue to do so until they are adolescents. Now he feels "conflicted," and in his commentary he reveals why. On the one hand Dr. Brazelton believes it is important to promote autonomy and independence by forcing infants and young children to sleep alone. He also worries about the temptations and dangers of sexual abuse. And he cannot shake from his mind the picture of the sexual fantasy life of young children (desiring the mother, hating the father, dreading genital mutilation) as portrayed by psychoanalytic theorists. He even acknowledges his own personal inhibitions and inability to sleep in the same bed with a small child, which he confesses are "due to deeply ingrained taboos and questions from my own past."

On the other hand Dr. Brazelton is well aware of all those apparently undamaged Japanese who have grown up co-sleeping with their parents. And he also finds himself faced with increasing numbers of American clients who feel a "need" to sleep in the same bed with their child. Dr. Brazelton is conflicted. He concludes by asking: "Should we re-evaluate our stance toward children's sleep?" His remarks appear in "Ab Initio: An International Newsletter for Professionals Working with Infants and Their Families." In such an international context, his roomy inclusive reference to "our stance" is fascinating. It suggests a) that Dr. Brazelton did not ponder what it would mean to address such a question to a truly international audience, whose stance on this topic could not be taken for granted, or b) that the readership of the newsletter is restricted to professionals from Europe and the United States, or c) that one measure of being acknowledged as an international "professional" in the infancy field is the adoption of an Anglo-American stance on questions about parent-child co-sleeping.

In any case, before adopting some stance toward co-sleeping arrangements, we might consider delving more deeply into the semantics and pragmatics as well as the form, function, and distribution of sleeping arrangements on a worldwide scale. The stance of the Anglo-American world on this topic is rather unusual in the international context of family life practices.

Although there have been surprisingly few systematic studies of co-sleeping between American children and their parents, a characteristic white middle-class practice does exist concerning who sleeps by whom in the family. Litt (1981) in a pediatric study of 119 children (age 6 and under) from white, middle-class, two-parent families in Cleveland, Ohio, found that only 3 percent of the children regularly slept in their parent's bedroom during the first year of life and only 1 percent did so after their first birthday. Rosenfeld et al. (1982) outlined similar results from an urban sample in California. Among members of the white middle class, the practice of regular, routinized, or customary parent-child co-sleeping appears to be exceedingly rare.

Studies of occasional or intermittent parent-child co-sleeping in the white middle class report higher percentages. Madansky and Edelbrock (1990) report that 21 percent of 2- and 3-year-olds in Massachusetts co-sleep with their parents one or more times a week. Lozoff, Wolf, and Davis (1984) report that 24 percent of children in Cleveland between 6 months and 4 years of age co-sleep with their parents at least part of the night at least three or more nights a week.

Although the practice of preferred parent-child co-sleeping is rare in the white middle class in the United States, it does appear to be more common in other American groups. Litt (1981) reports that in Cleveland 55 percent of African American children less than 1 year of age co-sleep with a parent every night and all night, and that 25 percent of African American children 1 to 5 years of age do so (also see Mandansky and Edelbrock, 1990; Lozoff, Wolf, and Davis, 1984). Abbott (1992) describes sleeping arrangements in a white predominantly blue-collar community in Appalachian Kentucky. Although parent-child co-sleeping was practically nonexistent for children over 9 years of age, the frequency of co-sleeping for younger children was quite high compared to the urban white middle class: 71 percent of children between 2 months and 2 years of age and 47 percent of children between 2 years and 4 years of age co-slept with a parent. Abbott does not explicitly state her definition of co-sleeping, although it appears to entail sleeping in a parent's bed or bedroom every night and all night. Abbott demonstrates that co-sleeping occurs even when there is ample space to sleep alone and that crowding and resource limitations are insufficient explanations of these co-sleeping arrangements. She argues that in many blue-collar Appalachian families, there is a preference for parent-child co-sleeping in the first years of life. That preference is articulated in terms of the moral view that the capacity to nurse and nurture are God-given blessings. Co-sleeping is justified as a palpable satisfaction and as an experience of profound "closeness," which enhances the long-term social bonds between parents and their offspring.

This limited research suggests that the sleeping practices of the white middle class have not been uniformly adopted by all groups in the United States. Nevertheless, there does seem to exist in white middle-class communities in the United States a family life practice in which, after darkness falls, the bedroom of adults is a private space guarded with taboos against children of all ages that is presumed to be essentially off limits (except for occasional medical problems and other emergencies), and children are expected to try their best to make it through the night alone.

Of course, anthropologists (see Whiting 1964, 1981; Caudill and Plath, 1966; also Burton and Whiting, 1961, LeVine, 1990; Lozoff and Brittenham, 1979) have long known that the ritualized isolation and solitude imposed on young children every night in middle-class Anglo-American families is a specialized kind of ordeal that is not practiced in most other regions of the world. In Whiting's 1964 survey of sleeping arrangements in 134 societies, infants and mothers were found to co-sleep most of the time. Commenting on the ethnographic record, Whiting (1981: 161) notes that "since in many cultures sleeping arrangements are a private affair, specific ethnographic accounts are often lacking and judgments are often made inferentially." Nevertheless, of the scores of the (mostly non-Western, mostly nonindustrial) communities around the world studied by anthropologists on which information about infant sleeping location is available (Barry and Paxson 1971), there is not a single community in which infants customarily sleep alone.

Indeed the historically evolved behavioral script calling for separation of child from parent that is re-enacted on a daily basis in

European and American families is often perceived as a form of child neglect in Africa, Asia, and Central America (see, for example, Morelli et al., 1992). Brazelton himself remarks that the Japanese think of Americans as "merciless" for forcing children to be off on their own and isolated in a dark room throughout the night. Adults in Orissa, India, express similar moral concerns about the practice, which they view as indicative of parental irresponsibility.

Advice Columns: Mirror of the American Middle Class

Most middle-class Anglo-Americans do not view their own sleeping practices as abusive and immoral. Quite the contrary, they are convinced that their arrangements are sound and healthy and promote the moral good. They are disturbed by the practice of parents and children bedding down together at night and nervous about its consequences. They are prone to the view that parent-child co-sleeping is pathological and perhaps even criminal or sinful. Here are two examples of queries and responses about parent-child co-sleeping that have appeared in expert advice columns in mainstream middle-class American newspapers such as the *Chicago Tribune:*

> Dear Ann Landers: I have three children, ages 2, 3 and 5. Here's my problem: All three end up in my bedroom during the night. Usually I know they are there but I sleep right through it . . . I'm newly divorced and there is no man in my bed, so the kids aren't disturbing anyone . . . My mother tells me I must make the kids sleep in their own rooms. She says sometimes children who want to sleep with their parents need to be taken to a psychologist

because their behavior indicates deeper problems. What do you say? Is it that big a deal when they are so young?

Dear Wondering: Usually, I tell parents to keep the kids out of their bed at night, but in your case I suspect the divorce has made them insecure. Talk to your pediatrician about the way to wean these kids away from this habit. You really do need professional guidance . . . Good luck, dear. You have your hands full. (January 14, 1992)

Dear Abby: I recently spent my first weekend at the home of my fiancé's parents. "Harold" warned me not to be shocked that his 14-year-old younger brother, "Nicky," sleeps in the same bed with their 50-year-old-mother. Needless to say I was appalled. I have always known that Harold's parents have had a troubled marriage and haven't shared a bedroom since 1980. Harold mentioned about a month ago that his younger brother hates sleeping with his mother, but that she threatens to spank him if he sleeps in his own bedroom. Harold has tried talking to his mother about this but she is very irrational and suffers bouts of depression. If the position were reversed and a 50-year-old man was forcing his 14-year-old daughter to sleep with him, I am sure that people's feelings would be different. But child abusers are not always men. Someone has to consider the interests of Nicky. I am honestly afraid that this sleeping arrangement could psychologically harm him. Would you please guide me on this issue?

Dear Really Worried: You are to be commended for caring enough to take a stand, because no immediate family member has been willing to become this boy's advocate.

Clearly, Nicky is being emotionally blackmailed, and his mother's behavior is inappropriate. You should report her to Children's Services. The number in Texas to call is . . . (April 21, 1992)

After reading such queries and responses, a middle-class Anglo-American reader might feel emotionally uncomfortable, morally distressed, and full of concern about issues of sexuality, excessive dependency, and the exploitation of children. Many of these readers would be prepared to accept without much reflection the supposition that the quality of a marriage can be gauged by whether a husband and wife sleep together, which is implicit in Really Worried's remarks. They would be offended by the perceived infringements on Nicky's autonomy and on his freedom of choice. They would stigmatize the mother and harbor doubts about her mental health or sexual morality. That is a normative and a culturally acceptable response for these readers. However, it would not be a normative or culturally proper response for readers from Japan. A typical Japanese observer of such practices would not worry about psychopathology or see a need to phone for help.

Co-Sleeping in Japan

The classic and most detailed anthropological study of sleeping arrangements in Japan is Caudill and Plath's 1966 research report "Who Sleeps by Whom?: Parent-Child Involvement in Urban Japanese Families." The data were derived from interviews collected in 1955 from 323 families in the cities of Kyoto, Tokyo, and Matsumoto. The Japanese case is instructive, as a lesson in the way cultural practices and individual psychological functioning (emotional appraisal, moral evaluation, self formation) are intertwined.

Caudill and Plath found that over a lifetime a typical Japanese person seldom sleeps alone and prefers not to do so. Parents feel morally obliged to provide their children with a parental sleeping partner and husbands and wives are willing to separate from each other in order to do so. Approximately 50 percent of urban Japanese children 11 to 15 years old sleep in the same bed with their mother or father or both, Japanese fathers are just as likely to sleep in the same bed with their daughters as with their sons, and only 14 percent of children this age sleep alone (they sleep with siblings if not with parents). A typical person is likely to sleep alone at only two points: in late adolescence, if unmarried and living away from home; and in late adulthood, if widowed and living without children or grandchildren.

Japanese sleeping practices documented in 1955 were not driven by crowding, limited resources, or lack of available space. By correlating an index of use density with an index of available space density, Caudill and Plath showed that variations in available space account for no more than 22 percent of the variance in actual space utilization. They found, for example, that three-person households consisting of two parents and an infant do not disperse for sleep even when space was available. Even in larger households, "Japanese prefer to sleep in clusters of two or three persons and prefer not to sleep alone" (1966: 349).

Caudill and Plath suggest that co-sleeping is a source of satisfaction for Japanese children and adults, that Japanese sleeping arrangements "emphasize the interdependency more than the separateness of individuals" (1966: 363), and that co-sleeping diminishes the tensions and separations between genders and generations. They even speculate that, given the way culture and psyche make each other up, the practice of sleeping alone is emotionally threatening to the Japanese sense of self and may be a cause of suicide and other psychopathologies.

The Myth of the Single Customary Sleeping Arrangement

The anthropological and pediatric literature on sleeping practices has limitations. The cross-cultural data portray sleeping arrangements in terms of the nuclear triad of mother (m), father (f), and infant or young child (c) without detailed attention to the gender of the child or the co-sleeping practices of older children. The research represents each cultural community with a single "customary" sleeping arrangement, such as mc/f (mother and child co-sleep, father sleeps separately) or mcf (mother, father, and child all sleep together), as though the concept of culture required the investigator to characterize the traditions of a cultural community in terms of some mandated single fixed behavior pattern for bedding down at night.

That is not the most satisfactory way to conceptualize a "culture" or to study the form and function of sleeping practices. The documentation of patterns of behavior—especially patterns of behavior that are traditional, invested with a moral force, and passed on from generation to generation—is an important first step in the study of culture. However, the study of culture is not reducible to the study of behavior patterns per se. A culture is a way of life, a world of meaning and value lit up by a series of conceptual schemes that are expressed, instantiated, and enforced in practice. The study of culture is largely about the historically activated and socially enforced categories, causal beliefs, preferences, values, and moral "goods" exhibited in the behavior of a group and about the types of resources that are required to sustain that distinctive way of life.

To provide a cultural account, one must establish a correspondence between behaviors and a particular kind of something else—a preference, a value, a moral good, an idea(l), a causal belief—exhibited in those behaviors. The entire exercise presupposes that values, meanings, concepts, idea(l)s, and causal beliefs are *analytically* external to and *theoretically* separable from the behaviors themselves. That is why in the study of Oriya sleeping practices, we conceptualized each recorded instance of who sleeps by whom on a particular night in Orissa, India, as a "choice" from a "logical matrix" of possibilities. The choice is constrained by a "moral grammar" (an ordered set of cultural preferences, values, goods, idea(l)s) that is expressed and realized through the sleeping arrangements.

In this chapter we use the following symbols to designate kinship statuses: f=father, m=mother, s=son, d=daughter, c=child, 1-n= age in years, /=separate sleeping spaces. Within any common sleeping space (co-sleeping on the same bed or mat), the ordering of symbols indicates the ordering of bodies. Thus for example, d7 s3 s8 indicates three co-sleeping children, with the 3-year-old son sleeping in between the 7-year-old daughter and the 8-year-old son.

Even when there are well-defined cultural values and ideals expressed and realized through the practice of who sleeps by whom, there may be no single, fixed sleeping pattern. For example, the nuclear relatives of different families might sleep as follows: f d6 / m d3 s4; f m d4 d7 d9; or f / m d14 d8 s3 / s16.[1] This type of data could be oversimplified to summary information about a prototypical nuclear triad (mother, father, child). However, even at that level, there is no single, fixed sleeping pattern that characterizes the Oriya community. In our record of single-night sleeping arrangements in 160 households, mcf, mc/f, and mc/fc patterns occur with about equal frequency (27 percent, 29 percent, and 25 percent, respectively) and even some instances of mf/c are observed (12 percent). (The other two possible patterns, m/c/f and fc/m, are relatively rare).

Nevertheless, we can understand the many sleeping arrangements that do occur in the Oriya community in terms of an ordered series of moral goods that define and constrain the "grammatical" variations in behavior that are exhibited. Just as a grammar of a language constrains but does not determine the particular linguistic expressions uttered on any occasion, the moral goods of a culture constrain but do not determine the sleeping arrangements in any particular household.

In other words, the reality and unity of Oriya sleeping practices do not reside at the level of description where we characterize a particular arrangement of bodies on the ground. Instead, the reality and unity of the practice reside at the level of description where we characterize the preferences, values, and moral goods realized and expressed by particular arrangements of bodies on the ground. There is absolutely no a priori reason to assume that a single ordered set of moral values requires everyone in a cultural community to arrange themselves in beds in a single way. Furthermore, even when two communities adopt the same sleeping pattern, there is no a priori reason to assume that their behavior realizes and expresses the same moral goods.

Framing the Debate: Should Parents and Children Co-Sleep?

Perhaps the most fascinating feature of the existing literature on sleeping arrangements is that it is packed with moral assumptions and evaluations. Researchers such as Abbott (1992), Caudill and

Plath (1966), Brazelton (1990), and Burton and Whiting (1961) have many ideas about the consequences of particular sleeping patterns for moral goods such as autonomy, individuation, privacy, group cohesion, and healthy gender identity. These moral goods are not always explicated or consistently addressed, but they are always relevant to the formulations and explanations offered in the literature.

For example, Whiting (1964) argues that husbands and wives customarily co-sleep in cold climates, for the sake of warmth. His analysis thereby presupposes that sleeping arrangements are selected to promote certain moral goods, such as a reduction of physical harm or pain. He implies that physical comfort (avoiding the cold) is a good reason for co-sleeping with a spouse and might even be the motive that explains why people in cold climates stay in bed together through the night.

A few researchers go a step further and take an interest in the moral reasons people adduce for their sleeping arrangements (see, for example, Morelli et al., 1992). It is not unusual for anthropological researchers to contextualize cultural sleeping practices by presenting readers with verbal justifications offered by local informants, although it is the rare study indeed whose central focus is the way members of a community think about the relationship between who sleeps by whom and the moral order. Abbott (1992: 34), for example, quotes a local Appalachian writer who justifies the practice of mother-child co-sleeping by remarking, "How can you expect to hold on to them in later life if you begin their lives by pushing them away?"

Other authors, such as Brazelton (1990) (and Ann Landers and Dear Abby, of course), bite the bullet and express their own views about whether a pattern of co-sleeping is justified. This type of moral discourse seems unavoidable if we are to credit the bearers of a cultural tradition with agency and with the capacity for responsible and rational action, unless we are prepared to defend the antirationalist proposition that "the examined life is not worth living." When Brazelton asks, "Should we re-evaluate our stance toward children's sleep?" he is raising a Socratic question that no responsible, autonomous, reflective participant in the life of a family can avoid. Although Dr. Brazelton's question should not be evaded, we do think it is best to put off answering it for a while. There is no point in engaging in a full-blown moral debate about who should sleep by whom until some empirical and conceptual foundations for the debate have been put in place.

With regard to these foundations, those who condemn (as well as those who justify) parent-child co-sleeping arrangements make many assumptions about objective means-ends connections. Yet systematic evidence is almost never presented (and may not exist) on whether, for example, co-sleeping in childhood per se deepens long-term familial cohesion or whether sleeping alone since infancy per se promotes independence and autonomy in adulthood or whether witnessing the primal scene per se is a cause of neuroses in adulthood (for discrepant opinions of the dangers of viewing the primal scene, see Dahl 1982 and Rosenfeld et al., 1980).

Particular sleeping practices may have no predictable long-term effects on individual psychological functioning and character formation. They may serve mainly as daily ritual enactments of the fundamental values and self-conceptions of the persons in some group or as a measure used by insiders for determining who should be accepted as a normal, responsible, consensus-sensitive, or cooperative member of that society.

Even if sleeping arrangements per se have no long-term effect on individual psychological functioning and character formation (Weisner and Garnier, 1992), sleeping arrangements may have long-term effects that are predictable once the local social meaning of the practice has been taken into account. In other words, the effects of a sleeping practice may be largely mediated by the moral meaning conferred on the practice by a group. Perhaps it is being confronted with a culturally deviant behavior in the bedroom (enforced isolation in a Japanese family; enforced co-sleeping in an Anglo-American family) that puts a child at risk.

It is also conceivable that any long-term effects of a particular sleeping arrangement on the emotional life of a particular individual are entirely idiosyncratic and involve a complex interaction between the details of the practice and aspects of personal temperament (see Kakar, 1990, for a relevant clinical case from India). Unfortunately, given the state of the research evidence, no one really knows. From an empirical point of view, all international moral advisors on sleeping arrangements are simply explicating their own local cultural intuitions while skating on very thin evidential ice.

From a conceptual point of view, the foundations for addressing Dr. Brazelton's question, "Who ought to sleep by whom in the family?" are no more secure. Those who condemn (as well as those who justify) parent-child co-sleeping arrangements make many strong and limiting assumptions about moral goods. Yet rarely are those moral considerations informed by a systematic examination of the range of moral values that are exhibited in the sleeping practices of different cultures around the world. Rarely is the problem of who should sleep by whom conceptualized as a problem in choosing between alternative moral goods or resolving a conflict among a multiplicity of moral goods. While the research outlined in this chapter does not provide an answer to Dr. Brazelton's question, it may supply a conceptual foundation for the moral debate that has already begun.

Who Sleeps by Whom in Orissa and Hyde Park?

Three types of data are discussed in this section: 1) the results of a "sleeping arrangement task" in which informants in Orissa, India, and in Hyde Park, Illinois, sort members of a hypothetical seven-person family into sleeping spaces under various resource constraints; 2) the results of a "preference conflict task" in which informants in the same locales evaluate and rank culturally deviant arrangements of members of the hypothetical family in terms of the relative seriousness of the breach; and 3) spot reports about who slept by whom on a single night in 160 households in the Hindu temple of Bhubaneswar in Orissa, India.[2]

EXTRACTING MORAL GOODS: THE SLEEPING ARRANGEMENTS TASK

In our view, sleeping arrangements are a joint product of cultural preferences (for example, the particular moral goods promoted by a people) and local resource constraints (for example, the amount of space or number of rooms available). Given our conceptualization of sleeping arrangements as symbolic actions, our main concern is to extract similarities and differences in cultural preferences, values, or goods as they are revealed in praxis, while taking account of similarities or differences that are driven primarily by limited space.

Oriya and American informants were presented with a sleeping arrangement task. For this task, a hypothetical family was constructed consisting of seven members: f, m, s15, s11, s8, d14, and d3. Nineteen Oriya adults (eleven women and eight men) and nineteen American adults (nine women and ten men) were asked to arrange and rearrange members of the family into separate sleeping spaces under hypothetical resource constraints ranging from one to seven rooms. At each resource level, the informant was free to declare that no sorting was possible or desirable. Informants were also asked to select their most preferred resource level. How many separate sleeping rooms would be ideal for this seven-person family?

An important first step in the cultural analysis of the proposed solutions to the sleeping arrangement task is the elaboration of a logical matrix. This is a characterization of all the logically possible ways to arrange the members of the family into one to seven sleeping spaces. Of course, there is only one way to sort seven persons into one room, and only one way to sort seven persons into seven rooms. But there are 63 logically possible ways to sort seven persons into two rooms, 301 ways for three rooms, 350 ways for four rooms, 140 ways for five rooms, and 21 ways for six rooms. (See Table 1.1, top half, for an example of the logically possible ways to sort seven persons into three rooms.)

It is a crucial fact about the force of cultural constraints on the practice of who sleeps by whom that very few of these 877 logically possible solutions were selected by any Oriya or American informant. For example, no one proposed such four-room solutions as f d14 / m s15 / s8 d3 / s11; or m / f d3 / s15 d14 / s8 s11 or f / m / d3 / s15 d14 s11 s8. No one proposed a two-room solution such as d3 / f m s15 d14 s11 s8. Indeed, perhaps 95 percent of the possible solutions in the logical matrix were ruled out as immoral, unacceptable, or otherwise ungrammatical by informants in both cultures. We would predict that even with a very large sample of informants, very few solutions (fewer than 15 or so, out of 877) would be selected with any frequency by informants in either culture. We would also predict that the small subset of solutions selected by Oriya Indians would not be coincidental with those selected by Americans.

Consider, for example, the Oriya and American solutions to the

Table 1.1   Distribution of Logically Possible and Selected Solutions under the Three-Room Constraint

Persons per space	1/1/5	1/2/4	1/3/3	2/2/3
Number of possible solutions (Total = 301)	21	105	70	105
Frequency of selection				
Oriya	0	0	2	17
American	0	0	1	17

Most favored 2/2/3 splits	Oriyas	Americans
f m / d14 d3 / s15 s11 s8	8	15
f m d3 / d14 s8 / s15 s11	4	0
f s8 / s15 s11 / m d14 d3	4	0
f m / s15 s11 / d14 d3 s8	1	1
s11 s8 / s15 d14 / f m d3	0	1

Note: f=father, m=mother, s=son, d=daughter, number following s or d =age of child, /=separation of sleeping space. Within a common sleeping space, the order of symbols is the order of sleeping positions.

sleeping arrangement task under the two-room constraint. Sixteen of nineteen Oriya informants offered a solution. Despite the fact that there were 63 possible ways to sort the family into two rooms, 75 percent of those Oriya informants selected one of two solutions: f s15 s11 s8 / m d14 d3; or f s15 s11 / m d14 d3 s8. In stark contrast, only seven of nineteen American informants offered a solution under the two-room constraint. Almost all of them converged on a sleeping arrangement that no Oriya would choose—namely, f m d14 d3 / s15 s11 s8.

Cultural Preferences. There is a small set of cultural preferences that help explain the unselected possibilities from the logical matrix. At least one of these preferences—summarized under the principle of incest avoidance—is familiar to all students of family dynamics. Within the family, sexualized unmarried males and females must not have sex with each other and should avoid all situations, such as co-sleeping, in which there may be sexual temptations or even suspicions about sexual contact. Incest avoidance is probably a universal moral preference, although allowances must be made for cultural variations in the scope of incest avoidance beyond the nuclear family and in the age of the people who must be separated.

Some of the other relevant moral preferences are more culture-specific. One such preference can be summarized under the principle of female chastity anxiety: in a culture such as India, where it is important in the context of marriage arrangements for unmarried sexualized women to be chaste, young unmarried girls are constantly chaperoned. Another preference can be summarized under the principle of respect for hierarchy: among sexually mature males, social superiority is expressed through deference and distance, which is incompatible with the intimacy, familiarity, and exposure of co-sleeping. A third culture-specific moral preference falls under the principle of the protection of the vulnerable: highly valued members of the family such as children are needy and fragile and should not be left alone at night.

Another preference can be summarized under the ideal of autonomy: highly valued members of the family such as children are needy and fragile and should be encouraged to be alone at night so they can learn to be self-reliant and independent and to care for themselves. A final moral preference falls under the principle of the sacred couple: when it comes to co-habiting adults, emotional intimacy, interpersonal commitment, and sexual privacy require that they sleep together and alone.

Interpreting Cultural Preferences. Each of these principles is a constraint on who sleeps by whom at night, although their interpretation and application leave room for local cultural discretion. For example, under Oriya interpretations, the incest avoidance principle requires separate sleeping space for at least these pairs: (f / d14), (m / s15), (s15 / d14). Under American interpretations, given the influence of certain ethnopsychological doctrines about the sexualized character of interactions between young children and adults, the moral preference for incest avoidance might also require separate sleeping space for (m / s11), (m / s8), (s11 / d14), (s8 / d14), and (f / d3).

For Oriyas there are four moral preferences implicit in their choices for the sleeping arrangement task: incest avoidance, protection of the vulnerable, female chastity anxiety, and respect for hierarchy. Thus, for example, a logically possible sleeping arrangement such as that proposed by an American informant—m f / s15 / d14 / d3 / s11 s8—is ruled out by Oriya informants because it is inconsistent with two important local moral preferences: female chastity anxiety (d14 cannot sleep alone) and protection of the vulnerable (d3 cannot sleep alone).

For middle-class Americans, in contrast, there are three moral preferences implicit in their choices for the sleeping arrangement task: incest avoidance, the sacred couple, and autonomy. Thus, for example, a logically possible sleeping arrangement such as the one proposed by an Oriya informant—m f s8 / d14 d3 / s15 s11—is ruled out by American informants because it is inconsistent with two important local moral preferences: the sacred couple (m and f should have exclusive co-sleeping space) and autonomy (each child should sleep alone).

Ordering of Moral Goods: The Preference Conflict Task

We are doubtful that the choices favoring a partitioning of sleeping locations in Oriya and American households are ever fully contravened by resource constraints. Even in a relatively confined space, members of a family can divide themselves into separate sleeping areas (using, for example, mats, beds, sections of a floor). Nevertheless, from an analytic point of view, imagining occasions when sleeping space is limited and members of a culture must make choices among their moral preferences is a useful exercise. The preferences for each culture can be arranged in precedence order.

We determined this ordering by presenting informants with the preference conflict task. In this task, four Oriya adults and sixteen American adults ranked a set of sleeping patterns selected to exemplify breaches of the moral preferences or goods in each culture. All the offensive arrangements referred to the same seven-person family used in the sleeping arrangement task. The preference conflict task was undertaken only after the groups' moral preferences and goods had been identified through the sleeping arrangement task. Table 1.2 lists the offensive arrangements presented to informants in Orissa and Hyde Park. They are ordered from most offensive to least offensive, based on the aggregate results from the preference conflict task in the two cultures.

Oriya moral preferences can be listed in order of importance as follows: incest avoidance, protection of the vulnerable, female chastity anxiety, and respect for hierarchy. For example, as shown in Table 1.2, a breach such as f d14 / m d3 / s11 s8 / s15 (a violation of incest avoidance) is judged by Oriyas to be more severe than a breach such as d14 / f / m d3 / s15 s11 s8 (a violation of female chastity anxiety), which in turn is judged to be more severe than a breach such as f s15 / m d14 d3 / s11 s8 (a violation of respect for hierarchy).

Given middle-class American moral preferences and the structure of our seven-person family, selecting a neatly discriminating set of breaches for the preference conflict task is not easy. We recognize that the particular set of offending arrangements presented to American informants (and shown in Table 1.2) is not ideal for determining the full ordering of American moral preferences. Nevertheless, we hypothesize that middle-class American moral preferences can be listed in order of importance as follows: incest avoidance,

Table 1.2 Culturally Offensive Sleeping Arrangements Ranked by Informants in Order of Severity of Breach

---

Orissa, India
f d14 / m d3 / s11 s8 / s15
d 3 / f / m d14 / s15 s11 s8
s8 d3 / f / m d14 / s15 s11
d14 / f / m d3 / s15 s11 s8
m / f / d14 d3 / s15 s11 s8
d14 s11/ f / m d3/ s15 s8
f s15 / m d14 d3 / s11 s8
f s11 /m d3 / s15 / d14 s8
f s15 / m d3 / d14 s8 / s11

Hyde Park, United States
f d14 / m s15 / s11 /s8 / d3
f m / s15 d14 / s11 /s8 / d3
f s15 / m d14 / s11 /s8 / d3
f / m / d14 d3 / s15 s8/ s11

Note: All these arrangements are offensive or "ungrammatical" to some degree in the relevant culture. Rankings move from most morally offensive at the top to least morally offensive at the bottom.

f=father, m=mother, s=son, d=daughter, number following s or d =age of child, /= separation of sleeping space. Within a common sleeping space, the order of symbols is the order of sleeping positions.

the sacred couple, and autonomy. One source of support for this hypothesis is Table 1.2, which shows a breach such as f m / s15 d 14 / s11 / s8 / d3 (a violation of incest avoidance) to be judged by Americans as more severe than a breach such as f / m / d14 d3 / s15 s8 / s11 (a violation of both the sacred couple principle and the principle of autonomy). A second source of support is the sleeping arrangement task, in which American informants often sacrificed the principle of autonomy while honoring the exclusive sleeping rights of the conjugal couple as required by the sacred couple principle.

Prioritizing Moral Preferences. Notice that there are both similarities and differences in the preferences implicit in the judgments of informants from Orissa, India, and Hyde Park, Illinois. The single most important moral preference in both cultures is the same: incest avoidance. All the other moral preferences differentiate the two cultures. For example, the second most important moral preference for middle-class Americans—what we have dubbed "the sacred couple"—plays no part in the choices made in Oriya culture. This American principle places such great constraints on possible solutions to the sleeping arrangements task that it rules out 92 percent of the 877 possible cells in the logical matrix; indeed, at certain resource levels, Americans can conceive of fewer solutions than the Oriyas. Thus, many Oriyas are willing to accept a two-room solution that divides males (f s15 s11 s8) from females (m d14 d3) and honors the incest avoidance principle. But this arrangement violates the sacred couple principle and thus most Americans find that solution unacceptable.

Moral Preferences and Resource Constraints. The results of our study make it apparent why, in constructing an analysis of a practice, it is imperative to distinguish between cultural preferences and resource constraints. Under particular resource constraints, the sleeping practices of two communities may look more similar than an analysis of cultural preferences would reveal. Thus, for example, Oriya Hindus and Hyde Park Americans converge in their solutions to the sleeping arrangements task under the three-room constraint, despite the fact that their choices are regulated by different moral preferences. Under the three-room resource constraint, both Americans and Oriyas favor f m / d14 d3 / s15 s11 s8 (see Table 1.1). This arrangement is only 1 of 301 logically possible ways to divide seven persons into three rooms, and it is only 1 of 105 logically possible ways to divide the persons into a two-two-three arrangement. Yet that one arrangement is preferred by a vast majority of American informants as well as by a plurality of the Oriya informants.

This particular sleeping arrangement is consistent with the two most important middle-class American moral preferences (incest avoidance and the sacred couple). Under a three-room constraint, most American informants seem willing to compromise on the autonomy of the children. The arrangement is also consistent with the three most important Oriya moral preferences (incest avoidance, protection of the vulnerable, and female chastity anxiety). (While there is no sacred couple principle in force in Orissa, the local culture does not prohibit exclusive parental co-sleeping, as long as culturally relevant principles are honored.) Under the three-room constraint, Oriyas seem willing to compromise on respect for hierarchy, although it might be argued that this principle applies only to the relationship of f and s15, in which case the willingness to accept co-sleeping for s15 s11 s8 may not be a compromise at all.

Under the three-room resource constraint, Oriyas do generate some solutions that middle-class Americans reject, such as f s8 / s15 s11 / m d14 d3 (see Table 1.1). Nevertheless, if one were only to observe the behavior of the two cultures at that one resource level, one might be misled into thinking that the two cultures were more or less the same. Only when one looks at behavior across a variety of resource constraints are true differences in cultural preferences revealed. The implication of this finding is important enough to warrant restating: in the face of any particular resource constraint, two different moral preference systems may give rise to similar "on the ground" sleeping arrangements; therefore, mere observation is insufficient as a method for determining true cultural differences.

SLEEPING ARRANGEMENTS IN THE TEMPLE TOWN: 160 SNAPSHOTS

How relevant is our account of Oriya preferences to "on the ground" sleeping arrangements in the temple town? To answer this question, we tested the Oriya and American packages of moral pref-

Table 1.3 Spot Reports of Previous Night's Sleeping Arrangement in Twelve
Oriya Households

Space	Sleeping arrangement	Persons per space
1	f d5 d7 m	4
2	f / s9 d6 d1 m	1/4
2	f / d12 s10 s 8 d4 m s15	1/6
2	f / s5 m s4 d7 d10 d13 d16	1/7
2	f s4 s7 / m d10 fm	3/3
2	f s9 m s6 / s18	4/1
3	f/ m d6 s10 / s16	1/3/1
3	f s6 / m s4 / fm	2/2/1
3	f m / s12 d7 d15 / ff	2/3/1
3	f s10 s6 / s20 / m (menstruating)	3/1/1
4	f / ff / m d10 d12 d14 / s12 s15 s16	1/1/4/3
4	f m d6 / s9 s14 / s16 s19 / fm	3/2/2/1

Note: The 12 households were randomly chosen from 160 spot reports. f=father, m=
mother, s=son, d=daughter, fm=father's mother, ff=father's father, number following s
or d =age of child, /=separation of sleeping space. Within a common sleeping space, the
order of symbols is the order of sleeping positions.

erences on our corpus of reports about who slept by whom the
night before in 160 Oriya households.

We conducted interviews with 160 children (ages 8 to 12) and
adults, who were asked to describe the sleeping locations of members of their family on the previous night. We relied on interviews rather than observations as it is not feasible to enter the inte-
rior spaces of a Hindu family compound to observe who sleeps by
whom. We will treat these spot reports as though they were a behavioral case record, although ultimately we have no way to assess
the degree of memory distortion, idealization, or error in this verbal record.

Table 1.3 lists twelve nighttime sleeping arrangements, randomly
selected from the data set. As the table shows, the family co-sleep-

ing networks in the temple town rarely fit the standard middle-class Anglo-American pattern.

Several decisions had to be made about how to apply the moral preference principles to the 160 cases at hand. These decisions were resolved in the following ways: 1) the Oriya female chastity principle is applied only to unmarried sexualized females, and the principle is not violated whenever an unmarried sexualized female shares a room with another family member, no matter who that is; 2) the Oriya respect for hierarchy principle does not apply between sons but only between father and son; 3) the incest avoidance principle does not apply to co-sleeping of grandparents and grandchildren; 4) the principles of incest avoidance, female chastity anxiety and respect for hierarchy are violated only if the child of relevance is 13 years of age or older. Finally, in order to simplify our analysis, we treated all indigenously recognized separations of sleeping space (different mats on two sides of a courtyard, different beds on two sides of a partition, different rooms) as equivalent separations.

In 87 percent of the Oriya households, sleeping arrangements were consistent with all four Oriya preferences The most important principle, incest avoidance, was violated in 8 of 160 households. An example of a violation of the incest avoidance principle can be found in Table 1.3 (line 3) where the mother and fifteen-year-old son co-sleep, although in the presence of four other children (f / d12 s10 s8 d4 m s15). Based on the results of our sleeping arrangement task, members of the local Oriya community ought to look askance at that particular arrangement, although within the terms of Oriya ethnopsychology it may not be easy to set precise age boundaries on the upper limits for nonexclusive parent-child co-sleeping. The second most important principle, protection of the vulnerable, was never violated. The third most important principle, female chastity anxiety, was violated in two households. The principle of respect for hierarchy was violated in twelve households.

It is a useful exercise to apply the package of American moral preferences to the Oriya sleeping arrangements. The American sacred couple principle was violated in 78 percent of Oriya households. Indeed actual sleeping arrangements in the temple town are consistent with all three American preferences in only 11 percent of the cases.

Conclusion: The Meaning of Practice

We began this chapter by examining two questions posed by the pediatrician Dr. T. Berry Brazelton: Should we re-evaluate our stance toward children's sleep, and who ought to sleep by whom in the family? It has not been our aim to answer these questions. Instead, we have pointed to conceptual work that needs to be done before those questions can be seriously addressed. Who sleeps by whom is not merely a personal or private activity. It is a social practice, like burying the dead or eating meals with your family or honoring the practice of a monogamous marriage, which (for those engaged in the practice) is invested with moral and social meaning and with implications for a person's standing in a community. Those meanings and implications must be taken into account if the issue of who sleeps by whom is to be treated not so much as a mindless habit or tradition-laden routine but as a deliberate act of rational choice motivated by an analysis of probable psychological and social costs and benefits.

In this chapter we present a method (the application of a logical matrix) for identifying moral and social meanings implicit in the praxis of who sleeps by whom. We examine similarities and differences in the preferred moral goods (for example, incest avoidance, the sacred couple, female chastity anxiety, the protection of the vulnerable) of two culture regions. Much work still remains to be done examining the effects of family life practices and the effects of social consensus on developmental competence in various domains of functioning (emotional, moral, interpersonal, cognitive) (see LeVine, 1990). Likewise, much work still remains to be done examining the developmental advantages, if any, of growing up in a family that engages in culturally consensual sleeping practices (co-sleeping if you are an Oriya child; sleeping alone if you are a middle-class Anglo-American child).

Nevertheless, on the basis of what we already know about the cultural meanings implicit in family-life practices, no informed discussion of parent-child co-sleeping can proceed unless those involved in the discussion first recognize that behavior per se is not what the action is about. The family order is part of the social order, which is part of the moral order—which is why all around the globe (in Japan, in India, even in middle-class America), a cultural analysis of local preferences, values, and moral goods is a necessary first step in making sense of who sleeps by whom.

The "Big Three" of Morality (Autonomy, Community, Divinity) and the "Big Three" Explanations of Suffering

with Nancy C. Much, Manamohan Mahapatra,
and Lawrence Park

Human beings apparently want to be edified by their miseries. It is as if the desire to make suffering intelligible and to turn it to some advantage is one of those dignifying peculiarities of our species, like the ability to cook or conjugate verbs or conceive of the idea of justice. Human beings, unlike other living things, want to go to school when they are miserable. They want answers: What caused this to happen? Why did this happen to me? Am I responsible? What can I do about it? What does this imply about my social relationships? What does this suggest about my personal rectitude? This chapter explores some of the ways human beings understand suffering and turn suffering to advantage, by blaming themselves for illness, disaster, and distress.

The chapter looks at the implications of imagining the world and the experience of suffering in terms of the moral metaphors of South Asia. (On the study of metaphors implicit in folk and scientific theories, see Lakoff and Johnson, 1980, 1986; Johnson, 1987; Lakoff, 1987).[1] In South Asia ideas about a sacred self, a sacred world, "karma" ("you reap what you sow; therefore suffering may be an index of moral failure") and what might be called "feudal ethics" exist both as folk theories and as highly developed technical theories. In the United States such ideas run counter to the official discourse of scientific explanation, yet persist as private intuitions experienced as mysteries or with embarrassment or as personal or communal counterdiscourses. Why do certain ideas, which are viewed as rational in South Asia and infused with publicly acknowledged social meaning, persist in our own culture despite the absence of a scientific ontology to support them and despite the preeminent prestige of a scientific-materialist discourse that disavows and disparages them?

Ideas about human experience that persist for a long time, are widespread, or become invested with social meaning and established as folk theories in a major region of the world are not likely to be merely primitive or superstitious. Such ideas illuminate some aspect of mind, experience, or society and can be put to use not only to construct a valid cultural psychology (Much, 1993; Shweder, 1991; Shweder and Sullivan, 1993) but to extend our moral imagination (Johnson, 1993). The chapter considers apparently primitive or superstitious ideas such as the notion that "old sins cast long shadows" and the related idea that illness is payback for spiritual debts. We spell out the wisdom that ideas about karma, the sacred self, the sacred world, and feudal ethics encode in their metaphors. We apply one of the central assumptions of cultural psychology: indigenous or folk theories (our own and others) should be taken seriously as cognitive objects and as potential sources of social scientific and practical knowledge (Much 1993: 6–7).

The Causal Ontologies of Suffering

To suffer is to experience a disvalued and unwanted state of mind, body, or spirit. The experience might be an acute disease, a recurrent nightmare, an obsessive thought, an incapacitating sadness, a skin rash, a miscarriage, or a cancer. It might be the experience of chronic fatigue or pain or a prolonged decline in physical integrity and personal autonomy.

One way to render suffering meaningful is to trace its genesis to some "order of reality" where one may point the finger at events and processes that can be held responsible, as suffering's cause. We shall use the expression "causal ontology" to refer to a person's or people's ideas about the orders of reality responsible for suffering.

TYPES OF ONTOLOGIES

Although the varieties of suffering of soma, psyche, and spirit that have been experienced by human beings range widely over an indefinitely large territory of afflictions, symptoms, and complaints, the types of causal ontologies that have played a major part in explanations of suffering are in fact relatively few. On a worldwide scale, there seem to be seven kinds of causal ontologies (and associated therapeutic institutions) for comprehending and responding to suffering. (We hasten to add that, because any taxonomy is discretionary, there may be other ways to classify causal ontologies and somewhat different verdicts on the overall count. We do not think seven is a "magic number," even allowing for the "plus or minus two.")

First, there is a biomedical causal ontology that is notable in its current official Western medical variety for its explanatory references to genetic defects, hormone imbalances, organ pathologies, and physiological impairments. It is notable in other non-Western or unofficial Western varieties (for example, Hindu Ayurvedic medicine) for its explanatory references to humors, precious bodily fluids and juices (semen, blood, ascorbic acid), and felicitous ecological transactions that enhance feelings of strength and well-being. Biomedical therapy focuses on the ingestion of special substances, herbs and roots, vitamins, vegetable compounds, and chemical compounds as well as on the direct or indirect mechanical repair (for example, via surgery or via message or emetics) of damaged fibers and organs.

Second, there is the interpersonal causal ontology which is notable in "traditional" societies for its references to sorcery, evil eye, black magic, spirit attack, poisoning, and bewitchment. We have our contemporary counterparts in harassment, abuse, exploitation, co-dependencies, and toxic relationships. This ontology is associated with the idea that one can be made sick by the envy or ill will of colleagues, neighbors, and associates. Therapy focuses on talismans and other protective devices, strategies for avoidance or aggressive counterattack, and, quite crucially, on the repair of interpersonal relationships.

Third, there is the sociopolitical causal ontology which is associated with the idea that suffering is the product of oppression or colonial (including ideological) domination or adverse economic or family conditions. Therapy focuses on altering one's life circumstances through social reform or, more typically, on achieving some local or immediate successes or gains.

Fourth, there is the psychological causal ontology which is associated with the idea that unfulfilled desires, frustrated intentions, or fear can make one suffer. Therapy focuses on a variety of intrapsychic and psychosocial interventions, including meditation, dialogue, therapeutic relationships, and realistic goal-setting. Freud is a noteworthy contemporary Western variant of psychological explanation, much absorbed into North American folk theory; but non-Western cultures, including South Asia, use psychological theories of causality as well.

The fifth causal ontology, astrophysical, is notable for its references to malevolent arrangements of planets, moons, and stars, and to auspicious and inauspicious periods of time. Therapy emphasizes the theme of waiting, with optimism, for some identifiable auspicious future time when recovery will occur spontaneously or remedial efforts can be effective. In the meantime certain protective or meliorative actions are often possible. This is a causal ontology that is foregrounded in many non-Western cultures. It is backgrounded or officially denied, yet very much present, in segments of the folk life of contemporary middle-class American culture (of European, African, or Asian origin).

Sixth, there is an apparently emergent causal ontology rooted in the metaphors of external stress, pressure, and environmental risk factors. This ontology seems contemporary in the forms of discourse with which we are all familiar. Along with CNN and Visa, the English word "stress" seems to have migrated to all parts of the world. It is possible, however, that this causal ontology has been around for a long time, but in terms we have as yet failed to identify. For example, aspects of Ayurvedic medicine, South Asian home remedies, and Indo-Tibetan social theory contain "ecological" causal relationships perhaps not entirely dissimilar to the terminologies of this ontology, and they recognize "de-stressing" tactics for remedial action. Stressors themselves may, of course, be of a social or a biochemical nature. Therapies emphasize the minimization of stress: relaxation, the creative use of leisure time, and the reduction of ambient hazards in one's environment through enlightenment, education, and foresight.

Finally, there is a moral causal ontology. That causal ontology is notable for its references to transgressions of obligation: omissions of duty, trespass of mandatory boundaries, and more generally any type of ethical failure at decision-making or self-control. It is associated with the idea that suffering is the result of one's own actions or intentions, that a loss of moral fiber is a prelude to misfortune, and that outcomes—good and bad—are proportionate to actions. You reap what you sow. Moral therapy focuses on unloading one's sin, purification, reparation, moral education, and the adoption of "right practices" sanctioned by a sacred authority (from the Pope to the Surgeon-General). Later in this chapter we take as an example a South Asian conception of moral causation, the theory of karma, and explore its implications as a viable moral metaphor for rethinking the discourse of morality and suffering in our own contemporary society.

The Idea of Causation in Folk Psychology

Within the intellectual framework of folk psychology, explanations of illness are instances of causal analysis. The idea of causation is recognized worldwide, though the folk use of the term has several distinguishing characteristics. In folk psychology the idea of causation does not rule out the possibility of influence at a distance. It does not rule out influence by unobservable forces. It does not treat all necessary conditions as equally relevant or as of the same kind. In contrast, logicians such as John Stuart Mills define causation as all the necessary conditions that are jointly sufficient to produce an event and empiricists such as David Hume reduce the idea of causation to directly observable events (for example, one billiard ball making contact with another) that are immediately coincidental in time and locally proximate in space (see Collingwood, 1961, originally 1938; Hart and Honore, 1961, originally 1956).

Quite crucially, the idea of causation in folk psychology is deeply shaped by human interests in assessing "normality," attributing responsibility or blame, and exercising control over future events. Thus, the numerous logically necessary conditions for the production of a given event do not all have equal status in the folk psychology of causation. Indeed, in folk psychology the elevation of a necessary condition to the status of an attributed cause is an act of selection and interpretation that can be understood only within the context of practices and institutions aimed at finding fault, righting wrongs, and gaining control over future events.

A classic account of the idea of causation in folk psychology can be found in Hart and Honore (1961: 333, 335). As these scholars note, distinctions are drawn in folk psychology (they call it "common sense" psychology) "between what is abnormal and what is normal in relation to any given subject-matter and between a free deliberate human action and all other conditions." For example, with regard to the distinction between normal and abnormal conditions, oxygen in the air is a necessary condition for a forest fire but it is a "normal" condition and is not viewed in folk psychology as a cause, while the lightening storm, although no more necessary than the oxygen, is an "abnormal" condition and hence is likely to be viewed as the cause.

And as Hart and Honore point out, with regard to the distinction between free deliberate human action and everything else, "we [folk psychologists] feel that it is not enough to be told that a man died from unusual quantities of arsenic in his body, and we press on for the more satisfactory explanation in terms of human agency." "Deliberate human action," Hart and Honore note, "has a special status as a cause [in folk psychology] and is not regarded in its turn as something which is caused."

In the folk concept of a cause, Collingwood (1961: 303,306) detects the idea of "a free and deliberate act of a conscious and responsible agent," which is best understood in terms of the ends the agent is trying to achieve and the means the agent believes are available for achieving them. For example, the cause of an event such as a miscarriage during pregnancy might be treated as equivalent to someone's motives for acting—in this case, for example, a neighbor is envious, intends to subvert the childbirth, and employs the services of a sorcerer. Indeed it is precisely by reference to the quality of those motives and intentions (are they good or bad) that the agent who caused the event can be held responsible or judged to be at fault, or even accused of being a witch.

Collingwood also notes a second sense of the idea of causation in folk psychology. In that second sense, "the cause of a given thing is that one of its [logically necessary] conditions which [some given person] is able to produce or prevent." Collingwood gives the following example:

> A car skids while cornering at a certain point, turns turtle, and bursts into flames. From the car-driver's point of view the cause of the accident was cornering too fast, and the lesson is that one must drive more carefully. From the county surveyor's point of view, the cause was a defective road surface, and the lesson is that one must make skid-proof roads. From the motor-manufacturer's point of view, the cause was defective design, and the lesson is that one must place the center of gravity lower.

Notice that in each case the selected necessary condition (the attributed cause) is relative to the potential range of control of the attributer. Notice that the attributed cause does not include everything that is logically relevant to a causal analysis but rather the one thing that is practically relevant because the attributer is in a position to set it right.

As we examine the causal ontologies of suffering available world-wide, it is helpful to keep in mind the aims of causal analysis in folk psychology: to set abnormal outcomes right by gaining control over abnormal conditions that are within the range of one's expertise and power, and to attribute responsibility and assign fault in a world of events presumed to be caused by "the free and deliberate acts of conscious and responsible agents."

Interpersonal, Biomedical, and Moral Explanations

Among anthropologists the cross-cultural study of the types and distribution of explanations of suffering with special reference to illness has a distinguished history (see, for example, Whiting and Child, 1953; Kleinman, 1986), although interest in the topic has been erratic. In 1980 George Peter Murdock published a survey of explanations of illness in 139 societies, as recorded in extant ethnographies. While the overall quality of that ethnographic data leaves much to be desired, Murdock's survey suggests that preferred or official causal ontologies for suffering are unequally distributed around the world and may cluster in broad geographically based "ideological regions."

In sub-Sahara Africa Murdock discerns a preference for explanations by reference to moral transgression (for example, violation of sexual taboos). In East Asia the folk seem inclined to the view that suffering is due to ancestral spirit attack and other interpersonal causes. Wikan (1989), for example, reports that "on the evidence of the souls of the dead themselves" 50 percent of all deaths in Bali are thought to be caused by black magic or poisoning by an intimate other. In the circum-Mediterranean region (Europe and North Africa), it is witchcraft that is favored in accounts of the causes of misery and death. Explanations by reference to organ pathology, hormone imbalance, or physiological impairment were, among the 139 societies surveyed by Murdock, never preferred.

A recent cross-cultural survey by Park (1992) reanalyzed some of Murdock's sources and recoded the data in several ways. The goals of Park's research were threefold: 1) to arrive at an estimate of the relative worldwide prevalence of six of the seven causal ontologies mentioned in this chapter (stress was not examined); 2) to assess the hypothesis that there is geographical clustering of different types of causal explanations of suffering into ideological regions; and 3) to examine the connection between specific illnesses and the particular types of explanations or therapies produced in response to illness.

In the present context we restrict our discussion to the prevalence rates of various causal ontologies for suffering and parallel therapies, although the third issue is relevant to our discussion as well. Thus, for example, Murdock's and Park's surveys suggest that particular afflictions (for example, a miscarriage, a rash, sterility) of particular parts of the body (the womb, genitals, the mouth, a visible part of the skin) incline the mind in the direction of particular causal ontologies and not others. Witchcraft explanations, where and when they are adduced, seem to be associated with issues of generativity and fecundity (crop failure, miscarriage, infertility). Murdock suggested that agent-blaming moralistic explanations crop up when suffering is preceded by violations of sexual or food taboos or by acts of disrespect to figures in authority (parents or gods).

Indeed it is tempting to speculate that sexual transgressions, dietary transgressions, and transgressions of the hierarchical ordering of things can have such a powerful influence on the way we think and reason that long-delayed misfortunes may be understood as punishments for prior sin, and as confirmation of the maxim that "ultimately the past catches up." A transgression such as disregard for one's parents or incest is most readily moralized if it is embedded in an intellectual framework such as an ethics of community and/or divinity, which carries with it the implication that the transgressor has violated the sacred order of things, as manifest in nature, society, or the self. The basic idea is that when things start to go bad in life, there is a special class of prior dreadful transgressions in one's life that are likely to leap out as suspiciously ill-begotten causes. For the moment, however, our main concern is the prevalence rates for causal ontologies of suffering.

On the basis of Park's reading of ethnographic reports from 68 cultures of the world, involving 752 illness episodes, interpersonal (42 percent), moral (15 percent), and biomedical (15 percent) causal ontologies serve as the three primary *explanations* of suffering worldwide. The most frequent *therapies* are biomedical (35 percent), interpersonal (29 percent), and moral (7 percent).

As a reminder, the interpersonal mode of explanation describes suffering as the result of the ill will of others, while the moral mode of explanation claims you reap what you sow. The biomedical mode of causal explanation sees suffering as a by-product of events and circumstances that take place outside the realms of human action, responsibility, or control. Strictly speaking, within the terms of a biomedical explanation, suffering is a material event. It should be understood in material terms. It should be controlled through material interventions. When it comes to the strict biomedical understanding and alleviation of illness, no further questions are asked about such ultimate issues as human society, social relationships, or personal rectitude. Pure biomedical explanations are by definition morally neutral and indifferent to the moral career of the sufferer or of others.

A second fascinating finding of Park's study is that sufferers are more likely to seek a biomedical therapy for a problem than to offer a biomedical explanation of it. This is not true of either of the other two modes of explanation and cure. Interpersonal therapies (repair of social relationships, counter-sorcery, exorcism) are less likely to be sought than interpersonal explanations of suffering are to be offered. Moral therapies (confession, sacrifice, austerities) are less likely to be sought than moral explanations of suffering are to be offered. Thus while there is a rough parallelism between mode of explanation and mode of cure—a tendency for biomedical explanations to lead to biomedical therapies, interpersonal explanations to interpersonal therapies, and moral explanations to moral therapies—when there is misalignment between explanatory ontology and therapeutic mode, the mismatch seems to be in the direction of using a biomedical therapy for an affliction believed to have an interpersonal or moral cause. This may have something to do with the perceived possibility for control. That is, when human beings suffer, an imperative may exist for direct, physical manipulation of the suffering body. Another reason for the slippage toward biomedical therapies may be the immediacy or relative efficacy of such cures. In any case, the drift toward biomedical therapies does not seem peculiar to our times or to our particular system of Western biomedicine.

The prevalence of interpersonal explanations of suffering suggests that the idea of victimization also is not peculiar to the contemporary United States with its particular social justice concerns. That choice of causal explanation may reflect an underinvestigated intuition of folk psychology—the attitudes and expressions of those around us, through various social-communicative and social control processes, are effective in inducing psychosomatic stress that can result in illness. Tibetan communities, for example, have the idea that the malicious or envious gossip of one's neighbors, without other intervening mechanisms such as sorcery or witch-craft, acts as a force capable of wreaking havoc with one's life and health (Mumford, 1989).

Let's look for a moment at moral explanations of suffering, ranked second in Park's survey, and moral therapies, ranked third in the survey. This estimate of the prevalence of moral thinking in health practices probably underestimates the role of moral agency in explanations of suffering. First, interpersonal explanations of suffering are often saturated with implicit secondary moral implications (for example, the ancestral spirit attack may have been related to an ethical failure to perform a ritual), which may not have been known to the ethnographer. Interpersonal causal explanations frequently involve moral features and moral offenses; there is some quarrel or bad feeling between the victim and the aggressor. Reparation of relationships and re-establishment of a just local order may be part of what sorcerers try to accomplish. Even in cases of pure victimization, the very notion of "victimization" is inherently a moral idea, which may place the victimizer in jeopardy of becoming sick.

Second, in areas such as South Asia and East India, biomedical and interpersonal therapies do not occur in "pure" form. Therapies are interlaced with religious elements similar to divine grace. Ayurvedic doctors and sorcerers alike may call upon the power of God to accomplish their work, and the act of healing may presuppose a moral relationship between the healer and the God (Much and Mahapatra, 1993). The third reason moral thinking may have been underestimated is that personal ruminations about moral reform take place without being announced in public and without being made available to ethnographers. Finally, an examination of the use of moral explanations and therapies in the context of an existing illness (where they can be viewed only as a response to distress) does not take into account the role of morality as a form of preventive medicine upholding right practices.

Perhaps the most noteworthy finding from Park's survey is that the biomedical causal ontology so prevalent in secular scientific subcultures in North America and Europe is the least frequently employed of the three most common explanations of suffering used worldwide (also see Murdock, 1980). Afflictions such as insanity or death, for example, are almost always explained in other-blaming interpersonal terms or agent-blaming moral terms rather than ascribed to biomedical events.

For most peoples of the world, there are no faultless deaths. As Hart and Honore remarked (1961: 333): "It is not enough to be told that a man died from the presence of unusual quantities of arsenic in his body; and we press on for a more satisfying explanation in terms of human agency." Death by arsenic or any life-terminating biological happening such as a stroke or heart attack would not take place without the push of human agency. Or so it is widely believed.

The "Big Three" of Ethical Discourse: Autonomy, Community, and Divinity

We now turn to a more detailed account of the way faults are found and agents blamed within the framework of some South Asian discourses of morality and health.

AN ANALYSIS OF MORAL DISCOURSE

Our analysis of the moral discourse of the residents of the city of Bhubaneswar is derived from interviews with forty-seven informants (twenty-nine males and eighteen females, mostly adults and mostly Brahmans). The thirty-nine incidents shown in Table 2.1 are brief descriptions of behavioral events representing actual or po-

Table 2.1 The Thirty-nine Incidents and Their Loadings on Autonomy, Community, and Divinity

Incident number	Thirty-nine incidents	Autonomy harm, rights, justice	Community duty, hierarchy, inter-dependency	Divinity sacred order, natural order personal sanctity
1.	A woman cooked rice and wanted to eat with her husband and his elder brother. Then she ate with them. (the woman)*	L	M	H
2.	In a family, a 25-year-old son addresses his father by his first name. (the son)	L	H	M
3.	In a family, the first-born son slept with his mother or grandmother till he was 10 years old. During these ten years, he never slept in a separate bed. (the practice)	M	M	M
4.	A woman is playing cards at home with her friends. Her husband is cooking rice for them. (the husband)	L	H	H
5.	A beggar was begging from house to house with his wife and sick child. A homeowner drove him away without giving anything. (the homeowner)	H	M	M
6.	A man says to his brother, "Your daughter's skin is dark. No one will say she is beautiful. No one will wish to marry her." (the man)	M	M	M
7.	The day after his father's death, the eldest son had a haircut and ate chicken. (the son)	L	H	M

Incident number	Thirty-nine incidents	Autonomy harm, rights, justice	Community duty, hierarchy, inter-dependency	Divinity sacred order, natural order personal sanctity
8.	A father said to his son, "If you do well on the exam, I will buy you a pen." The son did well on the exam, but his father did not give him anything, spending the money on a carton of cigarettes. (the father)	L	M	L
9.	A young married woman went alone to see a movie without informing her husband. When she returned home, her husband said, "If you do it again, I will beat you black and blue." She did it again; he beat her black and blue. (the husband)	L	H	M
10.	A letter arrived addressed to a 14-year-old son. Before the boy returned home, his father opened the letter and read it. (the father)	L	H	L
11.	A man had a married son and a married daughter. After his death his son claimed most of the property. His daughter got a little. (the son)	H	H	L
12.	You went to a movie. There was a long line in front of the ticket window. You broke into line and stood at the front. (you)	M	L	L

Table 2.1 (continued)

Incident number	Thirty-nine incidents	Autonomy harm, rights, justice	Community duty, hierarchy, inter-dependency	Divinity sacred order, natural order, personal sanctity
13.	Six months after the death of her husband, the widow wore jewelry and bright-colored clothes. (the widow)	L	M	H
14.	Immediately after marriage, a son was asked by his parents to live in the same house with them. The son said he wanted to live alone with his wife and that he and his wife had decided to live in another town and search for work there. (the son)	L	H	L
15.	Once a doctor's daughter met a garbage man, fell in love with him, and decided to marry him. The father of the girl opposed the marriage and tried to stop it, because the boy is a garbage man. In spite of the opposition from the father, the girl married the garbage man. (the daughter)	L	H	H
16.	There was a rule in a hotel: Invalids and disfigured persons are not allowed in the dining hall. (the rule)	H	M	M
17.	A widow and an unmarried man loved each other. The widow asked him to marry her. (the widow)	L	M	M

Incident number	Thirty-nine incidents	Autonomy harm, rights, justice	Community duty, hierarchy, inter-dependency	Divinity sacred order, natural order, personal sanctity
18.	A boy played hooky from school. The teacher told the boy's father and the father warned the boy not to do it again. But the boy did it again and the father beat him with a cane. (the father)	H	M	L
19.	At night a wife asked her husband to massage her legs. (the wife)	L	M	M
20.	A poor man went to the hospital after being seriously hurt in an accident. At the hospital they refused to treat him because he could not afford to pay. (the hospital)	H	M	L
21.	A wife is waiting for her husband at the railway station. The train arrives. When the husband gets off, the wife goes and kisses him. (the wife)	L	L	M
22.	In school a girl drew a picture. One of her classmates came, took it, and tore it up. (the classmate)	M	M	L
23.	One of your family members eats beef regularly. (the family member)	L	L	H
24.	Two people applied for a job. One of them was a relative of the interviewer. Because they were relatives, he was given the job although the other man did better on the exam. (the practice)	H	L	L

Table 2.1 (continued)

Incident number	Thirty-nine incidents	Autonomy harm, rights, justice	Community duty, hierarchy, inter-dependency	Divinity sacred order, natural order, personal sanctity
25.	A man had a wife who was sterile. He wanted to have two wives. He asked his first wife and she said she did not mind. So he married a second woman and the three of them lived happily in the same house. (the man)	M	H	L
26.	One of your family members eats dog regularly for dinner. (the family member)	L	L	H
27.	While walking, a man saw a dog sleeping on a road. He walked up to it and kicked it. (the man)	H	L	M
28.	After defecation (making a bowel movement) a woman did not change her clothes before cooking.	L	L	H
29.	A man does not like to use a fork. Instead he always eat rice with his bare hand. He washes his hand before and after eating. He does this when he eats alone or with others. (the man)	L	L	H
30.	A father told his son to steal flowers from his neighbor's garden. The boy did it. (the boy)	L	H	L
31.	A brother and sister decide to get married and have children. (the practice)	L	L	H

Incident number	Thirty-nine incidents	Autonomy harm, rights, justice	Community duty, hierarchy, inter-dependency	Divinity sacred order, natural order personal sanctity
32.	Two brothers are at home together. After they ate, the wife of the younger brother washed the dishes. (the wife)	L	L	M
33.	It was the king's order, if the villagers do not torture an innocent boy to death, twelve hundred people will be killed. The people killed the innocent boy. So the king spared the life of the twelve hundred people. (the people)	H	L	L
34.	A widow in your community eats fish two or three times a week. (the widow)	L	H	H
35.	You meet a foreigner. He is wearing a watch. You ask him how much it cost and whether he will give it to you. (you)	L	M	L
36.	Two men hold hands with each other while they wait for a bus. (the practice)	L	H	M
37.	A father, his eldest son, and his youngest daughter traveled in a boat. They had one life jacket. It could carry one person. The boat sank in the river. The father had to decide who should be saved. He decided to save his youngest daughter. The father and the eldest son drowned. (the father)	M	H	L

Table 2.1 (continued)

Incident number	Thirty-nine incidents	Autonomy harm, rights, justice	Community duty, hierarchy, inter-dependency	Divinity sacred order, natural order personal sanctity
38.	The day after the birth of his first child, a man entered his temple (church) and prayed to God.	L	L	H
39.	A woman cooks food for her family members and sleeps in the same bed with her husband during her menstrual period. (the woman)	H	L	H

L = low; M = medium; H = high;
Note: The potential transgressor is in parentheses.

tential breaches of codes of conduct. They were developed over a period of several months on the basis of ethnographic knowledge of community and family life in Bhubaneswar. The moral discourse to be analyzed was elicited during a structured interview described in Shweder, Mahapatra, and Miller (1987, also 1990). All of the incidents that are listed are considered to be breaches or transgressions, with the exception of incident #3 (co-sleeping child and adult), #9 (beating the insubordinate wife), #18 (caning the errant school boy), #29 (eating with your hands), and #36 (men holding hands with each other).

The basis for the analysis is the Oriya moral themes code, Figure 2.1, described by Much (1987). For the purpose of analysis, the rationales of all informants were pooled together to form collective transcripts for each of the thirty-nine incidents. The transcripts for each incident ranged from three to twenty-five pages of single-spaced text. Much developed the code through inductive iterative reading and classification of transcript contents, first generating a set of categories sufficient to exhaustively catalog the content of the transcripts at a meaningful level of discrimination, and then combining categories where justifiable to arrive at one parsimonious set. The purpose of the coding system was to identify the themes that occur in Oriya moral discourse and the ideas to which informants appeal when they give rationales for their moral judgments. The sixteen categories are not mutually exclusive.

A given stretch of text could instantiate more than one category. For example, if an informant expressed her moral condemnation of the events in incident #4 ("A women is playing cards at home with her friends. Her husband is cooking rice for them.") by stating, "The wife is the servant of the husband. The servant should do her work," that rationale would be coded as both "hierarchy" and "duty." After the texts were coded, a profile was calculated for each

Oriya Moral Themes

1   Virtue and merit: Acts that elevate and acts that degrade one's status as a human being, hence one's position in the social and cosmic (by karma) order. The development of a virtuous (elevated) nature.

2   Social order: Effects of action in the social structure, within the family or community. Maintenance of patterns of social organization, harmony within the social structure, and one's own position within the social order.

3   Souls and sentiments: Recognition of and respect for the nonmaterial self of oneself and others. Regard for the feelings and the sensibilities of others and the well-being of their soul or nonmaterial self. The goal and strivings of the spiritual self, hence individual will, desire and choice.

4   Tradition, custom, culture, relative dharmas: Hindu culture and traditional social law. The Hindu way of life. The relative dharmas of different castes, religions, nations, ages, and so on. The obligations one has by virtue of one's social identity, place, and time. Culture as an expression of the dharmic order; culture as an expression of natural law.

5   Duty: Role-based obligations within family and in society. The obligations that define one's particular role.

6   Sacred order: The laws of God, the acts of gods, human actions that please and displease God. Worship, devotion, sacred scripture, scriptural and other religious authority.

7   Interdependence, relationship: The interconnectedness of persons. One's own good as interdependent with the good of others. Asymmetrical reciprocity as bonding force in the social order.

8   Hierarchy: Respect for relative status within the family, in society, or in the cosmic order (for example, humans to gods). Patterns of behavior that signal acknowledgment of status differences.

9   Nature, biological order: Actions with intrinsic consequences for well-being, based on a conception of the biological order.

10   Justice, fairness, rights: Distribution of rewards, privileges, or punishments according to desert. One's rights and entitlements by various sources of entitlement.

11   Purity, sanctity, pollution: The maintenance of sanctity and purity of persons and environments. Actions, persons or animals, substances, or mental states that pollute sanctified persons or environments.

12	Harm, life, well-Being: Respect for life and material, biological well-being. Nonharming and protection of the life and well-being of others. Compassion.
13	Chastity: Sexual conduct in keeping with social or religious norms of rightful sexual unions and sexual behavior. In particular, the conjugal faithfulness of women and actions that signal a chaste attitude versus actions that signal an inclination to be unchaste.
14	Respect for possessions: Respect for ownership and personal or private property.
15	Truthfulness, honesty, trustworthiness: Telling the truth, speaking honestly, honoring commitments and vows, being dependable and undeceitful in dealings with others.
16	Transcendence: Spiritual goals or spiritual realities that transcend material or social categories or concerns.

Figure 2.1 Oriya moral themes

incident indicating the proportion of informants who had used each of the sixteen ideas listed in the Oriya Moral Themes code (see Figure 2.1). In effect, the degree of saturation was determined for each incident for moral ideas of particular kinds. For example, incident #2 ("In a family, a twenty-five year old son addresses his father by his first name") is highly saturated with ideas of hierarchy and duty and moderately saturated with other ideas, while some ideas are entirely absent from the collective transcript on this incident. On the basis of the themes profiles for the thirty-nine incidents, Much used statistical procedures including cluster analyses and stepwise discriminant analysis to distinguish three clusters of conceptually linked themes and to identify the degree of saturation of each incident by ideas from each cluster. The resulting three clusters are shown in Figure 2.2.

The first cluster (the ethics of autonomy) relies on regulative concepts such as harm, rights, and justice (see Oriya moral themes,

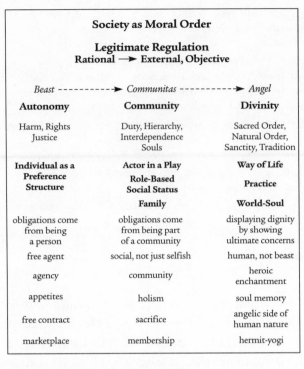

Society as Moral Order		
Legitimate Regulation Rational ⟶ External, Objective		
Beast ------→	*Communitas* ----------→	*Angel*
Autonomy	**Community**	**Divinity**
Harm, Rights Justice	Duty, Hierarchy, Interdependence Souls	Sacred Order, Natural Order, Sanctity, Tradition
Individual as a Preference Structure	**Actor in a Play** **Role-Based Social Status**	**Way of Life** **Practice**
	Family	**World-Soul**
obligations come from being a person	obligations come from being part of a community	displaying dignity by showing ultimate concerns
free agent	social, not just selfish	human, not beast
agency	community	heroic enchantment
appetites	holism	soul memory
free contract	sacrifice	angelic side of human nature
marketplace	membership	hermit-yogi

Figure 2.2 The "Big Three" of Morality

Figure 2.2, items 10 and 12). The second cluster (the ethics of community) relies on regulative concepts such as duty, hierarchy, interdependency, and souls (Figure 2.2, items 3, 5, 7, and 8). The third cluster (the ethics of divinity) relies on regulative concepts such as sacred order, natural order, sanctity, and tradition (Figure 2.2, items 4, 6, 9, and 11).

The ethics of autonomy aims to protect the zone of discretionary choice of individuals and to promote the exercise of individual will in the pursuit of personal preferences. Autonomy is usually the official ethic of societies in which individualism is an ideal. The ethics of community, in contrast, aims to protect the moral integrity of the various stations or roles that constitute a society or a community, where a "society" or "community" is conceived of as a corporate entity with an identity, standing, history, and reputation of its own. Finally, the ethics of divinity aims to protect the soul, the spirit, the spiritual aspects of the human agent and nature from degradation.

Presupposed by the ethics of autonomy is a conceptualization of the self as a individual preference structure, where the point of moral regulation is to increase choice and personal liberty. Presupposed by the ethic of community is a conceptualization of the self as an office holder. The basic idea is that one's role or station in life is intrinsic to one's identity and is part of a larger interdependent collective enterprise with a history and standing of its own. Presupposed by the ethics of divinity is a conceptualization of the self as a spiritual entity connected to some sacred or natural order of things and as a responsible bearer of a legacy that is elevated and divine. Those who regulate their life within the terms of an ethics of divinity do not want to do anything, such as eating the flesh of a slaughtered animal, that is incommensurate with the nature of the spirit that joins the self to the divine ground of all things.

Table 2.1 indicates the relative degree to which each of the thirty-nine incidents is saturated with ethical ideas from each of the big three types (autonomy, community, divinity) in the discourse of our Oriya informants. Incident #4 (the wife who is playing cards with her friends while her husbands cooks) is primarily conceptualized in terms of the ethics of community and the ethics of divinity. In several cases in which the reader might well reason in terms of harm, rights, and justice, our Oriya informants reason in terms of duty, sin, and pollution. We now turn to a more direct and "thicker" discussion of the three Oriya discourses and the themes that play a central role in the cultural construction of ethics and well-being.

METAPHORS FOR THE MORAL IMAGINATION: MULTIPLICITY AND DIFFERENTIAL SALIENCY

The three thematic clusters introduced in this chapter may be thought of as culturally co-existing discourses of morality.[2] Discourses are symbol systems for describing aspects of experience. More than one such symbol system may be applicable to any area of experience such as individual psychological development, ethics, health, or suffering.

There is no reason why one must select one and only one discourse to represent an area of experience. Indeed, there may be some advantage in possessing multiple discourses for covering the complexities of such an important area of human experience as ethics. No discourse corresponds so tightly to facticity that it cannot be separated from it. All discourses describe through interpretation and inference.

Experience is often so complex that its facticity is sometimes better described by one discourse and sometimes by another. Although different discourses in the social sciences and elsewhere—say behaviorist, cognitivist, and object relations schools of psychological development—often seem to be in competition for definition of a realm of experience, this is usually a sociological effect more than a logical one. It is often advantageous to have more than one discourse for interpreting a situation or solving a problem. Not only alternative solutions but multidimensional ones addressing several "orders of reality" or "orders of experience" may be more practical for solving complex human problems. An antidogmatic casuistry with multiple (but rationally limited) discursive resources may be the most effective method for meeting the vicissitudes of human ethical experience. It is useful to keep in mind the tenet that cognized reality is incomplete if described from any one point of view and incomplete if described from all points of view at once (Shweder, 1993c).

The three ethical discourses of Orissa work together to promote three different types of goods, which are meant to co-exist in the Hindu social order. The Hindu ethical worldview is incomplete without any one of the three. All three goods enhance human dignity and self-esteem. The rub, of course, is that the three goods are often in conflict. In the material world, the world of embodiment and constraint, there may never have been a place or time when all three goods have been or could have been simultaneously maximized. While it is true that they often come into conflict with one another and create moral dilemmas (Much and Mahapatra, 1993), in India these conflicts are often opportunities for personal ethical discrimination and spiritual growth.

In direct contrast to secular society in the United States, the discourse of autonomy and individualism is seemingly backgrounded in Hindu society, whereas the discourses of community and divinity are foregrounded, made salient and institutionalized. That does not mean that there is no personal experience of autonomy and individuality in India or no personal concern with those goods as essential to well-being. Instead, the themes of personal autonomy are often absorbed into the discourses of community and divinity in ways that we describe in this chapter.

Similarly, although ideas of community—and to an even greater extent, divinity—have been backgrounded and left out of much of the world-description produced and institutionalized by modernist Western social science, these communitarian concerns continue to live on, implicitly or explicitly, in the unofficial folk culture and its discourse.

Indeed, different cultural traditions try to promote human dignity by specializing in (and perhaps even exaggerating) different ratios of moral goods. Consequently, they moralize about the world in somewhat different ways and try to construct the social order as a moral order in somewhat different terms. Cultures differ in the degree to which one or other of the ethics and corresponding moral goods predominates in the development of social practices and institutions and in the elaboration of a moral ideology.

For example, in the United States today we are experts on the topic of the ethics of autonomy. We have extended the idea of "rights" to different domains such as education and health care. We have extended the class of rights holders to include children and animals. We have expanded the idea of this worldly autonomy to such an extent that we can imagine that children should be free to choose their parents. We wish to be protected from every imaginable harm, including secondary cigarette smoke and psychologically offensive work environments. Such all-embracing notions as harassment, abuse, and exploitation have great currency. We have stretched the notions of rights, autonomy, and harm even as we wonder nostalgically how we lost our sense of community and divinity and struggle to find a way to recover them. In rural India, on the other hand, the ethics of autonomy is much less salient, while the institutions and ideologies of community and divinity are highly elaborated and finely honed, which creates its own special distortions, of course.

One of the goals of this chapter is to suggest that there might be some advantages to expanding the moral discourse for health in Western scientific and popular culture. The potential for expanded discourse is latent in American folk culture. This chapter brings the relevant discourses into relief by showing how they have become "official," locally rational, institutionalized discourses in a South

Asian culture. We predict that some aspects of "traditional" thinking will appeal to many modern Americans.

Of course it is not our goal to persuade North American science to adopt the metaphysics and metapsychologies of Indian Brahmans and yogins. Rather we believe that by attending to explicit South Asian conceptions of the moral order, we will call attention to neglected ideas latent in our own cultural history and living contemporary culture. Ideas within one's own culture may be more easily seen by comparison with ideas from divergent cultures, which are the more obvious for the novelty of the ideational contexts in which they occur. We introduce in correspondence with our three domains of Oriya moral discourse (autonomy, community, divinity) three metaphors for the American moral imagination: the sacred self, feudal ethics, and the sacred world. Later we discuss a fourth overarching metaphor, the idea of karma.

AUTONOMY AND THE METAPHOR OF THE SACRED SELF

The three discourse domains of Oriya ethics represent three goods, each related to well-being. It is good to have personal autonomy and control. It is good to be part of an organized community and to have an identity or place(s) within its social structure. It is good to experience communication and to be on speaking terms with the divine. These discourses seem to represent distinct but interrelated conceptual contexts for moral discourse. In the interview texts from which the Oriya moral themes were derived, we found that each could be used alone or in combination with any of the others in an informant's argument concerning a particular incident or event.

We focus first on the ethics of autonomy cluster that most closely resembles the harm-rights-and-justice code that is prevalent in American culture, with its emphasis on the individual's claim to self-interest and noninterference. The themes of this cluster are by no means the most common discourse of Oriya moral argumentation. The discourse of cluster 1 represents the individual interests, desires, and preferences of the person. While it resembles the harm-rights-and-justice code of North America, there are also differences in the way that Oriya Hindus talk about the interests of individuals.

In Orissa, the idea of the individual is linked to the idea of a soul and its particular *dharma* or obligation. This soul (what contemporary secular Western scholars might refer to as a "transcendental ego") is an entity identified with the realm of divinity. Embodied, it exists under many limitations and constraints. But peal away the gross layers of illusion and what is left is pure God-essence, capable of merging directly with divine substrate of the phenomenal world. This ultimate (though not proximal) identity of the personal soul with God is what obligates respect for all living creatures, human and non-human, and what obligates tolerance of another person's free will. A concern for individual autonomy seems to act as a common denominator in the moral order and does not distinguish human beings from non-human animals, who are also regarded as having essentially the same soul and the same rights to protection from arbitrary harm or abuse and from interference with their natural needs and inclinations. Animal "souls" are not seen as particularly distinct from human ones, and souls may change places in transmigrations.

The following didactic or proverbial narrative from Shweder's interview texts illustrates the point. Such narratives are one of the preferred methods of moral discourse and moral instruction in Orissa (see Shweder and Much, 1987):

There was a dog that always slept on the doorstep of the house of a certain Brahman. [Because dogs are polluted and polluting animals, this was problematic for the Brahman, who might have to bathe before entering the temple or his own house after accidental contact with a dog.] One day the Brahman threw cold water on the dog in order to drive it away. The dog went to God and complained. It said, "I am a dog. It is my nature to sleep on the road [or in doorsteps]. When the Brahman threw water on me, I shivered [i.e., I suffered]. Let him take my sins and suffer as I suffer and let me take his merit." And God agreed. The Brahman became a dog. [from the Shweder interviews, Shweder, Mahapatra, and Miller 1987]

Any soul may be seen as having an individual *dharma*, designed for it either by God or by the precision of its own karma (the fruits of its work). One implication of this view of individuality is that there is a kind of specialness or even privilege to personal intuitions of right and wrong. Even odd and unconventional desires or overly adamant demands for normally forbidden things may be respected as possibly the utterance of the soul. They are apt to be understood as a command of the deity within, pertaining to a person's particular course of spiritual development, something that no one else can fully know.

This highly particularistic individual *dharma* exists in addition to the *dharma* or obligation assigned to the person by virtue of features of social position such as gender, caste, age, family relationships, and so on. Hindu obligation structures are complex. The first metaphor for the moral imagination is the sacred self, whose obligation it is to know or discover its own individuated *dharma*.

Community and the Feudal Ethics Metaphor

The second thematic cluster, the ethics of community, pertains to the discourse of obligations engendered through participation in a particular community. It is a discourse of roles and statuses and obligations in relation to other members of the community. The themes associated with this cluster are duty, hierarchy, interdependence, and souls (selves). Notice that the theme of the individual soul or self is more closely connected in Oriya discourse to the role structure of a community than to the themes of worldly self-sufficiency and individual freedom of choice. The identity of the person is defined in terms of community statuses. In Oriya Hindu discourse, personal identity is more closely associated with its statuses and relationships than with its individuality or distinctness.

Another reason for the association of souls or selves with relational concepts is that the protection and nurturance of the individual, and the satisfaction of individual desires, is most often discussed as somebody else's responsibility. Persons rely on those others to whom they are bound in institutionalized asymmetrical relationships to satisfy their needs. The person in the hierarchical position is obligated to protect and satisfy the wants of the subordinate person in specified ways. The subordinate person is also obligated to look after the interests and well-being of the superordinate person.

People often depend on others to satisfy their needs and desires. Even when they are capable of looking after themselves, they may not think it appropriate to do so. The understood moral obligation of the interdependent other in such a relationship is sensitive responsiveness to the perceived or expressed needs of one's interdependent self. Sons and daughters should be obedient to their parents; parents should be sensitive and responsive to the wishes, feelings, and inclinations of their children. Likewise wives should be obedient to their husbands, while husbands should be sensitive and responsive to the needs, desires, and inclinations of their wives. That is why the theme of selves or souls clusters with the themes of duty, hierarchy, and interdependence.

One might (somewhat tongue-in-cheek) refer to this second metaphor for the moral imagination as the idea of feudal ethics. It is a metaphor that is central to Oriya ethical argumentation in the context of communitarian concerns. What this discourse has to add to our own sense of community is the potential for rediscovery of some of the merits of the "feudal" mind.

Most Americans ideologically recoil at the idea of feudal ethics, which does not fit well with the philosophical underpinnings of our historically evolved political culture and our free market mentality. In true feudal systems, powerful persons take care of their subjects—family members, employees, fellow caste members. Along with hierarchy there is an obligatory responsibility for others. The less powerful respond with gratitude and loyalty that "sticks" when the chips are down. A cardinal principle of this ethic is "take care of one's own." Neither networking, which is too market oriented and ethically thin, nor social welfare, which is too impersonal and devoid of a sense of participation or alliance, are suitable substitutes for this concept.

A successful feudal lord or local big man *(bada loka)* uses his alliances sparingly. He tries to do more for others than they have done for him. That way he has a social "bank account" of debts due him when the really important issues arise. He cultivates alliances with those below him because they are the bedrock of his power. If he cultivates alliances only with superiors and equals, he will have no one to rule.

In a feudal social system, the lord (king, father, godfather) knows that his well-being is closely entwined with the satisfaction of his subjects. He knows that his understood obligation is to promote the satisfaction of those from whom he commands loyalty and that the obligation is proportional to his demands for allegiance and potential sacrifice. To do otherwise would be ultimately, if not immediately, self-destructive.

These policies are not necessarily easy for democratically minded Americans to appreciate. The contemporary American mistrust of hierarchy and ready-made association of hierarchy with tyranny, exploitation, and over-reaching entitlement reflect what happens to hierarchy in a democratic market society, in which "take care of one's own" is replaced by "survival of the fittest."

Nevertheless, in the cultural domain of health and well-being, the simple principle of "take care of one's own" might have far-reaching consequences, if it were taken seriously as an ethical obligation. The principle has a direct bearing on many social and psychological problems of the postmodern age, including community health problems such as isolation and alienation, the problem of young and elderly persons without family members to take care of them in times of ill health, the problems arising from the national health insurance question, and related issues of what employers owe to their employees in the way of health benefits and health-protective working conditions.

The particular wisdom of the South Asian discourse of community is that the well-being of persons who live or work together or share other life projects is interdependent. If your actions weaken those you depend on (whether in the upward or downward direction), they weaken you. This is true whether you are the lord or the servant. Loyalties of this kind require continuous cultivation, which means caring about what happens to others with whom you live or work, caring about larger units of which you are a part, and being taken care of in return. Our second moral metaphor from South Asia is then the feudal hierarchy, with its particular vision of allegiance, asymmetrical reciprocity, noblesse oblige, and ecological interdependence.

DIVINITY AND THE METAPHOR OF A SACRED WORLD

The third thematic cluster, the ethics of divinity, expresses the Indian belief that a sacred order is immanent in the world, that godliness permeates or interpenetrates the human social order as well as the natural world and interacts with both, that there are important communicative exchanges going on all of the time between persons and the realm of divinity. Matter (organic and inorganic) and all other forms—social hierarchies (parent, child, husband, wife), the tonal scales of music *(raga),* words *(mantra)*—are infused with spirit or divinity. This discourse is associated with the notion of a sacred tradition, the idea that a way of life—the Hindu *dharma*—is an earthly manifestation of divine design. Again there are partial (though not complete) correspondences with the orthodox Judaic vision of society (Spero, 1992). A view of this kind denies a radical separation between the secular and the sacred. Thus even family life is a sacramental event, which is why the breach of a seemingly mundane domestic procedure can be regarded as a kind of desecration.

The associated themes of the ethics of divinity are sacred order, sanctity, tradition, and natural law. The cluster represents the idea that sacred law and natural law are the same thing. Every entity in nature enjoys its particular right to exist and to be what it is according to its own nature, such that nothing is excluded from or contrasted to the moral order: everything is encompassed. This discourse ultimately brings one full circle, back to the origins of the sacredness of the individual, human or otherwise. The rights of human beings derive from and are protected under this same principle of a dharmic order in which every entity is entitled to be what it is and has its proper place in the order of things. That place is its protected realm.

Individuation also receives protection by this principle. Individual souls (selves) have desires that should be respected by others because those desires may be a form of wisdom that originates not in the discursive thoughts of the personal mind but ultimately in a kind of soul knowledge. Wishes and desires might be an indication from the divine order, which encompasses intimate knowledge of every individual soul. The wise sometimes feel it is better not to interfere with someone's wishes, especially if they are strong and persistent, even though the wishes may seem irrational or maladaptive. After all, one never knows what the true source of the wish may be. The divine order interpenetrates matter, social form, and mind. And any apparent form, no matter how lowly (for example, a dog is lowly in India), is in essence divine spirit. It may, in theory, "really be" a God, that is, manifest divinity in intensified form.

There are many such stories and myths. Lowly entities are always turning out to be something more than they appear. That is the classical test or trial of discrimination and genuine devotion that God imposes upon devotees. One kicks a dog. The dog turns out to be the Goddess in disguise and one is punished. One feeds a dog. The dog turns out to be the Goddess in disguise, and one is rewarded. A beggar or leper at one's doorstep turns out to be the Great God Siva in disguise, and so on. We are reminded of a similar idea expressed by the words of Jesus Christ, "As you did it to one of the least of these my brethren, you did it to me" (Math. 25: 31, 32).

The dignity of the individual person is also comprehended within the discourse of this ethics of divinity. It is represented in part by the idea of sanctity. This conception of sanctity is the basis of traditional social rank in Hindu society. It relates to one's ability to approach and communicate with the divinity, which in turn relates to social rank and personal fulfillment in the traditional Hindu social order. Individual dignity is also represented as the obligation to uphold the practices of a way of life (tradition) felt to originate in the design of a divine order. It is further represented by the possibilities for heroic expression of God-like personhood through concern with the ultimate aims of human existence and the disengagement from momentary temptations and sufferings of life.

The idea of divinity has in fact begun to re-enter the discourse of psychiatry and psychology, though at present it is still on the fringes. Spero (1992) has recently made an argument for considering personal relationship to divinity as an important psychological reality without reducing divinity to a psychological structure. Spero explains how early experiences of divinity could be objective phenomena that induce the development of a psychological God object and of one's personal relations with it. This experience may not originate (as is usually assumed) in the relationship with the parents. It may originate, Spero suggests, in the more mystical "oceanic" feelings of early infancy and receive later elaboration as God reveals the nature of divinity through parent-child relationships and other social structures.

An assumption of Spero's Halakhic metapsychology matches very well with an assumption of Hindu metaphysics: Divinity reveals and communicates itself through the objects and events of the world. Spero also argues that a personal relationship with divinity is a primary psychological good and a fundamental aspect of psychological development. Experiences of communication with a God object (which may be either concrete and personalized or abstract and formless) are among the fundamental psychological experiences that all people have. For Spero, divinity is a psychological construct but not reducible to psychology. He argues that psychology ought to include, as a fundamental aspect of human development, the development of a concept of divinity and one's relationship to it as a psychological object. William James would probably nod with approval at such a proposal.

The experience of divinity may or may not be theistic. It may or may not involve a personified God or Goddess. Mystical-aesthetic experiences of a more diffuse kind are also communications with divinity. The Hindu worldview is well aware of psychological differences among individuals that dispose them to relate better to one or another form of divinity. There are different forms for experiencing divinity suited to different personal qualities and understandings.

A particular feature of the Hindu worldview is the disposition to make connections between all aspects of secular, domestic, and psychological life and a sacred order that is the ultimate reference point for all sources of obligation. One might speak of a Hindu sense of "sacred world" (Much and Mahapatra, 1993). Thus, the third moral metaphor we invoke is the sacred world metaphor, the idea that persons communicate with the divine and the divine communicates with persons through actions in the world, whether special rituals, work, or ordinary domestic activities.

The three ethics (autonomy, community, divinity) and the three metaphors for the moral imagination (sacred self, feudal ethics, sacred world) represent an expanded repertoire of discourse for construing the grounds of obligation, the nature of particular obligations, and the consequences of remissiveness in matters of obligation. They represent an expanded discourse for considering the social, psychological, and behavioral context of health maintenance because they all relate to the kinds of responsibilities persons have to take care of themselves and others, and to treat the environment, the ecological matrix of personal life, with respect. We suspect that the development of similar discourses, in ways consistent with the beliefs, traditions, and roots of Western culture, would be a contribution to a postmodern reexamination of contemporary problems of personal well-being and social responsibility.

An Overarching Moral Metaphor: Karma and the Laws of Personal Responsibility

A fourth overarching moral metaphor, the Hindu idea of karma, is at its core a theory of personal responsibility: Fortune and misfortune are interpreted in terms of spiritual or moral merit and debt. This idea—that actions have inherent consequences—has been a topic for reflection and debate for many centuries (see, for example, Babb, 1983, Daniel, 1983, O'Flaherty, 1980; Kakar, 1978, 1982; Keyes and Daniel, 1983; Mahapatra, Much, and Shweder, 1991; Obeyesekere, 1980; Shweder and Miller, 1985). Here we examine the way the connection between morality and health is represented in the discourse of karma that is found in and around Bhubaneswar.

The South Asian theory of karma exists indigenously as a complex and technical subject matter. Karma is not, as Westerners sometimes suppose, a naive or primitive theory of immanent justice. In South Asia there are specific mechanisms postulated to account for its operation. These theories depend on a metaphysical ontology quite different from either the classical Judeo-Christian one or the materialist metaphysics of modern science (Much and Mahapatra, 1993). That metaphysical ontology includes, for example, the idea of a transmigrating soul, a mental self that goes on from one birth to another, taking with it its past deeds and the latent results of its actions. Karma pertains to several orders of reality, although most of this complexity is beyond the scope of the present discussion.

Like scientific Western biomedical theories, karma is part of an esoteric knowledge of indigenous experts; yet it also has its counterpart in widely disseminated folk knowledge that is closely but unevenly related to the expert's knowledge system. This discussion is concerned only with the form that karmic discourse takes in folk theory.

Despite the metaphysical mismatch, certain aspects of karmic conceptions translate well into ideas present in Western discourses of moral responsibility, cause and effect, and efficacy and control. As several ethnographers have observed (Babb, 1983, Mahapatra, Much, and Shweder, 1991, Much and Mahapatra, 1993; Wadley and Derr, 1990), karma has an operational quality of transference. That is, a person's karma affects not only the person's self, but also others who have relationships or transactions with that person.

Generally, the closer the relationship or transaction, or the greater the degree of participation in the sin or merit, the stronger the effect of one person's karma is on another. (There are subtle qualifications for all these rules of thumb. We give here only the most general outlines of the folk theory.)

For example, Western biomedical knowledge postulates that children of alcohol-addicted parents are a relatively high risk population for alcohol dependency and other socio-psychosomatic problems. The risk is created not only by genetic inheritance but by the behavioral patterns of alcohol-addicted parents and the participation of children in those patterns. Karma is similar to these kinds of complex causal relationships, though broader, including a more expansive discourse of obligation and encompassing more extended domains of cause and effect. Ethnographers (Babb, 1983; Daniel, 1983; Keyes, 1983; Wadley and Derr, 1990) have noted that some Indian conceptions of karma do not depend on a theory of transmigration: Karmic results can come within the life span. Even those who believe that karma operates across lives, such as our Oriya informants, also believe that it operates within lives, and they are able to narrate many local case histories of karmic cause and effect.

We focus here on karma as a theory of personal responsibility and its close connection to the idea of *dharma* (objective obligation or duty). This close connection between the two concepts, which has been noted by Wadley and Derr (1990) and others, denotes simultaneously natural law as well as a divine or sacred order to things.

The concept of karma as a law of personal responsibility may surprise Westerners who are familiar with karma as a theory of moral determinism (see Babb, 1983). It is ironic that Westerners often misinterpret karma as an excuse, freeing believers from responsibility by making them passive objects of the force of their past actions. Babb (1983) attributes this bias to the fact that karma was first studied intensively by Western scholars in the context of development economics, when it became perceived as a passive and fatalistic life view, encouraging acceptance of the status quo (for example, Kapp, 1963; Myrdal, 1968). What was missed was the powerful potential of karmic theory to generate prescriptions for agency and control.

In South Asian folk theories, the idea of karma creates a feeling of inevitability that one's actions will have proportionate consequences for the self, which lends a motivational force to the obligatoriness of the many demanding practices in Indian domestic, social, and ritual life. The use of the karma concept in folk theory may vary by region and by social position (Keyes, 1983; Babb, 1983; Wadley and Derr, 1990). Our own ethnographic information draws primarily on the accounts of Brahmans, sadhus, and serious devotees in Orissa. They are primarily high caste or traditionally educated persons with a relatively strong investment in the third code of moral discourse—the ethics of divinity. It is ironic that the idea of karma is often given a fatalistic interpretation in the West because the theory of karma not only contains many mechanisms for the remedy of situations but also numerous preventive procedures for exercising a willful control over one's life.

At the level of social thought, karma is a theory of responsibility (Mahapatra, Much, and Shweder 1991; Much and Mahapatra, 1993). Karma means "action" or "work" (the same word is used in modern Oriya for any task or work one does). In addition, karma implies the natural result or fruition of action. Generally speaking, the fruits (phala) of actions are proportionate to the action in quality and magnitude. The "quality" (for example, whether good or evil—finer distinctions exist but are not relevant here) relates closely to the three types of ethical obligations discussed earlier in this chapter.

The "teachings" of karma are disseminated in part through local narrative gossip. Narratives about the karmic events in the lives of other persons or in one's own life are locally circulated, told to intimates and friends, and commented upon. The principles of karma are also amply illustrated in mythology and in proverbial tales. Several examples follow:

> There was an old Bauri woman (the highest of the local formerly "untouchable," now "scheduled" or "Harijan,"

castes) who was suffering a painful and lingering death. She suffered for a long time but she could not die. Finally, her relatives asked her to remember if there was any sin that she had committed in her lifetime, and to confess. She confessed that she had once accepted boiled food (boiled food is more readily polluted than fried food) from a Kachara (Bangle-Seller). [Though the Bauris are an "untouchable" caste, they regard the Kachara as inferior to themselves in purity; and so the Bauri caste prohibits accepting boiled food from the Kachara.] She also confessed that on one occasion she had bound a cow in the cow shed and [as a result of the way she'd tied it and left it unattended] the cow had died during the night. After the woman had confessed these sins, she died peacefully. (local neighborhood narrative, Mahapatra, Much, and Shweder, 1991: 13)

The Bauri woman had breached the ethics of autonomy and of divinity by polluting herself with food offered by a person considered more impure than she. She had breached the second and third codes by carelessly binding the cow (a sacred animal in India), and then neglecting to look after it. She had allowed it to die during the night, unnoticed, while she was responsible for it.

There was a married woman in Old Town, who treated her mother-in-law cruelly. The mother-in-law was a widow, and her son took no interest in her well-being, so there was no one to protect her. Her daughter-in-law [who lived in the same house] tormented the old woman without pity. Having to bear this, the old woman cursed her daughter-in-law to have the same fate in her old age. As soon as the son's children were grown, the daughter-in-law became a widow. She is still living in the same sahi (ward) in Old Town. Now her children care nothing for her, but rather torment her just as she had tormented her mother-in-law. (local neighborhood narrative, Mahapatra, Much, and Shweder, 1991: 13)

The daughter-in-law breached the ethics of autonomy and community. She treated another person with cruelty. Worse yet, the person she treated with cruelty was her mother-in-law, a person whom she is obligated to respect and support.

A man and his wife lived with the husband's elderly father. The daughter-in-law was always thinking of how they could get rid of the old man. One day she had an idea. She told her husband, let us carry Father to Puri [a place of pilgrimage] in a basket. There we will leave him on the Great Road in front of the Temple of Jaganath [this road is a gathering place for the homeless and destitute. In those days there were no trains or buses, nor any other easy means of transport, so the old man would never be able to return on his own, but would have to remain where he was left.] The husband agreed to this plan. But their son had overheard everything. He first warned his grandfather of the plot. Then he went to his father and said, "Father, you leave Grandfather at Puri just as you have said. But please do not leave the basket. Bring the basket back. Otherwise, what shall I use to carry you to Puri when you become old?" Then the husband understood. He confessed everything to his father and begged his father's forgiveness. (proverbial narrative from the Shweder interviews, Shweder, Mahapatra, and Miller, 1987]

In each case, the wrongful treatment of others as well as the breach or neglect of some obligatory action covered by one or more of the three ethical codes (autonomy, community, divinity) predicts future suffering, including physical illness or pain, psychological suffering, and social disharmony. Many other narratives of this kind are to be heard in rural India.

As Babb (1983), O'Flaherty (1976), and Wadley and Derr (1990) point out, the karmic theory of causality entails indeterminacy, uncertainty, and unpredictability. In Orissa, persons who are suffering from an illness or misfortune may consult sacred specialists, holy persons, or oracles to ascertain the karmic causes of their suffering. Sacred healers may not only diagnose karmic problems but also prescribe remedial actions. This is especially true for illnesses or misfortunes that are not amenable to "immediate" or proximal remedial interventions (medicine, magic, or astrology).

> A man was blind in one eye. He consulted the oracle concerning this defect. The oracle told him that during his last life he had propitiated a certain Goddess. But, failing to obtain what he desired, he had spoken to her abusively, calling her "widow" [implying inauspiciousness and accursedness] and had torn out one eye from her image. Because of that, he now suffered blindness in one eye. The oracle advised him to bathe seven images of the goddess [a ritual bathing performed by a qualified temple priest] on seven Thursdays [the day sacred to the Goddess Laxmi]. Then he should prostrate flat on the floor before the [image of the] Goddess and beg her forgiveness. Calling her "Mother," he should remind her that he himself is her own son, so that she might be moved to forgive his error. After this, he should return to

the oracle for further instructions. (Mahapatra, Much, and Shweder, 1991: 16)

Karma can be viewed as a kind of economic account of accumulated ethical merit and demerit. Metaphorically speaking, one's karmic bank account affects one's overall circumstances and provides opportunities for improvement as well as constraints on improvement. When the accumulated demerit is great, meritorious action also becomes more difficult. Through immoral, adharmic actions, obstructions are accumulated.

The teleological presupposition of the doctrine of karma is that the natural aim of the soul is to recognize its own divine nature and so liberate itself from entrapment in the illusion that causes inappropriate impulse and action with its consequent suffering. In Western parlance, this could (roughly, and with some loss of meaning) be called a state of flourishing or optimal well-being. Adharmic acts create obstacles to this achievement.

Whatever one's present status in life, one can always improve it by achieving the *dharma* specific to one's existing capabilities and potentialities. A person's individual *dharma* is whatever is morally obligatory for that person, given the particular situation. This notion takes account of: 1) what it is possible for a particular individual to do in the particular case, and 2) the ideal conduct that is in accord with the three discourses of moral obligation. When the discourses of obligation come into conflict, features of context plus the resources and constraints of the agent enter into casuistic consideration of the principles that govern the case in point. Morality, therefore, is not simply a matter of following rules (see Shweder and Much, 1987). It involves personal effort of discrimination and judgment. It is a personal responsibility to cultivate this kind of knowledge and intelligence.

There are certain classes of action that are not obligatory but are meritorious by nature. One can perform these actions and so accumulate merit in order to better one's position in the future. These actions can be done as a kind of investment in one's future welfare.

Many of these measures involve either charity or the support of religious institutions. Sacrifice is a meritorious activity, and in some cases personal austerities are prescribed or considered efficacious. Acts of worship in themselves, as well as reading, reciting, and contemplating the scriptures, are meritorious. Many people in India do these things routinely. At the level of personal hygiene, there are many ways to maintain or enhance personal "sanctity." One may follow certain laws of purity, avoid polluting places or substances, and seek out those with beneficial effects.

Merit-producing actions exist for each of the three codes of ethical discourse. The effects of these actions (for example, going on pilgrimage, performing rituals) promote personal hygiene and dignity, contribute to social welfare, and enhance one's sense of spiritual inspiration.

"Karma yoga" (liberation by means of meritorious action) is, of course, a very long-term project. The classical karmic world view of South Asia envisions many lifetimes for the development of the soul. At the same time, certain known wrongs may be expiated in part or in whole by duly prescribed meritorious action. Local folk healers, especially sacred healers and ritual specialists, may prescribe meritorious actions that will benefit people who are suffering (Mahapatra, Much, and Shweder, 1991).

Thus our overarching metaphor for the moral imagination is karma. The significance of karmic discourse for our present argument lies in the way it rationally motivates responsible action for those who comprehend and internalize it. The fundamental presupposition is that traditional codes of ethics are part of the divine

and natural order of the universe and are established for the purpose of enhancing the well-being of persons in their worldly existence as well as the afterlife. In this view, morality and obedience to
the obligations and limits of the three ethical discourses directly affect physical and mental health, social harmony, status, and well-
being. Spero (1992) finds the same kind of reasoning in traditional
Judaic Halakhic metapsychology. We note in passing that the classical Hindu conception of the worthy and obligatory goals in life include *artha, dharma, moksha,* and *kama* (roughly, wealth, duty, liberation, and pleasure). We believe the three moral discourse realms of
autonomy, community, and divinity are related to the classical concepts of *artha, dharma,* and *moksha,* although we cannot expound on
these connections in this chapter.

According to the theory of karma, intended immoral action,
careless action, or even ignorant and misguided action is certain
to lead to personal suffering unless some intervening correction
can be made. In contrast, actions are often thought of as risk factors represented as probabilities in Western worldviews, and individuals are at liberty to perceive themselves as the improbable exceptions. To conceive of the world in karmic terms is to know *with
certainty* that the transgression of obligations will catch up with an
individual sooner or later unless that person does something to reverse the situation. Intervening corrections sometimes can be made
if the person has the insight to ask for help, but these interventions are costly and require great investments of effort and will.
Corrective efforts may have incomplete results, and the full effects
of these efforts may not be seen for a long time. Therefore, avoiding
problems in the first place is a better approach. The karmic metaphor emphasizes personal responsibility in regulating behavior and
wise investment in actions that accrue benefits to oneself in the
long run.

Theodicy and Public Health

This chapter examines ethical discourse realms and moral metaphors that are customary in many corners of South Asia with an eye toward enhancing the conceptual resources of Western culture for thinking about the connection between action, personal responsibility, and public health. We have assumed that one way to extend discourses for causation and morality is take account of the relevant indigenous theories of another complex culture that institutionalizes and supports intuitions that are suppressed or peripheralized by our own "official" scientific culture. We believe it is possible to show the relevance or partial translatability of these metaphors to our own ways of life and to raise questions about how South Asian ideas about autonomy, community, divinity, and karma might change our outlook on existential issues of universal importance: suffering, responsibility, and remedial change. In a sense, we have asked the reader to rethink the contemporary secular theodicy of Western biomedical and acknowledge both its limitations as well as its strengths.

Theodicy is the philosophical inquiry into the question of how the presence of "evil" in the world is to be explained. The presupposition of such an inquiry is that evil exists in the world, that it is distinguishable from good, and that the fact of its existence presents us with a problem. The prototypical problem formulated in terms of Judeo-Christian metaphysics is this: If God is good and omnipotent, then why does evil, which is antithetical to good, exist in the world? (O'Flaherty, 1976).

There are a variety of possible answers to this question. The philosophical possibilities include the conclusion that so far as "God" or "nature" is concerned, there is no distinction between good and evil and there is no reason to consider suffering as evil.

This theodicy is a relatively counterintuitive view of reality. It does appear in certain arcane philosophies (and sciences), but rarely as an ordinary folk intuition derived from the experience of an embodied human self. Suffering is organismically "felt" as a disvalued state, quite distinct from other felt valued states (well-being, happiness, pleasure). The intuitive distinction between good and bad, felt in the body as well as in the consciousness, seems to be a difficult distinction to dispel.

Another possible theodicy is that suffering, although painful, is not ultimately evil because it results in an end state that is good. People narratively interpret the benefits of their own suffering in a variety of ways. They may interpret suffering as a discipline through which human selves become wiser and stronger, for example, as a path of learning and personal growth, or as an experience that brings human beings closer to God. This interpretation is not necessarily counterintuitive. Some persons do seem to feel empowered by or benefit from their suffering. They experience themselves as stronger, wiser, better protected, and more morally fit than they were before. Some develop exceptional skills because they suffer.

The South Asian causal ontology has an explanatory advantage with respect to supporting this type of interpretation of suffering. It postulates a soul that continues its "life" through countless births until conditions are ultimately worked out for the good. The metaphor is the arduousness of acquiring wisdom and skillfulness and the sense of empowerment that comes from working off spiritual debts. Of course, in any society while some people will manage to transform suffering into growth, others will suffer and remain miserable.

A quite different interpretation of suffering is favored by much of the contemporary Western scientific community, at least in its official canons. That theodicy involves the disjunction of moral good and evil from large areas of the experience of suffering, including illness, adverse living situations, and behavior problems of various types. According to this theodicy, while suffering is real it is outside the domain of good and evil. It is outside the domain of the intentional agency of the sufferer.

One reigning metaphor of this contemporary official secular theodicy is chance misfortune. The sufferer is a victim, under attack from natural forces devoid of intentionality. Suffering is decontextualized and separated from the narrative structure of human life. It is viewed as a kind of "noise," an accidental interference with the life drama of the sufferer. It is as though suffering had no intelligible relation to any plot, except as a chaotic interruption. This image of suffering is most congruent with a theodicy that asserts that suffering is and must remain a mystery because it has no existential meaning or purpose. A metaphorical image associated with this view is suffering as an accident, as an event governed by chance.

Under this interpretation, suffering is to be treated by the intervention of second- or third-party agents who possess expert skills of some kind, relevant to treating the problem. The solution is sought at the proximal level of alleviating and curing a condition and not at any more fundamental level in which ultimate questions about "who is responsible" and "who is to be blamed" are asked. Under this interpretation, the way to deal with suffering is to treat it, not to ask where it came from or why someone in particular is suffering. This type of secular theodicy is pragmatic and in keeping with (at least parts of) the known observable facts of many mishaps, injuries, or illnesses, and in line with some of our powers to remedy them. It is well to keep in mind, however, that nothing is really "by accident" in a true sense and that "chance" is an illusory explanation, a distortion of a far more complex determinism. What "by accident" really means is that we do not and cannot know all of the specific events that have converged to create a causal chain.

If a person is hit by a motor vehicle while crossing the street, there is in fact a complex chain of events that led to that convergence. Our discourse of chance says these are irrelevant. The South Asian discourse of karmic causality says that each link in the chain is meaningful and related to responsible or irresponsible actions.

Even within the discourse of our own scientific causal discourse, the illness as accident metaphor is sometimes shown to be mistaken. For example, only several decades ago it was not known that cigarette smoking put people at high risk for very serious illnesses and was dangerous to fetuses. A genuine behavioral cause of suffering was missed because the linkage of action to outcome was not yet recognized by the scientific-medical community. At the same time there was a folk discourse that saw excessive smoking as an unsavory practice. It was said to be a "dirty" or "filthy" habit. There was a folk idea that women in particular ought not to smoke and there was a common discourse among smokers about "smoker's cough" and about addiction and other effects viewed explicitly as unhealthy and undignified by those who smoked and suffered. The respect for scientific authority and the absence at that time of a solid "scientific" linkage between cigarette smoking and serious health conditions enabled many people to ignore their own or others' experiential intuitions that excessive smoking was an unhealthy habit and damaging to the body. Although the "chance" view of suffering may sometimes be the best available representation, we suspect there may be many more linkages between behavior and suffering or well-being than are yet recognized by mainstream medical science.

From the sufferer's point of view, the "random catastrophe" explanation is about as appealing as is the invocation of "chance" as an explanation for a striking and world-altering series of "coincidental" events. Even with scientific sanction plus reasoned evaluation of known proximal causal factors, the idea of chance misfortune may not be felt by the sufferer to have much experiential validity. Especially in the case of catastrophic illness, the sufferer wants to make sense of an experience so intense that it should be meaningful. Yet even people who contract common colds and brief viral infections are often heard to say, "I guess I was supposed to slow down" or "I just wasn't supposed to go on that trip." Intuitively human beings often feel as though illness is a meaningful intervention in an intended course of action.

Health scientists in our culture increasingly recognize that the "chance" account of suffering is consistent with only a limited number of conditions. Many forms of suffering today are known to have multiple determinants, and at least some of those determinants (sexual behavior, food consumption, and so on) are under the control of the agent. In matters of health, it is no longer news that suffering is caused or mediated by one's own behavior: by ingesting dubious substances (smoke, alcohol, fatty foods), by engaging in sexual acts and other actions that bring you in contact with hazardous body fluids (semen, saliva, blood) or airborne viruses, by embarking on adventures that place you at risk (driving a car, entering a hospital). Given the connections between personal behavior and health outcomes, human beings should be willing to accept personal responsibility for their suffering and pain. In many cases, blaming yourself when you get sick is the rational thing to do.

Not surprisingly, there are major theodicies that locate the origin of evil in the realm of human action. Some theodicies hold that God created both evil and its antidotes as a challenge to humankind (Spero, 1992) to develop the character and will to choose good over evil. Other theodicies hold that suffering is evil and it is the human community, not God, that created it. A shared focus of these theodicies is the idea that God gave humankind free will (agency and intentionality) and the ability to choose good or evil.

This belief has had a long and fluctuating history in our culture's ideologies and discourses of suffering. We have gone from one extreme to the other in presuming or rejecting this explanation. At one extreme, every sufferer is at fault because of flaws of moral character and those who suffer have engaged in unwholesome practices that have led to the dissolution of personal integrity. At the other extreme, every sufferer is a victim and no one is at fault for their suffering. For believers at this end of the spectrum, suggesting that someone who suffers may be to blame for their own suffering is unethical, although that person may be represented as the victim of the evil actions of others or of unjust social environments. It is paradoxical to think that a person can be the victim of others' evil actions but not of his or her own. This is an issue not well worked out by that position.

Currently in the United States there is a mixed and perhaps changing discourse on suffering and fault. In many scientific circles, the most widespread discourse depersonalizes as many kinds of suffering as possible. It removes the idea of the agency of the sufferer as a relevant contributory factor. Attributions of "fault" to suffering persons are disparaged as "blaming the victim."

There is some wisdom in this, of course. We are only imperfectly capable of judging others, particularly little-known others, and it is presumptuous at best to infer moral defect from the fact of suffering. Perhaps our depersonalization of suffering is in part a form of self-criticism for any tendency to cast blame on people less fortunate than ourselves, persons from whom we would like to distance ourselves, or persons whose fates we fear.

There is a problem, however, when victimization becomes the

dominant account of suffering and when it becomes politically incorrect to ever hold people responsible for their misery. These descriptions of agents ironically depersonalize the sufferer, who is described as (and encouraged to envision himself or herself as) a passive victim—hardly a more health-inducing description than being called a villain. Victims who have no fault also have no control or responsibility for remedial action. A person's only recourse is reliance on the intervention of experts and on people with resources of power and knowledge that constitute the means for remedial action. The sufferer is seen as possessing no personal resources and capabilities that could ameliorate present conditions and future prospects.

Of course there are illnesses and other conditions of suffering for which the sufferer is not at fault. Some of these conditions are extremely serious and, as far as we know, biologically predetermined. There are also social or ecological environments in which only those with unusual psychosomatic gifts could flourish or survive. Far more frequently, however, biological predispositions and events, social-environmental conditions, and a person's actions all contribute to the state of suffering or well-being. The critical point here is not that people deserve punishment but rather that they deserve to be made aware of whatever degree of personal control they have over their own conditions. They deserve the acknowledgment that there may be something that they can and should do to change their state of being.

What is ironic about the rhetoric of (not) "blaming the victim" is how often the victim is the most difficult person to persuade of this position. The "no-blame" position seems, in fact, to be counterintuitive to sufferers. After all, suffering feels like punishment. There are deep intuitions linking suffering to emotions such as guilt and shame, which are emotions that presuppose that one has done something wrong. Highly educated, scientifically trained women have been shocked and overwhelmed by the unbidden and unwanted feeling that their miscarriages indicate they have done something "bad" or they are being punished for being a "bad person." Those intuitions are real experiences for suffers in the contemporary Western world, where those intuitions are judged irrational by the sufferer herself, just as they are for sufferers in other societies, where those intuitions make rational sense within the terms of an official karmic world view.

In a sense there is nothing surprising about the tendency of human beings to narratively link misfortune to personal agency and to blame or accept responsibility themselves when things go wrong. The experience of guilt and regret may be the affective side of a universal (and generally correct) human intuition that (in the aggregate and in the long run) outcomes tend to be proportionate to actions. These feelings may be merely the phenomenological corollary of the universal (and correct) intuition that personal effort deserves to be exercised in life precisely because it tends to be efficacious. When things go wrong, human beings acknowledge their sense of agency and power by wondering how they are at fault. What is surprising is the insistence with which so many secular-scientific scholars in the West choose to analyze that commonplace mental association as some kind of "problem" or "pathology" or "primitivism," rather than asking what kind of wisdom might be expressed by such recalcitrant human thoughts and attitudes. What is surprising is the way those intuitions are summarily disparaged in modernist discourse as "blaming the victim." Such a doctrine indeed ought to seem surprising because it violates the commonsense or folk psychology of most peoples of the world.

Recent policy-making and economic concerns over public health issues have double-edged implications for questions of personal control over health-related behavior. Risky behavior once was assumed to be the private concern of the individual. It was relatively easy to remain ignorant about the consequences of high-risk behaviors like cigarette smoking. Now individual health behaviors are being discussed in the context of community concerns. There is renewed attention to the economic and social problems of high risk behaviors and how they affect others. A communitarian discourse has re-emerged, expressed in terms of insurance rates, treatment facilities, family responsibilities, care for the uninsured, and the distribution of risk (for example, the effects of secondary cigarette smoke and sexually transmitted diseases). In a concurrent trend, personal health behaviors are being regarded in a community context. With increasing social pressures in the family and work place, people are being expected to develop feelings of community responsibility concerning their own health-related practices.

One possible outcome of this renewed communitarian discourse is that collective concerns will proceed in the direction of a form of "neo-Puritanism" (Shweder, 1993d), with escalating state controls over increasingly "medicalized" life practices. That is to say, more personal behavior will fall within the domain of the "medical," and medical issues will be subject to centralized control. The weaker the responsibility given to potential "victims" of suffering, the more sweeping may be the control taken by "protective" centralized social control mechanisms.

A more promising trend in the discourse of American medicine, which is of course a complex culture in and of itself, is the movement toward preventive medicine with its encouragement to participate in the responsibility for personal health. The rising public concern over how individual health practices affect groups and communities suggests that individuals and communities alike should cultivate a discourse of personal responsibility toward health-related behaviors. Informed by the moral metaphors of South Asia, we would prefer a scenario in which individuals consider their own health a life goal, a personal duty, and a good to be achieved, like a satisfying career, economic security, or a network of relationships. This vision is far better than the horrific alternative of a centralized medical hegemony in which individuals and even local communities lose the capacity to define the limits of a moral way of life.

The linkage of health and personal integrity, as we construe it, is not a simple one. We do not intend to say that healthy people are dignified and sick people are not. We acknowledge that the experience of illness can in some cases contribute to a sense of personal dignity. We are aware that suffering may be represented narratively or biographically as "trials" of moral strength, or as periods of personal growth, as an expansion of awareness and understanding, and even as a condition for the development of exceptional skills. As we engage the public health issues of the day, it is probably advisable to avoid a dogmatic preference for any one discourse of health, suffering, and well-being. Cultivating a casuistic flexibility in applying the appropriate moral discourse and theodicy to particular cases may be desirable. But doing this requires a general awareness of possibilities for expanding our discourses of health and responsibility. For this reason, one of our aims in this chapter has been to call attention to alternative discourse possibilities for considering questions of suffering and well-being, on the one hand, and questions of personal obligation and responsibility on the other. These possibilities already exist within various enclaves of our own contemporary culture, even though they have not been well represented as part of the official, institutionalized scientific model.

Yet there are signs that this is changing. At the very least, there is growing interest among social scientists and clinical theorists in folk wisdom and traditional world conceptions (for example, see Rozin and Nemeroff, 1990; Sabini and Silver, 1982, Spero, 1992) and in the role these play in psychological life and health-related behaviors. In this chapter we have attempted to bring forward what is culturally backgrounded in contemporary North America, by looking at how it is culturally foregrounded in contemporary South Asia and in the sensibilities of many premodern peoples in various regions of the world.

A Parting Prophetic Remark

An ethics of community and an ethics of divinity still flourish in South Asian villages and towns such as Bhubaneswar. The doctrine of karmic consequences and the idea that "old sins cast long shadows" flourish there as well. These ethics, doctrines, and ideas may seem antiquated; but as the United States enters a new phase in public health policy, we are likely to witness an increase in agent-blaming moralistic explanations of illness not unlike those discussed here. The connection between action and outcome (health, behavior, and illness) is going to be advertised, regulated, and evaluated in terms of social or community costs and the idea of a "sin tax" is going to enter collective consciousness and be enforced by the state. Whether our highly individualistic ethics of autonomy will give way to an ethics of community or divinity in a world full of anxieties about illness and contagious disease remains to be seen. Yet as we search around for postmodern ways to rethink our responsibilities to society and nature, it would not be surprising if we began to acknowledge the intuitive appeal of ideas such as sacred self, sacred world, karma, duty, pollution, and sin. It would not be surprising if we began to worry a lot about how those ideas are to be reconciled with the individualism that we value as well.

Cultural Psychology of Emotions:
Ancient and New

with Jonathan Haidt

Great, deep, wide and unbounded, the ocean is nevertheless drunk
by underwater fires; in the same way, Sorrow is drunk by Anger.

Translation of an unidentified Sanskrit stanza
from India in the early middle ages; Gnoli 1956:35

This chapter explores a cultural/sym-
bolic/meaning-centered approach to the study of the emotions, using some sources that are quite ancient (for example, a third-cen-
tury Sanskrit text, the "Rasādhyāya" of the *Nāṭyaśāstra*) and others
that are quite new. The chapter then examines the moral context of
emotional functioning and suggests that the character and meaning of particular emotions are systematically related to the kind of
ethic (autonomy, community, or divinity) prevalent in a cultural
community (Shweder, 1990b; Shweder et. al., 1997; Haidt, Koller,
and Dias, 1993; Jensen, 1995).

In recent years, major reviews of contemporary research have
compared emotional meanings across cultural groups (Good and

Kleinman, 1984; Kleinman and Good, 1985; Kitayama and Markus, 1994; Lutz and White, 1986; Marsella, 1980; Mesquita and Frijda, 1992; Russell, 1991; Scherer, Walbott, and Summerfield, 1986; Shweder and LeVine, 1984; Shweder, 1991, 1993a,b, 1994a; White and Kirkpatrick, 1985). Books and essays have also defined a new inter-disciplinary field for cross-cultural research on the emotions, which has come to be known as "cultural psychology."[1] For a discussion of the historical antecedents of cultural psychology, see Jahoda, 1991). In anthropology the two most notable forums for research on the cultural psychology of the emotions are the journals *Ethos: Journal of the Society for Psychological Anthropology* and *Culture, Medicine and Psychiatry.*

Cultural psychology attempts to spell out the implicit meanings that give shape to psychological processes, to examine the distribution of those meanings across ethnic groups and temporal-spatial regions of the world, and to identify the manner of their social acquisition. A related goal is to reassess the principle of psychic unity or uniformity and to develop a credible theory of psychological diversity or pluralism. Cultural psychology looks at how the human mind can be transformed and made functional in different ways that are not equally distributed across ethnic and cultural communities around the world. Hence the slogan, popular among some cultural psychologists, "one mind, but many mentalities: universalism without the uniformity," which expresses that pluralistic emphasis (see Shweder 1991, 1996a; Shweder et al., 1998).

One hallmark of cultural psychology is a conception of "culture" that is symbolic and behavioral at the same time. Culture, so conceived, can be defined as ideas about what is true, good, beautiful, and efficient that are made manifest in the speech, laws, and customary practices of a self-regulating group (Goodnow, Miller, and Kessel, 1995; Shweder et al., 1998; Shweder, 1999a,b). In research on cultural psychology, culture thus consists of meanings, conceptions, and interpretive schemes that are activated, constructed, or brought online through participation in normative social institutions and routine practices (including linguistic practices) (see, for example, D'Andrade, 1984; Geertz, 1973; LeVine, 1984; Miller et al., 1990; Shweder, 1991, 1999a,b). According to this view, a culture is that subset of available meanings that, by virtue of enculturation (informal or formal, implicit or explicit, unintended or intended), has become active in giving shape to the psychological processes of the individuals in a group.

A second hallmark of cultural psychology is the idea that interpretation, conceptualization, and other "acts of meaning" can take place rapidly, automatically, and unself-consciously. Examples of acts of meaning include the judgments that the human body may become polluted or desanctified because it is a temple for the soul, that illness is a means of empowerment because it unburdens a person of accumulated spiritual debts, or that shyness, shame, modesty, and embarrassment are good emotions because they are forms of civility. Indeed, these acts can take place so rapidly, automatically, and unself-consciously that, from the point of view of an individual person, they are indistinguishable from "raw" experience or "naked" consciousness itself (see, for example, Geertz, 1984, on "experience near" concepts; Kirsh, 1991, on "thought in action"; and Nisbett and Wilson, 1977, on the unconscious "knowing of more than you can tell"; also Fish, 1980). According to this view, many rapid, automatic, and unself-conscious psychological processes are best understood not as pure, fundamental, or intrinsic processes but rather as content-laden processes that are contingent on the implicit meanings, conceptual schemes, and interpretations that give them life (Markus, Kitayama, and Heiman, 1998; Nisbett and Cohen, 1995; Shweder, 1990; Stigler, 1984; Stigler, Chalip, and Miller, 1986; Stigler, Nusbaum, and Chalip, 1988).

In the context of the study of the emotions, the intellectual agenda of cultural psychology can be defined by four questions:

1. What is the generic shape of the meaning system that defines an experience as an emotional experience (for example, anger, sadness, or shame) rather than as an experience of some other kind such as muscle tension, fatigue, or emptiness (for example, Harre 1986, a,b; Lakoff, 1987; Levy, 1984a,b; Shweder, 1991; Smedslund, 1991; Solomon, 1976, 1984; Stein and Levine, 1987; Wierzbicka, 1986, 1992a)?

2. What particular emotional meanings (for example, Pintupi "watjilpa," Balinese "lek," Newar "lajja," Ifaluk "fago," American "happiness") are constructed or brought online in different ethnic groups and in different temporal-spatial regions of the world (see, for example, Abu-Lughod, 1985, 1986; Appadurai, 1985; Briggs, 1970; Gerber, 1985; Geertz, 1959; Lutz, 1982, 1988; Miller and Sperry, 1987; Myers, 1979a,b; Parish, 1991; Rosaldo, 1980, 1983, 1984; Schieffelin, 1976, 1983, 1985a,b; Stearns and Stearns, 1988; Swartz, 1988; Wierzbicka, 1986, 1990, 1997; Wikan, 1984, 1989)?

3. To what extent is the experience of various states of the world such as loss, goal blockage, status degradation, or taboo violation "emotionalized" (as sadness, anger, fear, or guilt) rather than "somatized" (as tiredness, chest pain, or appetite loss) in different ethnic groups and in different temporal-spatial regions of the world (Angel and Guarnaccia, 1989; Angel and Idler, 1992; Angel and Thoits, 1987; Kleinman, 1986; Levy, 1984a,b; Shweder, 1988)?

4. Precisely how are emotionalized and somatized meanings brought online, socialized, enculturated, or otherwise acquired; more specifically, what is the role of everyday dis-

course and social interpretation in the activation of emotionalized and somatized meanings (Bruner, 1990; Garvey, 1992; Miller and Sperry, 1987; Miller et al., 1990, 1992; Miller and Hoogstra, 1992; Ochs and Schieffelin, 1984; Schieffelin and Ochs, 1986; Shweder et al., 1998; Shweder and Much, 1987)?

Any comprehensive review of answers to these questions would have to address hundreds of years of theoretical arguments, empirical sightings, and philosophical reflections in the literatures of several different civilizations (see Dimock, 1974; Harre, 1986b; Kakar, 1982; Kleinman, 1986; Rorty, 1980; Shixie, 1989; Solomon, 1976; Veith, 1978). This chapter simply attempts to formulate the first two of these questions in ways that seem provocative and productive for future interdisciplinary research.

We start in the third century AD in India with a relatively detailed examination of a Sanskrit text (the "Rasādhyāya" of the *Nātyaśāstra*) that was written relatively close to the beginning of the historical record of systematic human self-consciousness about the emotions. It is through an analysis of this venerable text—an ancient example of a cultural psychology—that we address contemporary concerns.

The "Rasādhyāya" is a useful intellectual polestar on which to concentrate a discussion of the cultural psychology of the emotions for three reasons: 1) the text, although ancient, compares favorably with any contemporary treatise on the symbolic character of emotional experience; 2) the text, although famous among Sanskritists and scholars of South Asian civilization, is hardly known at all by emotion researchers in anthropology and psychology; and 3) the text provides the opportunity for an object lesson about the universally appealing yet culturally revealing character of all accounts about what is "basic" to the emotional nature of human beings.

Basic Emotions of the "Rasādhyāya"

In Sanskrit the word for existence and the word for mental state *(bhāva)* are the same, and mental states are said to "bring into existence the essence of poetry" (Gnoli, 1956: 63). So it is not surprising that between the third and eleventh centuries, Hindu philosophers of poetics and drama, interested in human emotions as objects of aesthetic pleasure, posited the existence of eight or nine basic emotions *(sthāyi-bhāva)*—four of which they viewed as primary—and developed a relatively detailed account of the symbolic structures that give them shape and meaning.

There is no standard English translation of the Sanskrit terms for the postulated basic emotions. Indeed there is no agreement about whether they should be translated as "emotions," "mental states," or "feelings" or about whether they are "basic," "dominant," "permanent," "universal," "natural," or "principal." The eight basic (or dominant) emotions (or mental states or feelings) are variously translated as 1) sexual passion, love, or delight *(rati);* 2) amusement, laughter, humor, or mirth *(hāsa);* 3) sorrow *(śoka);* 4) anger *(krodha);* 5) fear or terror *(bhaya);* 6) perseverance, energy, dynamic energy, or heroism *(utsāha);* 7) disgust or disillusion *(jugupsā);* and 8) amusement, wonder, astonishment, or amazement *(vismaya).* Some early medieval commentators mention an additional one: 9) serenity or calm *(sama).* To simplify our exegesis, we refer to the eight (or nine) as "basic emotions" and we label them sexual passion, amusement, sorrow, anger, fear, perseverance, disgust, wonder, and serenity. Of the basic emotions, four are privileged as primary basic emotions: sexual passion, anger, perseverance, and disgust (with serenity sometimes substituted or linked to disgust as a primary basic emotion).

The canonical Sanskrit text on the emotions, attributed to Bharata, is the sixth chapter, the "Rasādhyāya," of the *Nāṭyaśāstra,* which is a book about drama. Ancient and medieval Hindu thought specialized in "psychological" topics concerned with the nature of consciousness. Much of Sanskrit philosophy elevated the human mind and body to the status of sacramental objects, and was disinclined to draw sharp oppositions between the material, the sensate, the conscious, the poetic, and the divine. In Sanskrit drama the primary aim of the aesthetic experience was psychological as well; indeed, it was the symbolic representation of emotional states per se that set the stage for aesthetic and revelatory experience (see Dimock et al., 1974). The famous sixth chapter of the *Nāṭyaśāstra* is about the narrative structure (the causes, consequences, and concomitants) of eight basic emotional states and the most effective means (via facial expression, voice, posture, setting, character, action, physiological response) of their representation in the theatre.

The *Nāṭyaśāstra* was probably written between the third and fifth century AD. The most famous explication and commentary on the text—itself a critique of earlier explications and commentaries and the source of our knowledge of the earlier commentaries—derives from the tenth- and eleventh-century Kashmiri Brahman philosopher Abhivanagupta (for partial translations and contemporary commentaries, see Masson and Patwardhan, 1970 and Gnoli, 1956; also see Dimock et al., 1974 and Keith, 1924).

One major concern of the text and commentaries is to define the nature and significance (both aesthetic and theological) of an elusive meta-emotion called *rasa. Rasa* means to taste, to savor, or to sample; but when the term is used to refer to the grand meta-emotion of Hindu aesthetic experience, it is usually translated as aesthetic "pleasure," "enjoyment," or "rapture." It is a pleasure that lasts only as long as the dramatic illusion that makes *rasa* a reality. Because it is possible for members of the audience who witness a drama (the *rasiki*) to experience enjoyment or pleasure even from the apprehension of negative emotional states (disgust, fear, anger, sorrow), which in other circumstances they might want to avoid or repress, Abhinavagupta and others argue that *rasa* must be an autonomous meta-emotion, a *sui generis* form of consciousness.

A second major concern of the text and commentaries is to differentiate eight (or nine) varieties of *rasa*, each related to one of the basic emotions. The Sanskrit terms for these *rasa* are variously translated as 1) the erotic or love (*sṛṅgara*, the *rasa* of sexual passion); 2) the comic (*hāsya*, the *rasa* of amusement); 3) the compassionate or pathetic (*karuna*, the *rasa* of sorrow); 4) the furious or fury (*raudra*, the *rasa* of anger); 5) the heroic (*vīra*, the *rasa* of perseverance); 6) the terrifying or terror (*bhayānaka*, the *rasa* of fear); 7) horror, the loathsome, the odious, or the disgusting (*bībhatsa*, the *rasa* of disgust); 8) the marvelous, the awesome, admiration, or wonder (*adbhuta*, the *rasa* of wonder); and 9) the quietistic or calm (*śānta*, the *rasa* of serenity). When viewed from the perspective of their relationship to the basic emotions of everyday life, the *rasa* varieties are sometimes translated as the "sentiments" or "moods" of the theater.

A third major concern of the text and commentaries is to give an account of the precise relationship between the *rasa* and the basic emotions ("sthāyi-bhāva") to which they are said to correspond. In general, when the actor on stage effectively portrays a particular *bhāva*, the appreciative audience experiences the corresponding *rasa*. But is the relationship one of identity, such that the audience's experience of the *rasa* of fear is itself a real, everyday ex-

perience of fear? Or is the experience of the *rasa* of fear a mere sim-
ulation, imitation, or pretense of everyday fear? Or is it perhaps an
intensification or amplification of the basic emotion? Ultimately,
the idea is advanced that the experience of the *rasa* of a basic emotion is something entirely different from the experience of the basic
emotion itself.

Instead, the relationship of the *rasa* to the basic emotions is akin
to the relationship of an intentional state to its intentional object.
To experience *rasa* is to experience the pleasure or enjoyment (an intentional state) that results from the dramatically induced perception of the hidden or unconscious generic symbolic structures (the
intentional objects) that lend shape and meaning to the basic emotions in everyday life. Paraphrasing Bharata, in drama the basic
emotions are brought to a state of *rasa*. This happens to the very extent that their implicit symbolic codes are revealed and savored (or
tasted) as objects of pleasure and as a means of self-consciousness
and transcendence.

According to this line of reasoning, what colors the *rasa* and dis-
tinguishes the varieties from each other is that each has a different
intentional object, one of the basic emotions that all human beings
have at birth. At the same time, all the varieties share the pleasure,
delight, or rapture that comes from being artfully transported out
of time, place, and the immediacies of personal emotional experiences, beyond "the thick pall of mental stupor which cloaks one's
own consciousness" (Gnoli, 1956: 53) into the hidden depths of the
soul where one perceives, tastes, and savors the transcendental or
impersonal narrative forms that are immanent or implicit in the
most deeply rooted modes of human experience. Thus viewed, all
rasa possess that quality of pleasure or enjoyment that comes from
the tasting of a transcendent form that had previously been hidden
from the consciousness it had organized. It is that *sui generis* experi-

ence of delight, viewed as an intentional state aimed at the basic emotions as its intentional object, which explains how even disgust, anger, fear, and sorrow can be objects of pleasure when they present themselves as objects of aesthetic encounter.

This line of reasoning is suggestive of a parallel type of analysis of "empathy." Empathy might be viewed as a meta-emotion motivated by its own characteristic source of enjoyment or pleasure, which makes it possible to be responsive to another person's negative emotional states such as sorrow or guilt. Empathic sorrow or empathic guilt is not the same as the direct or secondary experience of sorrow or guilt. Instead, empathy is a dignifying experience precisely because, as a witness to someone else's emotional experience, one is transported out of one's self. Empathy is less detached than the experience of *rasa*, which comes from witnessing the generic symbolic structure that lends shape and meaning to a basic emotion; yet it is more detached than the experience of a basic emotion itself, which is the unwitnessed and all-too-immediate experience of everyday personal life. (For an account of the psychology of empathy, see Hoffman, 1990).

Having summarized a few key elements of the "Rasādhyāya" and subsequent commentaries, we are ready to ask two questions of the text: 1) What can the "Rasādhyāya" tell us about the symbolic structure of emotional experience? 2) What does it reveal about itself as a cultured (hence parochial or local) account of what is basic to human emotional experience? We treat the second question first.

The Wonder of the Sanskrit Emotions: A Cultural Account

Contemporary emotion researchers are likely to find the account of the basic emotions in the "Rasādhyāya" both familiar and strange.

If we compare the Sanskrit list of nine (eight plus one) basic emotions (sexual passion, amusement, sorrow, anger, fear, perseverance, disgust, wonder, and sometimes serenity) with Paul Ekman's well-known contemporary list of nine (six plus three) basic emotions (anger, fear, sadness, happiness, surprise, and disgust, plus interest, shame, and contempt), which Ekman derives from the analysis of everyday facial expressions (1980, 1984), the two lists are not closely coordinated, although they are not totally disjoint either.

Richard Schechner (1988: 267–289) in *Performance Theory* presents a series of photographs of facial expressions that he claims are iconic representations of the nine *rasa* of the *Nāṭyaśāstra*. The *Nāṭyaśāstra* never abstracts out facial expressions as the key markers of the basic emotions, but rather treats them as one element in an array of constituents; and there is every reason to believe that in Hindu drama, facial expressions unfold dynamically in a sequence of movements that are not easily frozen into a single frame. Nevertheless, Schechner posits direct analogies between six of his facial expressions for the *rasa* and the six facial expressions from Ekman's primary scheme (anger, fear, sadness, happiness, surprise, disgust). He equated, for example, Ekman's representation of the face of surprise with the face for the *rasa* of wonder (adbhuta) and Ekman's representation of the face of happiness with the face for the *rasa* of sexual passion (sṛṅgara). Schechner thinks he sees a universal pattern reflected in the two schemes. He (1988: 266) states, "Humankind has countless gods, but I would be very surprised if there were not some agreement concerning the basic emotions."

In our view several of Schechner's equations are dubious. For example, in Ekman's photo of the face of surprise, the mouth is wide open; it is not similar to the mouth of the *rasa* of wonder, which is closed and faintly suggestive of a smile. (The mouth is closed in all of the facial expressions of the rasa, which may be related to a cultural evaluation concerning the vulgarity of an open mouth.) And in Ekman's photo of the face of happiness, the eyes are directly frontal; they not similar to the eyes of the *rasa* of sexual passion, which are conspicuously averted to one side, perhaps suggestive of secrecy or conspiracy. More importantly, because Schechner's equation of American happiness with Sanskrit sexual passion seems peculiar from the start, it should also be noted that Ekman's photo of the face of happiness bears no resemblance whatsoever to the face of the *rasa* of amusement *(hāsya)*, which is the *rasa* one might have intuitively expected to be connected to the Western conception of "happiness."

We strongly doubt that most Americans could spontaneously generate accurate descriptions for the majority of the nine facial icons of the *rasa* displayed in Schechner's book. (Curiously one of the faces that American graduate students seem to identify easily is the Sanskrit face of serenity, which as far as we know is not a basic emotion on any Western list. In informal experiments conducted in classes at the University of Chicago, they also converge in their responses to faces of fear, disgust, and sorrow, but not to the others.) Indeed, we believe one can plausibly argue that happiness and surprise and most of the basic emotions on Ekman's list do not have close analogues among the basic emotions of the "Rasadhyaya," and any sense of easy familiarity with the Sanskrit list is more apparent than real.

As we read the "Rasādhyāya" and commentaries, three of the nine basic emotions (anger, fear, and sorrow) are genuinely familiar, in the sense of possessing an equivalent shape and meaning for medieval Hindus and contemporary Americans. Of course, to acknowledge those three points of dense similarity is not to suggest that those three emotional meanings must be cross-cultural universals. Wierzbicka (1992; also see 1990, 1997, 1999), an anthropological linguist and polyglot who specializes in the study of semantic universals and the language of the emotions, has brought to a halt facile claims about translation equivalence, by arguing that sadness as understood in European and American conceptions of the emotions is not an empirical universal and is neither lexicalized, important, nor salient in most of the languages of the world. She claims that from the point of view of the study of linguistic semantics of emotion terms, there are no basic or universal emotions.

Nevertheless, anger, fear, and sorrow are easy to recognize in the "Rasādhyāya." Sorrow, for example, is said to arise from misfortune, calamity, and destruction, and from "separation from those who are dear, [their] downfall, loss of wealth, death and imprisonment." "It should be acted out by tears, laments, drying up of the mouth, change of color, languor in the limbs, sighs, loss of memory, etc." Sorrow is said to be accompanied by other mental states, including world weariness, physical weariness, lifelessness, tears, confusion, dejection, and worry.

Anger and fear are also easy to recognize in the text. Anger, for example, is said to arise from provocative actions, insult, lies, assault, harsh words, oppression, and envy. The actions accompanying it include beating, splitting open, crushing, breaking, hitting, and drawing blood. "It should be acted out by red eyes, furrowing of the brows, biting one's lips and grinding one's teeth, puffing the cheeks, wringing the hands, and similar gestures." It is accompanied by other mental states, including an increase in determination or energy, rashness, violence, sweat, trembling, pride, panic, resentment, and stuttering (see Masson and Patwardhan, 1970: 52–53).

For three of the nine basic emotions described in the "Rasādhyāya," it is easy to recognize the underlying script, to see the self in the other and to arrive at a cross-cultural and transhistorical agreement about what is basic in emotional functioning, at least for them and us. Yet as one moves beyond sorrow, anger, and fear to disgust, amusement, wonder, perseverance, sexual passion, and serenity, the way in which consciousness is partitioned or hierarchically structured into basic and nonbasic states in the "Rasādhyāya" seems less and less familiar, despite any initial appearances to the contrary. This decline in familiarity is similar to the "gradient of recognition" that Haidt and Keltner (1999) found when studying facial expressions in India and the United States: some expressions are well recognized across cultures, some are less well recognized, and there is no clear or bounded set of "universal" facial expressions.

Thus it becomes clear on examination of the relevant Sanskrit texts and commentaries that medieval Hindu disgust differs from modern American disgust. Medieval Hindu disgust is partitioned into two subtypes: the first includes aspects of horror and disillusionment as well as the world weariness associated with the quest for detachment, transcendence, and salvation. The second includes horror at the sight of blood. Medieval Hindu disgust is, as the anthropologist McKim Marriott has suggested, more like a domain of the "loathsome," and it gathers together within its territory a broad range of human responses to the ugly, the nasty, and the odious. Rozin, Haidt, and McCauley (2000) argue that contemporary American disgust has a similarly broad and heterogeneous domain of elicitors, but that moral and interpersonal disgust are highly variable across cultures.

Medieval Hindu wonder is also not contemporary American surprise, but rather a state of mind closer to admiration than to startle or shock. Wonder has less to do with a sudden violation of expectations and more to do with one's reactions to the opportunity to witness heavenly or exalted feats, events, or beings (including, for example, the feats of a juggler). It is even possible to do such witnessing with your mouth closed, as long as your eyes are wide open!

Medieval Hindu amusement (which includes contemptuous, indignant, or derisive laughter at the faults and inferior status of others) is not contemporary American happiness, which has celebratory implications. Indeed, happiness, shame, indignation, arrogance, and some contempt-like emotions are explicitly mentioned in the "Rasādhyāya" for inclusion among thirty-three nonbasic ("accompanying") mental states. Thus it seems reasonable to assert that the basic emotion designated by medieval Hindu philosophers as "amusement" is not adequately translated as "happiness" or as "contempt." (While the text provides little basis for determining equivalence of meaning for the terms used to translate the thirty-three nonbasic mental states, there is good reason to doubt that "shame" or "happiness" have the same implications and associations, or play the same psychological role, in India as they do in the contemporary United States; see Menon and Shweder, 1994, on the positive qualities of "shame" in India, where it is a virtue associated with civility, modesty, and an ability to rein in one's destructive powers in support of the social order rather than with the diminishment of the ego; also Parish, 1991).

Finally, medieval Hindu perseverance is not contemporary American interest but is rather deeply connected to heroic determination and a willingness to engage in acts requiring endurance and self-sacrifice. In the context of the early medieval Hindu scriptures, when the Hindu goddess Durga (or Kali) endures trials and tribulations yet persists in a seemingly hopeless battle against uncountable demons in an effort to save the world, her efforts are said to display the heroic *rasa* of perseverance. Mere "interest" has very little to do with it. She would probably rather be doing something else.

In sum, the two lists of nine basic human emotions truly overlap at only three points. All the other points of similarity (amusement as happiness, their disgust as our disgust, wonder as surprise, perseverance as interest) turn out to be merely apparent; and for several of the emotions (sexual passion, serenity, shame, contempt), there is not even an illusion of transcultural equivalence. In the end most of the items cannot be easily mapped across the two lists.

There are other ways in which the "Rasādhyāya" presents us with a somewhat-unfamiliar portrait of the way consciousness is organized. One has to do with the way the text divides the basic emotions into primary basic emotions and secondary basic emotions. Thus according to the text and commentaries, the four primary basic emotions are sexual passion, anger, perseverance, and disgust. The four secondary basic emotions are amusement, sorrow, wonder, and fear. The ninth basic emotion—serenity—is sometimes viewed as a primary basic emotion and either substituted for disgust or associated with disgust (through a causal sequence that begins with horror and revulsion over attachments in the world and ends with the serenity of ego-alienation, detachment, and salvation). In commenting on this scheme, we should note, in passing, that Sigmund Freud might find much of value in a conception that treats sexual passion and anger (and perseverance and disgust) as the deepest aspects of human experience. One wonders whether Freud would have interpreted perseverance and disgust as analogs to the life and death instincts.

More notable, however, is the fact that the primary basic emotions are primary because they are the "emotions" associated in classical and folk Hindu thought with the four worthy ends or goals of life. One of those goals of life—pleasure (kāma)—is linked to sexual passion. A second goal—control, autonomy, and power (artha)—is linked to anger. A third goal—social duty and moral virtue (*dharma*)—is linked to perseverance. The fourth and perhaps highest goal—salvation or the attainment of divinity (*moksha*)—is linked to disgust or serenity. In other words, presupposed by this famous formulation about the organization of human emotions is a special theory of morality and human motivation and a specific way of life. Thus it is hardly surprising that this particular medieval South Asian conception of the hierarchical structuring of consciousness into basics versus nonbasics and primary basics versus secondary basics should seem somewhat strange to emotion researchers in America, and vice versa.

There is yet another way in which the "Rasādhyāya" presents an unfamiliar portrait of the organization of consciousness. The eight or nine items on the Sanskrit list are bound to seem like a disparate and anomalous collection, at least from the point of view of American folk and academic conceptions about how to partition consciousness into kinds of mental states (see D'Andrade, 1987). Indeed, one might expect American emotion researchers to recoil at the very suggestion that the Sanskrit list is really a list of basic "emotions" at all. American folk and academic psychologists do not classify serenity, wonder, sexual passion, amusement, or perseverance as definitive or clear examples of "emotions" (see Shaver et al., 1987). Sexual passion would probably be classified as a motive or alternatively as a nonemotional feeling. Serenity might be classified as a nonemotional feeling or a state of mind, although not as a motive. Perseverance would probably by classified as a quality of will or agency or perhaps a formal property of motivation. Amusement and wonder seem to be none of the above. Indeed after reading the text and commentaries and the various nonequivalent translations of *bhāva* and *rasa*—are they mental states, emotions, feelings, moods, sentiments, or what?—one might begin to suspect that in the "Rasādhyāya" one is faced with a somewhat different conception of how to partition a person into parts and how to divide consciousness into kinds.

It is of course possible, indeed likely, that in some ways the "Rasādhyāya" presupposes a partitioning of the person into parts that is not coordinate with our own conception of the person, and that is why it is so hard to settle on any single translation equivalent for the Sanskrit *bhāva* and *rasa*. This is a familiar kind of translation problem and it is encountered even across European languages and subcultures.

Wierzbicka (1989), for example, has analyzed in detail the many distortions of meaning that occur when the Russian word *duša* is translated into English. *Duša* is a lexical item that signifies a key Russian cultural concept that has to do with the partitioning of a person into parts. It is typically translated into English as "soul," or alternatively as "mind," "heart," or "spirit." None of those lexical mappings is adequate, because none of those English words signifies the full and equivalent set of meanings associated with *duša*. For example, Wierzbicka notes (1989: 52) that it is one of two parts of the person, that one cannot see it, that because of this part things can happen in a person that cannot happen in anything other than a person, that these things can be good or bad, that because of this part a person can feel things that nothing other than a person can feel, that other people cannot know what these things are if the person doesn't say it, that a person would want someone to know what these things are, that because of this part a person can be a good person and feel something good toward other people.

Similar issues concerning variations in the organization of consciousness arise in connection with the research of Steven Parish (1991) on conceptions of the mental life among the South Asian Hindu Newars of Nepal (also see Appadurai, 1990; Brenneis, 1990).

For the Newars, mental states such as memory, desire, feeling, thought, and emotion, which we would spatially differentiate between the head and the heart (and perhaps the gut and the skin), are all thought to be located together in the heart, and that heart of the mental life is thought to be animated by a God, who makes perception and experience possible. Consequently for the Newars "the efforts of individuals to monitor their inner life often draw on the sense of a divine agency" and "a person sees because the god sees through his or her eyes" (Parish, 1991: 316). So it would be surprising indeed if the set of meanings associated with the Sanskrit terms *rasa* and *bhāva* could be easily mapped onto the set of meanings associated with any single English term such as emotion, feeling, mood, sentiment, mental state, or consciousness. We look forward to the day when Sanskritists do for the concept signified by the term *bhāva* what Wierzbicka has done for the concept signified by the Russian word *duša*.

For the time being, however, we are not going to try to solve the very deepest of questions about the partitioning of the person into parts and the division of consciousness into kinds. Instead we are going to argue that it is helpful enough to know what the text tells us. What the "Rasādhyāya" tells us is that in drama the *sthāyi-bhāva* (we'll keep calling them "basic emotions") are brought to a state of *rasa*. More importantly, however, what the text tells us is that the *rasa* are nothing more than the union of three script-like or narrative components:

1. The determinants, causes, or eliciting conditions *(vi-bhāva),* which includes all the background information, settings, events, and action tendencies that might make manifest some state of the world and one's relationship

to it (for example, forced separation from something one cherishes; finding oneself powerless in the face of danger).

2. The consequents *(anu-bhāva)*, which includes eight types of involuntary somatic responses (sweating, fainting, weeping, and so on), and various action tendencies (abusing the body, brandishing weapons) and expressive modes (bodily movement, voice tone, facial expression).

3. The "accompanying" mental states *(vyabhicari-bhāva)*, which are a symptom list of secondary side effects, including emotions, feelings, and cognitive states such as weariness, reminiscence, panic, envy, dreaming, confusion, sickness, shame, and even death.

In other words, in the "Rasādhyāya" one finds a relatively elaborate account of the symbolic structures that give shape and meaning to a selected subset of mental experiences—which, because they have been privileged for symbolic elaboration, have become transformed into "basic" mental experiences for that culturally constituted world. In other words, in the "Rasādhyāya" one finds an ancient yet sophisticated text in the cultural psychology of the emotions.

Symbolic Structure of the Emotions

The strategy adopted in the "Rasādhyāya" is to define a basic emotion by the implicit symbolic structure that gives shape and meaning to that emotion (its *rasa*—the intentional object of aesthetic pleasure in the theatre) and then to define that symbolic structure by resolving it into its determinants, consequences, and accompanying side effects. This strategy is directly parallel to various contemporary approaches to the cultural psychology of the emotions.

One aspect of this symbolic (or, as some would call it, cognitive) approach is the view that kinds of emotions are not kinds of things like plants or animals. Instead they are (*rasa*-like) interpretive schemes of a particular script-like, story-like, or narrative kind that give shape and meaning to the human experience of those conditions of the world that have a bearing on self-esteem (see Shweder, 1993a,b, 1994a). The elements that are proposed as slots in the story may vary slightly from scholar to scholar, although most of the slots in use today can be found in the "Rasādhyāya."

Mesquita and Frijda (1992; also see Ellsworth, 1991; Frijda, 1986; Lazarus, 1991; Lewis, Sullivan, and Michalson, 1982; Lewis, 1989; Lutz, 1985b; Russell, 1991; Stein and Levine, 1987), for example, parse each emotion script into a series of slots including "antecedent events," "event coding" (type of condition of the world), "appraisal" (judged implications for self-esteem and well-being), "physiological reaction patterns," "action readiness," "emotional behavior," and "regulation." Shweder (1994a) suggests a parsing of emotion scripts into slots such as "self-involving conditions of the world" (for example, loss and gain, protection and threat), "somatic feelings" (muscle tension, pain, dizziness, nausea, fatigue, breathlessness), "affective feelings" (agitation, emptiness. expansiveness), "expressive modes" (face, posture, voice), and "plans for self-management" (to flee, to retaliate, to celebrate, to invest) (also see Shweder, 1991, where a slot is provided in the emotion narrative for variations in "social regulation" or the normative appropriateness of certain emotions being experienced or expressed).

The primary assumption of the symbolic approach is the same as the approach of the "Rasādhyāya": "Emotion" is not something separable from the conditions that justify it, from the somatic and affective events that are ways of feeling or being touched by it, or from the actions it demands. The emotion is the whole story—a kind of somatic event (fatigue, chest pain, goose flesh) or affective event (panic, emptiness, expansiveness) experienced as a perception of some antecedent conditions (death of a friend, acceptance of a book manuscript for publication, a proposition to go out to dinner) and their implications for the self (as loss, gain, threat, possibility) and experienced as a social judgment (of vice or virtue, sickness or health) and as a plan for action to preserve one's self-esteem (attack, withdraw, confess, hide, explore). The emotion is the simultaneous experience of all the components, or perhaps, more accurately, the unitary experience of the whole package deal.

The symbolic approach also claims that, for the sake of comparison and translation, any emotion is decomposable into its narrative slots. To ask whether people are alike or different in their emotional functioning (or whether emotion words in different languages are alike or different in their significations) is really to ask these more specific questions:

1. Are they alike or different in their somatic experiences (for example, muscle tension or headaches)? (somatic phenomenology question)
2. Are they alike or different in their affective experiences (emptiness, calm, pleasantness)? (affective phenomenology question)
3. Are they alike or different in the antecedent conditions of those somatic and affective experiences (infertility, job loss, winning the lottery)? (environmental determinants question)
4. Are they alike or different in the perceived implications of

those antecedent conditions for self-esteem (irreversible loss, fame, and recognition)? (self-appraisal question)

5. Are they alike or different in the extent to which showing or displaying that state of consciousness has been socially baptized as a vice or virtue or as a sign of sickness or health? (social appraisal question).

6. Are they alike or different in the plans for the self-management of self-esteem that are activated as part of the emotion script (celebration, attack, withdrawal from social contacts)? (self-management question)

7. Are they alike or different in the iconic and symbolic vehicles used for giving expression to the whole package deal (facial expressions, voice, posture, and action)? (communication question)

Given this type of decomposition of the definition of an emotion to its constituent narrative slots, the issue of translation equivalence becomes a matter of pattern matching, as one tries to determine whether the variables in each of those slots are linked in similar ways across cultures.

Bite Your Tongue: The Case of Hindu *lajja*

The contemporary Hindu conception of *lajja* (or *lajya*) has recently been explicated for two communities in South Asia, the Newars of Bhaktapur in Nepal (Parish, 1991) and the Oriyas of Bhubaneswar in Orissa, India (Menon and Shweder, 1994, 1998, in press). *Lajja* is often translated by bilingual informants and dictionaries as "shame," "embarrassment," "shyness," or "modesty," yet every one of these translations is problematic or fatally flawed.

For starters, *lajja* is something one deliberately shows or puts on display the way we might show our gratitude, loyalty, or respect. It is a state of consciousness that has been baptized in South Asia as a supreme virtue, especially for women, and it is routinely exhibited in everyday life, for example, every time a married women covers her face or ducks out of a room to avoid direct affiliation with those members of her family she is supposed to avoid.

Parish (1991: 324) describes *lajja* as an emotion and a moral state. It is by means of their *lajja* that those who are civilized uphold the social order, by showing perseverance in the pursuit of their own social role obligations; by displaying respect for the hierarchical arrangement of social privileges and responsibilities; by acting shyly, modestly, or deferentially and not encroaching on the prerogatives of others; and by covering one's face, remaining silent, or lowering one's eyes in the presence of superiors. Like gratitude, loyalty, or respect, *lajja,* is judged in South Asia to be a very good thing.

While *lajja* may be experienced by both men and women, it is an emotion and a virtue associated with a certain feminine ideal. It is talked about as a lovely ornament worn by women. *Lajja* is the linguistic stem for the name of a local creeper plant (a "touch me not") that is so delicate that, on the slightest contact, it closes its petals and withdraws into itself. To say of a woman that she is full of *lajja* is a very positive recommendation. Here is one reason why.

Perhaps the most important collective representation of *lajja* in various regions of Eastern India is the tantric icon portraying the mother goddess Kali, brandishing weapons and a decapitated head in her ten arms, eyes bulging and tongue out, with her foot stepping on the chest of her husband, the god Siva, who is lying on the ground beneath her. Based on interviews with ninety-two informants in Orissa, India, Menon and Shweder (1994, 1998, in press) have been examining the meaning of this icon.

The gist of the story, as it is narrated by local experts, is that

Figure 3.1 The Great Mother Goddess of Hinduism (as Kali)

once upon a time the male gods gave a boon to a minor demon, Mahisasura, to the effect that he could be killed only at the hands of a naked female. They thereby turned Mahisasura into a major demon who was able unimpeded to terrorize all the male gods. In order to destroy the demon, the male gods pooled all their energy and powers and created the goddess Durga and armed her with their own weapons. On their behalf they sent Durga into battle against Mahisasura, but they neglected to tell her about the boon. She fought bravely but could not kill the demon—he was too strong and clever.

In desperation Durga appealed for guidance from an auspicious goddess, who let her in on the secret. As one informant narrated the story: "So Durga did as she was advised to [she stripped], and within seconds after Mahisasura saw her [naked], his strength waned and he died under her sword. After killing him a terrible rage entered Durga's mind, and she asked herself, 'What kinds of gods are these that give to demons such boons, and apart from that what kind of gods are these that they do not have the honesty to tell me the truth before sending me into battle?'"

Durga felt humiliated by her nakedness and by the deceit. She decided that such a world with such gods did not deserve to survive and she took on the form of Kali and went on a mad rampage, devouring every living creature that came in her way.

The gods then called on Siva, who is Kali's husband, to do something to save the world from destruction at the hands of the mother goddess. Siva lay in her path as she came tromping along, enraged. Absorbed in her wild dance of destruction, Kali accidentally stepped on Siva and placed her foot on her husband's chest, an unspeakable act of disrespect. When she looked down and saw what she had done, she came back to her senses, in particular to her sense of *lajja*, which she expressed by biting her tongue between her teeth. She reined in her anger and became calm and still. To this day in Orissa, "bite your tongue" is an idiomatic expression for *lajja* and it is the facial expression used by women as an iconic apology when they realize, or are confronted with the fact, that they have failed to uphold social norms.

One moral of the story is that men are incapable of running the world by themselves even though they are socially dominant. They rely on women to make the world go round. Yet in a patriarchal society men humiliate women by the way they exploit female power, strength, and perseverance. This leads to anger and rage in women, which is highly destructive of everything of value and must be brought under control, for the sake of the social order. *Lajja* is a salient ideal in South Asia because it preserves social harmony by helping women to swallow their rage.

Decomposing *lajja* into its constituent narrative slots shows how hazardous it can be to render the emotional meanings of others with terms from our received English lexicon for mental states. See Geertz (1984: 130) on the difficulties of translating the Balinese term lek, which seems much like Hindu *lajja*. Geertz notes that *lek* has been variably translated and mistranslated and that "'shame' is the most common attempt." He tries to render it as "stage fright." *Lajja* does not map well onto words like shame, embarrassment, shyness, modesty, or stage fright.

From the perspective of social and self-appraisal, for example, to be full of *lajja* is to be in possession of the virtue of behaving in a civilized manner and in such a way that the social order and its norms are upheld. It is not a neurosis and it does not connote a reduction in the strength of the ego. Indeed *lajja* promotes self-esteem.

Of course, to be perceived or labeled as someone without *lajja*—as someone who encroaches on the station of others or fails to live up to the requirements of their own station—is unpleasant and arousing. Parish notes that to feel *lajja* is sometimes associated with blushing, sweating, and altered pulse (1991: 324), but I suspect that such a somatic phenomenology is a feature of the anxiety provoked by the social perception of the absence of *lajja* and is not definitive of *lajja* itself. To experience *lajja* is to experience that sense of virtuous, courteous, well-mannered restraint that led Kali to rein in her rage.

The environmental determinants of *lajja* as a sense of one's own virtue and civility are as varied as the set of actions that are dutiful and responsible, given one's station in life in a world in which everyone is highly self-conscious about their social designation (see Geertz, 1984 for a brilliant attempt to capture the dramatic qualities of such a world). They include events that we would find familiar (not being seen naked by the wrong person in the wrong context) as well as many events that might seem alien or strange (never talking directly to your husband's elder brother or to your father-in-law; never being in the same room with both your husband and another male to whom he must defer).

From the perspective of self-management, South Asian *lajja* may appear at first glance to be similar to American shame or embarrassment. It activates a habit or routine that sometimes results in hiding, covering up, and withdrawing from the scene. Yet what is really being activated by *lajja* is a general habit of respect for social hierarchy and a consciousness of one's social and public responsibilities, which in the context of South Asian norms may call for avoidance, silence, or other deferential, protective, or nonaggressive gestures and actions.

Finally consider the semantic structure of shame and *lajja* in the minds of informants. When middle-class Anglo-American college students are presented with the triad of terms "shame-happiness-anger" and asked "which is most different from the other two?" they are most likely to respond that either "happiness" or "shame" is most different from the other two, perhaps on the grounds that "shame" and "anger" go together because they are both unpleasant feelings, or that "happiness" and "anger" go together because they are both ego-expanding emotions. Neither response is typical of responses in the South Asian community where Menon and Shweder (1994) have worked, where *lajja* (shame?) and *suka* (happiness?) are thought to go together in the triads test and *raga* (anger?), perceived as destructive of society, is the odd emotion out. Here something seems to be amiss in the translation process. Something may well have been amiss in most past attempts to equate emotions across languages and across local cultural worlds (see Wierzbicka, 1992a).

Social and Moral Context of Emotional Experience

The case of *lajja* illustrates the dependence of emotional experience on its social and moral context. To understand *lajja*, one must understand the moral goods that Oriyas strive to achieve. This strategy of viewing emotions against the background of their associated moral goods can be extended to other emotions using a framework that has proved useful in recent cultural psychological work. Shweder et al. (1997; also Shweder, 1990; Haidt, Koller, and Dias, 1993; Jensen, 1995; Chapter 2 this book) suggest that moral goods do not vary randomly from culture to culture, but rather tend to cluster into three sets of related goods or three ethics, known as the ethics of autonomy, community, and divinity. Cultures rely on the three ethics to varying degrees. The relative weights of the three ethics within a culture appear to affect the experience and expression of emotion, as well as the way emotions are conceptualized by both local folk and local experts.

In cultures that emphasize an ethics of autonomy, the central object of value is the individual. Within that type of cultural world, the most salient moral goods are those that promote the autonomy, freedom, and well-being of the individual, with the result that nothing can be condemned that does not demonstrably harm others, restrict their freedom, or impinge on their rights. Haidt, Koller, and Dias (1993), for example, found that American college students (a population steeped in the ethics of autonomy) responded to stories about violations of food and sexual taboos (for example, eating one's already-dead pet dog) with disgust. Nevertheless these students felt compelled by the logic of their ethical stance to separate their feelings of disgust from their moral judgments. As a result, they held firmly to the view that their personal emotional reactions did not imply that the actions were wrong. They spoke exclusively in the language of the ethics of autonomy, pointing out that nobody was hurt, and that the people involved had a right to do as they pleased in a private setting.

Disgust plays an ambiguous role in such an autonomy-based cultural world (see Rozin, Haidt, and McCauley, 2000). In such a cultural world, the moral domain is constructed so that it is limited to issues of harm, rights, and justice (Turiel, 1983); and the emotions that are experienced as moral emotions (for example, anger, sympathy, and guilt) are those that respond to a rather narrow class of ethical goods such as justice, freedom, and the avoidance of harm. In such a cultural world, everyone's focus, folk and social scientists alike, is on individuals striving to maximize their personal utility (for example, Lazarus, 1991; Plutchik, 1980; Stein, 2000). Happiness, sadness, pride, and shame are viewed as responses to individual gains and losses, successes and failures. Other moral goods (such as loyalty, duty, and respect for status) that might be linked to the emotions are either lost or under-theorized.

In many parts of the world, the moral domain has been constructed so that it is broader than, or at least different from, an ethics of autonomy. In cultures that emphasize an ethics of community, ontological priority is given to collective entities (the family, guild, clan, community, corporation, or nation), and the central moral goods are those that protect these entities against challenges from without and decay from within (for example, goods such as loyalty, duty, honor, respectfulness, chastity, modesty, and self-control).

In such a world individual choices (what to wear, whom to marry, how to address others) take on a moral significance and an ethical importance (Shweder, Mahapatra, and Miller, 1987), and the successful pursuit of individual goals may even be a cause for embarrassment or shame. Haidt, Koller, and Dias (1993), for example, found that, outside of college samples, people of lower socioeconomic status thought it was morally wrong to eat one's already-dead pet dog or to clean one's toilet with the national flag. Even when these actions were judged to be harmless, they were still seen as objectively disgusting or disrespectful and hence morally wrong. In a cultural world based on an ethics of community, emotions may exist that are not fully felt or credited by those whose morality is based on an ethics of autonomy.

Lajja is a clear example, because it is not the type of emotion that will be experienced in a world that sees hierarchy and the exclusive prerogatives of others as unjust or as a form of oppression, rather than as a powerful and legitimate object of admiration or respect (Menon and Shweder, 1998, Chapter 5 this book). To select another example, "song," the righteous indignation of the Ifaluk (Lutz, 1988), may require a sense of close, valued, and inescapable community. While American "anger" is triggered by a violation of rights and leads to a desire for revenge, Ifaluk "song" appears to be triggered by violations of relationships, and it leads to a socially shared emotion that brings the violator back into voluntary conformity (Lutz, 1988).

Similarly, emotions related to honor and heroism may require a strong attachment and dedication to a collectivity or group, for whom the hero lays down his or her life. The *Nāṭyaśāstra*'s otherwise-puzzling inclusion of "perseverance" or heroism as a basic emotion, equal to anger and fear, seems more intelligible against the backdrop of the ethics of community. A James Bond–type hero may display perseverance as he battles to save the "free world"; yet we do not think he inspires the same *rasa* in an American audience that an Indian audience savors when a Hindi film hero battles to avenge the death of his father. Many older classic American films raised themes of family honor, but such themes have become less common in recent decades, as the ethics of autonomy has pushed back the ethics of community. Unlike Hindi films, modern American films rarely embed the hero in the thick traditions and obligations of family history. It is a rare movie indeed when we meet the hero's parents.

The ethics of divinity may have a similar differential activation and enabling effect on the emotional life. People (and sometimes animals) are seen as containing a bit of God within them, and the central moral goods are those that protect and dignify the person's inherent divinity. The body is experienced as a temple, so matters that seem to be personal choices within the ethics of autonomy (for example, food and sexual choices, personal hygiene) become moral and spiritual issues associated with such goods as sanctity, purity, and pollution.

Within the terms of a cultural world focused on an ethics of divinity, even love and hate may lose their simple positive versus negative hedonic valences. A modern spiritual guide (Yatiswarananda, 1979: 187) says that hatred and attachment are both fetters that "degrade the human being, preventing him from rising to his true stature. Both must be renounced." Hindu scriptures are full of stories such as that of Pingala, a greedy courtesan who sought incessantly for wealth. One day she was deeply disappointed that nobody came to give her gifts. "Her countenance sank and she was very much down in spirits. Then as a result of this brooding an utter disgust came over her that made her happy" (Yatiswarananda, 1979: 160, referring to *Bhagavatam* 11.8.27). While secularized Westerners can easily recognize these feelings of greed, attachment, and self-disgust, the story points to feelings about attachment and renunciation that may not be readily available to those who lack an ethics of divinity. Secularized Western folk may feel pride on giving up an attachment to cigarettes, or even to money; but if this renunciation is set within a script of personal accomplishment and health concerns, it is a different emotion (on the present account) than if it is a component of a script about the purification and advancement of the soul toward reunion with God.

Of course, the very idea of an emotion connected with renunciation seems paradoxical, because spiritual progress in many Eastern religions is measured by the degree to which one moves beyond the experience of emotions. Only once this paradox is grasped does the mysterious ninth emotion of the *Nāṭyaśāstra* make sense. Serenity or calmness is an important part of Hindu emotional life and emotional discourse precisely because of the centrality of an ethics of divinity in everyday Hindu life. Not surprisingly, it is on no Western lists of basic emotions.

Conclusion: The Cultural Psychology of the Emotions Anew

As we enter a new era of collaborative research among anthropologists, psychologists, and physiologists concerned with similarities and differences in emotional functioning on a worldwide scale, a major goal for the cultural psychology of the emotions will be to decompose the emotions (and the languages of the emotions) into constituent narrative slots. By decomposing the symbolic structure of the emotions, researchers can render the meaning of other peoples' mental states without assimilating them in misleading ways into an a priori set of familiar lexical items (for example, rendering Oriya Hindu *lajja* as English "shame").

It is one of the great marvels of life that, across languages, cultures, and history, people can truly understand each other's emotions and mental states. Yet it is one of the great ironies of life that the process of understanding the consciousness of others can appear to be far easier than it really is, thereby making it more difficult to achieve a genuine understanding of "otherness." Thus this chapter on the cultural psychology of the emotions and meditation on the venerable "Rasādhyāya" of the *Nāṭyaśāstra* is really a plea for a decomposition of emotional states into their constituent narrative slots (environmental determinants, somatic phenomenology, affective phenomenology, self-appraisal, social appraisal, self-management strategy, communication codes). Unless we take that step, we will continue to be prone to the bias that the emotional life of human beings is "basically" the same around the world. The truth may well be that, when it comes to "basic" emotions, we (medieval Hindus and contemporary Anglo-Americans, Pintupis and Russians, Eskimos and Balinese) are not only basically alike in some ways but also basically different from each other as well.

"What about Female Genital Mutilation?" And Why Understanding Culture Matters

Female genital mutilation (FGM, also known as female circumcision) has been practiced traditionally for centuries in sub-Saharan Africa. Customs, rituals, myths, and taboos have perpetuated the practice even though it has maimed or killed untold numbers of women and girls . . . FGM's disastrous health effects, combined with the social injustices it perpetuates, constitute a serious barrier to overall African development.

—Susan Rich and Stephanie Joyce,
"Eradicating Female Genital Mutilation" (n.d.)[1]

On the basis of the vast literature on the harmful effects of genital surgeries, one might have anticipated finding a wealth of studies that document considerable increases in mortality and morbidity. This review could find no incontrovertible evidence on mortality, and the rate of medical complications suggest that they are the exception rather than the rule.

—Carla M. Obermeyer, "Female Genital Surgeries" (1999)[2]

Early societies in Africa established strong controls over the sexual behavior of their women and devised the brutal means of circumcision to curb female sexual desire and response.

—Olayinka Koso-Thomas, *Circumcision of Women* (1987)[3]

In fact, studies that systematically investigate the sexual feelings of women and men in societies where genital surgeries are found are rare, and the scant information that is available calls into question the assertion that female genital surgeries are fundamentally antithetical to women's sexuality and incompatible with sexual enjoyment.

—Carla M. Obermeyer, "Female Genital Surgeries" (1999)

Those who practice some of the most controversial of such customs—clitoridectomy, polygamy, the marriage of children or marriages that are otherwise coerced—sometimes explicitly defend them as necessary for controlling women and openly acknowledge that the customs persist at men's insistence.

—Susan Moller Okin, *Is Multiculturalism Bad for Women?* (1999)[4]

It is difficult for me—considering the number of ceremonies I have observed, including my own—to accept that what appears to be expressions of joy and ecstatic celebrations of womanhood in actuality disguise hidden experiences of coercion and subjugation. Indeed, I offer that the bulk of Kono women who uphold these rituals do so because they want to—they relish the supernatural powers of their ritual leaders over against men in society, and they embrace the legitimacy of female authority and particularly, the authority of their mothers and grandmothers.

—Fuambai Ahmadu, "Rites and Wrongs" (2000)[5]

On November 18, 1999, Fuambai Ahmadu, a young African scholar who grew up in the United States, delivered a paper at the American Anthropological Association Meeting in Chicago that should be deeply troubling to all liberal, free-thinking people who value democratic pluralism and the toleration of differences and who care about the accuracy of cultural representations in our public policy debates.[6]

Ms. Ahmadu (2000: 283) began her paper with these words:

> I also share with feminist scholars and activists campaigning against the practice [of female circumcision] a concern for women's physical, psychological and sexual well-being, as well as with the implications of these traditional rituals for women's status and power in society. Coming from an ethnic group [the Kono of Eastern Sierra Leone] in which female (and male) initiation and "circumcision" are institutionalized and a central feature of culture and society and having myself undergone this traditional process of becoming a "woman," I find it increasingly challenging to reconcile my own experiences with prevailing global discourses on female "circumcision."

By Rites a Woman: Listening to the Multicultural Voices of Feminism

Coming-of-age and gender-identity ceremonies involving genital alterations are embraced by, and deeply embedded in the lives of, many African women, not only in Africa but in Europe and the United States as well. Estimates of the number of contemporary African women who participate in these practices vary widely between 80 million and 200 million. In general, these women keep their secrets secret. They have not been inclined to expose the most intimate parts of their bodies to public examination, and they have not been in the habit of making their case on the op-ed pages of American newspapers, in the halls of Congress, or at academic meetings. So it was an extraordinary event to witness Fuambai Ahmadu—an initiate and anthropologist—stand up and state that the oft-repeated claims "regarding adverse effects [of female circumcision] on women's sexuality do not tally with the experiences of most Kono women," including her own (Ahmadu 2000: 308, 305). Ms. Ahmadu was 22 years old and sexually experienced when she returned to Sierra Leone to be circumcised, so at least in her own case, she knows what she is talking about. Most Kono women uphold the practice of female (and male) circumcision and positively evaluate its consequences for their psychological, social, spiritual, and physical well-being. Ms. Ahmadu went on to suggest that Kono girls and women feel empowered by the initiation ceremony, and she described some of the reasons why.

Fuambai Ahmadu's ethnographic observations and testimony may seem astonishing. In the social and intellectual circles in which most liberal Americans travel, it has been so politically correct to deplore female circumcision that the alarming claims by anti-FGM advocacy groups (images of African parents routinely and for hundreds of years disfiguring, maiming, and murdering their female children and depriving them of their capacity for a sexual response) have not been scrutinized with regard to reliable evidence. Nor have these claims been cross-examined through a process of systematic rebuttal. Quite the contrary. The facts on the ground and the "correct" moral attitude for "good guys" are taken to be self-evident. This is unfortunate because this case is far less one-sided than it appears—the "bad guys" are not really all that bad, the values of toleration and pluralism should be upheld, and the "good guys" may have rushed to judgment and gotten an awful lot rather wrong.

Six months before Fuambai Ahmadu publicly expressed her

doubts about the prevailing global discourse on female circumcision, readers of the *Medical Anthropology Quarterly* observed an extraordinary event of a similar yet (methodologically) different sort. Carla Obermeyer, a medical anthropologist and epidemiologist at Harvard University, published a comprehensive review of the existing medical literature on female genital surgeries in Africa, in which she concluded that the claims of the anti-FGM movement are highly exaggerated and may not match reality (also see Larsen and Yan, 2000 and Morison et al., 2001)

Obermeyer (1999: 80) began her essay by pointing out, "The exhaustive review of the literature on which this article is based was motivated by what appeared as a potential disparity between the mobilization of resources toward activism and the research base that ought to support such efforts." When she took a closer look at that research base—a total of 435 articles were reviewed from the medical, demographic, and social science literatures, including every published article available on the topic of female circumcision or female genital mutilation in the Medline, Popline, and Sociofile databases—Obermeyer discovered that in most publications in which statements were made about the devastating effects of female circumcision, no evidence was presented at all. When research reports containing original evidence were examined, Obermeyer discovered numerous methodological flaws (for example, small or unrepresentative samples, no control groups) and quality control problems (such as vague descriptions of medical complications) in some of the most widely cited documents. "Despite their deficiencies, some of the published reports have come to acquire an aura of dependability through repeated and uncritical citations" (Obermeyer, 1999: 81).

In order to draw some realistic (even if tentative) conclusions about the health consequences of female circumcision in Africa,

Obermeyer then introduced standard epidemiological quality control criteria for evaluating evidence (Obermeyer, 1999: n24). For example, a research study was excluded if its sampling methods were not described or if its claims were based on a single case rather than a population sample. On the basis of the relatively small number of available studies that passed minimum scientific standards (for example, eight studies on the topic of medical complications), Obermeyer reported that the widely publicized medical complications of African genital operations are the exception, not the rule; that female genital alterations are not incompatible with sexual enjoyment; and that the claim that untold numbers of girls and women have been killed as a result of this "traditional practice" is not well supported by the evidence (Obermeyer, 1999: 79).

In the liberal academy, even among typically skeptical and normally critical public intellectuals, there has been an easy acceptance of the anti-FGM representations of family and social life in Africa as brutal, barbaric, and unquestionably beyond the pale. Several moral, political, and feminist theorists even suggest that these coming-of-age and gender-identity ceremonies of African women deserve a place on the list of absolute evils, along with human sacrifice, the Holocaust, rape, lynching, and slavery. "Frankly, I don't give a damn if opposing this is a violation of someone's culture. To me, female genital mutilation is a violation of the physical and spiritual integrity of a person," states Tilman Hasche, a political asylum lawyer (quoted in Egan, 1994), summarizing a common view among public intellectuals in the United States and Europe.

Much of the press in the First World similarly has been swayed. Media coverage that affects American opinion about African customs has been influenced extensively by anti-FGM activists and advocacy groups who represent the African practice of female genital alteration as a scourge that needs to be eradicated and who write books with stirring titles such as *Women, Why Do You Weep?* "Here is a dream for Americans, worthy of their country and what they would like it to be," writes A. M. Rosenthal, the distinguished columnist for the *New York Times.* "The dream is that the U.S. could bring about the end of a system of torture that has crippled 100 million people now living upon this earth and every year takes at least two million more into an existence of suffering, deprivation and disease. . . . The torture is female genital mutilation" (Rosenthal, 1995: A25). In his op-ed essay Rosenthal then proudly advertises three advocacy groups, including the organization that publishes *The Hosken Report* (Hosken, 1993), an anti-FGM document that has been widely distributed to opinion makers in the United States and has impressed many journalists.

Equally noteworthy, however, is that these judgments seem precipitous and fundamentally misinformed to many anthropologists who study gender, initiation, and life stages in Africa. Many researchers who work on these topics have long been aware of discrepancies between the global discourse on female circumcision (with its images of maiming, murder, sexual dysfunction, mutilation, coercion, and oppression) and their own ethnographic experiences with indigenous discourses and with social and physical realities at their field settings (for example, Abusharaf, 2001; Boddy, 1989, 1996; Gruenbaum, 1996, 2001; Johnson, 2000; Kratz, 1994, 1999; Obiora, 1997; Parker, 1995; Shell-Duncan and Hernlund, 2000a; Walley, 1997).

Perhaps the first anthropological protest against the global discourse came in 1938 from Jomo Kenyatta, who, prior to becoming the first president of postcolonial Kenya, published a doctoral thesis in anthropology at the London School of Economics and Political Science (Kenyatta, 1938). He described both the customary premarital sexual practices of the Kikuyu (rather liberal attitudes toward adolescent petting and sexual arousal) and the practice of female and male circumcision.[7]

Kenyatta's words have an uncanny contemporary ring and relevance. First he informs us:

> In 1931 a conference on African children was held in Geneva under the auspices of the Save the Children Fund. In this conference several European delegates urged that the time was ripe when this "barbarous custom" should be abolished, and that, like all other "heathen" customs, it should be abolished at once by law. (Kenyatta, 1938: 131)

Kenyatta goes on to argue that among the Kikuyu a genital alteration, "like Jewish circumcision," is a bodily sign that is regarded "as the *conditio sine qua non* of the whole teaching of tribal law, religion and morality"; that no proper Kikuyu man or woman would have sex with or marry someone who was not circumcised; that the practice is an essential step into responsible adulthood for many African girls and boys; and that "there is a strong community of educated [K]ikuyu opinion in defense of this custom" (Kenyatta, 1938: 133,132).

Nearly sixty years later, echoes of Jomo Kenyatta's message can be found in the writings of Corinne Kratz, who has written a detailed account of female initiation among another ethnic group in Kenya, the Okiek. The Okiek, she tells us, do not talk about circumcision in terms of the dampening of sexual pleasure or desire, but rather speak of it "in terms of cleanliness, beauty and adulthood." According to Kratz, Okiek women and men view "genital modification and the bravery and self-control displayed during the operation as constitutive experiences of Okiek personhood" (Kratz, 1994: 346).

Many other examples could be cited of discrepancies between the global discourse and the experience of field researchers in Africa. With regard to the issue of sexual enjoyment, for example, Robert Edgerton (1989: 254, *n*22) remarks that "Kikuyu men and women, like those of several other East African societies that practice female circumcision, assured me in 1961–62 that circumcised women continue to be orgasmic." Similar remarks appear in other field reports (for example, Lightfoot-Klein, 1989; Gruenbaum, 2001: 139–143).

With regard to the global discourse that represents circumcision as a disfigurement or mutilation, Sandra Lane and Robert Rubinstein (1996: 35) offer the following caution:

> An important caveat, however, is that many members of societies that practice traditional female genital surgeries do not view the result as mutilation. Among these groups, in fact, the resulting appearance is considered an improvement over female genitalia in their natural state. Indeed, to call a woman uncircumcised, or to call a man the son of an uncircumcised mother, is a terrible insult and noncircumcised adult female genitalia are often considered disgusting. In interviews we conducted in rural and urban Egypt and in studies conducted by faculty of the High Institute of Nursing, Zagazig University, Egypt, the overwhelming majority of circumcised women planned to have the procedure performed on their daughters. In discussions with some fifty women we found only two who resent and are angry at having been circumcised. Even these women do not think that female circumcision is one of the most critical problems facing Egyptian women and girls. In the rural Egyptian hamlet where we have conducted fieldwork some women were not familiar with groups that did not circumcise their

girls. When they learned that the female researcher was not circumcised their response was disgust mixed with joking laughter. They wondered how she could have thus gotten married and questioned how her mother could have neglected such an important part of her preparation for womanhood.

These ethnographic reports are noteworthy because they suggest that, instead of assuming that our own perceptions of beauty and disfigurement are universal and must be transcendental, we should consider the possibility that a real and astonishing cultural divide exists around the world in moral, emotional, and aesthetic reactions to female genital surgeries. No doubt, of course, our own feelings of disgust, indignation, and anxiety about this topic are powerful and may be aroused easily and manipulated rhetorically with pictures (for example, of Third World surgical implements) or words (for example, labeling the activity "torture" or "mutilation"). If we want to understand the true character of this cultural divide in sensibilities, however, we need to bracket our initial (and automatic) emotional-visceral reactions and save any powerful conclusive feelings for the end of the argument, rather than have them color all objective analysis. Perhaps we can develop a better understanding of the subject by constructing a synoptic account of the inside point of view, from the perspective of those many African women for whom such practices seem both normal and desirable.

Moral Pluralism and the Mutual Yuck Response

People recoil at each other's practices and say "yuck" at each other all over the world. When it comes to female genital alterations—or lack thereof—the mutual yuck response among peoples is particularly intense and may even approach outrage or horror. From a purely descriptive point of view, this type of physical modification is routine and normal in many ethnic groups: for example, national prevalence rates of 80 percent to 98 percent have been reported for Egypt, Ethiopia, the Gambia, Mali, Sierra Leone, Somalia, and the Sudan (Shell-Duncan and Hernlund, 2000a: 10–12). In African nations where the overall prevalence rate is lower—for example, Kenya (50 percent), Côte d'Ivoire (43 percent), and Ghana (30 percent)—it is typically because some ethnic groups have a tradition of female circumcision while others do not. Thus, for example, within Ghana ethnic groups in the north and east circumcise boys and girls, while ethnic groups in the south have no tradition of female circumcision.

In general, for both sexes the best predictor of circumcision (versus the absence of it) is ethnicity or cultural group affiliation. Circumcision is customary for the Kono of Sierra Leone, for example, but for the Wolof of Senegal it is not. For women within these groups, one key factor—their cultural affiliation as either Kono or Wolof—trumps other predictors of behavior, such as education level or socioeconomic status. Among the Kono, even women with a secondary school or college education (such as Fuambai Ahmadu) are circumcised, while Senegalese Wolof women—including the illiterate and unschooled—are not. Notably, most African women do not think about circumcision in human rights terms or as a human rights violation. Women who endorse female circumcision argue that it is an important part of their cultural heritage or their religion, while women who do not endorse the practice typically argue that it is not permitted by their cultural heritage or their religion (see, for example, El Dareer, 1983).

Moreover, among members of ethnic groups in which female circumcision is part of their cultural heritage, approval ratings for the custom are generally high. According to the Sudan Demographic and Health Survey of 1989–90 conducted in northern and central Sudan, of 3,805 women interviewed, 89 percent were circumcised. Of the women who were circumcised, 96 percent said they had or would circumcise their daughters. When asked whether they favored continuation of the practice, 90 percent of circumcised women said they favored its continuation (see Williams and Sobieszyzyk, 1997: Table 1).

In Sierra Leone, the picture is pretty much the same and the vast majority of women are sympathetic to the practice and appear to feel at home in their way of life. Even Olayinka Koso-Thomas, an anti-FGM activist, makes note of the high degree of support for genital operations, although she expresses herself with a rather patronizing voice and in imperial tones:

> Most African women still have not developed the sensitivity to feel deprived or to see in many cultural practices a violation of their human rights. The consequence of this is that, in the mid–80's, when most women in Africa have voting rights and can influence political decisions against practices harmful to their health, they continue to uphold the dictates and mores of the communities in which they live; they seem in fact to regard traditional beliefs as inviolate. (Koso-Thomas, 1987: 2)

When it comes to maintaining their coming-of-age and gender-identity ceremonies, Koso-Thomas does not like the way many African women vote. While she thinks she is enlightened about human rights and health and that these women remain in the dark, Koso-Thomas indeed recognizes that most women in Sierra Leone endorse the practice of circumcision. (For recent evidence of high approval ratings among Mandinka women in the Gambia, see

Morison et al., 2001.) Amy Kendoh, a member of the women's secret society in Sierra Leone, where more than 90 percent of adult women have been initiated, put it this way: "I have grown up to the age of fifty years, and this is the first time anyone has come forward to ask me why we do these ceremonies. It doesn't matter what other people think because we are happy with our customs. We will carry on with our lives" (French, 1997: A4).

Further, although ethnic group affiliation is the best predictor of who circumcises and who does not, the timing and form of the operation are not uniform across groups. Thus, there is enormous variability in the age at which the surgery is normally performed (any time from birth to the late teenage years). There is also enormous variability in the traditional style and degree of surgery— from a cut in the prepuce covering the clitoris to the complete "smoothing out" of the genital area by removing all visible parts of the clitoris and all external labia. In some ethnic groups (for example, in Somalia and the Sudan), the smoothing out operation is concluded by stitching closed the vaginal opening with the aims of enhancing fertility, tightening the vaginal opening, and protecting the womb (see Boddy, 1982, 1989, 1996; Gruenbaum, 2001). The latter procedure, often referred to as *infibulation* or Pharaonic circumcision, is not typical in most circumcising ethnic groups, although it has received a good deal of attention in the anti-FGM literature. The procedure occurs in an estimated 15 percent of all African cases, although it is rare or nonexistent in many of the ethnic groups in which some form of genital alteration for both males and females is culturally endorsed.

In places where the practice of female circumcision is popular, women believe that these genital alterations improve their bodies and make them more beautiful, more feminine, more civilized, and more honorable.

Circumcised genitalia are thought to be more beautiful because the body is made smooth and a protrusion or "fleshy encumbrance" removed that is thought to be ugly and odious to both sight and touch (see, for example, Abusharaf, 2001; Koso-Thomas, 1987: 7; Lane and Rubinstein, 1996, quoted herein; Meinardus, 1967: 394; El Dareer, 1982: 73). Here a cultural aesthetics is in play among circumcising ethnic groups—an ideal of the human sexual region as smooth, cleansed, and refined—that supports the view that the genitals of women and men are unsightly, misshapen, and unappealing if left in their natural state.

Circumcised genitalia are thought to be more feminine because unmodified genitals (in both males and females) are perceived as sexually ambiguous. From a female's perspective, the clitoris is viewed as an unwelcome vestige of the male organ, and its removal is positively associated with several desirable things: attainment of full female identity, induction into a social network and support group of powerful adult women, and, ultimately, marriage and motherhood (Ahmadu, 2000; Meinardus, 1967: 389). Many women who uphold these traditions of female initiation seek to empower themselves by getting rid of what they view as an unbidden yet dispensable trace of unwanted male anatomy.

Circumcised genitalia are thought to be more civilized because a genital alteration is a symbolic action that says something about one's willingness to exercise restraint over feelings of lust and self-control over the antisocial desire for sexual pleasure.

Circumcised genitalia are thought to be more honorable because the surgery announces one's commitment to perpetuate the lineage and value the womb as the source of social reproduction (see, for example, Boddy, 1982, 1989, 1996).

As hard as it may be to believe (and I recognize that for some of us this is *really* hard to believe), many women in places such as

Mali, Somalia, and Egypt are repulsed by the idea of unmodified female genitals, which they view as ugly, unrefined, undignified, uncivilized, and hence, not fully human. They associate unmodified genitals with life outside or at the bottom of civilized society. They think to themselves, "Yuck, what kind of barbarians are these who don't circumcise their genitals?"

The yuck is, of course, mutual. Female genital alterations are not routine for members of mainstream populations in Europe, the United States, China, Japan, and other parts of the world, and it is not a common practice in the southern parts of Africa. For members of these cultures, the very thought of female genital surgery produces an unpleasant visceral reaction—although for many of us the detailed visualization of any kind of surgery—a bypass operation, a sex change, a face lift, or even a decorative eyebrow or tongue piercing—produces an unpleasant visceral reaction.

Saying "yuck" to the practice has become a symbol of opposition to the oppression of women and of one's support for their emancipation around the world. Eliminating this practice thus has become a high priority for many Western feminists, some human rights activists in Africa (who very often, although not invariably, come from noncircumcising ethnic groups), and for some human rights organizations (for example, Amnesty International and Equality Now). Even some international organizations such as WHO and UNICEF have agreeably responded to the anti-FGM call to arms and have felt justified in expanding their mission statements to include the extermination of female circumcision. The technique for mission expansion is simple and direct. If the organization's official aim is to rid the world of sickness, female circumcision is classified as a health hazard or a disease. If the official aim is to protect political prisoners from torture, African parents are classified as "torturers" and African children defined as political prisoners held captive, coerced, and "mutilated" by their relatives.

Outside of Africa, especially in the United States and Europe, righteous opposition to female circumcision has become so commonplace and so politically correct that until very recently most critiques of the global discourse have been defensive, superficial, or suggestions on how to improve "eradication tactics." For example, activists Susan Rich and Stephanie Joyce give this recommendation on how to gain the trust of African villagers in areas where circumcision is customary: bring them "malarial medicine, radios, and other gifts to 'smooth the path'" but wait until the sixth visit before you drop any hints about why you are really there (Rich and Joyce, n.d.: 4).

Under such circumstances, the potential for counterproductive activism is great. For example, Daniel Arap Moi, the president of Kenya, has twice tried to ban female circumcision and without great success. His second attempt was in 1989. In a top-down gesture of political authority (and perhaps with an eye toward the West), he denounced the custom, and the next day thousands of girls from ethnic groups with a tradition of circumcision stepped forward to be initiated, as a form of social, moral, and political protest.

There have also been occasional complaints that anti-FGM campaigns displace attention and take resources away from battles against social injustice in the United States and Europe (for example, Tamir, 1996). And there have been expressions of concern about the anguished state of mind of African children living in the United States who are told by the media and by social service agencies that their own mothers are "mutilated" and potentially dangerous to them too (Beyene, 1999).

But these types of criticisms do not go very deep. In general, the purported facts about female circumcision go unquestioned, the moral implications of the case are thought to be obvious, and the query "What about FGM?" is presumed to function in and of itself as a knockdown argument against both cultural pluralism and any inclination toward tolerance.

So What about FGM?

The practice of genital alteration is a poor example of gender inequality or of discrimination against women. There are few cultures, if any, in which genital surgeries are performed exclusively on girls, although many cultures perform such surgeries only on boys or on both sexes. (Male genital alterations often take place in adolescence and can involve major modifications, including subincision, in which the penis is split along the line of the urethra.) Considering the prevalence, timing, and intensity of the relevant initiation rites and viewed on a worldwide scale, one is hard pressed to argue that this is an obvious instance of a gender inequity disfavoring girls. Quite the contrary; social recognition of the ritual transformation of both boys and girls into a more mature status as empowered men and women often is a major point of the alteration ceremony. In other words, when and where female circumcision occurs in Africa, society is treating boys and girls *equally* before the common law and inducting them into responsible adulthood in parallel ways.

The practice is also a poor example of patriarchal domination. Many patriarchal cultures in Europe and Asia do not engage in genital alterations, or (as in the case of Jews, many non-African Muslims, and many African ethnic groups) deliberately exclude girls from this highly valued practice and perform the surgery only on boys. Moreover, the African ethnic groups that circumcise both females and males are very different from one another in kinship, religion, economy, family life, ceremonial practice, and so forth. Some are Islamic, and some are not. Some are patriarchal, and some—such as the Kono, a matrilineal society—are not. Some have formal initiations into well-established women's organizations, and some do not. (On the connection between circumcision and entrance into powerful women's secret societies in Sierra Leone, see Ahmadu, 2000.) Some care greatly about female purity, sexual restraint outside of marriage, and the social regulation of desire, but others (such as Kenyatta's Kikuyu) are more relaxed about premarital sexual play and are not puritanical.

Indeed, in cases of female initiation and genital alterations, the practice almost always is controlled, performed, and most strongly upheld by women, although male kin provide material and moral support. Typically, however, men have little to do with these female operations, may not know very much about them, and may feel it is not really their business to tell their wives, mothers, aunts, and grandmothers what to do. Rather, the women of the society are the cultural experts in this intimate feminine domain, and they are not inclined to give up power or share their secrets.

In those cases of female genital alterations with which I am most familiar (having lived and taught in Kenya, where the practice is routine for some ethnic groups; see Kenyatta, 1938; Kratz, 1994; Thomas, 2000; Walley, 1997), adolescent girls who undergo the ritual initiation look forward to it. The ordeal can be painful (especially if done without anesthesia), but it is viewed as a test of courage. This is an event organized and controlled by women, who have their own view of the aesthetics of the body—a different view from ours about what is civilized, dignified, and beautiful. The girls' parents are not trying to be cruel to their daughters. No one is raped or tortured. Indeed, a celebration surrounds the event.

What about the devastating negative effects on health and sexuality so vividly portrayed in the anti-FGM literature? Relatively few methodologically sound studies exist on the consequences of female genital surgeries on sexuality and health. As Obermeyer (1999) discovered in her medical review, most of the published literature is data-free or else relies on sensational testimonials, secondhand reports, or inadequate samples. Judged against basic epidemiological research standards, much of the published empirical evidence—including some of the most widely cited publications in the anti-FGM advocacy literature (including the influential 1993 *Hosken Report*)—is fatally flawed (see Obermeyer, 1999).

The anti-FGM advocacy literature typically features long lists of short- and long-term medical complications of circumcision, including blood loss, shock, acute infection, menstrual problems, child-bearing difficulties, incontinence, sterility, and death. These lists read like the warning pamphlets that accompany many prescription drugs, which enumerate every negative side effect of the medicine that has ever been reported (no matter how infrequently). They are scary to read, and they are misleading. Nevertheless, there is some science worth considering in thinking about female circumcision, which leads Obermeyer to conclude that the global discourse about the health and sexual consequences of female circumcision is not sufficiently supplied with credible evidence.

Obermeyer's conclusions converge with the findings of the recent large-scale Medical Research Council study of the long-term reproductive health consequences of female circumcision (Morison et al., 2001). The study, conducted in the Gambia, compared circumcised and uncircumcised women. In this country the surgery typically involves a full clitoridectomy and either partial or complete excision of the labia minora. More than 1,100 women (ages 15 to 54) from three ethnic groups (Mandinka, Wolof, and Fula) were interviewed and also given gynecological examinations and laboratory tests. Very few differences were discovered in the reproductive health status of circumcised versus uncircumcised women. As noted in the research report, the supposed morbidities (such as infertility, painful sex, vulval tumors, menstrual problems, incontinence, and most endogenous infections) often cited by anti-FGM advocacy groups did not distinguish between circumcised and uncircumcised women. The authors of the report caution anti-FGM activists against exaggerating the morbidity and mortality risks of the practice (see also Larsen and Yan, 2000).

These findings are consistent with Edgerton's comments about female circumcision among the Kikuyu in Kenya in the 1920s and 1930s, when Western missionaries first launched their own version of "FGM eradication programs." As Edgerton (1989: 40) remarks, the operation was performed without anesthesia and hence was very painful, "yet most girls bore it bravely and few suffered serious infection or injury as a result. Circumcised women did not lose their ability to enjoy sexual relations, nor was their child-bearing capacity diminished. Nevertheless the practice offended Christian sensibilities."

In other words, the standard alarmist claims in the anti-FGM advocacy literature that African traditions of circumcision have "maimed or killed untold numbers of women and girls" (Rich and Joyce, n.d.: 1) and deprived them of their sexuality may not be true. Given the most reliable (even if limited) scientific evidence at hand, these claims should be viewed with skepticism and not accepted as fact, no matter how many times they are uncritically recapitulated on the editorial pages of the *New York Times* or poignantly invoked on PBS.

If genital alteration in Africa really were a long-standing cultural practice in which parents, oblivious to intolerably high risks, disabled and murdered their pre-adolescent and adolescent children, there would be good reason to wish for its quick end. Carla Obermeyer's review suggests that this line of attack on the practice may be as fanciful as it is nightmarish, or, at the very least, dubious and misleading.

In their reactions to this African cultural practice, the anti-FGM advocacy groups behave much like yesterday's missionaries. Given the importance of accurate information in public policy debates in liberal democracies, now would be a good time for them to either revise their factoids or else substantiate their claims with rigorously collected data. An organization such as Amnesty International (USA) discredits itself as a balanced and reliable source of information when it recycles pseudo-evidence, posting website bulletins such as, "In Egypt the practices of clitoridectomy and excision predominate and dozens of FGM-related deaths have been reported in the press."

With regard to the consequences of genital surgeries, the weight of the evidence suggests that the overwhelming majority of youthful female initiates believe they have been improved (physically, socially, and spiritually) by the ceremonial ordeal and symbolic process (including the pain) associated with initiation. Evidence indicates that most of these youthful initiates manage to be (in their own estimation) "improved" without disastrous or major negative consequences for their health (Larsen and Yan, 2000; Morison et al., 2001; Obermeyer, 1999). This is not to say that we should not worry about the documented 4 percent to 16 percent urinary infection rate associated with these surgeries, or the 7 percent to 13 percent of cases in which there is excessive bleeding, or the 1 percent rate of septicemia (see Obermeyer, 1999: 93). (It would be instructive to compare these rates with those of infection and bleeding for other types of less controversial Third World surgeries.) These medical complications that arise from unsanitary surgical procedures or malpractice can be corrected without depriving others of rites and meanings central to their culture, personal identities, and sense of well-being. What I do want to suggest, however, is that the current sense of shock, horror, and righteous Western indignation directed against the mothers of Mali, Somalia, Egypt, Sierra Leone, Ethiopia, the Gambia, and the Sudan is misguided and disturbingly misinformed.

The Enlightened First World versus the Dark Continent

Fifty years after the end of colonial rule, many First World intellectuals still think of Africa as the Dark Continent and imagine that genital surgery is a Dark Age practice supported mainly by those who are unenlightened, uneducated, ignorant, and unsophisticated. Yet, contrary to expectations, not only the uneducated, rural, or poor women of Africa promote the gender identity of their children and grandchildren and celebrate their coming of age in this way. As Jomo Kenyatta pointed out long ago, in many African ethnic groups, even high-status, highly educated members of the community remain committed to these ceremonies (see Ahmadu, 2000). Meinardus (1967: 393) notes that in the eighteenth and nineteenth centuries, female circumcision was "universal in Egypt and that it was adhered to by members of all social classes extending from Lower Egypt to Aswan." From the viewpoint of education, urbanization, and economic development, a good deal has changed in Egypt since the eighteenth century. The prevalence rate of female (and male) circumcision, however, has remained pretty much the same. Obermeyer (1999) points out that female genital alterations are common even among the most educated groups of women in a number of countries. She notes that one cannot assume that more schooling necessarily will result in a dramatic reduction in the prevalence of genital surgery in a population for which it has been a customary practice. She indicates a 90 percent prevalence rate in Egypt for women with a secondary school education or beyond.

Dirie and Lindmark (1991: 70) make a similar point with regard to Somalia, noting, "Early studies have revealed that education and economic status have no influence on the practice of female circumcision, and the present study supports these findings." It is probably a mistake to expect that women are going to give up a practice central to their sense of personal dignity and cultural identity just because they have received a high school diploma or even a Ph.D.

The following historical observation appears in a research report about circumcision in Nigeria (Olamijuto, Joiner, and Oyedeji, 1983: 581).

> In December 1929, a British parliamentary committee, formed to study conditions of women and children in the crown colonies, strongly lobbied the British Government to take steps to, among other things, abolish circumcision of girls in Africa. In his contribution to the British effort, A. C. Burns, the then Deputy Governor of Nigeria, expressed optimism that the practice would disappear with advance in education.

The authors point out that the British deputy governor's prediction has not come true, despite fifty years of top-down political pressure and a sharp rise in literacy since free primary education was introduced in 1955. The customary practice of female circumcision has turned out to be highly resistant to either coaxed or forced change. This is true even for sophisticated and educated members of society (Kenyatta, 1938; Ahmadu, 2000; Thomas, 2000).

Jewish circumcision practices have a similar profile. Throughout millennia, Jews have continued to circumcise sons regardless of the historical context of their lives, the proclaimed medical benefits or harms (the medical establishment has not been consistent), and dominant opinion, which at times has viewed them as "mutilators" of babies and their practice as "barbaric" (see Gilman, 1999; Gollaher, 2000: ch. 1). Among Jews, when it comes to circumcision, it does not matter whether you are rich or poor, urban or rural, educated or uneducated, religious or secular. And it does not really matter what the medical establishment or Amnesty International or the Save the Children Fund happen to think. If you are Jewish, you circumcise your son. The practice has to do with a covenant between Jews and their God, and it has to do (as Kenyatta put it) with "the whole teaching of tribal law, religion and morality" (Kenyatta, 1938: 133).

One should not expect less from other cultural traditions, especially those that are already equitable in their ritual treatment of the sexes. It is not ignorance that keeps the practice of female circumcision going, any more than it is ignorance that has kept male circumcision going for over three thousand years.

First World "Lessons" on Normal Bodies

When considering the connection between education and attitudes toward circumcision, we might ask ourselves, "What might we teach these women that would change their minds about the importance and benefits of circumcision?" Here I confess that I find it hard to imagine and to describe such a curriculum without sounding sardonic, or at least ironical, but I will try.

For example, we might teach them about Dr. Sigmund Freud, who claimed that women really want to be men and suffer from something called *penis envy*. On second thought, this is probably not a good idea, as Freud's thesis is a disempowering claim that circumcised African women may well have proved wrong.

Perhaps we might teach them that enlightened human beings do not engage in cosmetic surgery. Yet, could we say that with a straight face, when there are thousands of aesthetic surgeries licensed by the American Medical Association, including face lifts, tummy tucks, and clitoridectomies for young women who don't like the way their genitals look or feel.

The lesson might be that a genital alteration makes it impossible to enjoy sex—but one suspects that this claim derives from our own ethno-anatomical folk beliefs rather than from any hard science. Most First World intellectuals underestimate the true size and anatomical depth of the clitoris: about 50 percent of its tissue structure is internal and thus remains intact after any external modification of the genitals (Shell-Duncan and Hernlund, 2000a: 26–27). Indeed, in spite of a lack of systematic investigations into this topic, circumcised African women have talked about their sexual experiences in ways that strongly suggest that they can and do enjoy sex (Ahmadu, 2000; Edgerton, 1989: 254; Lightfoot-Klein, 1989; Gruenbaum, 2001: 139–43).

Or perhaps we could teach these women that the medical risks of circumcision are too great to tolerate. Yet it seems likely that the risk of death associated with these operations compares quite favorably with the risks associated with many activities that are routine in our own lives, such as driving a car. Moreover, circumcised African women likely know that most initiates do not suffer medical complications from the surgery, as Obermeyer (1999) has shown (see also Morison et al., 2001). Malpractice does occur, of course, and these and other Third World operations certainly are not risk-free: Asma El Dareer (1982: iii) had a bad experience with circumcision, having developed an infection that was then treated with five injections of penicillin administered by the registered Sudanese nurse who performed the operation. Yet her experience is atypical.

Most circumcised African women know that unsafe procedures can be made safer—without doing away with the practice.

Or we could teach African women that without anesthesia a circumcision ceremony is extremely painful and will leave them with scars—but the pain and scarring are a part of the initiation ceremony of which they are fully aware, because the rite is a test of their courage and a proof of adulthood. This gives them an opportunity to prove to themselves and to others, including their parents, that they are tough enough to be adults.

Moreover, where female genital alterations are customary, the women don't view their scars as mutilations. With regard to West Africa, Koso-Thomas (1987: 55) writes,

> [The scar] may even be a stamp of identification for admission to other branches of the [women's secret] society, and, therefore, may be sought after. It is traditional for youths to mark and scar themselves as a sign of courage and endurance; women's initiation societies also include training in these qualities. Thus they see no disadvantage in being scarred.

Is our lesson that sexual behavior has nothing to do with honor or fertility? The anthropological literature on female circumcision contains useful discussions of cultural variations in conceptions of the body and in the socially constructed ideals of sexual gratification associated with personal well-being (Parker, 1995: 519–20; Boddy, 1982, 1989, 1996; see also Lâm, 1994). For women in many societies, the womb is thought to be the body part that is the biological essence of femininity and is treasured because of its association with fertility, fecundity, and the project of social reproduction. This is not true for all women, particularly in the United States and Europe. As a result of the women's liberation movement in the 1960s, a variation on the ethnoanatomy of femininity was constructed according to which the womb was devalued precisely because it was associated with "bad" things, such as big families, domesticity, and a sexual division of labor in which women stayed at home and were not paid for their work. A new body part—the clitoris—was valorized and reconceptualized as the biological essence of femininity and associated with "good" things such as autonomy, sexual freedom, orgasm, and even an independent capacity for pleasurable self-stimulation.

In effect, for a particular subculture of women in the West, the clitoris became the ultimate symbol of female emancipation from men, marriage, and the domestic life. During the 1960s, 1970s, and 1980s, this conception of femininity and its symbolic anatomy emerged and was embraced by many in the professional and white middle class in the United States and Europe. It was even embraced by women who in any other context would strongly oppose all forms of "essentialism" and "biological reductionism" and reject the idea that there is only one way to have normal sexual relations, or only one ideal body type for all women.

I am not raising an objection to the aims of the women's liberation movement, or to the view that love and sex can be separated from marriage and pursued for their own sake. Nor am I criticizing the doctrine of hedonism. I am simply reiterating a central message of many gender studies programs at colleges and universities in the United States. Definitions of femininity (or masculinity) and of normal sexual relations are essentially contestable. There is no single, inherent, or universally binding objective ideal for femininity or masculinity. Hence, it is hard to see why any one particular set of aims, views, and doctrines about sex, marriage, and femininity should be embraced by all rational human beings, regardless of cultural or religious background. Where and when norms are essentially contestable, education is not going to make difference go away.

Finally, to bring this travesty of education to an end, is our lesson that uncircumcised genitals (male and female) are really beautiful? I am not even sure that most educated people in Europe and the United States believe that. Besides, what we teach in our finest (and most liberal) colleges is that "beauty is in the eye of the beholder," and that Western eyes (or Christian missionary eyes or American feminist eyes) are not the only ones that count.

If the West really does have some lessons to teach, these lessons should focus on correcting erroneous beliefs. Some African men, for example, have fantastical views about what happens to a woman's clitoris (its ultimate size) if she is not circumcised. There are also African men—as well as many American men and women—who do not understand the anatomical structure of the clitoris and thus do not realize that circumcised women can enjoy sex. Perhaps also some women in Egypt, Somalia, or the Sudan choose infibulation because of a groundless belief in the hazards of an unprotected or open vagina for reproduction and fertility. Challenging such beliefs is a good idea. Nevertheless, it will not bring an end to genital surgeries, because the main reasons for those surgeries and the initiation ceremonies in which they play their part have little to do with such mistaken beliefs.

IMPERIAL LIBERALISM AND ITS TOTALITARIAN IMPLICATIONS

In his book on the foundations of political liberalism, the philosopher John Rawls (1993: 61) cautions us, "it is unreasonable for us to use political power, should we possess it, or share it with others, to repress comprehensive doctrines [conceptions of the world elaborated from different standpoints] that are not unreasonable."

Rawls contrasts *political liberalism* with *comprehensive liberalism*. Political liberalism means the minimum ground rules for social cooperation among free and equal citizens in a genuinely pluralistic democracy. Comprehensive liberalism is a particular and single-minded doctrine about the proper selection and ordering of values, and about ideals for a good life. I wish to invoke a further contrast between political liberalism (as Rawls defines it) and *imperial liberalism*.

Imperial liberalism holds that it is desirable for us to spread and enforce our liberal conceptions and ideals for the good life in all corners of society and throughout the world. More specifically, imperial liberalists claim that all social institutions and dimensions of social life (not just political but associational and family life as well) should be ruled by principles of autonomy, individualism, and equality—and by the particular ordering of values and ideals for gender identity, sexuality, work, reproduction, and family life embraced by liberal men and women in the United States today. As a corollary, this doctrine claims that liberal principles and conceptions should be upheld using the coercive power of the state and, if possible, exported to foreign lands using the coercive powers of international institutions (such as the World Bank, the IMF, NATO, and the United Nations).

From such a stance of imperial liberalism, Susan Okin (1999: 14), for example, implies that virginity, domesticity, childbearing, and fidelity to marriage should not be selected as high ideals anywhere in the world. From the same imperial stance, Katha Pollitt (1999: 29–30) suggests that secular governments around the world should empower children to be autonomous and free of their parents' influence and religious beliefs. Pollitt especially would like to empower children against illiberal Muslim parents who subscribe to such notions as female modesty, family honor, and sexual restraint, and therefore want their daughters to wear a head scarf, or hijab, in school. This is the same stance, to cite a third example, that leads Olayinka Koso-Thomas (1987: 2) to discredit the women of Sierra Leone for choosing to perpetuate the customs of their ethnic groups and to admonish them for not using their full voting rights and political power to liberate themselves from "tradition."

The imperial messages of this type of comprehensive liberalism are simple and powerful, and they appeal to many progressive secular individualists and cosmopolitan elites in the postmodern world. These messages may be summed up as follows.

1. Acknowledging social distinctions is invidious and implies vicious discrimination.
2. Where there are ethnic groups and social categories, let there be individuals.
3. Where there are individuals, let them transcend their tradition-bound commitments and experience the quality of their lives solely in secular and ecumenical terms (for example, as measured by health or wealth or years of life).

Given that particular imperial liberal view of the world, Fuambai Ahmadu's self-empowering act of initiation into Kono womanhood, West African–style, can only seem retrograde, like a glimpse at some unwelcome and archaic past, when the marks of social, cultural, and gender identity ran deep into both body and soul.

Political liberals, I believe, ought to be concerned about the totalitarian implications of imperial liberalism. They should worry about the coercion that would be needed to enforce the doctrine that our gender ideals are best, that our ideas about sexuality and reproduction are best, that our ideas about work and family are best, and moreover, good for everyone. They should be especially cautious with such an emotionally charged and poorly understood issue as circumcision (both male and female), because the temptation to demonize others and impose one's will is especially great and there is a general reluctance to recognize the particularity, even the peculiarity, of one's own point of view.

But to reasonably debate the issue, we need first to discount, or at least bracket, our own culturally shaped visceral reactions to female genital alterations. We must do so to have a fair, informed engagement with the voices of the African women who think that an eradication program, a threat to withdraw foreign aid, or a prison sentence are not appropriate responses to their valued way of life and may be more a measure of our brutality and barbarism than theirs.

Should We Tolerate It Here?

Any public debate in the United States about female genital alterations must address the question: How much toleration of the practice is reasonable here? Should we permit each other enough space to live and let live, and to disagree reasonably? Liberal free-thinking people in the United States need to debate openly whether a politically liberal, pluralistic society should accommodate both circumcising and noncircumcising ethnic groups and their associated cultural commitments and religious beliefs.

A real cultural divide clearly exists in the world in moral, emotional, and aesthetic reactions to female (and male) genital alterations. What is thought to be virtuous, rational, beautiful, and normal by most members of some ethnic groups is seen as vicious, ignorant, ugly, and abnormal by most members of other ethnic groups. As a result of labor migration and the flow of political refugees, this cultural divide has reproduced itself within several European countries (for example, France and Norway) and in the United States, to the detriment of those minority groups who uphold the practice.

Witness, for example, the adverse reaction of middle-class feminists in the United States to a Seattle hospital proposal to allow Somali immigrant parents—with the informed consent and approval of their daughter—to safely and painlessly perform a minor and culturally meaningful genital surgery (see Coleman, 1998). From a medical point of view, the proposed procedure (a small cut in the prepuce that covers the clitoris) was less severe than a typical American male circumcision. Nevertheless, the mainstream response to the unfamiliar practice was intensely negative, and the proposal was discarded. The practice, however, is not unfamiliar for most in the Somali immigrant community, and many Somalis, male and female, living in the United States, deem a genital alteration to be practically and emotionally essential for their sense of dignity and well-being.

Despite evidence that suggests circumcision is a source of esteem for many African men and women and that women are not typically injured or sexually incapacitated by the surgery, the practice of female circumcision continues to offend the sensibilities of majority populations in the First World. If that evidence is reliable (and clearly we need more and better research on these issues), then every "political liberal" has a responsibility to ask whether an offense to his or her own culturally shaped sensibilities alone is sufficient reason to eradicate someone else's way of life.

Medical Tradition. On the medical front, the issue is straightforward. Genital alterations for both girls and boys can be done safely, hygienically, and without major risks to physical health. Cosmetic genital surgeries for women are not customary in the United States, but cosmetic surgeons know how to do them. Given the state of our medical sciences, unwanted pain can be controlled or elimi-nated. For some young women, however, enduring the pain may continue to be part of the point of the experience, just as it is for others who endure tests of courage and character, such as running a marathon.

Another relevant, less obvious scientific fact has to do with the justification of male circumcision and its bearing on claims about gender equity. One widely held folk belief in the United States is that surgical removal of the foreskin of the penis protects the health of men, but this is not strongly supported by evidence. Dur-ing the 1990s, about 65 percent of male babies in the United States were circumcised, and the medical establishment did little to discourage the dubious claim that circumcision is salubrious for males. In fact, the medical case for male circumcision is so flimsy that in other English-speaking countries such as Canada, England, and Australia, doctors do not typically recommend the operation and only about 10 percent to 15 percent of infant boys are circum-cised.

A relatively recent set of recommendations of the American Academy of Pediatrics (as of March 1, 1999) reads as follows: "The weight of the evidence would have to be significant for the academy to recommend an elective surgical procedure on every newborn male, and the evidence is not sufficient for us to make such a rec-ommendation." The authors of the AAP recommendations recog-nize, however, that not all decisions about a normal or properly de-veloped body can be reduced to medical or health criteria. They do not therefore recommend against the elective surgery for males, ac-knowledging that the decision really rests on religious and cultural grounds, not medical ones.

Thus, on the basis of our medical traditions the following two conclusions may be drawn, both of which will have a bearing on the question of tolerance for female genital alterations: genital surgeries for both males and females can be done safely; and if there are good reasons for the common American practice of male circumcision—as I believe there are—such reasons remain beyond the realm of modern medicine.

Legal and Moral Traditions. United States Supreme Court Justice William Brennan (*Michael H. v. Gerald D.,* 491 U.S. 110, 141 [1989], dissenting) has written, "We are not an assimilative, homogeneous society, but a facilitative, pluralistic one, in which we must be willing to abide someone else's unfamiliar and even repellent practice because the same tolerant impulse protects our own idiosyncrasies." Justice Brennan's pluralistic ideals may be theoretically appealing; but in the case of customary African genital alterations, the initial impulse in our society has been intolerant, single-minded, and assimilative in the extreme.

In September, 1996, the Congress of the United States, without holding public hearings or seeking expert testimony and certainly without any attempt to understand the "native point of view," passed a statute targeted at the practice of female genital surgery among African immigrants. United States Representative Patricia Schroeder played a significant part formulating and lobbying for the legislation. The law, which went into effect in March, 1997, criminalizes "female genital mutilation" and penalizes with fines or a prison sentence (up to five years) anyone who knowingly engages in surgery on any part of the genitals of a female under eighteen years of age. Exceptions are made for established medical practitioners engaging in surgical procedures necessary for the woman's health (for example, surgery to facilitate the delivery of a baby). The law explicitly states that, in punishing offenders, no account shall be taken of their belief that the surgery is required as a matter of custom or ritual.

In February, 1999, a court in Paris went a step further and sentenced Hawa Greou, a Malian immigrant who is a ritual circumcisor, to eight years in prison. She is a woman whose services as an expert surgeon had been sought by other women in her ethnic group. The stiff prison sentence was imposed by the court despite the fact that neither Hawa Greou nor most other Malians believed she was morally culpable or had done any harm.

The *New York Times* journalist Celia Dugger writes that when passing The Federal Prohibition of Female Genital Mutilation Act, the U.S. Congress also required "United States representatives to the World Bank and other international financial institutions that have lent billions of dollars to the 28 African countries where the practice exists to oppose loans to governments that have not carried out educational programs to prevent it" (Dugger, 1996: A1). Further, in recent years the State Department's Annual Report on Human Rights has been publishing a list of African governments that have officially banned female genital alterations. Through the use of carrots and sticks, various First World international agencies and ambassadors have been actively trying to induce or force the political leaders of Africa to comply with our desire to eradicate their custom. Indeed, in response to pressure from international benefactors, some African governments (for example, Egypt, Senegal, Togo, Côte D'Ivoire) have agreed to prohibit female circumcision. The list of formally compliant African governments grows. Understandably, this gesture is not appreciated by a considerable number of women (and their male kinsmen) in these countries, which may explain why many African officials under pressure from the First World pass the required laws, take the money, and then do not do anything. This is one way that tactical African leaders react to an unwelcome, unpopular, or difficult-to-implement yet unavoidable external demand combined with enormous material enticement or unequal bargaining power.

This rush to criminalize and penalize African female genital surgeries is distressing for several reasons. First, as we have seen, the decision is based on unsupported claims about the consequences of the genital surgery and highly dubious representations of African customs.

Second, the federal statute in the United States appears to be targeted at and causes selective injury to African immigrant and minority groups. The law treats their ritual life (and associated ideas about beauty, honor, marriage, and family life) with official contempt. The ban thereby causes distress to relatively powerless African immigrant families while allowing more highly placed citizens to make use of the coercive power of the state to further their particular single-minded vision of the good life.

Finally, by selectively criminalizing and penalizing female but not male genital surgeries, our lawmakers have overlooked several important normative issues that ought to guide any just consideration of this provocative and controversial case.

Moving Forward. How might a fair consideration of the case proceed? To start such a discussion, I need to distinguish between types of body alterations: consensual versus nonconsensual alterations; major versus minor alterations; and reversible versus nonreversible alterations. With these distinctions in place, the following type of argument can be made for limited toleration.

Principle 1. Certain types of genital alterations are permissible for boys. Parents can surgically remove the foreskin of a male infant, even though the infant has not given consent, even though the procedure is irreversible, and even though no compelling medical justification exists for performing the operation. Circumcision is permissible in this case because the alteration is minor in two senses. From a medical viewpoint, the procedure is easy to perform and, aside from some short-term pain (in the absence of anesthesia), the operation is inconsequential with regard to its effects on basic biological functioning. The procedure also is minor from the viewpoint of social and psychological functioning, in the sense that circumcised males remain perfectly capable of attaining mental health and participating in a normal social life.

Male circumcision in infancy also is permissible because we are willing to respect the cultural and religious traditions of the family. We are also willing to make room for family privacy and leave child care to parents rather than to the state, except under extreme circumstances. Indeed, in the case of infant male circumcision, the procedure is so commonplace and tolerated that a sufficient reason for conducting the surgery is that the father does not want his son's genitals to look different from his own, or simply because he thinks it looks good.

I am not suggesting that this principle is incontestable or has never been contested. There are activists who view the removal of the foreskin as a mutilation and as a wrong that outweighs claims of religious freedom, cultural rights, family privacy, or pluralism. This is not a new phenomenon. Various historical attacks on Judaism (for example, the severe penalties imposed on mohels and mothers of circumcised infants by Antiochus Epiphanes, the ruler of Judea in the second century BC; and the English "Jew Bill" of 1753) have been associated with assaults on the practice of male circumcision (Gollaher, 2000: 15, 28).

Moreover, it is quite possible for a minor surgical procedure to be substantial in its social implications. Imagine if Jews lived as a small minority group in a society where only Jews circumcised their sons. Imagine also that as a matter of cultural aesthetics and individual taste, most non-Jewish women in this society were disinclined to marry a circumcised male and most Jewish women disinclined to marry an uncircumcised male. Then this minor medical procedure in effect would amount to a significant parental and cultural influence on the personal marriage choices of children and effectively would help perpetuate a sense of in-group identity and social distinction.

Sander Gilman (1999: 53), in a critique of some intellectual tempers that are much like the stance of imperial liberalism, quotes an Italian physician of the late nineteenth century who writes:

> I shout and shall continue to shout at the Hebrews, until my last breath: Cease mutilating yourselves: cease imprinting upon your flesh an odious brand to distinguish you from other men; until you do this you cannot pretend to be our equal. As it is, you, of your own accord, with the branding iron from the first days of your lives, proceed to proclaim yourselves a race apart, one that cannot, and does not care to, mix with ours.

Under such circumstances, in which the distinctive family life practices of different ethnic groups result in the development of divergent tastes that then function as personal inhibitions to marrying outside the group, would we want the government to step in to level the playing field? Under the banner of justice and equality in marriage choices, the law might require all American citizens to circumcise their sons or, alternatively, the government could criminalize the ancient custom and start throwing Jewish circumcisors in prison along with Malian women. In either case, the government would be trying to ensure that men and women from different ethnic backgrounds find each other attractive so that patterns of preferential in-group marriage (like marrying like, on the basis of tastes and preferences acquired by virtue of ethnic background) would disappear from society. In either case, the state in effect would be promoting the cultural assimilation of minority groups bound together by selective marriage preferences related to their distinctive ways of life. Perhaps even some imperial liberals might balk at that prospect.

Nevertheless, principle 1 as stated allows for minor genital alterations for boys, regardless of any social implications that may follow (unless the surgery makes it impossible for the person to have a meaningful and rewarding social life, in which case the social consequences of circumcision cannot be overlooked).

Principle 2. Major body alterations are permissible if you know what you are doing and why such alterations are being done. In other words, someone who has reached the appropriate age for autonomous decision making (or the age at which discretion is permitted, with parental consent) can alter his or her body in ways that are more substantial than would be allowed by principle 1 alone.

At some point in growing up, we are granted rights of discretion over our own bodies. If a girl is old enough to get pregnant, we grant her considerable discretion (either on her own or with parental backing) over any decision to abort the fetus. If she is old enough to experience her own body as ugly or distressing (or even just ordinary) and if she is mentally healthy and aware of the costs and benefits of altering her body, we grant her considerable discretion to do so (either on her own or with parental permission) in major or irreversible ways.

If children have the support of their parents (and even in some cases if they don't), they do not have to wait until they are eighteen to have a breast implant or nose job, pierce their nipples, radically stretch their earlobes, or even engage in a sex-change operation. These more major body alterations are permitted because of *con-*

sent. We believe that people who are old enough to care about themselves ought to be able to have the things they want that make them "happy," by their own lights. This holds true even if the things they want done do not make us happy, as long as the body alterations they bring on themselves cause us no greater harm than offending our tastes or deviating from our idea of correct body politics.

Principle 3. No major irreversible alterations of the body should be permitted without consent. In other words, we should have a strong presumption against nonconsensual alterations of the body that have major consequences for either normal biological functioning or participation in a meaningful and fulfilling social life, and even more so if such alterations are irreversible. (There are some circumstances in which even this strong presumption might be overturned—for example, if someone is unconscious and certain to die unless a leg is amputated.)

If we can agree on those three principles, the prevailing First World intolerance and repressive attitudes toward African genital alterations deserves review. We should at least be willing to listen to the claims of those African immigrant mothers (see Coleman, 1998; Obiora, 1997) who believe that, in a tolerant pluralistic society such as the United States, there ought to be room for their conceptions of femininity, family life ideals, and ideas of the good life.

For example, if genital alterations are permitted for boys on the grounds of family privacy, religious freedom, and the fact that they are not harmful to health or sexual functioning (principle 1), then to the extent that the same conditions hold, genital alterations should be permitted for girls as well. The determination of which types of procedures or styles of surgery should be allowed should rest entirely on scientific and medical evidence concerning the consequences of different procedures. There is no doubt that there are existing forms of female genital surgery which already are (or can be made to be) no more consequential for health and sexual functioning then the typical male operation as currently practiced in the United States.

Imagine an African mother who believes that her daughters as well as her sons should be able to improve their looks and their marriage prospects, enter into a covenant with God, and be honored as adult members of the community via circumcision. Imagine that her proposed surgical procedure is as minor medically as the customary American male operation. Why should we not extend the option of circumcision to, for example, the Kono parents of daughters as well as to the Jewish parents of sons? This is basically what was proposed at the Harborview Medical Center in Seattle, Washington, until U.S. Representative Patricia Schroeder objected and raised the possibility of a violation of federal law (Coleman, 1998). Nevertheless, principles of gender equity, due process before the law, religious and cultural freedom, and family privacy would seem to support the option. The constitutional status of the federal prohibition remains untested.

And if body alterations such as breast implants or sex change operations are allowable with consent at an appropriate age (principle 2), then why not consensual genital alterations aimed at enhancing beauty and confirming appropriate gender identity (which, for some African immigrants, means getting rid of the male element in the female, and the female element in the male), as long as the procedure is done safely and is compatible with sexual and reproductive functioning? As Obermeyer's (1999) review of the medical evidence suggests, such procedures are not only feasible but available now.

Needless to say, there is plenty of room for argument about the appropriate age of discretion and the conditions for establishing informed consent. In ethnic groups with a heritage of both male and female circumcision, the psychological burden of being uncircumcised (of feeling ugly, sexually ambiguous, immature and unmarriageable) is likely to intensify as a child begins to sexually mature, so perhaps such maturation might be a lower bound for an age of discretion (with permission from one's parents). But such issues are not unique to this question. Policymakers should consider the age at which young people are permitted (with parental consent) to have a breast implant or an abortion or a sex change operation.

There is also plenty of room for argument about what counts as a major body alteration and what counts as minor. Some types of body alterations may be benign from the point of view of health and sexuality and yet radically reduce a person's chances of having a rewarding social and family life. The more uncertainty there is about whether a body alteration will ruin a child's life, the more the procedure should be viewed as major rather than minor, and the more the need for informed consent (principle 3). In the case of circumcision (for both males and females), the judgment about what is good for your child not only affects, but also depends on, what is considered beautiful or ugly, normal or monstrous, by others in the community. There is little risk that parents will circumcise their children in the absence of a community of relevant others who share the same tastes. Fortunately, there are many ways for men and women to live meaningful social lives without securing universal agreement about the aesthetics of the human body, especially when the body parts in question are private. If happiness in life depended on being physically attractive to all members of the opposite sex, happiness would be in short supply.

Under this scenario, all circumcisions would be either minor (and hence permissible at an early age) or would have to wait until some reasonable age of consent. Infibulations of young children would be out of the question, although that procedure might be freely chosen after the appropriate age of discretion. Infibulation is a relatively infrequent procedure even in Africa, so it seems unlikely that in the United States it would emerge as a popular style of genital alteration. Of course, who would have predicted ear lobe plugs, tongue or nipple piercings, or elaborate tattoos to become fashionable? If we grant to others various freedoms (of choice, association, expression, religion) and various protections (of bodily privacy), what they do with and to themselves may offend our (Christian or feminist or bourgeois) sensibilities. It is the price you pay for freedom and equality in a politically liberal democratic society. Under such circumstances, it is the virtue of tolerance that makes it possible for people to be quite different from one another, yet socially cooperate with each other at the same time.

Imagine a 16-year-old female Somali teenager living in Seattle who believes that a genital alteration would be "something very great." She likes the look of her mother's body and her recently circumcised cousin's body far better than she likes the look of her own. She wants to be a mature and beautiful woman, Somali style. She wants to marry a Somali man, or at least a man who appreciates the intimate appearance of an initiated woman's body. She wants to show solidarity with other African women who express their sense of beauty, civility, and feminine dignity in this way, and she shares their sense of aesthetics and seemliness. She reviews the medical literature and discovers that the surgery can be done safely, hygienically, and with no great effect on her capacity to enjoy sex. After consultation with her parents and the full support of other members of her community, she elects to carry on the tradition. What principle of justice demands that her cultural heritage should be eradicated?

African Customs and Political Persecution

In recent years in the United States, two political asylum requests related to female circumcision have been highly publicized—the

1996 case of Fauziya Kassindja, a refugee from Togo, and the 1999 case of Adelaide Abankwah, a refugee from Ghana. These cases are worth examining, in part, because of their peculiarities. (For a more comprehensive discussion of the circumstances surrounding both cases, see Kratz, 2002.)

The concept of political persecution as it has evolved in political asylum law has little relevance to the circumcision and initiation experiences of most African men and women. As we have seen, African men and women from ethnic groups with a heritage of circumcision generally endorse and identify with the practice and do not construe their own coming-of-age ceremonies as forms of political terror. Nevertheless, it is not impossible to imagine extreme or unusual political situations in which either a fear of being forcibly circumcised or, alternatively, of persecution for performing a circumcision (the former Soviet Union penalized Jews for circumcising their sons) might be grounds for an asylum request. Whether that was the case in either of the two most celebrated recent cases is quite another matter.

Legitimate requests for political asylum are supposed to be based on "a well-founded fear of persecution [in one's native land] on account of race, religion, nationality, membership in a particular social group, or political opinion" (*Abankwah v. INS,* U.S. 2d Circuit Court of Appeals, No. 98-4304). Persecution means unreasonable harm and from which no relief is possible short of migration.

The selective use of the coercive power of the state directed against particular ethnic groups in a country is an obvious example of persecution. In addition, people may be vulnerable to persecution by organizations other than those of the state, especially if the state is in no position to protect them. In Kenya, male circumcision (customarily done in adolescence) is embraced and upheld by all ethnic groups, with the notable exception of the Luo. Imagine the following hypothetical situation. The Kenyan government adopts a policy of forced circumcision of Luo males, rounding them up in adolescence and removing their foreskins. Perhaps they do this with the aim of promoting intermarriage between Luos and everyone else, or because health officials convince them that male circumcision reduces the risk of AIDS. Such an action might justify a request for political asylum in the United States.

The merits of political asylum cases are contestable. Is the coercive action unreasonable, or, for example, can the use of government force be justified in light of a population or health crisis? Is the coercive action arbitrary, discriminatory, or unfair to particular categories of persons, or is it applied to all members of society regardless of race, religion, nationality, or political opinion? Are remedies possible through normal political and legal institutions within the country of origin? Given that race, religion, and nationality are explicitly admissible grounds for establishing "a well-founded fear of persecution," should gender be included as admissible grounds as well? Is a person automatically a member of "a particular social group" simply by virtue of his or her sex?

These are the types of tough-minded questions that need to be asked in such cases. Unlike the formal legal restrictions on male circumcision in the former Soviet Union, however, African coming-of-age and gender identity ceremonies and procedures are not matters of government policy. In African ethnic groups in which both male and female circumcision is part of the cultural landscape, the surgery is a customary part of family life and social practice. It may occur so early in life that it never enters consciousness. Or it may occur in middle childhood, where it unfolds as a routine expectation in which parents entice, coax, or force their children to do what well-intended adults in Africa believe is in their children's best interests (just as we entice, coax, or, if necessary, force our children to go to school, have their teeth drilled, or undergo a beneficial medical procedure, even when we know it may be painful). Or the operation may occur just before or during adolescence and unfold as a test of courage, a source of personal empowerment, and an eagerly awaited step into mature adulthood (see Kratz, 1994; Johnson, 2000). Uncircumcised adult women are not typically placed in an intolerably coercive situation in which political asylum from their country of origin is the only remedy. Political asylum requests for uncircumcised African females are few and far between, and they tend to arise under strange (and in some instances, unbelievable) circumstances.

Adelaide Abankwah comes from an ethnic group in Ghana in which women are not circumcised, in a country where a majority of ethnic groups have no tradition of female circumcision, and the government does not endorse the practice. She claimed that she was going to be forcibly circumcised as punishment for not being a virgin, and that she could not receive protection in Ghana. Anti-FGM advocacy groups such as Equality Now were moved by her incredible and unique story (most of which was undocumented and almost all of which, including her name, turned out to be fraudulent; see Branigin and Farah, 2000). Instead of first doing some basic fact-checking, these groups rallied to her side and enlisted celebrity, senatorial, and White House support to grant her asylum (see the case of *Adelaide Abankwah v. INS* and related news coverage; see also Kratz, 2002).

Other cases seem more meritorious, but they appear to arise from unusual circumstances and reveal little about characteristic features of the local African scene. Fauziya Kassindja is a sympathetic figure from Togo. She asked for political asylum due to an unusual domestic situation in which one part of the family endorsed a tradition of female circumcision while her own parents did not. As a teenager, she grew up with no expectation or anticipation of being circumcised. Nevertheless, when her father died, her father's siblings arranged for her to be married into a family where female circumcision was part of the family tradition. She fled Togo and landed in Newark, New Jersey, where in 1994 Kassindja was arrested for entering the United States illegally (see Kratz, 2002). Two years later, just after she was granted political asylum and then heralded by anti-FGM advocacy groups as a feminist heroine who had been liberated from the "oppressive and barbaric" customs of Africa, Fauziya Kassindja was interviewed on Ted Koppel's television program "Night Line." In that interview, Kassindja surprised her host by announcing that most young women in Togo are happy to be circumcised and "think it is something very great." She spoke the truth, but her response did not compute within the terms of the global anti-FGM discourse. Because African genital alterations are torture and everyone must want to flee Togo—the basic assumption of the program—Koppel pressed on with his prepared story line (Walley, 1997: 421). It remains to be seen whether other liberal, free-thinking Americans—all of "us"—will be more able to "break frame," open our minds, uncover our ears, and listen.

Conclusion: Being Slow to Judge the Unfamiliar and Having a Hard Second Look

I can think of no better way to conclude than by quoting the legal scholar Lawrence Sager (2000), who writes:

> Epistemic concerns and the principle of equal liberty require that we be slow to judge the unfamiliar, and that we take a hard look at our own factual beliefs and normative judgments before we condemn culturally endorsed practices. They also require that extant legal cate-

gories of excuse and mitigation be open to the distinct experience of cultural minorities. Finally, they require that our robust tradition of constitutional liberty—including the rights of speech and belief, the right of parents to guide their children's development, and the right of people to be free from governmental intrusion into decisions that ought to be theirs alone—be available on full and fair terms to cultural minorities.

As a matter of epistemic concern, this chapter has suggested that we should be skeptical of the anti-FGM advocacy literature and global discourse that portrays African mothers as mutilators, murderers, and torturers of their children. We should be dubious of representations that suggest African mothers are bad mothers, or that First World mothers have a better idea of what it means to be a good mother. We should be slow to judge the unfamiliar practice of female genital alterations, in part because the horrifying assertions concerning the consequences of this practice (that is, claims about mortality, devastating health outcomes, and loss of a capacity to enjoy sex) are not well supported with credible scientific evidence. That is reason enough to take a hard second look and hesitate before even using the epithet "FGM" to describe the coming-of-age and gender identity practices embraced by many millions of African women. African women too have rights to personal and family privacy, to guide the development of their children in light of their own ideals of the good life, and to be free of excessive and unreasonable government intrusion.

This chapter also has claimed that merely posing the question, "What about FGM?" is not an argument against cultural pluralism. Tolerance begins with seeing the cultural point of these practices for those who believe in them and getting the scientific facts straight. Our cherished ideals of tolerance (including the ideal of having a "choice") would not amount to much if we were merely willing to eat each other's foods and to grant each other permission to enter different houses of worship for a couple of hours on the weekend. Tolerance means setting aside readily aroused and powerfully negative feelings about the practices of immigrant minority groups long enough to get the facts straight and engage the "other" in a serious moral dialogue. It should take far more than overheated rhetoric and offended sensibilities to justify a cultural eradication campaign. Needless to say, the question of toleration versus eradication of other people's ways of life is not just a women's issue.

The controversy over female circumcision in Africa is not an open-and-shut case. Given the high stakes involved, cultural pluralists who are knowledgeable about African circumcision practices have a responsibility to step forward, speak out, and educate the public about this practice. Many African women, out of a sense of modesty, privacy, loyalty, or a well-founded fear of political persecution, may hesitate to speak for themselves. Everyone, anti-FGM activists and cultural pluralists alike, has a responsibility to insist on fairness and the highest standards of reason and evidence in any public policy debate on this topic—or at least to insist that there is a public policy debate, with all sides and voices fully represented.

The Return of the "White Man's Burden" and the Domestic Life of Hindu Women

with Usha Menon

This chapter characterizes the life course images and domestic life of Oriya Hindu women living in extended households in the temple town of Bhubaneswar in Orissa, India. The chapter is divided into three parts.

The first part examines Oriya women's conceptions of the ideal phases in a woman's life. Oriya women do not conceive of a middle phase of life defined by chronological age (for example, 40–65) or by markers of biological aging (poorer eye sight, menopause, loss of muscle strength) that would correspond to the English phrase "middle age." Yet Oriya women do have a well-differentiated conception of the normal and desirable phases in a woman's life. Their ideal life course scheme includes a phase called *prauda* or "mature adulthood," which begins when a married woman takes over the management of the extended household and ends when she relinquishes control and social responsibilities to others. Although *prauda* is a phase that a married Oriya woman is likely to achieve by her early thirties and be finished with by her late fifties, age and biology per se are not the defining characteristics of Oriya life-phase transitions. The underlying logic of the five-phase scheme elaborated here is one of social responsibility, family management, and moral duty.

In the second part of the chapter, we review recent anthropological representations and moral evaluations of the lives of rural Hindu women more generally. Since the 1970s, a growing number of anthropological studies have examined the lives of Hindu women (to name but a few, Fruzetti, 1982; Dhruvarajan, 1988; Papanek and Minault, 1982; Sharma, 1980; Roy, 1975; Jacobson, 1982; Jain and Bannerjee, 1985; Liddle and Joshi, 1986; Wadley, 1980; Wadley and Jacobson, 1986i; Bennett, 1983; Kondos, 1989; Minturn, 1990; Jeffrey et al., 1988; Raheja and Gold, 1994). Many of these studies are implicitly, if not self-consciously, "feminist" in orientation and rely on moral concepts such as social inequality, patriarchal oppression, and subjugation to depict Hindu women, their lives, and their situations. In explicating and critiquing the feminist view, we identify two kinds of ethnographic portraits—the passive victim and the clandestine rebel—that have emerged from such studies.

The third part of the chapter raises some doubts about these recent representations and moral evaluations of the situation of rural Hindu women. We recover a set of local moral meanings that have been lost in the writing or invention of a feminist ethnography of Hindu family life. In this effort, we rely on Oriya women's descriptions of their workaday lives and their own ratings of psychological well-being and physical health. We also make use of observations of daily life in the family, of cooking and worship, of events like births and marriages, and the everyday conversations that one of the authors (Usha Menon) had with these women outside the interview context. We relate women's daily routines to the different phases in an Oriya woman's life, and we contextualize the lives of Oriya "housewives" and trace connections between family statuses over the life course and the achievement of a sense of personal well-being *(hito)*.

Our strategy in this final part of the chapter is to rely on indigenous and locally salient Oriya moral concepts to reveal a hidden presupposition implicit in many portrayals of Hindu women. That unexamined presupposition is the tenet of the moral superiority of the West, the presumption of a white man's (or white woman's) burden to liberate others from the darkness of their cultural traditions. We describe the ways in which Oriya Hindu women derive meaning, purpose, and a sense of power from their family life practices, and we point out some of the important differences between the moral sensibilities of Westernized feminist writers and the moral sensibilities of the non-Westernized Hindu women whose lives they have sought to depict.

As we shall see, the overriding moral significances of the domestic life of Hindu women perceived by many Westernized ethnographers (and projected into their writings about exploitation, victimization, and resistance) are not the moral significances constructed by local Oriya women, whose voices and subaltern notions of the good (including their ideas about service, duty, civility, and self-improvement) articulate a vision of life in society that Westernized feminists appear ideologically unprepared to represent sympathetically.

Our investigation was conducted in the neighborhood surrounding the Lingaraj temple in Bhubaneswar, Orissa, the "Old Town" as it is known locally. This medieval temple dating from the tenth or eleventh century is one of the contemporary residences of the Hindu god Siva and his divine family. The temple is a necessary stop in the itinerary of pilgrims on their way to the famous Jagannatha ("juggernaut") temple forty miles away in the coastal town of Puri.[1]

In 1991, Usha Menon interviewed ninety-two Oriya Hindu men

and women about their conceptions of the life course and about the kinds of events and experiences that they considered typical or significant in a person's life. They were also asked to assess their past and present life satisfaction and their expectations for the future.[2]

The results of this initial research highlighted three important issues. First, Oriya Hindus tend to describe life in terms of changes in roles, duties, and responsibilities. They rarely speak of life in terms of the growth and development of a child's capacity to speak or walk and they never mention first menstruation or menopause, although the former is marked by explicit rituals and marks the beginning of restrictions on girls' movements, apparel, and companions. Second, Oriya Hindus have well-articulated conceptions of two-, four-, and five-phase models of the life course.

Third, Oriya Hindu women of all ages tend to see mature adulthood as, relatively speaking, the most satisfying period in a woman's life. This finding appears to be distinctive of the Oriya Hindu cultural world; for instance, it differs quite remarkably from research done with American women.[3] According to Paul Cleary's unpublished results (Figure 5.1), American women exhibit a steady, linear decline in anticipated future life satisfaction as they move from young adulthood to advanced middle age. According to our results (see Figure 5.1), however, Oriya Hindu women have different expectations. In fact, unlike American women, who view young adulthood—the period of life when individual capacities for autonomous, independent action are at their peak—as the more satisfying period in life, mature adulthood is the period that elicits from Oriya Hindu women the greatest anticipation of positive life satisfaction. As we shall see, there are indigenous meanings and understandings that can help us understand their evaluations.

Those findings from the fieldwork in 1991 provided the back-

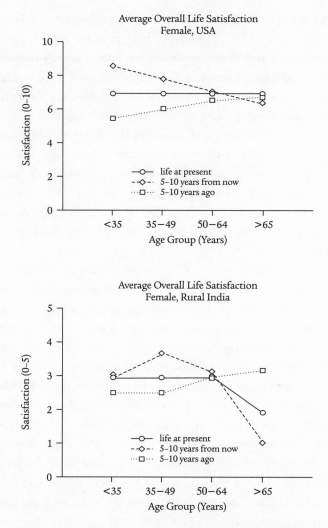

Figure 5.1 The American data were collected and analyzed by Paul Cleary and his associates at Harvard University. I am grateful for the opportunity to use this unpublished material as a point of comparison with the data from India.

ground for a second spell of fieldwork conducted by Menon in 1992–1993. Because Oriyas tend to describe their lives in terms of changing roles and responsibilities, the later research focused on women at different phases in the life course who were occupying different family roles, performing different duties, and bearing different responsibilities. The second set of interviews and observations explored the values and meanings that these women attach to mature adulthood and the ways they define "satisfying life experiences." Because we believe that shifts in these women's roles, responsibilities, and personal well-being can be most clearly witnessed within the context of joint living arrangements, informants for the second spell of fieldwork were selected from extended households.

Joint living arrangements (a three-generation family consisting of adult brothers, their parents, wives, children, and unmarried sisters) are a phase of the developmental cycle of all families in the temple town of Bhubaneswar. One significant difference between joint and nuclear living arrangements in India lies in the fact that joint families are most certainly the cultural ideal. Indians prefer such living arrangements whenever they are possible. In Old Town, joint families usually break up when either the old father or grandfather (the head of the household) dies or when the old widowed mother or grandmother dies. At that time, the adult sons set up their own nuclear families with their wives and their children. Yet with the marriage of their sons and the birth of their grandchildren, their families extend and become complex, and the cycle of joint living arrangements begins again.

Our sample of Oriya informants for this phase of the research consisted of thirty-seven Hindu women belonging to ten extended households, ranging from 19 to 78 years old. These women follow traditional age-related family roles, those of "new" daughter-in-law, wife, mother, "old" (or senior) daughter-in-law, mother-in-law, grandmother, widow. A couple of unmarried adult daughters also form part of the sample; they were interviewed to provide a same-age control group and counterpoint to the experiences of new daughters-in-law.

Of the ten families selected, seven are Brahman; one is a Chassa (a cultivating caste), another a Teli (a merchant caste) and the last a Maharana (a caste of carpenters). Except for one Brahman family, the families are fairly well off: they own agricultural land and other property—houses and shops—that earn rent. Signs of this relative wealth can be seen in the fact that all families have at least one motor scooter, perhaps two, as well as televisions, refrigerators, and other household appliances.

The number of members in these families vary from six to twenty, with the average being thirteen. Of the thirty-seven women, there are twenty-two daughters-in-law, thirteen mothers-in-law, and two daughters; two of these daughters-in-law belong to four-generation households and so are mothers-in-law to the newest generation of daughters-in-law. In terms of education, a generational effect is clearly noticeable: mothers-in-law rarely have more than three or four years of education while almost all the daughters-in-law have completed ten years of formal schooling. There are, moreover, five mothers-in-law who state that they are unable to read or write; of these, three are non-Brahmans while two belong to a caste (Badus) whose status as Brahmans is contested by other Brahmans in the community.

Using open-ended, loosely structured interview schedules, women were asked to describe their daily routines, the degree of control they exercised over their own actions and bodies as well as the actions and bodies of others, their sense of belonging to their families and being part of a meaningful communal life, and the extent to which they felt they had achieved well-being. In order to measure the extent to which these women experience well-being, responses are keyed to the following mode of estimation. Ordinary folk in Old Town often speak of having "not even one *anna* of control over what happens in life"[4] or of having "fully sixteen *annas* of happiness in childhood," and so when it came to asking women how healthy they were or how much well-being they thought they had, we framed the question in these commonplace terms. The answers we typically heard were, "six *annas* of good health [*svasthya*]" or "four *annas* of well-being [*hito*]."

Almost without exception, the women were candid, articulate, and eager to participate; consequently, the interviews are long and detailed. None lasted for less than an hour. Some went on for more than two hours. The reasons for this candor and eagerness are not hard to understand. We believe most women saw the interviews as an opportunity to engage in a kind of therapy or a criticism of family members. They permitted themselves to speak their minds with relative freedom to an interested stranger who spoke their language but who did not share the constraints of their lives. While most interviews were one-on-one conversations in secluded rooms, the feeling that the rest of the family was close at hand, within earshot, was not easy to shake off. Often, when the women felt that they were saying something particularly critical of other family members, their voices would drop, but at other times they would deliberately raise their voices so that their complaints could be heard by other members of the family. Thus, most new daughters-in-law spoke in low undertones while mothers-in-law and sometimes old daughters-in-law spoke loudly and self-confidently, often even aggressively. All interviews were in Oriya, audiotaped, and later transcribed and translated.

Between Birth and Death in Orissa

Figure 5.2 shows the phases of life *(avastha)* as described by sixty-six women (predominantly Brahman) living in extended households in the summer of 1991. During the interviews, they were presented with sheets of paper on which there were two dots, designated "birth" and "death." The women were asked to fill in the space between the two dots by narrating the most significant events and experiences in a typical person's life and in their own lives as well.

Some women initially resisted the request, indicating that it is really boring to talk in broad generalities about things that are obvious about life. As one elderly woman put it (a woman who was in the fifth and last phase of life, the *briddha avastha,* or stage of completion), "What can I tell you about those kinds of things? You know about them. Everyone does. You are born, you grow up, you grow old, you die. Do you want to hear that?" Other women were initially skeptical about the task on the grounds that "each person's life is different from everyone else's" and that "it depends on what kind of family you are born into, what your caste is, whether you're a boy or girl, whether you are the oldest child or the second or whatever, what your capabilities are, what karma you have brought with you." Nevertheless, Oriya women are quite adept at storytelling, and with just a bit of coaxing, they had much to say about how a woman's life proceeds between life and death in rural India.

The tales told by these women reveal an alternative cultural conceptualization of the phases of the life course, one based on the logic of social responsibility, family management, and moral duty. In their narrations, Oriya women divide the life course into two,

	Lifeline				
	Birth	Knows right from wrong (7–9)	Marriage (18–20)	Takes over family management (30–39)	Relinquishes family management (55–60) — Death
Two-stage model	bapa gharo (Life in father's house)				sasu gharo (Life in mother-in-law's house)
Five-stage model	pila (undisciplined child)	kishoro (morally formative youth)	jouvana (sexually active)	prauda (mature)	briddha (completed)
Quality of role	Pet	Guest	Servant	Manager	Dependent
Rank in family	High	High	Low	High (peak)	Low
Control over others	High	Low	Low	High (peak)	Low
Assimilation in the family	High	High	Low	High (peak)	Declines
Served by others?	Yes	Yes	No	Yes	Uncertainty
Restrictive life?	No	Yes	Yes (peak)	Yes	No
Burden of responsibilities	Low	Low	High	High	Low
Worry about welfare of others	No	No	Yes	Yes (peak)	Disappears
Perceived stress	Low	Low	High (peak)	High	High
Karmic consequences of one's actions	Low	High	High	High (peak)	High
Capacity to reason	Absent	Present	Present	Present (peak)	Declines
Time of suffering?	No	No	Yes	No	Yes
Perception of life-satisfaction trajectory		I will be worse off in next phase	I was better off in last phase and will be much better off in next phase	I was worse off in last phase and will be worse off in next phase	I was much better off in last phase and will be much worse off in next phase

Figure 5.2 Oriya women's conception of the life course.

four, or five phases. These three types of conceptualizations (the two-, four-, and five-phase models) form a nested hierarchy of differentiated cultural models of the life course. The two- and five-stage models are schematically represented in Figure 5.2.

In the context of our general concern with documenting the breadth versus the narrowness of the cross-cultural and historical distribution of the idea of "middle age," the four- and five-phase models interest us the most because within these models there is a life phase known as *prauda* or "mature adulthood." First, though, we turn to the most rudimentary Oriya model of a woman's life, in which the life course is partitioned into only two phases: life spent in "my father's house" *(bapa gharo)* and that spent in "my husband's mother's house" *(sasu gharo),* the most common bipartite characterization among Oriya women who divide their lives into only two phases.

In extended households in Orissa, India, married sons continue to stay at home with their parents, but daughters, after an arranged marriage, move out. From the point of view of the daughter who is marrying out, the marriage ceremony is the most significant phase boundary in her life. It is at this point that an Oriya woman's socially recognized status shifts from being "a child who is some man's daughter" *(jhio pila)* to being "a sexually active female who is some other woman's daughter-in-law" *(bou).* As a *jhio pila,* an Oriya female is assumed to be sexually dormant (even after she is biologically mature) and lives under her father's protection. As a young *bou,* she is expected to be reproductively and sexually active and live under her mother-in-law's command.

Ideally, this fundamental phase shift from father's house to mother-in-law's house takes place between 18 and 20 years of age. However, age per se does not mark the boundary between these two basic phases in life. Rather, it is marked by the numerous changes in social responsibilities attendant upon marriage, including, among other things, the responsibility to serve and be sensitive to the in-laws' needs and to become sexually active for the sake of reproducing the family line. Unlike young American females, who want to be referred to as "women" (rather than "girls") as soon as they move out of their parents' homes and into a college dormitory, a sexually inactive Oriya 30-year-old who is still unmarried and lives under the protection of her father is socially categorized as a "child." She becomes a "woman" by getting married and by willingly and dutifully placing herself under an older woman's authority.

For the women in our study, the story of the life course, then, is the story of domestic life in someone else's house (first father's, then mother-in-law's). The fact that Oriya women are housebound, however, is not viewed by them as a mark of their oppression. Quite the contrary. The domestic realm is highly valued in Oriya culture, and domestic space *(ghare)* is understood as a kind of sacred, uncontaminating space and is contrasted with public, or outside, contaminating space *(bahare)*. Men spend time outside the home and, therefore, are always at risk of becoming coarse *(asabhya)* and uncivilized *(abhadra)*. It is by virtue of being able to remain indoors that Oriyas, both men and women, believe that women are more refined than men, more capable of experiencing civilizing dispositions such as "humility," "restraint," and "shame" *(lajya),* and less likely to display crude emotions such as "anger" *(raga)* or "mocking laughter" *(hasa)*.

The four- and five-phase models elaborate on life in the two houses, presenting a more differentiated view of a woman's life course. In the five-phase model, life in one's father's house is divided into two phases: first, the undisciplined early childhood phase *(pilaliya),* when the daughter is indulged as a kind of adorable yet uncivilized family pet, and the second, the morally formative yet tender youthful phase *(kishor avastha),* when the daughter-child becomes a kind of resident guest in training and is given anticipatory instruction in the social responsibilities and duties of married life. The first phase ends at approximately 7 to 9 years of age. The daughter-child is now thought capable of praying on her own, of distinguishing right from wrong, and of being sufficiently mature to have a conscience about the social responsibilities associated with domestic life. The second phase ends at marriage. (The four-phase model joins the first two phases and labels them *"pila."*)

Life in the mother-in-law's house is divided into three phases: the first is *jouvana*, or young adulthood, when the sexually active young daughter-in-law is expected to have children and to serve the needs of her husband's family members; the second is *prauda*, or mature adulthood, when a woman takes over all the responsibilities for family management, including planning and control; and the third is *briddha*, or the age of completion, when a woman gives up the management of the family, becomes dependent on her kin, and begins to anticipate life in yet another house, the house of *Yama*, the house of the god of death.

Figure 5.2 lists some of the characteristics of each life phase as revealed in these women's narratives. We have focused on those that are potentially relevant to perceived life satisfaction or well-being, for example, assimilation into the family, dominance within the family, being served by others, and having control over the actions of others. The women in our sample represent four of the five life phases. As a measure of perceived life satisfaction, they were asked to estimate the ratio of good and bad events in their current lives, in the past five to ten years, and five to ten years into the future. The perceived life satisfaction of the fourteen oldest women (those over 60 who are in the last phase, that of *briddha*) can be summarized as follows: "My life was much better off in the past and it will be much worse off in the future." The perceived life satisfaction of the nineteen young daughters-in-law, those women under 30 who are in phase 3 *(jouvana)* can be summarized this way: "My life was better off in the past and it will be much better off in the future." Neither *jouvana* (the early married phase) nor *briddha* (the last phase of life) are valued times for women in this community. It is the *prauda* (mature adulthood) phase that is highly prized. Married women in their twenties look forward to it with anticipation. The elder women look back on it as that phase of life that preceded their decline.

Prauda may seem vaguely reminiscent of "midlife" or "middle age." Yet that impression is surely misleading, for mature adulthood is not defined by biological age and does not normally extend beyond the ages of 55 or 60. *Prauda* begins when a married woman takes over the management of the extended household and ends when she relinquishes control and social responsibilities to others. According to these Oriya women, *prauda* is the phase in life when dominance, control, and responsibility for others are at their peak. The perceived life satisfaction of the twenty-eight women who are in the *prauda* phase can be summarized this way: "Compared to where I am now I was worse off in the past and I will be worse off in the future." In absolute terms it is when Oriya women are "mature adults" that they report the greatest life satisfaction.

Writing about Domesticity: The Moral Foundations of Ethnographic Representation

In recent scholarly literature, the "native point of view" of Hindu family life and the domestic careers of Hindu women has either been subordinated to, or appropriated by, the moral framework of the currently popular "feminist" point of view. First we discuss the two types of constructions of the lives of Hindu women that are most prevalent in feminist ethnography. Then we offer an alternative construction derived from an alternative Oriya women's point of view.

FEMINIST DISCOURSE ABOUT HINDU WOMEN

Feminist scholarship is, of course, neither uniform nor homogeneous in its goals or beliefs. Nevertheless, in the context of South Asian studies, there are certain assumptions that seem to be widely held among anthropologists who approach their subject matter from a feminist point of view: that is, that patriarchy is bad and is responsible for the subordination of women; that women can be grouped into a unitary, coherent category made up of gendered persons who have the same objective interests and similar subjective desires; that male dominance and female subordination are not only morally outrageous but also seem to exist in almost every context; and that Hindu cultural meanings systematically and regularly devalue women.

Armed with these tenets, scholars who study India from a feminist point of view seem to divide into two camps: those who view Hindu women as passive victims of patriarchy, and those who view Hindu women as active rebels against it.

The scholars who portray Hindu women as passive victims (for example, Kondos, 1989; Dhruvarajan, 1988; Jeffrey et al., 1988) focus on the differences that they, as Westernized observers, see in the life circumstances of the female Hindu "other," and they are sensitive to (and feel great empathy for) the situations of the most unfortunate of Hindu women.

There is much that these scholars dislike or even disdain in Hindu society. For example, they blame Hindu religion (which they interpret as mere ideology rather than as a sacred and factual explanation of social and physical phenomena) for the "subordination and subjection" of women (Kondos, 1989: 162); for clouding the consciousness of its victims; and for withholding from Hindu women a political discourse of protest, insurgency, and victimhood. Such feminist writers tend to project an image of "the Hindu woman" as tame, domesticated, bound by tradition, intellectually unsophisticated, and sexually constrained. In this view, she is a woman who has little control over her actions or her body, a woman whose life is completely contingent on others.

Thus, Dhruvarajan, while describing her book's objective, writes:

> By elaborating on the philosophical underpinnings and
> the beliefs regarding the nature of men and women [they

are] based on, [my book] shows how women's dependent position on men is legitimized, how the ideology manipulates the motivational structure of women to accept their position as underlings of men, and how it strips them of the willpower necessary for self-reliance and personal growth. (1988, 108)

Kondos, in her study of upper-caste Nepali Hindu women, concludes that "feminine success is predefined and not open to variation, for a woman cannot be successful in any other way or in any other terms except those specified by the structures (the domicile, the laws, the cultural imperatives to produce sons and to die before her husband)" (1989: 190). Jeffrey et al. reveal their intellectual predispositions when they write that "Swaleha (one of our research assistants) responded to Patricia's exasperation over women's self-abnegation with the comment: 'But you see, the men here have subdued their women so completely that the idea has perched in women's minds that they are indeed inferior'" (1988: 157).

The image of the Hindu woman as passive victim is set in sharp contrast to another representation that is implicit in the writings of these feminist scholars: the image of the Western or Westernized academic woman as educated and cosmopolitan, as having control over her body and her sexuality, as autonomous, and as having the freedom to make informed decisions on her own. The message conveyed by these authors is that the discrepancy between the two images is a measure of the failure of Hindu society to recognize and live up to a set of obvious and universally binding moral ideals (autonomy, equality, privacy, individual rights, and social and economic justice), which have been recognized and are being institutionalized in the West. In ethnographic constructions of this sort, the native point of view remains unvoiced or tends to be subordinated to a feminist point of view.

Yet not all scholars who study India portray Hindu women as passive victims. There is an alternative construction or invention—the Hindu woman as active rebel. Those who represent Hindu women this way, as proto-Jacobins or cryptorevolutionaries, perceive a set of "liberated" attitudes and reactions against patriarchy that are very much like their own. These ethnographers detect "subversion" and "resistance" in Hindu women's songs, poetry, and ordinary conversations. They portray Hindu women as having a bawdy sense of humor, taking pleasure in their sexuality, and relishing their female nature. They represent these symbolic actions as ways for women to express their disenchantment with patriarchy and as indications of an incipient or clandestine movement aimed at undermining received gender roles (see Raheja and Gold, 1994).

According to this representation of South Asian moral attitudes and beliefs, Hindu women speak in multiple voices and elaborate both dominant male and subversive female perspectives. At some fundamental level, however, Hindu women, share with Western feminists the insights that enable them to identify the ultimate cause as well as the proximate instruments of their oppression—patriarchy and men. In ethnographic constructions of this sort, the native point of view is equated with, and thereby appropriated by, the feminist point of view.

IS THERE A DISTINCTIVE (NONFEMINIST) "NATIVE POINT OF VIEW"?

The cultural practices of rural India in general and the family life practices of rural Hindu women in particular are a challenge to the cognitive, moral, and aesthetic sensibilities of Euro-American observers. For example, most married Oriya Hindu women living in the temple town of Bhubaneswar are sequestered in family compounds, where they assume a major responsibility for the humdrum routines, tasks, and duties of domestic life. Chandrama, a 23-year-old Oriya woman who has been married for the last five years and is the oldest daughter-in-law in an extended household of twelve, tells us about a typical day in her life. What she has to narrate about her daily routine is typical of a day in the life of an Oriya woman in the *jouvana* phase of life:

> As soon as I get up, I sweep out the house and then I go to the bathroom. I clean my teeth, have a bath, and then I start the breakfast. Once the breakfast is done, people come in one by one to eat. I serve each of them breakfast. Once that is done, we have our breakfast together. *Bou* [husband's mother] and I eat together. And then, I start preparing lunch—what we'll be eating at two in the afternoon. Once that is done, again people come in one by one to eat. By three, we would also have eaten and I would have washed up after lunch. Then, I come and sleep in the afternoon. I sleep for an hour. I get up at four. I again sweep out the house and then I go down to start making something to eat with tea. I knead the *atta* [wheat flour] and make *parathas* or *rotis* [different kinds of bread]. Again, people come one by one to eat. I serve them and then it would be sundown by now and I offer *sandhya* [evening worship] before I start cooking the night meal. I am usually cooking till nine in the night. Then I go and watch the serial on TV. After that, at about 9:30, everyone will come to eat and I serve them. And then we eat. After finishing eating, we go to bed. The dishes are left as they are till morning. I just keep them till the morning when I wash them. In the morning, the first thing I do is take out and wash the *ointha* [polluted by leftovers] dishes, then I leave them out in the sun to dry, while I sweep out the

kitchen, wash it out, and then take the vessels back in again.

Q. Would you like to add anything more to what you've just said?

A. No, nothing else.

Q. What about *puja* [worship]? In the morning do you do *puja* after your bath? Give water to the *tulasi* [basil leaf, representing the goddess] or offer water to *surjya* [sun god]?

A. No, I do nothing. *Bou* does all that. All I do is wash the feet of our *burhi ma* [husband's father's mother] and drink the water after my bath and before I go to make breakfast. I used to do it for *bou* and *nona* [husband's mother and father; the use of the term "bou" to refer to husband's mother is not its literal meaning—the word means "son's wife" or "daughter-in-law"—but it is colloquial usage in these Oriya households] in the beginning but they stopped me from doing it. They said that it was enough to do it for *burhi ma* and get her blessings. But apart from that I don't do any *puja*. I offer *sandhya* but that is only in the kitchen—*bou* offers it in the *puja* room and over the rest of the house.

As every interpretive anthropologist knows, a storyteller's intent is not always equivalent to a listener's response. From the point of view of "authorial intent," Chandrama's chronicle of her daily routine is a narrative saturated with locally salient yet universally recognizable moral meanings about her self-conscious engagement in a project of doing *sewa*, or service, for her husband's family. Her narrative is about the positive moral implications of voluntarily enduring the specific life phase (and hence temporary) responsibilities of a family *sevaka* (a devoted servant of the divine).

One of the things this storyteller, Chandrama, does not know, however, is that some of her listeners are cosmopolitan, "liberated" Westernized scholars who reflexively perceive her *sewa* as humiliating subservience, oppressive subjugation, or abusive exploitation. Minimally we can expect that the daily routine of an Oriya "housewife" as described in this narrative will appear to give new meaning (both literal and figurative) to the idea of the "daily grind."

First impressions can be misleading, especially when those impressions have been formed under the influence of a relatively thin theory of moral goods, such as the honorable yet incomplete (and hence "partial" or "biased") "ethics of autonomy" privileged by Western liberal thought. In this case the (objectively) partial yet (subjectively) totalizing moral significances projected (and then perceived) by Western and Westernized feminist ethnographers as they gaze upon the lives of "unliberated" Hindu women are almost neocolonial in character, for those significances carry with them the implications of a moral imperialism or a white (wo)man's burden to emancipate and uplift Hindu family life and to disenthrall "uneducated" and "superstitious" Hindus of their "unjust" and "oppressive" gender roles.

In fact, the Oriya Hindu women of the temple town of Bhubaneswar are neither passive victims nor subversive rebels, but rather active upholders of a moral order that Western feminists have largely failed to comprehend. High on the list of virtues and values in the moral order upheld by Oriya women are chastity, modesty, duty, self-discipline, the deferment of gratification, self-improvement, and the ideal of domestic "service" *(sewa)*. Low on the list are liberty and social equality.[5]

The women display cultural agency as they go about their daily

lives—agency that supports and affirms rather than denies or un-
dermines the cultural order. These women are not cultural robots
who go through life mechanically and unthinkingly. Rather, they
are self-reflecting people who acknowledge the constraints they live
with, recognize the choices available to them, and are well aware of
the costs and rewards of conforming to cultural norms.

Hito, the Oriya term for well-being, is an analytic category familiar to the women who participated in this study. Defined very
broadly, it refers to the state of being satisfied with the way one's
world has turned out. A more nuanced definition, one that includes the indigenous meanings that this term conveys to Oriya
women, will emerge during the course of this chapter. It is that
nuanced definition that enables us to critique the rather dismal
feminist representations of the lives of Hindu women and to relo-
cate Oriya domestic life within an alternative moral order. (On the
idea of plural moral goods such as autonomy, community, or divinity and alternative moral orders, see Shweder, 1990, 1994b; Shweder
et al., 1990; Shweder et al., 1997; Haidt, Koller and Dias, 1993; Jensen,
1995; Chapter 2 this book. On the idea of plural moral goods such
as fairness, sympathy, duty, and self-improvement and alternative
moral orders, see Wilson, 1993.)

Our representation of women's lives in Oriya households high-
lights the way a woman's access to and achievement of well-being
(hito) systematically varies across the life cycle. There are periods
when an Oriya housewife is so valued within the family, when her
activities are so significant for the material and spiritual prosperity
of the entire household, that her own sense of well-being peaks.
There are also periods when she is less essential to the household's
well-being and her own sense of well-being declines. No Oriya
Hindu woman's life is uniformly a success or uniformly a failure,
just as there is no woman in this community who always makes her

own decisions or one who never does. These are facts well recognized by the women themselves. Oriya women will tell you that success or failure, control or lack of control, well-being or distress characterize different phases in a person's life and ultimately mesh together to form the fabric of a self-disciplined life.

Understanding Gender in a Hindu Temple Town

For the sake of this analysis we define a "culture" as a reality lit up by a morally enforceable conceptual scheme or subset of meanings instantiated in practice (Shweder, 1996a). This part introduces the alternative cultural reality of gender relations in the temple town of Bhubaneswar and some of the concepts, beliefs, and practices that make Oriya gender relations a justifiable moral reality.

To an outside observer, the women who live in the temple town may at first glance seem docile, withdrawn, and relegated to the background—women without voices. But appearances can deceive, revealing more about the observer than the observed. A closer acquaintance suggests a radically different picture, for these Oriya women do not see themselves as powerless, and they confidently believe that it is they who hold families and society together. Oriya men share this view.

Sudhir Kakar's comment that, in Hindu India, "the preferred medium of instruction and transmission of psychological, metaphysical and social thought continues to be the story" (1982: 1) accurately describes much of indigenous cultural discourse in the temple town of Bhubaneswar. Oriya men and women frequently use stories from the various Puranas (texts about the old times, the often times), as well as regional Oriya folk tales to give logic and meaning to everyday or mundane experience. For most of the Oriya women who spoke at length and in intimate detail about their lives, the stories from the Puranas are far more real and relevant to everyday life (and thus more worthy of repetition) than events reported in the daily newspapers.

The female protagonists (divine and human) of these stories— Durga, Kali, Kunti, Draupadi, Sita, Radha, Savitri, Anusuya—exemplify womanly virtues. Their experiences elucidate a woman's *dharma* (duties, life path) and define a woman's *prakriti* (*svabhava,* her nature). Their qualities *(guna)* tell them what it means to be a Hindu woman. Women see these figures as paradigmatic, partly because they represent ideals worthy of emulation and partly because, by virtue of being female, these heroines and ordinary Oriya Hindu women share the same configurations of female substance.

In addition to the Puranic orientation in the temple town, the *Sakta* tradition is also strong.[6] Oriya Hindus, both men and women, are liable to say that women embody, as the goddess does, *sakti* (vital energy or power or strength) and that they have more of the *gunas* in terms of absolute quantities than do men, which is why women can turn the *asadhya* (undoable) into the *sadhya* (doable), the *asambhav* (impossible) into the *sambhav* (possible). Women are commonly described as *saktidayini* (givers of vital energy or strength) and as being *sampoorna sakti* (full of vital energy or strength). Women are depicted as *samsarore chalak* (controllers or directors of the family and the flow of life in this world), as those whose duties include satisfying everyone *(samasthonku santhusta koriba),* maintaining the family *(samsaroku sambhaliba),* and ensuring peace and order *(shanti shrunkhala rakhiba).*[7]

Most Oriya Hindus in the temple town believe that social reproduction is the primary task of any group. And they believe that the family represents the most appropriate site for social reproduction. For most Oriyas the idea of a voluntarily childless marriage is a contradiction in terms. (Why would anyone marry, Oriyas ask, if they had no intention of having children and contributing to the reproduction of the group?) Both men and women say, "We are born into this world to play our roles in *samsara,* to participate in the ebb and flow of life, to build families, to raise children." They emphasize the impermanence of all things in this world, the fact that continual change is the only stable feature of life. They believe that only through procreating and raising children to responsible adulthood does a group achieve immortality.

It is thus not surprising that Oriya Hindu women, and their menfolk too, regard the home and the family—the domestic do-main—as a more important sphere of human action than the pub-lic domain. Because women control and manage all household ac-tivities, whether what men earn is used effectively depends on the sagacity and capability of the women of the household, particularly the senior-most woman. Men readily acknowledge that women shoulder many more responsibilities than they do *(striro daitya purusa opekhya jyateshtha adhika)* and that the work women do is six times as much as men have to do *(stri jatinkoro karma chho guna adhika).* As a 60-year-old husband, a father, and one of the most ar-ticulate of informants says:

> Look at a 20-year-old man, a 20-year-old child, he knows nothing, he just roams here and there, but a 20-year-old girl, she has become the mother of two children, she runs her household and family, she cares for the cows and calves under her care, the children and the house, she cooks and serves her husband, she cleans the children, dresses them, and sends them to school, makes sure that they are well. She manages the parents of her husband, she cleans the house. Compared to a man's, a woman's

responsibilities are far more. When you compare men
and women of the same age, that is what you find.

In contrast to the premises of modern liberal thought, the view
of the world espoused by Oriya women and men is built on a logic
of difference and solidarity rather than on equality and competition. The popular Oriya recognition of the worth of women's work
and widespread acknowledgement of greater female effectiveness is
not a local idiomatic Oriya expression of a feminist viewpoint—for,
quite emphatically, neither women nor men in Orissa believe that
women and men are equal.

Indeed, most Oriya women and men find the notion that one
should be indifferent to gender or treat the genders as though they
were the same as either incomprehensible, amusing, or immature.
For these Oriyas, the most common metaphor for society is the human body: no organ is exactly substitutable for any other and yet
all work together so that the body functions efficiently while life
endures. Most Oriya women and men believe that of all the *jatis*
(castes) in the world, male and female are the only authentic only
because male and female are the only two *jatis* whose fundamental
differences cannot be transcended.

For Oriya Hindus then, difference and interdependency are
givens. Yet, this difference and the character of the interdependence
are not fixed or global. The prerogatives and privileges enjoyed and
the power exercised by women and men are fluid, varying, as A. K.
Ramanujan (1990) has said, with particular contexts. Men, in terms
of the constitution of their bodily substances, have disproportion-
ately more of the *sattva guna* (qualities of transparency, lucidity,
coherence) and so are regarded as "purer" and because of this relative purity enjoy certain privileges in some situations (for example,

they can approach divinity with fewer restrictions); while women, because they possess more of all the *gunas* in absolute terms, exercise considerable power and control in other situations (for example, they manage household finances and activities with little interference).

THE EXPERIENCE OF WELL-BEING

This section relies on the voices of thirty-seven Oriya women from our broader sample to construct a representation of the way personal well-being is understood and defined by women who belong to this orthodox Hindu community.

Family role (rank and status) appears to be the significant variable in determining an Oriya woman's well-being. As noted earlier, considering the fabric of adult life across the life course, access to personal well-being is at its maximum when an Oriya woman enters the managerial stage of *prauda* (typically as either an old daughter-in-law or as a married mother-in-law). And while most Oriya women achieve this rank or status some time between thirty and forty years of age, biological age per se is not a crucial variable.

Similarly, the sense of well-being reported by daughters and new daughters-in-law varies according to their particular family roles. In Hindu extended households, unmarried adult daughters and new daughters-in-law live in the same family compound and are often of approximately the same age (both may be in their early twenties). Yet their well-being assessments vary widely, with unmarried daughters reporting strikingly higher levels of *hito*.

Because an Oriya woman's duties, responsibilities, social status, and ways of being enmeshed in interpersonal relationships seem to be the major factors giving her meaning, purpose, and fulfillment in life, ethnographers of Hindu family life must be able to characterize local moral meanings and understand how access to those moral meanings is related to personal well-being.

DAILY GRIND: THE MORAL MEANINGS OF SERVICE

In most societies as a woman ages, the restrictions under which she lives relax (cf. Brown and Kerns, 1985). While this may be true on a worldwide scale, it would be a mistake to infer that increased autonomy is the central moral good that explains the association between personal well-being and *prauda* in our sample. We believe that in the temple town a woman's sense of well-being hinges on the particular kinds of family relationships she has succeeded at developing or has failed to develop as she ages.

An important part of the story about *hito* concerns the values and meanings that Oriya Hindus attach to the roles of old daughter-in-law and married mother-in-law. By incorporating such indigenous values and meanings, we can construct an ideal-typical model of the development of well-being among Oriya women. We believe this model is culturally salient, although because this model is an idealization, summarizing and typifying thirty-seven Oriya voices, it does not necessarily coincide with the lived experiences of each and every woman.

The most striking feature of the daily routines of these Oriya women lies, we think, in the ways such routines highlight social relational patterns within families. These daily routines bring to the fore the ways in which duties, responsibilities, and opportunities are distributed among women according to the needs of the family. Exploring these social relational patterns requires an examination of five family roles: daughter, new daughter-in-law, old daughter-in-law, mother-in-law, and widow.

We begin with the daughter of the family. As an unmarried adult, an Oriya Hindu girl enjoys a carefree and relatively irresponsible life. She is far more carefree, in fact, than even her brothers, for whom, given the unemployment statistics in India, the pressure to obtain an adequate source of livelihood makes these years of early adulthood very difficult. An unmarried adult girl is indulged. She has no prescribed duties. Whatever she does, she does voluntarily. The daily routines of the two daughters in the sample make this abundantly clear. (Although there were only two unmarried adult women in our sample, over the years, the authors have observed this pattern of behavior in scores of families.) As Sudhangani, one of the unmarried adult daughters, says, "After eating rice, I may stitch something or I may knit or if I wanted to, I may watch some TV or I may go to sleep. I do things like that."

And as the other daughter, Ameeta, says explicitly, daughters have no responsibility toward anyone in their fathers' households. "My responsibility? What responsibility? I have no responsibility. As long as my father and mother are alive, I have no responsibility toward anyone."

At the same time, however, they are aware of their positions as temporary residents in the *kishoro* stage of life; their permanent homes are elsewhere. Although these unmarried girls have few illusions that life in the homes of their mothers-in-law is initially going to be anything less than strenuous, the interviews communicate clearly the sense of anticipation they feel as they look ahead to becoming daughters-in-law.

Now let us consider the situation of a new daughter-in-law. The differences in well-being between daughters and daughters-in-law are quite striking. Daughters report almost double the level of personal well-being reported by daughters-in-law. This reflects, perhaps, the comfort, the sense of belonging, that daughters feel in their fathers' homes, a feeling of comfort that new daughters-in-law lack during their initial years in their husbands' homes. Be-

cause these two groups are of roughly the same age, the relationship is clearly not between age and well-being but between the family role occupied and well-being.

Unlike an unmarried daughter of the house, a new daughter-in-
law is in the *jouvana* phase and has explicitly understood duties.
She is put through something like the domestic Oriya version of
military boot camp. The most important of these duties lies in doing *sewa*—service to members of her husband's family. Such *sewa*
has, in the Oriya Hindu context, very concrete dimensions. She has
to do all the cooking and some of the serving of the food and much
of the cleaning and washing, and she must perform explicit rituals
of deference to her husband's mother and father. These rituals include massaging their feet daily, drinking the water used to ceremo-
nially wash their feet before eating, and eating out of the *thali*
(metal plate) previously used by either her mother-in-law or her father-in-law.

The meaning of these rituals is easily misunderstood if they are
evaluated only within the moral framework of Western individual-
ist liberationist ideals. From the native point of view, these rituals
of family life are culturally defined ways available to a daughter-in-
law for reconstructing (see Lamb, 1993) her physical substance and
for expressing her solidarity with the patrilineage into which she
has merged through marriage. This is not to say that every Oriya
newlywed is temperamentally inclined to life in a boot camp or tol-
erates harsh treatment without suffering and physical distress.
However, within the framework of indigenous South Asian understandings, such rituals of deference continue the process of reconstruction of the bride's bodily substance begun explicitly during
the marriage ceremonies and symbolized by the new name given
the bride at marriage (see Inden and Nicholas, 1977). In keeping
with Hindu notions of the body, which emphasize the relative

openness to external influences (Marriott, 1976), the new given name, the marriage ceremonies, and the rituals of deference mark the continual reconstructions that a woman's body undergoes as her bodily substance slowly becomes that of the patrilineage into which she has married.

Such rituals contribute directly to an increase or decrease in a daughter-in-law's sense of well-being. Thus when an angry mother-in-law withholds permission to perform such rituals, all daughters-in-law interpret such refusal as a rejection by the family to her assimilation and experience that rejection with considerable sorrow and distress. The cognitive and emotional reactions of Westernized feminist scholars to such practices do not further—indeed they obscure—our understanding of the local moral world supporting extended family life in India.

Most new daughters-in-law echo Chandrama with only minor variations. In the early years of marriage, daughters-in-law do not worship any gods. For them, it is enough to worship their mothers-in-law and fathers-in-law, earthly gods having the power to withhold or bestow blessings. As Sabitiri, a new daughter-in-law, married for just four months, reports, "At my time in life, it is appropriate that I worship *bou*. What need is there for me to worship any other god? She is my god."

These new daughters-in-law are working up a spiritual ladder to the gods. At this point in their moral careers, they regard the opportunity to worship their husbands' mothers and fathers rather than the gods as opportunities for promotion, not a deprivation. At this stage in the life course, given their position in the family hierarchy, new daughters-in-law appear to have few other responsibilities. As Chandrama says further along in her interview, "For the moment, I have no responsibility. There are so many people older than I am—they take all the responsibility of this household."

Nevertheless, as she herself is aware, *daitva*, or responsibility, is never completely absent. A competent daughter-in-law has to learn to be adept in maintaining harmony among the younger members of the family. She must take on the role of friend and advisor to them. She may even intervene as an intermediary between them and her mother-in-law, when the latter's consent and approval is required but unlikely. And it is this capacity to, as she says, "understand what lies in the minds of the *nanad* and *diyoro*" (husband's younger sisters and brothers) that is the distinctive mark of a successful daughter-in-law, trusted by her affinal family.

Further in the interview, Chandrama describes the fairly severe restrictions under which she lives. She rarely goes out; she meets hardly anyone but family members. Her trips to her father's house are infrequent and depend on the wishes of her husband's mother and father. Even within the house, she is unable to move freely because, given the pattern of avoidance relationships within the family, she has to hide from (avoid) those male affines senior to her husband. As Sandhyarani, another new daughter-in-law, says, "All that one does in the house of one's *sasu* [husband's mother] is hide."

Given the stressful circumstances in which new daughters-in-law in the *jouvana* phase live their lives, it is not surprising that only a couple of them claim to have achieved substantial (fifteen to sixteen *annas* of) well-being. The ones who do experience high levels of *hito* live in relatively small families with only seven or eight members and their mothers-in-law are both noninterfering and undemanding. At the other extreme, there are two daughters-in-law who appear to suffer considerable distress, one claiming to have no well-being at all and the other to have only two *annas* of well-being. For the most part, daughters-in-law have rather low feelings of well-being: if sixteen *annas* indicates complete well-being, a new daughter-in-law, typically has less than eight *annas* of well-being.

A notable and distinctive feature of these interviews with new daughters-in-law is the evidence for the somatization of emotional distress. New daughters-in-law who give themselves low scores on well-being complain of night fevers, chest pains, and swooning. Such somatization is explicitly recognized in local discourse. There are new daughters-in-law who say that they are so sad that they cannot digest their food and this leads to chest pains that cannot be explained by the doctors they consult. Their husbands' mothers and sisters say that these women make no effort to integrate with the rest of the family, that they are angry and resentful of everyone else, and that this anger and resentment hinders digestion of food, leading to chest pains.

There are also daughters-in-law who feel so unappreciated in their husbands' homes, so diminished in respect, so anxious to receive regard, that they experience (by their own accounts) a fall in their blood pressure that leads to fainting. Of course, all these accounts have to be seen against the background of a strong cultural aversion to excessive self-concern and reflection about oneself. Generally speaking, people in Old Town believe that too much thinking (i.e., worrying about oneself) is deleterious. They believe that attention to oneself leads in and of itself to illness and physical distress—one makes oneself vulnerable to disease by thinking about oneself too much.

Thus there are multiple explanations for the somatic symptoms of emotional distress, and they vary depending on who is speaking—whether it is the new daughter-in-law or the mother-in-law or the husband's sister. Nevertheless, these multiple explanations have one common thread. They all ascribe the lack of well-being not to the severity of the restrictions under which new daughters-in-law live nor to their having to perform deference, but to their incomplete assimilation into their husbands' families. Oriya women say quite categorically that the greater the assimilation, the greater the well-being that is experienced.

Before a new daughter-in-law gives birth to children, she receives more from the family than she gives to it, and she does not control any of this exchanging. Oriya women state that a new daughter-in-law has to learn to open herself, during this phase, to influences from the family and learn to become as permeable as she can so that her reconstructing and assimilation can occur rapidly and effectively. Those women who are unable to open themselves—and Oriya women recognize such a possibility, saying that often *lajya* (modesty, a heightened awareness of oneself) makes such opening painful and difficult—cannot make use of the opportunities available, even during *jouvana*, for achieving well-being and so feel less well off.

Let us now consider the situation of an old daughter-in-law. With age, the birth of children, and the entry of younger daughter-in-laws, a woman progressively attains a status that is referred to as old daughter-in-law—*purna bou*. *Purna* is an interesting word because it also connotes completeness and, in a sense, it is when a woman matures, becomes a mother, and becomes senior to others like herself that she finally becomes the complete daughter-in-law. While maturing and seniority happen on their own, women actively complete themselves as daughters-in-law by giving birth to children. By providing new members for the families they have married into, they are entrenching themselves within the household, embedding themselves in the families, and laying claim to being heard in family debates and discussions.

In reading the daily routines of these women, it is possible to detect a gradual relaxation in some of the restrictions women experience as new daughters-in-law. The insistence by their seniors that they do a substantial part of the cooking declines. The restrictions on movement, on meeting people who do not belong to the family, become fewer. Even the emphasis on the performance of explicit rituals of deference grows steadily weaker.

Thus, Dukhi, a 40-year-old *purna bou,* makes very clear her promotion out of the kitchen. When asked if she helps her husband's younger brother's wife *(sana ja)* in the cooking, she says, referring to herself as a *sasu* (husband's mother), "No, no. I don't have anything to do with the cooking. The *sana ja,* she does all that. We *sasus* don't even enter the kitchen. She will do all the work, won't she? She does the cooking, doesn't she? Why should I do all that? I don't cut the vegetables, I don't grind the *masala.* I don't touch the cooking utensils."

And Pranati, a 33-year-old *purna bou,* says, "If people drop in, then it is my responsibility to serve tea to them, snacks, talk pleasantly to them, till whoever they have come to see is ready to meet them."

Most old daughters-in-law do not strictly observe the rituals of deference toward the mother-in-law. Most *purna bous* explain it as merely a result of increased familiarity with one's mother-in-law, a consequence of the passage of time and a function of the number of years they have lived within their husbands' families. An alternative, perhaps more plausible, interpretation would appear to be that such rituals are no longer needed: *purna bous* have completed their reconstructions into fully acknowledged members of their husbands' patrilineages. Indeed, nonperformance of such rituals figures as a factor playing into their sense of well-being by underscoring their sense of finally belonging to their husbands' families. As *purna bous,* it is not a question of being prevented from performing such rituals (as new daughters-in-law sometimes are) but rather that such rituals are no longer needed, having served their purpose of completing the reconstruction of the newlywed into a real daughter-in-law.

With the passage of time and the birth of children, old daughters-in-law merge with their husbands' lineages. Although they are still some time away from being the senior-most woman of the household, they see themselves as well on the way to it. They have begun to take advantage of the privileges that that position is likely to bring with it, privileges that include commanding those subordinate and junior to themselves. A concomitant of this improved position within the family is greater well-being: on the average, a *purna bou* states that she has thirteen *annas* of well-being.

Let us now consider the situation of a mother-in-law. For the average Oriya Hindu woman, her position reaches its apogee when her sons marry and a new generation of daughters-in-law enter the family.[8] A reading of the following daily routine brings home the shifts that occur in duties and privileges when a woman becomes a mother-in-law. Priyambada, a 62-year-old mother-in-law who lives with her own mother-in-law, her husband, four sons, two daughters, daughter-in-law, and two grandsons, describes her day in the following manner:

> Getting up in the morning. We get up at 3:30 or 4:00 in the morning. As soon as we get up we wash our faces and then we bow our heads to god. We then clean our teeth, go and defecate. After defecating, we may do some polluting work. And then we go for our baths. While we are returning from our baths, we pluck a few flowers for god. After we return, we pray to god, we light a lamp, *agarbatti* [incense sticks], offer flowers, repeat a few *slokas* [verses] and after that we have some tea to drink. After tea, I arrange the *thali* [tray] that I will be taking to the temple later on. Once I have finished arranging, I turn my attention to cutting vegetables or grinding *masala*—I have to do all that. It varies from day to day. Once that is done, I have to go to the temple. Once I have gone around the temple and returned, I have to see who has come, who has eaten,

who has gone out, who is in the house, and then again, I
have the job of arranging the flowers and other things for
god. And then, I may sit down, go from this room to that,
look out of the front of the house, whatever needs to be
done in the house—that has to be settled, this has to be
cleaned and washed. And then comes the business of serving food and seeing people eat. All the business of running a house.

And then the children return home from tuition and
it's time to see to their eating, their studies—this would be
about three in the afternoon. Sometimes it may be a little
later but my work of arranging things for the temple goes
on. I make the wicks for the temple lamps, I make gar-
lands with flowers for the deity. I gather together whatever
will be necessary for tomorrow, and then I move around
the house, from here to there and then we have tea. I join
in the cutting of vegetables for the evening meal. After tea,
I offer *sandhya* [evening worship]. Once I've given *sandhya*,
I go and lie down. I cover myself and lie down right here. I
only get up at about 9:30 or 10 at night. I eat food then
and go to bed soon after. Nowadays, because it's cold, I
cover myself and lie down, but even in summer, I lie down
and close my eyes. After all, the food won't be ready till 10
o'clock—so what is there to do but lie down and close
one's eyes?

Q. As you were saying, before you go to the temple in the
   morning, you bow your head to god?
A. As soon as we get up, early in the morning, as soon as
   we have washed our faces with water, we turn to the
   one or two photos we have of god and we bow our

heads three times. Then we clean our teeth, after that
we defecate. After defecating, before going for our
baths we may clean out the house, throw out the gar-
bage, do all that kind of polluting work and then we
go for our baths. On the way back from Bindusagar,[9]
we pick a few flowers and, after returning home, there
are again prayers in the *puja* room upstairs. After doing *puja*, I water the plants that we grow and then I
come down for tea.

Clearly, this daily routine's emphasis is quite different from that
of the earlier ones. Priyambada is freed from the strenuous work of
cooking and feeding a large family; in fact, she does more than
most mothers-in-law. When she says, "I turn my attention to cutting vegetables or grinding *masala*. I have to do that," she is subtly
directing our attention to what she sees as her daughter-in-law's in-
competence, her inability to manage the kitchen independently.
Furthermore, her work now is more of a supervisory nature, of ensuring that her little community runs efficiently. She has considerable geographical mobility: she goes alone for her daily bath to the
temple pond, she worships everyday at the Lingaraj temple, she ad-
mits that, during the day, she looks out of the front of the house,
watching the world going by—all activities that are strictly forbidden a new daughter-in-law and often limited even for an old daughter-in-law.

Most important, however, is her regular communication with
god and her uninterrupted association with offerings meant for divinity. This privilege of approaching divinity without reservation is
a direct consequence of her ability to maintain her physical body's
purity, an ability that is relatively recent for her and the direct result of two factors.

First, among Oriya Hindus of Old Town, when a son marries and brings his wife into the family, his parents usually cease being sexually active. The job of reproduction has been passed on to the son and his wife. Many Oriya adults are disgusted or feel desanctified by the idea of two generations copulating under the same roof. Priyambada is no exception to this custom and she believes that this cessation of sexual activity makes it easier for her to maintain bodily purity.

Second, she is past menopause, and so there is no time of the month when she is *mara,* polluted or impure. Both of these reasons make it appropriate that as the mother-in-law she is the intermediary between the family and god, a position that she enjoys considerably and that is the source of a substantial sense of well-being; the average score for mothers-in-law among our survey is twelve *annas* of well-being. In fact, there are three married mothers-in-law in the sample who say that they have fully sixteen *annas* of well-being.

Let us now consider the situation of a widow. It is as a married mother-in-law that an Oriya Hindu woman's position is least assailable. Yet with old age and widowhood there is usually a sharp reversal in a woman's situation. As an old widow, a woman is often relegated to the background, expected to contribute nothing to the family and expecting to get little in return.

Sociologically speaking, a widow in Old Town is a nonperson. During the funeral rites for her husband, there are several rituals that emphasize this erasure of her social existence and that mark her entrance into the status of a perpetual mourner whose preoccupations ought to be both transcendent and otherworldly. This erasure of social standing is symbolized by her lack of a family name: as a widow, a woman can no longer use her husband's family name and is known only by her given name (the one given at marriage, not birth) and the title *bewa,* a local contraction of *vidhwa* or widow.

Harsamani, age 78, has been a widow for thirty-six years, and her poignant story of an ordinary day's activities typifies this particular experience of widowhood among Oriya Hindu women of Old Town:

> I get up at three in the morning. I put some water for heating and then I go and defecate. After that I bathe. People would be still sleeping—it would be dark, some people may be awake but others would be sleeping. After bathing, I get back into bed. I cover myself up and go to sleep. I get up only when the tea comes. With tea, there would be something to eat—whatever they had made, maybe some *upma* [dish of farina] or whatever—they will call me and I get up. But I eat lying in bed—do you understand? Sometimes I sit and eat but sometimes I lie and eat. These days the weather is cold and so I wrap myself and go and sit in the doorway. By about ten or eleven, they would have finished cooking and they come and call me. My daughter would have come, she goes to the kitchen and serves for me and herself and the two of us eat together. We eat here in this room. After eating, we go and wash our hands and then we come back to this room. If daughter is not there, they serve me and bring the food here. On days when I'm not feeling well, I get back into bed after eating, I eat *paan* [betel leaf] and I lie down once more. But on days when my mind is active, I sit in the doorway and chew *paan*. I see you going by sometimes, sometimes I see an aunt going by, sometimes a mother, sometimes a grandmother, and they will say, "You're sitting here?" After sitting for some time, when I again feel cold, I get back into bed, I cover myself and lie down. Then again tea and snacks will come and I will eat,

again my middle daughter will be here and we have tea and snacks together. And then dusk falls, once dusk falls, there is no work whatsoever. You understand? Daughter will put the mosquito net over my bed and once again I lie down all covered up. In the middle of all this the evening meal arrives. At night, whatever comes, if I feel like it, I eat it. I eat a little of it and then I lie down. *Parathas* [fried breads], milk, curry, fried vegetables, whatever they have made, that is what is served. After eating, then again I make myself some *paan*, I eat one and keep one under the pillow. I lie down. I have no work to do, neither night nor day. At no time during the day do I have any work. I have nothing to do. When I get up in the morning, again I put water for heating, I shit, clean my teeth, I bathe. This is the month of *Magha* (January/February), all the women get up early, bathe, go to the temple, they do what they want to after bathing, I go back to bed. The *nathani-bou* [grandson's wife], she comes and calls me, "Ma, you've fallen asleep, get up, get up, here's your tea and breakfast." Again the tea and something to eat—some days it's *suji* [cream of wheat], some days it's *parathas*.

Q. When do you pray?

A. There's no more praying for me. Why? Do you want to know why? Our gods are kept upstairs. By the time I walk up those stairs, my strength disappears. God is taken care of nowadays by the *bous* (sons' wives). Now that they do all that, what is left for me to do? On days when I have the strength I pour a little water on the *tulasi* [basil leaf] at the back but otherwise all I do is put a few drops of *nirmaliya* in my mouth.[10] Everyday, everyday, I put a few drops of *nirmaliya* in my mouth and then I lie down. Then the same things happen every day—over and over again, the same things.

Q. How often do you go to the temple?

A. I can't go to the temple. It is now two years since I went to the temple. My strength is declining, my body trembles, I may fall down somewhere, and then people will say, *Hou, hou,* people will criticize me for that.

Harsamani appears to have been effectively marginalized by age and widowhood. She is forbidden to provide sustenance to the family, for she is not allowed to cook for and feed others. She is forbidden to provide spiritual sustenance, for she is not allowed to intercede with divinity to ensure the health and prosperity of family members.

The "Auspicious Heart of the Family"

In one of the interviews about roles and responsibilities across the life cycle, an articulate Oriya woman described a mature, married woman as the "auspicious heart of the family" *(parivararo mangaliko antahkarano)*. That particular description seems apt as one reads and rereads these accounts by Oriya women of their daily round of activities and their feelings of well-being. As the interviews demonstrate, a new daughter-in-law gradually becomes an old daughter-in-law, and her access to and enjoyment of greater well-being occurs almost imperceptibly as she attains the domestic managerial responsibilities associated with *prauda* [mature adulthood]. A period in which she has many juniors and still commands all sustenance in a household, *prauda* is a peak period in the lives of each of these women.

For a daughter-in-law to grow old (and well), she has to move out of the kitchen. This move out of the kitchen need not be complete or even substantial, but the possibility that she could move out if she wanted to has to exist. However, her ties to the kitchen continue to be strong enough to make her the primary server of food—a responsibility steeped in prestige that emphasizes the central nature of her role within the family. Through ensuring that each member of the family gets his or her fair share of food, she sustains, very concretely, the life and health of the family. If someone should come to the house for social or business reasons and if the men of the family are otherwise busy, she entertains them. She represents the family, underscoring once more her importance. She performs less and less frequently the rituals of deference, indicating her full assimilation into the family. Finally, she begins to represent the family in its relations with divinity: one of the first tasks of any ritual significance that an old daughter-in-law does is to offer *sandhya*, a ceremony performed at sunset that seeks to keep malevolent spirits at bay while inviting Lakshmi, the goddess of wealth and auspiciousness, into the home.

Of course, other factors, physiological and cultural, limit this involvement in household worship: usually, an old daughter-in-law is young enough to menstruate. She is sexually active and she is still involved in the care of her children, feeding and cleaning them. All these factors make it difficult for her to maintain bodily purity and compromise her ability to approach the divine. It is as a married mother-in-law that these factors begin to lose their salience.

With daughters-in-law entering the household, the business of reproduction is passed on to the younger generation. The older couple withdraw from sexual activity, enabling the mother-in-law to maintain bodily purity more easily. This is also the time when one is no longer involved in taking care of the very old or the very young. One's own children are past needing such care. One's own mother-in-law and father-in-law are either dead or their care has been handed over to the newest daughter-in-law. At this time of life, most Oriya women go through menopause, which eliminates impurity caused by menstruation. Finally, for a postmenopausal Oriya Hindu woman, it is both culturally and physiologically appropriate to go to the temple whenever she wishes, to pray whenever she wishes, to perform the daily *puja* for her family without hindrance, and to function as the intermediary who seeks divine blessings for every member of the family.

Apart from this, an older married woman is also relieved of the physical labor of cooking and cleaning for a large family. While she still retains the responsibilities and privileges associated with *prauda,* she continues to administer the affairs of the household and remains aware of everything that happens to family members. The possibility of geographical mobility, of traveling, of going on pilgrimages, and of visiting relatives also contributes in some measure to her heightened sense of well-being. As a mother-in-law, explicit deference is paid to her by the junior women of the household. While this explicit display of social power must surely increase her sense of well-being, it also provides her with a forum in which to express her opinions. By refusing to accept a daughter-in-law's deference, she conveys unmistakably her feelings of displeasure and disapproval without saying a word. A mother-in-law, therefore, has greater opportunity to express negative feelings about other family members, and this perhaps does make her feel better. Unlike the other women in the family, she does not have to control what she says or does for the sake of family harmony.

There are of course anxieties that may work to reduce a mother-in-law's feelings of well-being. First, there is the prospect of widowhood and all the connotations that Oriya Hindus attach to that condition. Second, there is the process of growing old and losing the ability to care for oneself physically. While the junior wife has to shake off the constraints that are attached to being new to gain in well-being, the mother-in-law loses some of her wellness because she is looking to an uncertain future.

A Culturally Salient Model of Well-Being

In general, women expect the middle phase of their lives, that of mature adulthood, *prauda,* to afford them the most satisfying experiences. According to their accounts, during this phase, they are either the senior-most woman in the household or the next-to-most senior. As such, a woman is dominant—she has control over her own body and her actions, but more important, she has considerable control over the activities of others within the family. She is also very productive during this phase—she is likely to feel and to be felt central to the order and material prosperity of the family. Finally, she feels coherent—her connections and communication with divinity are now regular and uninterrupted. Dominance coming from seniority, productivity emerging from centrality within the family, and coherence resulting from the capacity to approach divinity without restriction are thus three salient measures of well-being for an Oriya Hindu woman. All imply controlling and managing the transactions and exchanges she has with those above, around, and below her, within the household, between the household, and beyond.

There is another, subsidiary aspect of women's well-being that needs to be mentioned here—the skill and competence with which a woman manages and controls these processes and transactions. In Bhubaneswar, as Lamb (1993) reports for Bengali women, the processes of reconstruction and deconstruction that women undergo as they marry, give birth, undergo affinal assimilation, mature, age, and become widows, require them to skillfully manage change if they are to achieve well-being. Those women who are less competent at managing these processes experience low well-being even during the middle phase of their lives, while those who know when and how to expand and encompass others and when to curtail their transactions, withdraw into themselves, or minimize their exchanges are more likely to achieve higher levels of well-being during all phases of their lives.

Furthermore, we suggest that these three measures (dominance, productivity, and coherence) of well-being are not competing but complementary. Having control over one's own activities and the activities of others makes one central to the family's well-being and enables one to control one's interactions with divinity and to approach the gods in a coherent, ordered way. When a woman achieves all three, usually during the middle phase of mature adulthood, her well-being is complete.

VARIATIONS AROUND THE IDEAL MODEL

What we have described is, of course, an ideal model extracted from our interviews. However, even thirty-seven interviews are enough to make the point that this ideal rarely fits perfectly with anyone's lived experience. There are women in other family roles who claim to have achieved substantial well-being as well as some married mothers-in-law and old daughters-in-law who claim to be miserable. For instance, Priyambada, a married mother-in-law, says that she does not even have two *annas* of well-being. She ascribes her lack of well-being to the conflicts within the family, which she believes result from the lack of respect that younger members display toward their elders:

> Everyone thinks he is the superior of the other, everyone
> thinks he is the family elder, everyone thinks he has to
> speak out, that he has to say what his opinion is. . . .
> I'm not preventing others from talking, I'm only saying,
> "Think of everything, the person who is talking and the
> consequences of your talking back before you answer."

In a community in which asymmetry of privilege and responsibility has such salience, lack of respect leads to diminishment of well-being. Priyambada might also have used the interview to inform others in the family of her displeasure with what she perceived as discord within the family. Her daughter-in-law definitely interpreted her statements to indicate just that. This daughter-in-law believed that her own conduct was the focus of the mother-in-law's criticism. The daughter-in-law's attribution seems plausible. At the time of the interview, it appeared possible that Priyambada was using her low assessment of her own well-being as a means to arouse the younger woman's guilt at being an "unsatisfactory" daughter-in-law.

And the reverse, too, occurs. There are widowed mothers-in-law who continue to be valued and respected members of the family. There are sonless (Kondos, 1989, 185) mothers who become the mainstay of their husband's families. There are new daughters-in-law who dominate household affairs almost as soon as they step across the threshold. Even in this small sample, such examples can be found, demonstrating, we think, quite conclusively that one must be suspicious of simplistic feminist representations (see, for example, Kondos, 1988: 108). Kondos claims that Hindu women lead such contingent lives that only those who produce sons and who predecease their husbands are deemed successful. The following excerpt, from an interview with a 72-year-old widow, Labanya, whose husband died almost forty years earlier, holds particular relevance here. She describes her day:

> I get up in the morning. I clean my teeth, I have tea. After having had tea, it's necessary to make sure that the children have gone to school and I go and do that. And then, maybe someone comes over, like you have come over, and I sit and talk. I have become the elder *(murabbi)* in the family, when people come over, I have to sit and talk to them, we discuss things. They may have tea, I may have some more tea. And then, I go for my bath. After my bath, the cooking would be almost finished, and so I eat. After eating, I take some rest, I lie down. I rest till afternoon. At about four, I get up and again, if people come over, I sit and talk to them. I talk to them till the sun sets. After the sun sets, once more tea is made, I drink some tea and then ... [Long pause] I have no work. So right here, I take some rest. While I'm resting, the children will come, the *bous* will come and they will say, "Ma, come, eat your rice," and so, I go and eat. And then, I go to bed—what else is there to my day? ...

Q. Do you do *pujas* to God?

A. [Long pause, then finally, hesitantly] Yes, yes ... This elder *bou,* she does all that. I have become an old woman. I can't have a bath that early in the morning. They all have their baths early and then they pray to God. Eldest son, he bathes, he is the *kalasi* [medium through whom the goddess speaks] at the *Thakurani mandir.* He goes there. ...

Q. Do you offer *sandhya* in the evening?

A. No. I don't offer any sandhya. I don't have that responsibility anymore. That is a responsibility that the *bous* have and that they fulfill. I no longer touch the cooking vessels, they do and so they offer *sandhya*. This *bou* offers *sandhya* or if this one can't, then the other or the other or one of the granddaughters, they offer *sandhya*. That is a burden that has slipped from my head.

Q. Do you tell them what to cook?

A. No. no. I don't bother my head with all that. When they first came to this house then I had to teach them everything. "*Arre, ma,* do this like this, do that like that," I used to tell them. "This food won't be enough" or "That is too much," but now I have grown old and they have all raised their families. What is there for me to teach them now? Now that I am old, I eat a fistful of rice that they give me and I sit. What else is left for me in life? Why should I continue to keep all that in my head?

Q. When did you give up giving directions?

A. It is now thirty years since I left all that. Once this eldest *bou* came into the house, a few years after that, I stopped running the house. A few years after eldest *bou* came, another *bou* came into the house, and a few years later, another *bou* came. In this way, three *bous* came. They gave birth to children, and they managed running the house. Why should I try to keep the nuisance and trouble of running the household on my head? All that I do nowadays is soothe my grandchildren when they cry, carry them on my hip when they're small, clean them when they're dirty, see that they go to school regularly. Or when someone wants

advice or when someone wants to give or take money,
I do that—that's my business now. . . .
He [eldest son] keeps nothing. He comes and gives me
everything. I keep all the money, when he needs
money, he asks me. He needs 5,000 rupees or 6,000
rupees to pay the laborers who are repairing this house,
he comes to me, I give him the money. Vegetables have
to be bought, I give the grandsons the money to buy
the vegetables. I keep all the money. When I go away
to Unit VI to be with my middle son, then I leave
some money with eldest *bou* for household expenses
but the rest of the money is still with me and he [el-
dest son] will come to Unit VI when he needs money.

One can see that Labanya is barely involved in the day-to-day activities of the household and has little contact with divinity. But
even a casual reading of her daily activities makes clear how she
continues to be the center of her family. She holds the family purse
strings. Her sons choose to give her all their earnings. No expense is
incurred without her knowledge. More importantly, according to
her account, her sons and her daughters-in-law make it explicit
that they care for her: they are concerned that she relish what she
eats, that her clothes are decent. They desire her comfort.

And then there is Pranati, an old daughter-in-law, mother of
three daughters, who recognizes that she has disappointed her
mother-in-law and father-in-law by not providing sons for the
kutumba (lineage). This affects her sense of well-being, her score of
eight *annas* being the lowest among all the old daughters-in-law.
While this score may reflect her sorrow at not having had sons, that
inadequacy clearly does not cramp her style when it comes to running the household. She is not relegated to some corner of the

house, ignored and despised because she is sonless; instead, as one reads her interview as well as those of her mother-in-law and her younger sister-in-law, it becomes quite clear that the entire household depends on her for its efficient functioning. She decides what will be cooked. She shops for the entire family, selecting the clothes the others will wear. She entertains guests and relatives when they visit. She plays the lead role when it comes to arranging her husband's younger brother's wedding. Sonlessness, though a matter for personal sorrow, does not determine her position within the family; in fact, it does not even define her as inauspicious. For these women, success and failure are not predefined. Being a widow or sonless are constraining circumstances, but they do not absolutely define success or failure.

Labanya's and Pranati's lives provide examples of ways in which "culture and psyche make each other up" (Shweder, 1991: 73). Cultural meanings and possibilities are picked up by these women, each according to her particular talents; they then create their own life situations. Labanya is not just a widow; she is also the loving mother who single-handedly raised her three sons to adulthood. As such she is entitled to their respect and devotion, an entitlement that she appropriates in full measure. Pranati is not merely a sonless mother. She is also the dutiful daughter-in-law who has never stinted in her performance of *sewa*. As such, she has extended her influence through the family, making her its single most important member. According to Kondos's formulation, these women would be "failures," and yet, by all accounts, they participate fully in running their households and raising their children. More importantly, they feel good about themselves.

SUBVERSION OR RESISTANCE IN OLD TOWN?

On the basis of our experience in Old Town, we suspect that the representation of the Hindu housewife as a rebel or subversive is largely a projection of critical ethnography grasping at straws. Quite baldly stated, almost nothing we have encountered in our interviews and observations implies a deep political critique of family or social life or the desirability of subverting the social system. There is an absence of subversive voices in Old Town. While complaint could, perhaps, be regarded as a language of "subversion" and the dragging of feet while performing household chores as acts of "resistance," only old daughters-in-law and mothers-in-law do so. New daughters-in-law who have the most to gain from subverting the system do not complain and rarely drag their feet. It is true that they are trained to suppress their words, to anticipate negative consequences from expressing themselves. It is also true that their positions within the family are fragile, and that they have yet to accumulate power or exercise substantial influence. Only an old daughter-in-law or a mother-in-law, secure in her position within the family, could engage in such verbal and nonverbal displays of discontent with impunity.

We believe, however, that neither complaint nor feet dragging can be credibly viewed as subversion or resistance. In Old Town they are just the ways in which confident women express their dissatisfaction or displeasure with what is happening within the family—they do not indicate a desire for radical change.

Ultimately extended families do break up. Each brother lives separately with just his own wife and children. This is the nuclear beginning for a fresh cycle of joint family living. A catalyst is usually needed to set this breakup into motion. Often this is the death of the father or of both father and mother. Yet joint family living remains the ideal. Daughters-in-law, both new and old, continue to live jointly because they are realistic and pragmatic about the options open to them. They make the best of whatever resources they have, realizing that they often gain thereby. Apart from the advantages that these women themselves mention when explaining why they continue to live within the joint family—those of greater economic, social, and personal security and the sharing of household chores and child rearing—an important reason lies in the fact that there is room for maneuvering, for achievement, and for working toward personal goals such as increased power within the family, a greater say in the process of family decision-making, a sense of getting newly recruited women and their children to do what one wants them to do, and the possibility of ensuring the future success of one's children.

What is remarkable and worth noting is not the insurgency of these women but rather their attitude of active acceptance. Sudhangini, a daughter who was to be married just six weeks after the interview, in talking of her future life in her mother-in-law's home, says:

> In truth, however affectionate the new family, I will feel sad for some time remembering this home but then as one day passes and then another and then another, the sense that this is mine will begin even with respect to the other home and the people there. . . . One has to accept everything as one's own. *Nona-bou* [father-mother] haven't given us our *karma,* they have given us only *janma* [birth]. They have given me birth, and they have also given me *sikhya* [learning], they have given me *jogyata* [competence], that is my good fortune. Now with that, if I decide to do good work in their house, then it will arouse their appreciation, but if I don't do good work, they will criticize me and that I will have to endure. But it is all in my own hands—my *karma* is in my hands. If I want to do good and gain appreciation, it is in my hands.

Most people in the Old Town hold to this future-oriented notion as a major aspect of the karmic process. This sense of having control over what happens in one's life, of being responsible for one's own destiny, this belief that "human intentions really do matter" (Babb, 1983: 180) runs through several of the other interviews, though perhaps no other woman articulated the idea so fluently. All these women—daughters, daughters-in-law, and mothers-in-law—recognize the givens in each of their situations. They recognize the factors that they cannot change. But they also realize that it is possible to work within an emerging situation for success. In fact, these women see such compromise and accommodation as admirable signs of maturity.

Furthermore, these women share with other Oriya Hindus a particular way of looking at life. They look on family life as a process, one that is continuously shifting and changing, never complete or static. And so, when they marry and enter a household, they do not see themselves as new daughters-in-law for the rest of their lives. They can see in front of them women at different stages in the life course. They see themselves as occupying those positions in the not-too-distant future. To understand their motivations and actions, one has to assume their future-oriented, developmental perspective. They do not see themselves as victims. They are looking ahead into the future, perhaps ten or fifteen years, seeing themselves contributing to and controlling family decisions. Even the very old do not lack this future orientation. Indeed, most people in Old Town see death as merely a punctuation mark in the process of living numerous lives, and they are clearly busy at work preparing the way for the life they expect to come next.

OPPRESSORS AND VICTIMS?

Among Oriya Hindus in the temple town of Bhubaneswar, men and women recognize members of the other sex as social actors, equal in importance and effectiveness, whose activities complement their own. To cast men as oppressors and women as victims is to try to establish a false dichotomy, one that does not exist within the Oriya point of view. If one wants to organize Oriya social life in terms of those in control and those controlled, then it makes much more sense to discuss the matter generationally, with the older generation controlling the activities of the younger generation. But even here one needs to temper this statement because age is not valued in and of itself. Only those older people who care for and are responsible for the welfare of others are respected and their opinions valued.

Furthermore, as anyone familiar with life and society in Hindu India knows, men (especially younger men) as well as women live with major constraints. Most Oriya men and women, just like most Hindu men and women in other parts of the subcontinent, do not decide entirely for themselves what Westerners would regard as the two most crucial decisions of a person's life: their professions and their marriages. This is not to say that there is no difference between men's and women's lives, for, most significantly, men can move and interact with others quite freely.

Whether women regard this freedom as an unmitigated advantage is doubtful. Many women pitied Usha Menon's interviewer's predicament, one that necessitated "wandering from door to door looking for people to talk to." One widow, in responding to whether she planned to send her 17-year-old daughter to college, said good-humoredly, "Why? So that she will become like you, going from door to door talking to people?"

SAKTI: WHAT IT MEANS TO BE A WOMAN IN THE OLD TOWN

Even today, most Oriya Hindus believe that female power *(sakti)* energizes the natural and social world. In ordinary, everyday conversations, women in Old Town describe a woman as the embodiment of *adya sakti* (primordial power), *matru sakti* (mother power), and *sri sakti* (woman power). According to these women, such *sakti* is harnessed for the good of society and the family. It is power reined in, power that is controlled from within, power that is exercised responsibly. A woman is said to hold the destiny of her husband's family in the palm of her hands. If she is irresponsible in her management of the family's resources, the household does not prosper. If she commits adultery, the family disintegrates.[11] These women say that a woman maintains her chastity not because she lives in a joint family and others exercise a watchful eye over what she does, but because she disciplines herself. This is a remarkable assertion, quite unlike what Derne (1993) found among Hindu men in Varanasi, who relied on family structure and external forces to control their behavior. For Oriya Hindu women, to be truly effective, control has to come from within; only this effort ensures the spiritual and material prosperity of the family.

It is relevant to mention here some of the understandings that Old Town residents have about a popular icon of the goddess Kali in which she is shown with her foot placed squarely on the chest of a supine Siva (for a detailed description of this study, see Menon and Shweder, 1994; also Chapter 3). Men and women describe the protruding tongue of the goddess as the mark of her "shame" (*lajya* or *lajja*) (more accurately translated as "respectful restraint") at having stepped on her husband, her personal god. Acknowledging her husband's social and ritual superiority enables her to become calm, to rein in her power to destroy. Many of those knowledgeable about this icon say that Siva does not do anything to stop her, because, in fact, he can do nothing to stop her (Kali is far too powerful). Rather, she chooses to recognize what she owes her husband in terms of respect and deference and so stops her destruction. According to the Oriya Hindus of Old Town, her choice is an entirely autonomous act.

From the perspective of many Oriya Hindus, Ortner's formulation (1974) nature:culture::woman:man (nature is to culture as woman is to man) seems unnatural. For them, a woman derives her strength and power from her closeness to nature. She, like nature, creates and reproduces, but such power gathers its full significance only because it is subject to cultural, ultimately moral, control that originates from within her. As Ramanujan points out, the Levi-Straussian opposition between nature and culture is itself culture bound. In the Hindu alternative, "culture is enclosed in nature, nature is reworked in culture, so that we cannot tell the difference" (Ramanujan, 1990: 50). This is yet another of the "container-contained relations" (ibid. 50) that extend to other Hindu concepts and ideas.

So, Oriya Hindu women think of themselves as intrinsically powerful. Simply by being female, by sharing the gendered physiology of the great goddess of Hinduism, they believe they share her power to create and destroy. But they also recognize that unrestrained exercise of such power inevitably leads to destruction. Such power has to be curbed not by an external force but from within, through a voluntary, autonomous act of self-discipline. We believe that it is this self-discipline that those who perceive the world through Westernized lenses misinterpret as subordination.

Culturally Available Means to Power

Personal growth, then, for these women is not conceived to be some kind of process of self-realization that involves detaching themselves from others. Instead, it is a power that involves an increasing denseness in one's relations with others. It depends on one becoming a strong weaver of the fabric of the family.

An Oriya Hindu woman achieves this kind of personal growth in a variety of ways. Behavior that from a Western perspective is an index of subordination and passivity often becomes something quite different when seen from a Hindu perspective or understood in terms of local meanings. The Hindu notion of the body emphasizes (Kakar, 1982; Zimmerman, 1979) its relative openness to both improvement and contamination. Thus when a new daughter-in-law takes orders from her mother-in-law or eats her leftovers or massages her feet or drinks the water that has been used to wash the older woman's feet, these practices are not a measure of her subordination or passivity. Rather they are ways she takes into her body potent substances from a superior. Ultimately these internalized substances empower her. Progressively, with time, such behavior increases her influence and control within the family.

Again, *sewa,* or service to others, is a culturally significant way of achieving power. When a woman cooks, serves, and takes care of members of the joint family, she is building relationships in very concrete ways. Many women compared cooking and serving to acts of *bhakti* or devotion, requiring the same degree of concentration and attention to detail as that involved in worshiping God and leading to similar feelings of serenity and contentment.

Self-abnegation or self-denial is yet another culturally salient way of gaining moral authority. While from a Western perspective, self-abnegation can be interpreted as a kind of deprivation, that is not what it means to an Oriya Hindu woman. Fasting, eating last, and eating leftovers are seen as ways to garner moral authority. And when, after years of self-denial, a woman requests or decides or commands that something should be so, her husband and her adult sons cannot but accede to her, for no man in the family equals her in moral stature.

Conclusion: The Moral Discourse of Anthropology

Think of the Oriya Hindu woman's life as a movement in three dimensions: outward and upward with time being the third dimension. Her life moves outward because with time she is no longer restricted to the kitchen, and she can ultimately move freely within the house and sometimes go outside the house accompanied by only a child. Her life moves upward because with time it becomes socially and physiologically possible for her to approach divinity.

A new daughter-in-law is essentially locked into the kitchen, which is often referred to as the heart of the household, because it is the place where the ancestral spirits (*pitru loku*) reside and are fed. But with time and age, when she begins to play a greater role in making decisions within the family, she moves to other spaces within the house. She has access to the *puja* room and "higher" gods, the household deities (*ishta devata*). With old age and widowhood, this outward movement is completed, and old widows, who are now peripheral to household affairs, often live in an outer room that overlooks the street. On the other hand, the upward movement is temporarily halted, for although old widows continue to pray, they are relatively inauspicious members of the family who are no longer involved in family rituals. They are free to absolve themselves of their own accumulated spiritual debts for the sake of their own personal salvation but little more.

To represent women's lives in different social contexts and cultural worlds is a difficult and complex task. If anthropology as a discipline views itself as a means of understanding one's self and one's own culture by journeying through other selves in other cultures, it is important that anthropologists understand the complexity of the dialectic in which they are engaged. At the moment, the intellectual insights of feminist anthropology cannot be easily disentangled from the political agenda, for there is a transparent attempt in feminist literature to narrate a story of "emancipation," universalize the idea of women's oppression, and indulge in myth-making for political ends. If anthropology is a discipline that studies differences, it is necessary that feminists devise the means to analyze and interpret differences that they find personally disturbing without distorting and thus dishonoring the objects of their study (see Boon, 1994). To ignore the alternative moral goods emphasized and made manifest in family life practice in India, to presume that inner control, service, and deferred gratification amount to subordination and acceptance of oppression, to represent Hindu women in South Asia as either victims or subversives is not only to dishonor these women—it is to engage in little more than a late-twentieth-century version of cognitive and moral imperialism.

Culture and Mental Development in Our Poststructural Age

In this essay I discuss some of the major changes that have taken place over the past thirty years in how we view mental development. I take account of the current interest in cultural processes of child development by drawing a contrast between the once fashionable structural (primarily Piagetian) picture of mental development (which left rather little intellectual space for the study of cultural psychology) and various pictures of mental development from our current poststructural age (which make room for almost everything, including "culture").

Piaget's Grand Structural Picture of Mental Development

Thirty-six years ago, in 1966, when I entered graduate school in the Department of Social Relations at Harvard University, the mind and spirit of Jean Piaget was a vibrant presence in William James Hall and his "structural" stage theory of cognitive development was the rage in most leading centers of developmental psychology in the United States (see Piaget, 1954, 1967, 1970). Here is the version of

Piaget's theory that was current and quickly passed on to students in those days.

For one thing, Piaget studied *cognitive* development. Although the relevant contrast set was often left a bit vague (cognition versus what? Behavior? Conation? Emotion? Non-representational thought?), our teachers made clear that Piaget's study of cognitive development meant at least these two things: 1) he studied the mind of the child the way one might study the mind of an ideal scientist or a logician, and 2) from a Piagetian perspective, growth or development had something to do with endorsing true propositions.

The study of cognitive development was thereby differentiated from the study of development in noncognitive domains, such as emotional development or the development of moral character. In those noncognitive domains, we were told, development did not amount to endorsing true propositions but rather amounted to doing what is right or good (as in the case of having moral character) or amounted to experiencing appropriate feelings and desires in various kinds of social situations (as in the case of being emotionally competent or mature). Feeling, desire, and moral commitment were thus placed outside the territory of the cognitive domain, whereas scientific, logical and propositional reasoning were placed securely within the field of cognitive studies.

We learned that Piaget studied the development of scientific and logical capacities in the child by carefully observing children striving to figure out what causes what, striving for consistency among ideas, striving to build up or construct for themselves a set of principles (for example, the logic of inductive science and experimental reasoning, the idea of necessary truths) for regulating their own thought and for avoiding intellectual mistakes. Heroic images were presented to us of Piaget on a kind of researcher's Odyssey to the most unlikely of places in his quest for a grand, all-encompassing theory of mental development—images of Piaget playing marbles with children in the playground, of Piaget as the assiduous chronicler of the sucking behavior of infants in the nursery.

We were told that Piaget had traced the ontogenetic history of children's scientific and logical understandings through four self-constructed stages: the sensorimotor, preoperational, concrete operational, and formal operational stages. At each stage new mental structures were said to emerge: the idea of an object during the sensorimotor stage, the idea of reversibility and transitivity during the concrete operational stage. Thus, for example, a preoperational 4-year-old was supposed to lack the requisite mental structures for constructing the perspective of others, as evidenced by the following interview (reported by Peter Wason) with a 4-year-old: "Do you have a brother?" "Yes." "What's his name?" "Jim." "Does Jim have a brother?" "No."

In 1966, psychology in America had long since lost its institutional connection to philosophy. Perhaps that is why no one bothered to point out to us that the core ideas examined by Piaget (number, object, cause, space, time, morality) were more or less the same ideas identified by Immanuel Kant as synthetic *a priori* truths and as the necessary preconditions of empiricism. Without some *a priori* idea of number, object, cause, space, and time the very notion of "having an experience" (the supposed source of all knowledge for empiricists) makes no sense. Perhaps that is why no one bothered to boggle our minds and disrupt the Piagetian developmental story by asking, "how is it possible for a young infant to experience anything at all (including your experimental manipulation) if he or she does not already have at hand (or in its mouth) the ideas that Piaget says are not available until 18 months or 6 years of age or what have you?"

What we did learn was that, according to Piagetian theory, immature thinking was characterized by a cluster of correlated attributes. Immature thinking was supposed to be undifferentiated (versus differentiated), concrete (versus abstract), egocentric or subject-dependent (versus impersonal or objective), context-bound (versus context-free), inconsistent (versus consistent), incomplete (versus complete), intuitive (versus reflective), implicit (versus explicit), complexive, associative, or functional (versus taxonomic), percept-driven (versus concept-driven), animistic (versus causal), temporal (versus logical), affective in tone, and concrete in its imagery. Young children were said to be unaware of any perspective but their own. They were said to be unable to distinguish a word or name from its referent, unable to know the difference between objectivity and subjectivity.

Moreover a kind of master developmental narrative was built, in which the French Enlightenment's opposition between religion-superstition-irrationality versus logic-science-rationality was used to tell a story—indeed, the very same story—about the differences between children and adults, between primitive peoples and civilized peoples, and between premodern peoples in the West (for example, people in the "dark ages") and modern peoples in the West (peoples who benefited from the French "enlightenment").

The basic theme of the narrative, which was sometimes explicit and sometimes covert, went like this: In contrast to mature thinkers or the "enlightened" elite (we presumed that meant us), all those "others" (children, contemporary primitive peoples, and historical peoples from the premodern period in the West) are relatively confused or undifferentiated about a lot of things. They are confused about the relationship of language to reality (for example, they believe in "word magic" or the idea that symbols are part of the reality they describe). They are confused about the relationship of the moral order to the natural world (for example, they believe in "immanent justice" or the idea that suffering is punishment for your sins). They are confused about the relationship of the social order to the natural world (for example, they tend to think that their duties, obligations, and social roles are objective emanations or have been handed down by God). And so forth.

Pictures of Mental Development from out of Our Poststructural Age

I think that any American psychologist who is unfeigned in his or her assessment of the recent history of child development studies must admit that interest in the Piagetian picture of mental development had largely waned by the early 1980s and that today, at least among developmental psychologists in the United States, Piaget's research agenda is now more or less moribund. It is not even clear that his spirit lives on, although knowledge of some standardized and watered-down version of his stage theory may still be required to pass a licensing exam in child psychiatry in some states or an introductory psychology test at some university.

Today, rightly or wrongly, at most leading centers of cognitive developmental psychology in the United States, students are told a different story from the poststructural age. Perhaps it is the master narrative of an age that is suspicious of all master narratives and totalizing world views and does not worry quite so much as did Piaget about the role of self-monitoring, rational justification, and contradiction in fostering conceptual (and behavioral) change. Piaget was a modernist and we live in a postmodern age.

The current poststructural story has many themes and no one has integrated them into a single plot (which may be part of the point of the story), but some of the themes go something like this:

1. The mind is not a structured whole. If we examine the cognitive functioning of individuals across a series of tasks, we discover that no single operational level is a generalized property of an individual's thought. Thus, as the poststructural story goes, Piaget exaggerated the stage-like character of cognitive growth.

2. The mind should not be conceptualized as a central processing unit organized by means of abstract operational structures. The mind is decentralized, modular, and concrete. What you think about is decisive for how you think. Thus, Piaget misjudged the role of "mere content" and domain-specific knowledge in reasoning, judgment, and memory.

3. The mind of the child is differentiated and complex from the start. Kant's synthetic *a priori* truths (object permanence, number, time, space, causality) are hard-wired as innate ideas. The newly born already know a lot from the deep past. Thus, as the story goes (and here arguably the story is more premodern than poststructural and how the various themes fit together remains to be seen), Piaget underestimated the intellectual sophistication and operational capacity of infants and young children. We come into the world old, not young.

4. There is no property of thought that can serve as a general index of intellectual immaturity. The various properties of thinking (concrete versus abstract, intuitive versus reflective, functional versus taxonomic, context-bound

versus context-free, temporal versus logical, emotion-laden versus affect-free, and so on) that were supposed to serve of indicators of mental development do not necessarily correlate with each other, and out of context they are not reliable measures of mental immaturity. There are advanced modes of thought in which performers are expert and sophisticated precisely because they are concrete, percept-driven, imagistic, context-bound, and emotion-laden. Thus, as the poststructural story goes, Piaget mythologized and totalized the unidirectional nature of progressive conceptual change.

According to the story told these days it is an open question whether the newly born come into the world with an overabundance of specific and contradictory propensities, some of which are selected for and others suppressed by cultural practices in the course of development (the "maintenance-loss" approach to socialization; Werker, 1989), whether the newly born come into the world (as Piaget believed) with only a few specific propensities (for example, a sucking reflex) that are then elaborated and generalized in the course of development, or whether the newly born come into the world with either a lot or a few highly general propensities (for example, to "categorize"—treat like cases alike and different cases differently) that are then specified and given character in the course of development.

I have contributed to this story. I like this story. I even believe in this story. There are themes in this story that I have narrated before in other publications. Nevertheless there is, I believe, at least one motif that has yet to receive sufficient attention in the poststructural literature: the tension between rationalism and pluralism in Piaget's account of mental development. In the remainder of this chapter, I suggest that any credible poststructural theory of mental development must find a way to marry rationalism and cultural pluralism, which is a match that Piaget was disinclined to make.

Is It Possible to Be a Developmentalist and a Cultural Pluralist at the Same Time?

Any credible poststructural story about mental development must engage and come to terms with Piaget's rationalistic conception of the process of mental development. As a rationalist who studied conceptual change, Piaget believed that what *deserved* to be called mature thinking (or correct mental functioning) could be characterized in terms of strictly objective ideals or standards (for example, the rules of logic, the abstract principle of justice). Piaget thus believed that what *deserved* to be called mature thinking was the same across cultures and history. He believed that when people disagree about what is true, there are principles, methods, or procedures that can reconcile their differences and produce agreement. Most developmentalists who take "culture" at all seriously have some difficulties with this aspect of Piaget's rationalism. So I am going to try to soften the idea of objective standards and rational justifiability. By doing so, I can highlight the relevance of a developmental perspective to cases in which the standards and ideals that guide development and define mature thinking are contingent, contestable, plural, culture-specific, and thus not universally binding.

The remainder of this commentary is thus about Piaget's rationalistic conception of the process of mental development, which I believe is separable from his monistic view of the mature product of that process. Piaget believed that the route to mature thinking (mental development) was 1) a temporal process (it took time to become a mature thinker); 2) a progressive process (over time, more mature understandings superseded less mature understandings); and 3) an active process (over time, more mature understandings superseded less mature understandings because individuals are self-reflective knowers who try to work out and see for themselves the rational justification for their own understandings). In praise of this aspect of Piaget's theory, I argue that his very Hegelian conception of the process of mental development is entirely right-minded and is so alien to the philosophical assumptions of both empirical psychology and poststructural thinking in the United States that it has largely been overlooked or misunderstood.

Before I offer some tokens of respect for aspects of Piaget's rationalism, however, I have two other confessions to make. My first is that I am an anthropologist. More specifically, I am an anthropological pluralist interested in different modes of thought and understanding among adults in different cultural traditions around the world. Over the years I have given special attention to Brahmanical Hindu traditions in India and secular liberal humanist traditions in the United States.

Anthropological pluralists are distrustful of applications of the Piagetian principle that what deserves to be called mature thinking (or correct mental functioning) is the same across cultures and history. They become especially suspicious when a developmental theory is proposed by the lights of which the thinking (or mental functioning) of full-grown adults in other cultures begins to look very much like the thinking of young children in our own.

For example, in his account of a Swiss child's idea of "immanent justice," Piaget makes it quite clear that he believes that there is a *universally binding* rational standard or ideal that defines mature thinking in this domain. In particular, this rational standard or ideal is attained by endorsing the proposition that "wickedness may go unpunished and virtue remain unrewarded." Because the belief in "immanent justice" consists of endorsing the alternative proposition that "justice is a law of nature according to which for every transgression there is some natural catastrophe that serves as its punishment," the endorsement of immanent justice is viewed as an immature or less developed mode of thought. Yet as every anthropologist knows, something very much like a belief in immanent justice can be found not only in the thinking of Swiss 5- and 6-year-olds. It can also be found in the thinking of several hundred million South Asian Hindu adults who believe in the idea of karma and among adults in many other cultures of the world. Are we to say that the beliefs of Hindu adults are immature or child-like? Are we to draw the opposite and equally invidious conclusion that Northern European children begin life as sophisticated Hindus and then fall into immaturity or regress as they age?

Anthropological pluralists are deeply suspicious of this kind of application of developmental theory, in which by means of some presumptively universalized standard for rational or mature thinking, adults in other cultures are analogized to children in our own, with the implication that they are intellectually immature. Margaret Mead (1932) long ago argued this point with Piaget over the issue of animistic thinking. She argued that among the Manus people of New Guinea, the adults rather than the children are the animists. In the cultural perspective of Manus adults, it is European adults who appear to be intellectually immature because they think like Manus children. She preferred to view both Swiss adults and Manus adults as intellectually mature, each in their own way. Her view was that certain kinds of applications of developmental standards (presumptively universalizing the standard) smack of ethnocentrism and give developmental theory a bad name.

One obvious implication of Mead's critique is that there are certain kinds of culture-specific standards or ideals for development that should not be applied or generalized to other populations. But it also seems to me that a second and less noted implication of her pluralistic view is that, within a particular interpretive community or cultural context, those very same ideals can serve perfectly well as developmental standards for children and adults trying to work through for themselves (self-construct) the rational basis of their own traditions. Presumably it would be a matter of some concern among the Manus if their children never intellectually matured and constructed for themselves a defensible and locally rational animistic interpretation of the causal forces of nature.

This discomfort among anthropological pluralists with certain types of applications of developmental theory arises with respect to many other areas of knowledge. For example, adult thinking in much of Hindu society about the status and meaning of dreams (they are not thought to be merely subjective), about the power of words to influence biological and physical nature (mantras, kirtans, and other verbal formulas are thought to be effective), and about the moral basis of hierarchy ("autonomy" is not privileged over "heteronomy") is reminiscent of early Piagetian accounts of the ideas and understandings of Western children. Indeed, I suspect that one reason Piaget himself moved from those earlier accounts (which were focused on children's understandings of dreams, words, and punishment) to the later stages of his research (where he focused on children's understanding of number, chance, and logical necessity) was to accommodate criticism.

In the process of constructing his own theory of the world, he found a way to hold on to the view that what deserves to be called mature thinking can be characterized in terms of strictly objective ideals and standards and is the same across cultures and history.

His way of doing this was to radically narrow the types of domains of knowledge (experimental reasoning—yes, dream understandings—no) to which his type of developmental analysis should be applied. In effect he adopted the premise common to all "structural" approaches: Human beings would all think the same way (reason the same way, make the same judgments) if it weren't for differences in the content of their thought. Looking back on his own early research informed by his subsequently constructed "structural" theory, I suspect Piaget must have viewed those early investigations of children's ideas about dreams, word meanings, and immanent justice as somewhat misguided studies of mere content. Mere content, he might have reasoned, is not proper grist for developmental structural analysis.

Piaget's Challenge to Anthropology

I must also confess that I have been a critic of Piaget (e.g., Shweder, 1982, 1984). I have gone so far as to suggest that research on mental development in children can be advanced by inverting his assumptions ("standing Piaget on his head") and by paying far more attention than did Piaget to assisted learning, to the discretionary or extralogical aspects of mental development, to the way content is part of the process of thought and thus what you think about is decisive for how you think, and to the socialization of cultural ideals for development.

Nevertheless there are two appealing features of Piaget's conception of mental development to which I want to draw attention. Piaget believed that "logic is the morality of thought just as morality is the logic of action." While this may be too narrow a view of the "morality of thought," Piaget's formulation makes it clear that 1) in his view the study of mental development is primarily a prescriptive rather than a merely descriptive discipline; 2) having good reasons and justifications for what you think and do is a driving engine of conceptual change; and 3) "logic" is not just another domain of knowledge or specialized module of mind.

I do not discuss point 3 in this context, except to note that it is quite fashionable these days to argue that "logic" is just one more specialized module of thought or domain of knowledge, like recognizing faces or speaking a natural language. The alternative view is that "logic" is an essential, even if incomplete, part of the rationality internal to any domain of knowledge. This view has credibility because it is hard to understand how the *justification* of reasoning and decision making in any domain of knowledge could proceed without the presence within that domain and every domain of something like a logic device.

Piaget's commitment to the study of mental development as a prescriptive science and to the process of self-justification as an engine of conceptual change are the features of his thinking that I believe are most worthy of praise. He recognized that the idea of human development implies much more than change over time, that it implies some desirable state of mental functioning the ultimate attainment of which is a mark of progress.

These aspects of Piaget's thinking are especially challenging for my own discipline of anthropology, which is well known for its emphasis on the existence of plurality or diversity in the descriptive norms of cultures around the world. Thus, for example, anthropologists will tell you that it is "normal" (in the descriptive sense) for Samburu girls and boys in Kenya to be circumcised during adolescence, that it is "normal" (in the descriptive sense) in India for widows not to be invited to a wedding ceremony because their presence is thought to be inauspicious, that it is "normal" (in the descriptive sense) for American midlife adults to put their own parents out to pasture in an old age home rather than care for them in their own household. Speaking as an anthropologist, if I were to describe for you "normal" medical cognition in rural India, I would start by pointing out that given the "normal" metaphysical belief system subscribed to by hundreds of millions of Hindus, when physical or mental suffering occurs the diagnostic situation is, from the native point of view, understandably quite complex. For one thing, there is not just one world to deal with but three: the society of the gods (who are a major presence in nearly every household and community), the society of the spirits, including the spirits of dead ancestors (who are also a major presence in almost every household and community), and the society of human beings. Moreover these three worlds all interact in a universe governed by the principles of *dharma* (objective obligations emanating from God) and the laws of *karma* (the idea that nature guarantees that in the long run for every action there is a just and proportionate reaction).

Notice, however, that these anthropological claims about the existence of plurality or diversity in the norms of different cultures amount to little more than the proposition that there is variety in what people around the world believe and desire. They do not come close to touching on the far more challenging issues raised by Piaget rationalism: Is there variety in what is believable, not just in what is believed? Is there plurality in what is desirable, not just in what is desired? Is it really possible for mental states that are pathological, irrational, or immature in one community to be healthy, rational, and mature in another?

Piaget's strict notions of objectivity and rational justifiability blocked him from seeing how the answer to these questions might be "yes." Ironically most poststructural pluralistic anthropologists who might intuitively believe that the answer to those questions is "yes" have yet to realize that issues of justification are at the heart of cultural analysis. They have yet to realize that the mere existence of variety in cultural beliefs and desires does not imply that it is possible to be mentally developed and intellectually mature in culturally divergent ways.

Piaget's challenge to anthropology is to demonstrate how particular cultural understandings and practices can seem well-founded and compelling precisely because they have been developmentally constructed out of the self-reflective processes of rational individuals. His challenge to anthropology is to show how autonomous reason depends on cultural tradition to exercise its critical powers. His challenge to anthropology is to formulate an ideal of rationality (and an account of the role of metaphysical beliefs in the construction of our sense of reality) that will make it credible to be a developmentalist and a pluralist at the very same time. We are currently in the thick of a revival of cultural psychology as a discipline (see, for example, Bruner, 1990; Cole, 1996; D'Andrade, 1995; Goodnow, Miller, and Kessel, 1995; Greenfield, 1997; Jessor, Colby, and Shweder 1996; Markus, Kitayama, and Heiman 1997; Miller, 1997; Much, 1992; Rogoff, 1990; Shore, 1996; Shweder, 1991; Shweder and Sullivan, 1993; Shweder et al., 1997; Stigler, Shweder, and Herdt, 1991; Wierzbicka, 1991, 1992b). Nevertheless, it will not be until Jean Piaget's challenge has been substantially met that cultural psychology will have fully come of age.

7

A Polytheistic Conception of the Sciences and the Virtues of Deep Variety

"Can we actually 'know' the universe? My God, it is hard enough finding your way around in Chinatown" is a line from one of Woody Allen's books. The line seems appropriate on this occasion, and when we have been asked to react to Professor E.O. Wilson's conception of consilience and unity of science. I think there are many problems with the gospel of consilience. I have doubts about its "unification metaphysics" (material determination, all the way down) and its "unified learning" pedagogy (with its emphasis on one particular, even peculiar, "natural science" conception of knowledge) (Wilson, 1998:5,3). And I confess that I am quite dubious of attempts to spread the word of "science" or promote the quest for knowledge in the human sciences under its name.

Members of the faith of consilience believe that we are now (for the first time, or finally, or is it once again?) on the threshold of (as T. S. Eliot put it, skeptically summarizing the creed) "rolling the universe up into a ball" (quoted in Converse, 1986). Perhaps that is why I experienced Professor E.O. Wilson's lecture on "The Unity of Knowledge: The Convergence of Natural and Human Science" as a kind of "good news" monotheistic sermon. In effect Professor Wilson invited us to return to an old-time state of pre-Kuhnian, pre-Wittgensteinian, pre-Quinean, pre-Rortyean innocence (see Kuhn, 1962; Quine, 1953, 1969; Rorty, 1991; Wittgenstein, 1953, 1969). Listening to that homily on the nature of human understanding and intellectual curiosity, one might forget that the Enlightenment idealization of the sufficient conditions for producing knowledge ("an innocent eye" plus a logic machine) has pretty much been dismantled (or at least seriously critiqued) over the past 200 years. One might never have thought to doubt the speaker's conviction that unification and convergence of belief are the criteria of maturity in scholarly disciplines. Where T. S. Eliot was skeptical, Professor Wilson remains pious.

There are other skeptics. Clifford Geertz is a cultural anthropologist who specializes in the interpretation of behavior and who describes his intellectual aim as "ferreting out the singularities of other peoples' ways-of-life" (Geertz, 2000:xi). As a psychological anthropologist and cultural psychologist, that is my goal as well. Professor Geertz writes about the field of psychology (which was once known as the science of the soul, is now called the science of the mind, and is scripted to become the science of the body in Professor Wilson's augury for the future) as follows: "We are not apparently, proceeding towards some appointed end where it all comes together, Babel is undone, and Self lies down with Society."

Apparently Professor Wilson disagrees and his visions stretch far beyond psychology per se. He still dreams Enlightenment dreams of connecting anything and everything (Chinatown and the whole universe) "in a common skein of cause-and-effect explanation" (Wilson, 2000): validity, simplicity, and unity "all rolled up in a ball." In his book entitled *Consilience: The Unity of Knowledge*, Professor Wilson writes of it as an "epiphany" or an "enchantment" that freed him from his Southern Baptist upbringing. I have my doubts. He describes the typical devotee of "consilience" as being "under the spell" (his expression) of "a hoped-for consolidation of theory so tight as to turn the science into a 'perfect' system of thought, which by sheer weight of evidence and logic is made resistant to revision." He has described the natural sciences of the new millennium as having nearly reached a state of perfect "consilience" (Wilson, 2000). He expressed his conviction that the social sciences and humanities could be similarly unified, with each other and with the natural sciences, under the banner of biology. He wagered that the royal road to such a comprehensive consilience—a resistant-to-revision, eternal, or final solution to all debates and disputations about culture and mind, what might be called the academic "end time"— would come through work on brain science, human genetics, cognitive psychology, and biological anthropology.

I have my doubts. I would suggest that the idea of consilience— the idea of a seamless coherency and of systematic interconnections across culture, mind, and body, across intellectual disciplines and across units of analysis neatly arranged into decomposable levels of material organization—is far more fictional than factual. At the very least I would suggest that consilience is not a very good description of the current intellectual scene across the human and the nonhuman sciences.

I recognize, of course, that rather than dismissing the idea of consilience as a fanciful description of the current intellectual scene, it is possible to construe the notion merely as a utopian ideal for guiding research. Even so, I would hope that the aspirations of the members of the church of consilience remain denominational in character and that those ideals are understood to be useful for some intellectual projects but not for others. Why? Because Professor Wilson's ecumenical and monotheistic quest for a consilient unification of knowledge overidealizes one very special and rather limited (even limiting) type of knowledge—the type of knowledge in which observations and logic alone make it resistant to revision. There is no universally binding reason to privilege that particular ideal of knowledge and that ideal, while perhaps serviceable in some contexts, may get in the way of many valuable forms of systematic inquiry in the human sciences, and perhaps even in the nonhuman sciences as well. Or at least that is the pluralistic or polytheistic conception of human understanding that I would like to put on the table for discussion.

Polycentrism or Consilience?

It is instructive (by way of contrast to the dogma of consilience) to take a closer look at Clifford Geertz's description of the state of play these days—the realities of scholarship and the way interpretative communities are functioning—in the sciences and the humanities. In his recent collection of essays entitled *Available Light* (compare to the tone and implication of the title of E.O. Wilson's book), Professor Geertz (2000: 145-146) writes, "The homogenization of natural science, both over time and across fields, as a constant other, an 'opposing ideal' permanently set off from other forms of thought, as Richard Rorty has put it, 'by a special method [and] a special relation to reality,' is extremely difficult to defend when one looks at either its history or its internal variety with any degree of circumstantiality." He continues: "There is indeed some evidence from within the natural sciences themselves that the continental image of them as an undivided bloc, united in their commitment to Galilean procedures, disengaged consciousness and the view from nowhere, is coming under a certain amount of pressure" (Geertz, 2000: 150).

Professor Geertz is impressed by the "localness" of the knowledge systems constructed by different cultural communities (including scientific communities). He is clearly suspicious of both fanatics and infidels in the academy. In the place of both the hypermodernist total systems builders and the radically skeptical antiscience postmodernists, he asks us to take seriously the image and the reality "of a loose assemblage of differently focused, rather self-involved, and variably overlapping research communities in both the human and natural sciences."

Professor Geertz invites us to abandon a conception of "two continental enterprises, one driven by the ideal of disengaged consciousness looking out with cognitive assurance upon an absolute world of ascertainable fact, the other driven by the ideal of an engaged self struggling uncertainly with signs and expressions to make readable sense of intentional action." In other words, the story of the academy is not about two cultures (the "sciences" versus the "humanities"). Nor is it about just one imperial culture (to pick some random examples, human genetics, sociobiology, or cognitive neuroscience) taking over all the others. Reflecting on claims about the "unity of knowledge," Clifford Geertz doubtfully asks (quoting the philosopher Richard Rorty), "What method is common to paleontology and particle physics? What relation to reality is shared by topology and entomology?" Such questions, he argues, are hardly more useful than asking, "Is sociology closer to physics than to literary criticism?" or "Is political science more hermeneutic than microbiology, chemistry more explanatory than psychology?" (Geertz, 2000:150).

I share Professor Geertz's view of the current intellectual scene. When invited by the New York Academy to attend a conference on "The Unity of Knowledge: The Convergence of Natural and Human Science," I wrote: "I am pleased to accept your invitation, although

I feel that I should give you some warning that I am quite skeptical of much that is presupposed and implied by the title and sub-title of the meeting. I do not think there is unity either between or within the social and natural sciences. I am not even confident there is unity within biology, although there certainly are similarities between the way certain sorts of biologists and certain sorts of social scientists think about the world."

The similarities and sorts I had in mind were the reductive systems—building modernists in the natural sciences and human sciences. They share a mode of explanation and style of research. Nonreductive "top down" holists, interactionists, and contextualists in the natural sciences and human sciences share a mode of explanation and style of research as well. So there are parallel or comparable splits within the natural and the human sciences. The field of plate tectonics, for example, according to the geologist Frank Richter (1986), makes "no reference to laws of motion even though it describes motion," is bound to historical circumstances, and has more in common with some varieties of social science scholarship then with some versions of physics.

Biology is not homogeneous either. There are conflicts over some rather fundamental issues in that territory of knowledge. There appear to be a few items on the "nature-nurture" agenda that remain unsettled: minor things, such as how to think about the distinction between genes and environments, what precisely it means to say "it [intelligence, a fear of snakes, Catholicism] is all in your genes," and how to properly measure gene-environment interactions, assuming the distinction between genes and environments can be made precisely and coherently in the first place (which, according to some biologists, is very much in doubt).

One thing that is not in doubt is that it is an oversimplification to say that there are only two types of biologists, although at least there is more than just one. The first type includes biologists who conceptualize phenotypes in terms of "epigenetic complexity." They focus their research on interactions "between genes, between genes and gene products (proteins), and between all these and environmental signals, including, of course, the individual organismal experience" (see Strohman, 1993: 114). (Richard Strohman has written a critique of the genetic paradigm in biology and medicine in which he points out that 98 percent of diseases are not monogenetic and that, although there is a genetic basis for "speaking French," there probably are no "speaking French genes"—or if there are "speaking French genes," it is only in the sense that there is a genetic basis for being a human being who is capable of learning French. This is a very old point but apparently it still needs to be made).

The second type includes biologists who talk the talk of "genetic reductionism" and speak the language of direct gene-trait pathways (whether monogenetic or polygenetic, whether simple or complex—in principle, if not in practice, they think they can handle, which means simplify, any complexity that comes along). The distinction between these two types of biologists is revealing. Many of the (type 1) epigenetic biologists are suspicious of genetic interventionism and have ambivalent feelings, at best, about the human genome project. Many of the (type 2) genetic reductionists believe that they can make the world a better place through selective alterations in the genetic endowment of particular members of our species. So they promote the human genome project as the paradigm for medical and behavioral research. My main point, however, is that whether you are for them or against them, or whether you believe or disbelieve (like or loathe) the message that successful people and their offspring do better in life because they have better genes, there is more than one contentious voice out there, even in biology.

I concluded my response to the NYAS invitation to attend this "Unity of Knowledge" conference as follows: "And I have some doubts about whether the ideal of substantive 'unity' across the natural and human sciences is any more attainable today than 200 years ago. I even think it is an open question whether (for the sake of human progress and the progress of knowledge) the ideal of substantive unity of belief is even truly desirable. Given those caveats I look forward to a lively meeting in June."

Available Light contains a similar vein of thought. Focusing on the field of psychology, broadly conceived, Clifford Geertz sees little consilience. He writes: "Paradigms, wholly new ways of going about things, come along not by the century, but by the decade, sometimes, it almost seems, by the month. . . . It takes either a preternaturally focused, dogmatical individual, who can shut out any ideas but his or her own, or a mercurial, hopelessly inquisitive one, who can keep dozens of them in play at once, to remain upright amidst this tumble of programs, promises and proclamations" (Geertz, 2000: 188).

Programs, promises, proclamations. The Unity of Knowledge. The Convergence of the Natural and Human Sciences. The New Synthesis. What Geertz thinks we are witnessing, at least in psychology and the cognitive sciences, is not some deep unification of knowledge but rather a rapid proliferation of what Thomas Kuhn called disciplinary matrices: "loose assemblages of techniques, vocabularies, assumptions, instruments and exemplary achievements," some of which are original and creative, some of which are incommensurate with each other or semi-independent of each other, some of which are mutually stimulating. No common project—rather "half-ordered, polycentric collections of mutually conditioned projects" with no ultimate consilience in sight.

The contrast between Professor Wilson's and Professor Geertz's conceptions of human knowledge and knowledge of humans is dramatic. Unreconstructed and unfazed in substance, monotheistic and modernist in spirit, Professor Wilson (2000) offers us the Enlightenment picture of science as a distinctive and superior mode of thought that is leading us to a new synthesis linking culture, mind, and body. This time around (and we have been around this issue many times both before and after the Enlightenment), it would appear that the bygone and misconceived idea of a reductive "social physics" is going to be replaced with the fashionable new idea of a reductive "social biology," based on a set of universal truths generated out of cognitive neuroscience, human genetics, biological anthropology, and a species-typifying cognitive psychology. (As an aside, the expression "it is not rocket science" has not yet been replaced in popular discourse by such phrases as "it is not brain science" or "it is not genetic engineering." Perhaps this is just a case of cultural lag and the popular recognition of a shift in scientific prestige from nuclear physics to microbiology is only a matter of time. Or perhaps the public is waiting to see whether the human genome project is going to realize its quite benevolent medical dreams or will turn out instead to be a eugenics nightmare or just a very expensive dead end.)

In any case, whatever one thinks of Professor Wilson's Enlightenment picture of how science works or ought to work—or of its potential public relations appeal, for example, to funding agencies or to readers of the *New York Times*—I submit it is not a good depiction of the current intellectual scene. Clifford Geertz's polycentrism (rather than E.O. Wilson's consilience) is the descriptive and normative term that rings more true. I shall briefly illustrate what I take to be the polycentric realities of the current scene with some casual glances in a couple of directions.

A Nonconsilient Truth

Let me confess first that the most rock-bottom truth in my own conception of the human relationship to knowledge (including knowledge of human beings) is fundamentally nonconsilient. I associate this truth with an approach to understanding I call Confusionism (not to be confused with Confucionism). According to this nonconsilient Confusionist truth, the knowable world is incomplete if seen from any one point of view, incoherent if seen from all points of view at once, and empty if seen from nowhere in particular.

Given the choice among incompleteness, incoherence, and emptiness, the best option is to opt for incompleteness, staying on the move between different points of view. The best option is to go ahead and see what each point of view (each genuine cultural tradition, school of thought, theoretical position) illuminates and what each hides, while keeping track of the plural (some might say, polytheistic) character of the humanly knowable world. Coherence can sometimes be achieved but only within the limits of particular points of view. Findings of great generality across all human beings can also sometimes be uncovered. However, in the human sciences at least, these universal generalizations are often bought at the price of describing the world of culture and mind at a level of abstraction so distanced from lived realities that they are devoid of sufficient content and meaning and have little predictive utility.

For example, the psychologist Charles Osgood long ago proposed a simple universal code for characterizing the way all human beings evaluate objects and events in the universe. We do it, he proposed, by asking of every object and event three questions: "Is it good or bad?" (Osgood called this the "evaluation" dimension), "Is it strong or weak? (the "potency" dimension) and "Is it fast or slow?" (the "activity" dimension) (Osgood, May, and Miron, 1975). The problem is that this universal code is theorized at such a high level of abstraction that it classifies God and ice cream as equivalent, because they are both judged to be good, strong, and active. As you can see, a bit too much gets lost in this type of search for universally valid generalizations. That is a common shortcoming (the shortcoming of emptiness) of propositions in the human sciences that are designed to be statements about culture and mind true of all human beings.

The consilient aim of synthesizing different points of view is, of course, not inherently evil; but it is equally important to recognize that if different points of view could be fully integrated or synthesized, they would not count as different points of view. There *are* times when the difference between two or more points of view is illusory and a limited "unification" of knowledge may be possible. But this is not true always or even often when it comes to the types of issues that arise when one examines the links between culture, mind, and biology. In this very broad domain, the so-called mind/body (or the mind/brain) problem continues (along with other major issues) to be a major concern, and, despite many claims to the contrary, no real resolution is in sight. That is one reason why all interdisciplinary meetings that bring together brain scientists interested in "organic matter" (and how it functions) with humanists and social scientists interested in "matterings," meanings, and mental states (and how they function) do indeed seem very much like the tower of Babel. Or else at such conferences a fake sense of consilience is achieved by actively repressing any real tower of Babel effect. Typically this fake sense of consilience is a byproduct of either 1) not knowing or caring very much about what other researchers are doing or what they think (just paying attention to the things you are looking for can also produce a sense of unity); or 2) formulating propositions at such a "view from afar" level of abstraction that most of the things that are of interest to social scientists and humanists disappear from sight; or 3) by sharing words in common— like "mind," "mental," "cause," or "behavior"—without asking what those words precisely mean.

Minds and Brains in Bremen

So here is my first glimpse at the current scene. While residing in Germany (where I was a Fellow at the Wissenschaftskolleg zu Berlin), I attended a major interdisciplinary conference held in Bremen on the subject of voluntary action. The experience typified for me the way consilience works (or more accurately does not work) as a description of the current intellectual scene in the cognitive sciences. The conference featured philosophers, cognitive neuroscientists, psychologists, and anthropologists. All were there ostensibly to explain the fact (or is it just the phenomenal experience? That is the question!) of voluntary action.

Voluntary action is a nice topic for an interdisciplinary meeting. As the conference organizers (Wolfgang Prinz, Gerhart Roth, and Sabine Maasen) brilliantly pointed out in their invitation, voluntary action

> poses a severe challenge to scientific attempts to form a unitary picture of the working of the human mind and its relation to the working of the body. This is because the notion of mental causation, inherent in the received

standard view of voluntary action, is difficult to reconcile with both dualist and monist approaches to the mental and the physical. For dualist accounts it has to be explained what a causal interaction between mind and matter means and how it is possible at all. Conversely, for monist approaches the question of mental causation does not arise and therefore appears to denote a cognitive illusion at best. Dualist and monist accounts can be found in all the disciplines mentioned above [cognitive psychology, neuropsychology, philosophy, ethnology], albeit in different phrasings and/or theoretical frameworks. Moreover, in virtually all disciplines this seemingly insurmountable opposition is [a] subject of ongoing debate.

So voluntary action is a challenge for both mind/body monists and mind/body pluralists (of which mind/body dualism is just one variety). If you are a mind/body monist (and at such conferences the monists are all materialists; apparently the idealists are either hard to find or are not invited) then the voluntariness of voluntary action must be an illusion. That, of course, is the spectacular and breath-taking (or, should we say, dis-spiriting) implication of mind/body monism—namely, the renunciation of all of folk psychology and the claim (*involuntarily* arrived at and offered, I suppose, at least according to mind/body monists) that mental states, including one's own truth claims about mental states, are epiphenomenal and have nothing to do with the chain of real events that causes behavior.

You raise your hand in a situation in which you thought that your desire to signal the teacher that you wanted to try to answer the question he or she just posed to the class was the reason that you deliberately, willfully or "voluntarily" raised your hand. In a folk psychological sort of way, you might think that deliberately communicating an intention to answer a question was what the hand-raising action was all about. "Not so!" says the mind/body monist. The hand raising was the end product of material determinants at the neural level, where a human will (and indeed even a human self) cannot be observed, and where ideas qua ideas do not exist, and hence can play no causal role in the movement of your hand. Given our contemporary received understanding of the nature (physics, chemistry, and biology) of the material world, that is how mind/body monists think they must talk about so-called voluntary action. They talk of it as an epiphenomenon.

But this leaves the mind/body monists (it's all body, no mind) with a whole lot of explaining to do. Why should such a complex epiphenomenal system (amounting to all of human consciousness and its products) exist at all? How could it evolve, if it plays no causal role in behavior? Are the ideas of agency, virtue, and human responsibility then incompatible with the consilient teachings of the physical and biological sciences? Should folk psychology (including all the literary, moral, legal, and social science disciplines premised on such notions) be banished from the unified curriculum, except perhaps as examples of error, ignorance, and superstition?

Mind/body dualists fare no better when it comes to making sense of voluntary action. As an aside, almost all cognitive neuroscience research programs become tacitly dualist as soon as they treat something mental as an independent variable and something neurological as a dependent variable, or vice versa. In other words, just to carry forward their research agenda, they implicitly, usually unself-consciously, distinguish thoughts (or ideas) from things (or neurons) and identify them using ontologically distinct types of criteria.

In any case, if you are a reflective mind/body dualist, you must explain how something that is immaterial (for example, the mental state associated with choice, planning, free will, and intentionality) can have an effect on something that is physical (the movement of one's hand). So there is a real and deep problem here with our current understanding of voluntary action, and at Bremen an interdisciplinary conference was organized to make some progress on resolving it, in the light of recent research in cognitive neuroscience, psychology, and anthropology, with some assistance from the philosophers. Here is the way consilience operated in that context.

The philosophers were really good at defining the mind/body problem. And each philosopher was terrific at arguing in favor of one of the incompatible solutions (such as interactionism, psychophysical parallelism, and reductive materialism) that have been contenders, while at the same time advancing compelling criticisms against all other solutions. Not much convergence took place among the philosophers, but at least they knew what the problem was and they tried to address it.

The neuroscientists, on the other hand, came armed with lots of colorful slides, showing this or that brain part lighting up when this or that kind of action took place or sentence got spoken. They named lots of brain parts and they spoke with great confidence and with a sense of pride and excitement about the technological revolution that had taken place on their watch, which had finally made it possible, or so they thought, to empirically solve the mind/body problem. After about ten slides, I began to realize that they probably had never read Descartes and seemed to think that he would be surprised to find out that when thinking occurs something happens somewhere in the nervous system. After about twenty slides, I began to realize that they did not really know what the mind/body problem was in the first place. But they had an imagined solution to the problem, which seemed to excite them a great deal. Upon examination, this "solution" was simply a form of question-begging in which the very real puzzle of how a nonmaterial thing and a material thing can causally interact is solved by substituting a Humean notion of causation for the sense of causation that makes the problem a problem in the first place.

Here I merely restate a philosophical commonplace. David Hume was a radical empiricist for whom knowledge had to be based on sensory experience to count as knowledge at all (and hence only "seeing is believing"). According to Hume's epistemology, the belief in any underlying causal process is illusory and causal claims are just reified projections of mental associations. In other words, the empirical world (the perceivable world) is devoid of underlying causes and causal claims are merely psychological habits or manners of speaking about subjective impressions that are formed by the perceptions of things and events that are co-occurring in time and space. For David Hume, that is all that counts as knowledge—things and events that are observed and located in time and space. The cause itself, however, cannot be seen, and hence for Hume, the radical empiricist, it is excluded from Hume's positive "science." The neuroscientists "solved" the mind/body problem by being Humean in their conception of causation, because for them mind/body causation amounted to little more than the observation that the brain lights up here and there when a person does this or that. This, of course, is hardly a *theoretical* advance over Descartes. But they kept going, slide after slide demonstrating that the mind/body problem had been empirically solved! After 100 slides, the only ones awake in the audience were the other neuroscientists, who were legitimately interested in questions about the details of brain localization, and a few others who liked the pretty pictures.

Then there were the psychologists and the anthropologists. They generally *presupposed* the reality and causal powers of mental states and their ideational content (in other words, they had not expunged folk psychology from their scientific work), and they described the operation of that folk psychology in some detail. One psychologist did present reaction time evidence, all of it equivocal, trying to prove that mental states are unreal and have no causal powers. In the end, the mind/body problem remained unsolved, when acknowledged, or it remained untouched; but it was innocently thought to have been solved by the new technologies for mapping the brain. In the end, the everyday experience or reality of voluntary action remained as mysterious and fascinating as ever.

"Matter" and "Matterings" in the Human Sciences

My second glimpse is a quick look at the crisis literature in the human sciences. This worry about the state of the human sciences compared to the natural sciences goes up and down; and when it is up, there emerges a crisis literature. Before examining this literature, however, let me state up front that I think that social science research institutions are pluralistic hot beds of creative and useful activity. I myself share with Philip Converse (1986) and others the view that disciplined inquiry (use the honorific term "science" if you like) consists of "the systematic decoding of observed regularities and the reduction of the regularities to more parsimonious and general principles that account for wide ranges of phenotypic detail." There is plenty of this type of work going on in the social sciences; and whether or not it moves in the direction of con-silience, much of this work is exciting and useful.

I myself have tried to contribute to the enterprise in various ways. I work on the cultural psychology of morality, of the emotions, of gender, of illness and suffering; as well as on the meaning of family life practices (such as sleeping patterns, dietary practices, and coming of age ceremonies for boys and girls); and on various other issues concerned with the character and social origins of *differences* in psychological functioning across cultural communities. Reports on the substance of this work are available (see, for example, Shweder, 1991, 1996; also Shweder and LeVine, 1984; Shweder and Fiske, 1986; Shweder et al., 1997; Shweder and Haidt, 2000; see Chapters 2 through 5); but my concerns today go well beyond the discussion of this or that discovery. Any consideration of the substantive issues or questions that concern me—the "big three" domains (autonomy, community, divinity) of moral reasoning around the world, or the way moral ideas are made manifest and expressed in mundane social practices such as who eats with whom and who sleeps with whom (that story, by the way, goes well beyond the "incest taboo"), or why the emotions that are most valued are not the same from culture to culture, or how the experience of loss does not result in the same psychological or somatic response from society to society or even person to person—must wait for another, less weighty, occasion.

However, one of the things I have discovered is that the ideal of systematically observing and decoding regularities does not imply that the most useful, significant, or even discoverable generalizations in the social sciences are going to be those that characterize all human beings. As Edelson (1984) has remarked, "not all hypotheses of interest to a scientist are universal generalizations." Indeed I believe that some of the most reliable, useful, and significant generalizations in the social and psychological sciences are those that are restricted in scope and are "firmly wedded," as Philip Converse (1986) might have expressed it, to historical, cultural, and institutional circumstances. Rural Oriya Brahmans in India will react this way for these reasons under these circumstances, which is not the way middle-class Anglo-Americans will react, and for these reasons.

When undertaking a project of disciplined inquiry in the human sciences, one cannot assume that real things must exist independently of a point of view if they are be considered "really real." The realm of culture is a realm occupied and preoccupied with real things—touchdowns, in-laws, child abuse, weeds, the Christmas season—that do not exist independently of the point of view of some specific interpretive community. That is one of the reasons that some of the most reliable and predictively useful generalizations about human behavior are restricted in scope.

Nor can one assume that the reality of such things is adequately captured from a purely "naturalistic" or "materialistic" point of view. Professor Wilson (2000) states: "*After all*, mind and culture, which are the subjects of the social sciences and humanities, are material entities and processes. They do not exist in an astral plane above the tangible world, and are therefore intrinsically open to analysis in the natural scientific mode" (my emphasis).

I find this statement both remarkable and revealing. The current discourse across the sciences and humanities about the character and reality status of culture and mind is far from consilient. Yet Professor Wilson seems so untouched by this discourse that a proposition that has been problematic for 3,000 years and soundly rejected by many, perhaps most, interpretive social scientists, and for good reason, is asserted as though it were common-sense ("After all . . ."). What do cultural meanings as meanings (for example, the idea of "sin") or cultural meanings as made manifest in cultural artifacts (for example, a "weapon" or a "weed") look like from a purely material point of view? Is it from a purely material point of view that their very identity is established? For example, a "utensil" and a "weapon" could be exactly the same object from a purely material point of view. Reference to some nonmaterial element such as a human purpose, a human aim, or a human practice is required to identify the object in the first place.

This is not a topic I can examine here in any detail—although you can see the shadow of the mind/body problem once again and you can see how readily many empirical scientists manage to avoid the central issues. Here let me simply invoke the work of Karl Popper, the well-known twentieth-century philosopher of science, as a corrective to Professor Wilson's (in my view) dubious assertion that the subjects of the social sciences and humanities are tangible, material, and intrinsically open to naturalistic inspection. Karl Popper believed in three worlds (a world of material objects, of subjective mental states, and of collective meanings), not just one. And he was deeply critical of monistic World 1 approaches of the type advanced by Professor Wilson (Popper and Eccles, 1977).

"Mind" and "culture" refer to ideas or meanings accessible to the mental processes of individual human beings and made manifest in the practices—including linguistic practices—of interpretive communities or social groups. If mind and culture exist at all in the sense that those who study mind and culture think they exist, then they exist in a way that is different from the mode of existence of mere material objects. That of course is one big part of what the 3,000-year-old argument about the reality status of ideas is about. Can a World 1 science go all the way? The argument is about whether ideas and the mental processes that make them available to human beings have more than just a World 1 material existence and need to be understood in a different way, as ideas and mental processes per se. It seems to me that reference to an "astral plane" over and above the material world, Popper's World 3 (for example), may not be a bad way to index all that. It is certainly no more mysterious and wondrous than the experience of consciousness itself. Perhaps the ideas made manifest in cultural practices exist in an astral plane not very far away from the place where Gottlob Frege and some philosophers of mathematics think the truths of logic and mathematics exist (or subsist) before they are discovered. The concept of "zero" is not a material thing. But enough said on that score in this context. This is not consilient intellectual territory in which "after all . . ." is the best way to open a conversation. The mind/body problem is not solved, any more (here moving to the other side of the fence) than issues of salvation are addressed by taking a picture of the brain activity of sinners in a confessional booth.

My main point, however, is that creative and useful science goes on in social science research centers despite the fact that across and within such research institutions there is a conspicuous absence of consilience and considerable disagreement about whether the unification of knowledge is even a worthy ideal. Most researchers, even those who are totally out of sympathy with each other and find it difficult to credit or make sense of what each other is doing, believe that progress is being made on the problem on which they are working. And, I would suggest, in many cases they are right.

Crisis Literature in the Social Sciences

Finally then here is that second glimpse of the current intellectual scene, this time in the social sciences. If you take a look at the crisis literature in the social sciences, you find four types of complaints, of which I focus on three (see Shweder and Fiske, 1986).

COMPLAINT #1

Social science generalizations are typically restricted in scope. The modal social science generalization is bound to a particular population studied at a particular historical time in a particular culture, and often restricted as well to the particular methodology used in the investigations (so-called method effects). In other words, as Lee Cronbach (1975) has noted, in the social sciences "generalizations decay" (as you move from one population to another or across historical eras or across methods). Or, as Donald Campbell (1972) has noted, in the social sciences (including psychology, that ambiguously and ambivalently "non-social social science") "higher-order interactions are the rule, and main effects, ceteris paribus generalizations, the rare exception." For a sustained critique of the quest for abstractionism in the social sciences, see Jerome Kagan's book *Three Seductive Ideas* (1998).

Here I might add that, given that "main effects' are the rare exception, rushing to generalizations about all human beings is generally hazardous in the social sciences. I suspect that Professor Wilson has been tempted in that direction in his interpretation of animal phobias. I do not think we really know very much about animal phobias around the world. We need much more ethnographic and experimental evidence on this topic. But I will bet a quarter that when the cross-cultural developmental evidence is in, it will be far more complicated and qualified than Professor Wilson has suggested. Even with the limited evidence that is now available, it is not obvious that there are universal biologically driven rules, readily understandable from a Darwinian adaptationist point of view, for the acquisition of specific animal phobias.

What we know about animal phobias comes mainly from research done in Europe and North America. In that limited database, 90 percent of those adults who have animal phobias are women. So even in those populations, the inclination is restricted to a small subset of one half of the members of the species. More importantly, the list of animals that women with phobias fear the most is not predictable from a Darwinian point of view. What does

Darwinian theory predict about which animals should be on the list of phobic objects (and which should not) for specific populations of people? North American and European women who have animal phobias are afraid of snakes, spiders, and mice. They are also afraid of frogs and birds, yet they are not afraid of wolves, lions, or elephants. Biological adaptationists (it is all about getting your genes into the next generation) need to tell us a lot more about what their theory predicts about the evolution of fears for specific populations. They need to do so before making claims about how the current evidence on animal phobias confirms the theory.

COMPLAINT #2

Social science theories and schools of thought do not converge over time. Multiple paradigms persist, and the set of concepts and theories that guide research and the interpretation of evidence are as various today as they were 50 years ago or even 100 years ago.

COMPLAINT #3

Meanings, intentions, ideas, values, emotions, and all other aspects of human consciousness, phenomenological experience, or subjectivity cannot be studied scientifically, because they are not the types of things (observable material entities that can be located in time and space) that science was designed to study. In other words, some social scientists (those who are the most humanistic) believe that the subject matter of the social sciences puts them outside the proper realm of science. Professor Wilson's response to this is to argue that their subject matter is not what these humanists thought it was and that meanings, intentions, and all the other stuff of consciousness is inherently material and hence the "matter" of the natural sciences, after all. Lurking behind these types of complaints are presuppositions about the criteria that distinguish mature science from proto-science from non-science from nonsense; and those presuppositions make a big difference in whether one perceives a crisis at all.

For example, Philip Converse (1986) has argued that "a model of science that suggests that either we can, in T. S. Eliot's words, 'roll the universe into a ball' with one grand summary expression like E = MC², or we are not engaging in science is a false model." He argues that there is a different "texture" to different fields of rigorous disciplined inquiry depending on their subject matter.

A related point has been made by Roy D'Andrade (1986). D'Andrade presents an ethnographic account of the diversity of models and ideals of science that he finds among practicing researchers. He argues:

> that the sciences contain at least three very different
> world views, that of the physical sciences, that of the natural sciences, and that of the semiotic sciences; . . . that
> the pursuit of "general laws" is characteristic primarily of
> the physical sciences; . . . that some of the natural sciences, such as biology, have done well despite the fact
> that they have not found general laws; . . . that in the social sciences there is a considerable division between the
> natural science approach and the semiotic approach
> [which involves the interpretation of what something
> "means"] without a reasonable synthesis in view. . . .

Where D'Andrade reports plural scientific world views and a division between natural science and interpretive social science, Professor Wilson senses that a new age of consilience is close at hand.

My answer to all this, as you have perhaps already realized, is to suggest that plurality is inherent in science (just as it is in religion, culture, and society). Evidence and logic alone are not sufficient conditions for the development of knowledge systems. Reality testing is a metaphysical act, which relies on various aspects of the imagination, including category systems, background assumptions, metaphors, and so on. Hence I do not expect scientific debate and controversy about fundamental issues to ever come to an end. Because I do not believe that convergence in belief is a mark of the maturity of a scholarly discipline, I do not worry, as some do, about the future of the social sciences.

I believe that either 1) our current account of the nature of the material world is incomplete (because it cannot handle the role of "meaning" without terrorizing or eliminating the concept of meaning itself) or else 2) human beings have a nature that takes them beyond the material world, in which case reference to other worlds—Popper's World 2, the mental world, and his World 3, the world of ideas—must play a central part in any science of human action. Given the central role of meaning as a causal factor for human beings, the restriction of scope of generalizations in the social sciences and humanities is thus entirely expectable. And the discovery of such meaning-dependent or context-dependent regularities is highly respectable, because it honors the truth.

The "Queep" and the "Deep" of Life: Meaning and Divergence in Science

Here is a small but powerful example of what happens when meaning enters our nervous system. The example comes from Benjamin Lee Whorf's book *Language, Thought and Reality* (1956: 257). Whorf is famous for his work on linguistic relativity, but he was fully aware of the existence of some species typifying affective or synesthetic responses to stimuli of various kinds. He notes that the semantically meaningless sound pattern "queep" elicits a universal set of affective or "feeling-tone" associations when it interacts with the human nervous system. Whether you are in the highlands of New Guinea or in Manhattan, whether you speak English, Guugu Yimidhirr, or Russian, "queep" is judged to be fast (rather than slow), sharp (rather than dull), light (rather than dark), narrow (rather than wide). Our affective response to "queep" is automatic and may well be preprogrammed, a feature of our common biology.

But notice what happens when semantic meaning enters the picture. Whorf asks us to consider the sound pattern "deep." As a material thing (and as a pure sound pattern) "deep" is very similar to "queep." For speakers of languages in which "deep" is a nonsense syllable (that is, most languages of the world), the sound pattern "deep" elicits exactly the same set of affective or feeling-tone associations (fast, sharp, light, narrow) as does "queep." But "deep" is not just a physical entity (or pure sound) for English speakers. It is a word in our language. It has semantic meaning. And that meaning totally overrides its impact as pure physical sound (the sound merely becomes the vehicle of the meaning) and completely reverses our nervous system response. For speakers of English only, "deep" is judged to be slow, dull, dark, and wide. That is one of the reasons that so many interpretive social scientists are prepared to argue for the duality of human nature, of meaning and mind over and above mechanism and body, of the angel over and above the beast. There is something more to our nature than just the material realities that meet the ear (or the eye) plus the nervous system that is common to us all. The challenge for the humanities and the social sciences has always been to get "ideas" and our capacity to be sensitive to what things "mean" into the picture without completely reducing the "mental" to the "material" or "matterings" to "matter." Contemplating a human being as "a hairless gorilla with a big brain" does not quite do the trick.

Finally, let me conclude by telling you why I do not view the social sciences as "soft" with their feet in the sand in comparison to the "hardness" of the natural sciences, with their feet set in bedrock. Some do worry, however, about being soft, or about being too low on the hardness hierarchy. Thus, when I talk to psychologists, sociologists, or cultural anthropologists, they sometimes confess that what they do is soft science (if they are willing to grant that it is science at all) and that the real hard scientists are the physical scientists (or perhaps the microbiologists). When I go talk to the physical scientists who are meteorologists or geophysicists, they tell me that what they do is soft science and that the real hard scientists—those closest to bedrock reality—are the physicists. And so it goes. The experimental physicists, feeling a bit soft, send me in the direction of the theoretical physicists, who point me to the mathematicians, among whom the linear algebraists, feeling like their feet are in the sand, point me to the hard cutting edge, the topologists, who more often then not tell me that ultimately their work is intuitive and discretionary, and basically mystical. So for starters, bedrock is hard to find. And that is where I will end.

Fundamentalism for Highbrows:
The Aims of Education Address at the
University of Chicago

"No one ever died of homesickness" were the most comforting words told to me during my first days at college. I remember the moment vividly because I actually thought I was going to die. Back in those days, I was an athlete as much as an intellectual. My metaphor for basic survival was "just take one hurdle at a time. Do not think all at once and at the same time about everything that is to be done in life, or in the next four years, or tomorrow morning. Just take one hurdle at a time."

These days, I have a son who attends an intellectually intense liberal arts college—sort of a miniature University of Chicago—where the school slogan is "guilt without sex." I have a daughter who is entering her senior year at the University High School and has had college on her mind, and in her backyard, since she was in the womb. And I have just discovered that, if you go through life just taking one hurdle at a time, suddenly you find yourself on a pulpit in Rockefeller Chapel, looking at yourself thirty years earlier. You find yourself wondering if there is anything you can offer another generation, the adored generation of your own children, by way of some sage advice. So I am going to start by telling you that no one ever died of homesickness. I am going to tell you that, at the University of Chicago, many believe that the brain is an erogenous zone and that provocation is a fundamental virtue. That means there is plenty of sex and very little guilt here, and you are going to have an astonishing time. And I am going to provoke you.

There is actually a bit more to be said about the sex thing. We meet today in Rockefeller Chapel. There is a story about this place that goes back to the years of Robert Maynard Hutchins, who became President of the University in 1929 at the startling age of thirty and remained President until 1951. Rockefeller Chapel used to be open twenty-four hours a day; Hutchins ordered the building closed at night. When asked why, he remarked, "Unfortunately, more souls have been conceived at Rockefeller Chapel than have been saved there." My theme this evening is going to be a kind of postmodern reflection on the "saving of souls," in the hope that, if enough souls get saved in this building, perhaps we can get the place open again at night.

The soul I want to save is the soul of liberalism—as in the L-word, as in Liberal Arts Education—and I think there is good reason to think it needs to be saved, or at least resuscitated. Perhaps at a place like the University of Chicago, it merely needs to be constantly defended.

Liberalism is sometimes identified with the spirit of open-mindedness, yet the idea of an "open mind" is notoriously difficult to define, and it is easy to get the specifications wrong. Consider, for example, Kurt Vonnegut's description of his education in open-mindedness four decades ago at the greatest of all American universities. This is what he recounts in his novel *Slaughterhouse Five:* "I went to the University of Chicago for a while after the Second World War. I was a student in the department of anthropology.

They taught me that nobody was ridiculous or bad or disgusting."
Vonnegut goes on to say he never wrote a book with a villain in it
because that is what they taught him at college. They taught him
there are no villains. They taught him that whatever is, is okay. It is
precisely open-mindedness of that sort that led our late colleague
Allan Bloom to strongly recommend closing the American mind.

Although provocation is a virtue at the University of Chicago,
Allan Bloom's book *The Closing of the American Mind* drove most of
his reviewers, and even some of his colleagues, wild. The incitement
in the book was not so much his ridicule of Woodstock, which he
likened to Nazi rallies at Nuremberg, or of rock music, which he
viewed as obscene. The real instigation was the claim that the basic
distinction between good and evil, between culture and barbarism,
had gone out of style on American campuses. College students,
Bloom complained, have become so open-minded that they don't
make moral judgments and feel embarrassed when others do. They
have become so tolerant that they have lost their sense of taste.
They are so enamored of the idea that beauty, goodness, and truth
are in the eyes of the beholder that they have become blind to
things of genuine worth. They ascribe no greater value to the dia-
logues of Socrates than to those of Beavis and Butthead.

Cole Porter, the famous social critic, composed lyrics to go with
Bloom's thesis. "Good authors, too, who once knew better words, /
Now only use four-letter words. / Writing prose, anything goes."
That "anything goes" attitude is sometimes called nihilism or sub-
jectivism. Bloom called it relativism. One of the wittiest reviews of
The Closing of the American Mind appeared in *Rolling Stone* magazine,
where the book was described as "fundamentalism for highbrows."

(Incidentally, I am told that, soon after the publication of
Bloom's book, the admissions office received at least one phone call
from a concerned parent of a prospective student asking whether it
was true that rock music was prohibited on the University of Chi-

cago campus! In fact, one of my favorite images of the spirit of the university is the undergraduate woman I saw last spring, wearing a walkman, listening to Widespread Panic, eating a croissant from the Medici, and reading Aristotle while walking across 57th Street in traffic. I much prefer that image to those earnest, patriarchal portraits hanging in Hutchinson Commons, which seem so perfectly designed to terrify any young visitor to our community. Those austere glances from off the wall are meant to guard the secret that, inside its Gothic exterior, the University of Chicago is really an informal place where people have fun.)

Now, I am not particularly a fan of Bloom's thesis. I am far more concerned about the Puritanism on American campuses than the relativism. But I do like that idea of "fundamentalism for highbrows." Every other community has its sacred principles that give life to its profane activities, so why shouldn't we? Why not think of fundamentalism for highbrows as something like a ten commandments for saving the soul of liberal education? To get the project started, I propose to list a few fundamental qualities of the liberal academic spirit at the University of Chicago as I have experienced them. For rhetorical reasons, I will call them "commandments."

(Actually, I find it a little hard to believe that God could only come up with ten commandments. I suspect she had hundreds in mind, but only ten could fit on those tablets. The soul of liberalism rests on far more than six principles. Fortunately, I have been given less than an hour to discern what they might be. Here are the first six that come to mind. None of them are written in stone.)

First Commandment: Don't Stand Up When Your Professor Enters the Room

I do research in a Hindu temple town in India. A few years ago, I invited a friend and scholar from that temple community to visit my temple community, the University of Chicago. It was his first trip abroad, so he came to the United States quite fresh. I invited him to attend my section of the Social Science Core. He noticed things we take for granted. He noticed that, as I walked into the classroom, the students did not stand up and show their respect for my status. He noticed that males and females were sitting together. He noticed that I encouraged the expression of opinions from my students. All those things went against his notion of what the practice of teaching is about.

Such observations by an "outsider" helped me recognize a fundamental message of the organization of the classroom in our intellectual community. The message has something to do with the autonomy of voice. We participate in the community as individuals, not as social categories. We try to detach our evaluation of the ideas that are voiced from the social identity of the person who voiced them.

There are many ways to lose your voice or to have it taken from you. Laryngitis is just one of them. I have lost my voice twice in recent years, both at academic conferences. On the first occasion, one of the main speakers at the conference declined to participate in round-table discussion with the males in the room on the grounds that her only interest in men was as sexual objects. It was her way of telling a story about the loss of voice. On the second occasion, a speaker denounced the musical "West Side Story" on the grounds that it had been produced by "successful white males" who, she argued, had no authority to represent the Puerto Rican–American experience. When a wounded female fan of the show pointed out that "West Side Story" was a variation on "Romeo and Juliet," a play created by a successful white male who was neither Italian nor a citizen of Verona, the speaker denounced William Shakespeare as a racist.

Confrontations of that type raise fascinating questions about the authority of a voice to speak about particular topics. Earlier, I said this was going to be a kind of "postmodern" reflection on the saving of souls, but I did not tell you what that term "postmodern" really means. You are going to hear that term a lot around this university (just as you are going to hear the term "positivism" a lot). You have four years to figure out "postmodernism" for yourself. I am not going to spoil the fun, but I will give you a hint. Postmodernism is not modernism, and it is not premodernism either. In case you think that is not much of a hint, here is one of the ways you can tell the three modernisms (pre-, post-, and pure) apart.

In a premodern frame of mind, there are "insiders" and "outsiders," and it is easy to tell which is which. All knowledge is parochial and owned by those who are insiders. Only insiders have the authority to speak about themselves. The Old Testament is the private property of the tribes of Israel. Only Afro-Americans are entitled to rap or sing the blues.

So much for premodernism. Let us move on to modernism, the mentality of the French Enlightenment. Modernism has been the dominant mentality of our academic culture, at least until recent times. The modern mind believes that the only knowledge worth having is universal knowledge. What is true for one is true for all. If two people disagree, for example, about whether it is blasphemous for Salman Rushdie to write *The Satanic Verses,* then, according to the modernists, at least one of them must be wrong. The message of modernism is that, if we stick to pure reason and hard facts (logic and science), all disagreements and conflicts between peoples can be resolved. If you believe the world would be a better place if there were just one language to speak (for example, Esperanto or Arabic), you are probably a modernist. Perhaps you think it should be English.

The postmodern mentality is a bit different. Let me define it by illustration. I have in my files an item about a prominent member of an East African tribe who was professionally trained in Western philosophy. He had an interest in reviving the traditional practices of his ethnic group. As it turned out, the old ways had been forgotten even by the elders of his community. The main repository of knowledge about his tribal past was located in books published in Europe and the United States. The East African philosopher realized he needed a Western anthropologist as a consultant. He had no difficulty finding several Westerners eager to take the job.

The East African philosopher and the Western anthropologist collaborating to keep each other's valued differences alive is an example of open-mindedness in the postmodern world. In a postmodern world, your ancestry is less important than your travel plans. "Ebony" and "ivory" do not rise above their differences to realize their essential nature; instead, they trade places. Let's call this postmodern liberalism. Here are some scenes from the postmodern liberal world: German linguists teaching Sanskrit to Indian Brahmans; Bengali writers feeling disappointed when they journey to England and discover that the prose of Byron, the prose to which they are accustomed, is not spoken on the streets of London; the indigenous elite in Kenya and Jamaica teaching the English how to be properly English; American baseball financed by the Japanese; Japanese rice production financed by General Mills; an Afro-Caribbean scholar translating ancient Greek texts; Janis Joplin singing the blues.

I think there is a message to be drawn from these examples, and it is this: The authority of a voice has a lot to do with what is said and very little to do with who says it. In other words, you do not have to be a Westerner or a male to articulate a Western or masculine perspective, and most Westerners and most males are not very good at it, anyhow. Authoritative voices speak for the zen of things not because of who they are, least of all because of their social designation, but because what they say binds you to a reality. Indeed, "insiders" in the old premodern sense are not necessarily the best ones to speak about themselves. That is why some of the best books about social life in the United States have been written by "outsiders" from Asia, Africa, and Europe. It was an observation by a friend from India that got me to pay attention to the first commandment of the liberal soul: never sacrifice the autonomy of your voice.

Second Commandment: Seeing Is Not Believing

When I entered college, I believed that seeing is believing. I was pretty hard-nosed about it. "I'll believe that when I see it," I used to say, especially in arguments about the existence of God or miracles or elves. Then someone showed me a photograph of a leprechaun, looking just like the little Irish elf of my imagination. The photograph, which was astonishing and very natural-looking indeed, came accompanied by a notarized letter from someone at the Kodak Company swearing that the photo was authentic. I have now learned through much schooling that seeing is believing only if I am already prepared to believe.

This insight has been confirmed for me by an experiment I have conducted over the years with students in the social sciences Core. I have asked my students whether levitation has ever occurred. The students divide into three groups. There are those who are convinced that levitation has occurred but have never seen it. There are those who think levitation is theoretically impossible and would not believe it, no matter what they saw. They have already seen levitation in magic shows and on the movie screen and they think deception, hallucination, or mirage is more likely than genuine levitation. And then there are those who are so open-minded, they think anything is possible. In all three cases, actually seeing it has little to do with believing it.

That insight was confirmed for me in a second way. A few years ago, a famous theoretical physicist was confronted with some puzzling evidence from a carefully conducted scientific experiment. He announced, "I'll believe that data only when I have a theory that makes it plausible."

It is precisely because our views of reality are not literal that so much time is spent at the University of Chicago provoking conversations in which our assumptions get challenged. You will find that one of the maxims, if not commandments, of the place is "no statement shall go unanalyzed." Some people think this maxim is simply a variation on "the unexamined life is not worth living." I happen to think there is a lot to be said for the unexamined life, but I can assure you that one of the most popular University of Chicago campfire songs is "anything you can do I can do meta."

Third Commandment: Students Shall Not Sleep; They Need Time to Worry about Right and Wrong

Hannah Arendt, a former member of our faculty, is well known for an idea called the "banality of evil." The motives that move human beings in administrative bureaucracies to commit atrocities, she claims, are themselves average or commonplace, like the desire for a promotion or the fear that government funding might be lost. In 1961, Hannah Arendt (being a University of Chicago type) wrote a provocative essay about the trial of Adolf Eichmann in Jerusalem. She argued that the Nazi who was in charge of the Final Solution was an ordinary and rather uninteresting bureaucrat who had no particular hatred of Jews and was in possession of a normal conscience. His motives in life were entirely banal.

Now, one of my friends and colleagues at the University of Chicago is Frank Richter. He is chair of the Geophysical Sciences department. (You will discover that, at the University of Chicago, conversations cut across bureaucratic academic divisions.) One evening, as we found ourselves arguing about Arendt's thesis, Richter asked, "What about the evil in banality?" He wanted to stand Hannah on her head. I think he had a point, this point: Courage (and other high motives) is in short supply these days. Perhaps it always was. Still there remains a "demonic profundity" to the absence of heroism in the contemporary world. It is a devilish world when mundane (and hence popular motives) can lead human beings so astray. Just reflect for a moment on the shameful events in Waco, Texas, when several bureaucracies and prominent national leaders managed, in a routine way, to produce an atrocity, while everyone else, from the American Civil Liberties Union (where they do not like guns) to the National Conference of Christians and Jews (where they do not like "cults"), stood by silently and watched.

Perhaps it is because courage is in such short supply that we have students at the University of Chicago. Do not forget to remind those of us with too great a stake in mundane things that there is "evil in banality" and in bureaucratic motivations. Keep us alert. Engage the issues of the day. Examine their moral foundations. How do you feel about the human genome project? Do you know what it is? If there is to be a new world order, how are the forces of internationalization to be reconciled with the forces of separatism, and local cultural and religious revival? You are now college students. That means you are members of an ancient order of fellows who never sleep, just so you can have more time to worry about right and wrong.

Fortunately for everyone's sleep, there can also be irony and humor in the evil of banality. In the late 1960s, I knew a South Asian woman, married to an American man, who applied for United States citizenship so that her father, who had lived his entire life in the Third World, could join the American Peace Corps. (By the way, the preferred term these days for the former Third World is the Southern World now that the former Second World, the Soviet Union, has disappeared. Only a few troglodytes persist in calling it the "underdeveloped world.") In any case, at the final stage of being "naturalized" in New York, the immigration officer asked my Indian friend, "Do you swear you will bear arms in defense of the Constitution of the United States?" Compounding the irony of her situation (her aim was to get her father into the *Peace* Corps), she replied, "No, I won't do that!" The immigration officer asked, "What do you mean?" She said, "I am a pacifist. I don't believe in killing." He said, "Who taught you that?" She said, "Mahatma Gandhi." He said, "Who is he?" She said, "A great Indian religious leader." He said, "Well, you'll have to get a note from him." She said, "I can't. He is dead." He said, "Well, get a note from whoever took his place." The evil of banality flourishes because, in the thick of a horde of utterly compelling everyday concerns (promotion, profit, good grades, the flow of government funds), no one dares to step forward to take "his" place.

Fourth Commandment: Don't Believe What They Tell You about the Core

(I threw this one in just in case you are still musing about getting Rockefeller Chapel open at night. Well, maybe there is more to it than that.)

A curriculum in which there is a set of readings of old or seminal or at least "original" texts, common to all incoming students, taught entirely in a discussion section format by regular full-time members of the faculty has probably never existed at the University of Chicago. It certainly does not exist now.

Here is one way you can do the university a service. When you are asked why you came to the University of Chicago, do not humor the administration by telling them what they told you about the university, because they may believe you. Do not tell them you came here for the Core. There are better reasons for coming. Tell them you "came for the waters" or for "Da Bulls." Tell them you came because you heard that, in Hyde Park, the brain is an erogenous zone and provocation is a virtue. Those are good reasons for coming because, if you came for those reasons, you are going to be very happy. It is good to be happy.

That is not to say you won't be happy in the Core. You may be. You may even learn some useful things there. Learning is a curious thing. It is very hard to do entirely on your own. Even the simplest things are hard to induce by trial and error or by observation without coaching. For example, I played squash regularly for several years without understanding the game. One day, another friend of mine, Bill Meadow, who is a member of our medical faculty and a former college squash player, took me aside on a court in the fieldhouse and said, "Let me tell you what this game is about. The point is not to hit the ball as hard as you can down the center of the court. The idea is to gain position in the T, and you do this by keeping the ball deep along the wall." That took about thirty seconds. My game improved 600 percent in thirty seconds.

I had a similar experience with bagels, which I assure you should be sliced before, not after, you place them in your freezer. That one took even more years to learn, and the insight was achieved only because slicing bagels before freezing them was the standing practice in someone else's house and they didn't guard their secret. They shared their knowledge as a free good.

Of course, I may be a slow learner, but I think there is another conclusion you might draw from these examples. Just as it is good to be happy and to have friends, it is good to have traditions. They protect you from the down side of trial-and-error learning. You do not have to figure out everything on your own. A deep tradition—for example, the tradition of free inquiry and provocation at the independent-minded private colleges of our land—may even be an antidote to tyranny. You are going to learn some practical things at college. No Chicago police officer is ever going to pull you over on Lake Shore Drive and ask you for your definition of "postmodernism," but you are going to learn some practical things nevertheless.

Here are a few practical things I hope you will be lucky enough to learn from the tradition of teaching associated with the Core: that the world is incomplete if seen from any one point of view and incoherent if seen from all points of view at once; that if you have no starting point in life, you will never get started; that it is our prejudgments, sometimes disparaged as prejudices, that make it possible for us to see; that just because there is honor among thieves does not mean that theft is honorable; that the authority of a voice has a lot to do with what was said and very little to do with who said it; that seeing is not believing; that banality can be evil; and that you shouldn't believe everything they tell you about the Core. If you are not taught those things, switch sections. Better yet, ask your instructor for a definition of "postmodernism."

Fifth Commandment: Never Take a Puritan to the Monty Python Show

A puritan is someone who exaggerates a virtue until it becomes a vice. Puritans come clad in straight laces rather than in the untied sneakers that are the footwear of the liberal soul on our college campus. There are puritans of the left and of the right. There are as many kinds of puritans as there are kinds of virtues, because any virtue can be overdrawn. Try this thought experiment: Imagine a world governed by some perfectly enforced virtue. Whenever I engage in the exercise, I reason myself into a horror show.

Justice, for example, is an important virtue. It is deeply offensive to the human spirit when like cases are not treated alike, or when effort and accomplishment go unrewarded. Many people spend their lives feeling indignant about injustice. A few even succeed at bettering the world. This is admirable. Perhaps if you are lucky, your generation will develop a permanent sense of itself as the nineties generation because of the role you play during your college years in standing up for what is just. My generation has that sense of itself. Many of us who were students in the 1960s continue to feel proud of the role we played opposing the war in Vietnam and marching on Washington for the extension of civil rights. One of us kept marching right into the White House.

A world of perfect justice, however, would be a nightmare. In such a world, every error, indiscretion, or dark desire would show up on your "permanent record card." Actions and outcomes would be exactly correlated. You would reap what you sowed and only what you sowed. Forgiveness and redemption would be impossible. There would be no such thing as luck. You could not start over in another town. The past would always catch up. To enforce perfect justice, someone would have to be watching all the time. It would be a world run by accountants and prosecutors. Too great an emphasis on accountability can be stifling to the human spirit and dangerous to the life of the free university. Let us hope the lesson of the Lani Guinier case is not to keep your scholarly mouth shut so that one day you can make it in Washington. What is the lesson?

As you know, the biblical text the Book of Job addresses the question of justice. It is one of those exuberant texts that resists any single interpretation of its deepest meanings. Nevertheless, I would hazard this reading. In the Book of Job, an all-powerful God refuses to enforce a principle of perfect justice. God then refuses Job's demand for an explanation why. Could it be that God is not an accountant or a prosecutor after all? Could it be that she knows just how important it is for us to achieve that understanding of her nature on our own?

Protecting people from harm is also a virtue. It is deeply offensive to the human spirit when the vulnerable are exploited by those who should be caring for them. Yet even here, puritan alchemy is capable of turning a virtue into a vice. A world comprehended only in terms of harm would be a disaster. If you exaggerate too much the idea that you should be protected from harm, you have a recipe for creating a society of thin-skinned complainers. For every parody, lampoon, or personal slight (you "snake," you "pig," you "animal"), there would be an accusation of "harassment" or "abuse." For every act of criticism, someone would rise up to claim they were being "victimized." Hate groups and anti-defamation leagues would quickly organize and keep each other in business. Eventually, the members of such a society would learn to keep their mouths closed, their ears covered, and their doors shut for fear of the consequences. Then someone would surely complain that the people they detest will have nothing to do with them.

Even provocation can become a vice if it is the only virtue in a puritanical town. There is no dignity in provocation if its only aim is to celebrate your freedom to humiliate others or convict them of inferiority. Provocation is an act of love, not of hate. It serves the pursuit of truth and of justice and protects from harm those who use it wisely. But like anything else of value, it must be handled with care.

As you undoubtedly know, there is no such thing as "political correctness" at the University of Chicago. If there were, it would be a unique form of "P.C.," because everything we do at the University is "unique." "Postmodernism," "positivism," and "unique" are three words you are going to hear a lot here.

Of course, these days it has become very hard to know what it means to be "politically correct." Is it politically correct to be in favor of government regulation or against it? Is it politically correct to celebrate the differences between men and women or to deny that there are any differences?

In the contemporary, postmodern political world, even the old distinction between left-wing and right-wing attitudes seems outdated. Libertarians and anarchists are bedfellows. Moral Majoritarians and Old New Dealers want the government to be more involved in our lives. There is an old joke about "the three great American lies." The first lie is "The check is in the mail." The second lie is "Hi, I am here from the government. I am here to help you." These days it is hard to predict who is going to laugh at the joke. I remember the political scene a few years ago when the "left-wing" government of Angola employed Cuban troops to defend oil fields owned by American corporations against a Maoist revolutionary supported by the Reagan administration. It is hard to be politically correct when the world starts to look like Monty Python's Flying Circus.

Yet let me not be evasive. Curiosity about variety, diversity, and difference is a mark of a liberal, open mind. So is the celebration of difference. So is the criticism of difference. If "political correctness" refers to the tenet that "nobody is ridiculous, bad, or disgusting," then it is an exaggeration of the virtue of tolerance, which makes it a form of Puritanism, which is not a good thing. If it refers to the idea that the only reason some people are not as accomplished as others is because they have been victimized, then P.C. diminishes some of the pleasures of the brain. But of course you won't find any of that at the University of Chicago. Or if you do, it will be "unique," which may make it okay.

It is not the exaggeration of some single virtue that makes an open mind. Open-mindedness is a balancing act involving several virtues. This annual address is entitled *The Aims of Education*. I have been invited to address the question, "What are the ends that an excellent college education ought to promote?" The ability to make intelligent choices? The recognition of one's true interests, talents, and goals? A sense of community and the public good? A desire to feel justified in the eyes of other open-minded women and men? The good taste and judgment to go beyond simply being well informed? The title of the address presupposes that there are certain ends that, if achieved, would lead you to say that the process that helped produce them was an excellent process. One of those ends, I believe, is to cultivate an understanding of the balance of intellectual functions and virtues that makes the life of an open mind possible. That balance of intellectual virtues is what my *Aims of Education Address* is about.

The idea of balancing several virtues may remind you of the idea of seeking the golden mean. The two ideas may be related, but I don't think they are identical. Things in balance protect each other from the distortions of exaggeration, but they do not blandly average each other out.

Many classical societies subscribed to the idea of natural aims in life. They believed there was a divine plan behind the organization of roles and functions in their community. It was the expectation of those ancients that there would be a division of labor within society, but that all roles and functions would be valued and esteemed as part of the plan.

I am uncertain whether that very premodern idea is entirely

correct. Nevertheless, in a postmodern world eager for any ironic turn, we should be willing to revalue certain aspects of premodern thought. Here is an image of a divine plan for the liberal arts college. I leave it to you to decide whether it is truly divine. I leave it to you to ponder what term other than "divine" you would rather use to speak about things that are elevated and have worth. Even if seeing is not believing, I do hope you still believe in fairies.

In the great, fabulous intellectual court of my imagination, there are four functions, or roles, in balance with one another. There is a king or queen. There is a loyal opposition. There is a jester. And there is a secret society.

The king or queen stakes out some starting point and tries to make his or her perspective the reigning view of things. It is important to the life of an intellectual community that someone play this part. The king or queen tries to establish some reigning view of things (such as rational choice theory, Marxism, reader response criticism, feminist criticism, or structural analysis). He or she tries to push it as far as it can credibly go (and perhaps even beyond that). Reigning views become objects of debate or criticism. Occasionally, they even become targets for rebellion and revolution, although one of the things you don't learn in school is that even the most appealing of revolutionaries usually turns out to be a frustrated king or queen.

Debate and criticism is in the hands of the loyal opposition. Members of the loyal opposition look for kinks and inconsistencies in what the king or queen has to say. They become disturbed if things are not functioning in an orderly way (the king or queen is usually amazed that there is any order at all, and grateful for it).

The jester, on the other hand, plays the part of deconstructionist, questioning deep assumptions, letting the court know how ridiculous it is to think there can ever be a reigning vision, sawing off, with a blade of irony, the branch upon which the king sits. (That last sentence, in which, with some effort, I avoided ending the sentence with a prepositional phrase—sawing off, with a blade of irony, the branch the king sits upon—reminds me of Winston Churchill's quip about that rule of grammar. When told he should not end his sentences with prepositional phrases, Churchill replied, "That is something up with which I shall not put." Parenthetical digressions are one of the jester's many tricks. Have you kept count of them in my talk? Which role am I playing tonight?)

Then there is the secret society. The secret society is a safe haven for the human imagination. The secret society protects the mind from premature cross-examination. It protects the mind from difficult and stifling questions that it is not yet prepared to answer. It protects the mind from embarrassing public scrutiny for the sake of human creativity. There is a private, secret part to the human mind that it is imperative to protect. Nothing should be forced to come out of the closet until it is ready.

You can think of the secret society as a function that includes all the more private aspects of the liberal, open-minded intellectual community. It includes private clubs, research groups, and spheres of personal association where birds of a feather flock together and where various versions of thick ethnicity are practiced. In its secret societies, the university community is a microcosm of the world. In dining halls, dormitories, and private clubs on and off campus and at various recreational activities, it is likely that some form of voluntary separation will be witnessed. If you decide to spend all your private time with other star-bellied sneetches, or if you decide to form a private club where men and women are segregated during social occasions or where only women meet to worship the Mother Goddess of the universe, you are probably going to succeed. Personally, I think it would be highly edifying, even ennobling, to be randomly assigned to meals throughout the year with a cross-section of members of the community, male and female, who come from different racial, ethnic, national, and religious groups. Nevertheless, the soul of liberalism is not saved by mandating against the spontaneous separations and free associations of everyday social life. Quite the contrary, without the secret society, the soul of the liberal community is bleached of some of its creativity.

In the non-Puritanical world of an open mind, there is dignity associated with each of those four intellectual roles. On my list of the great achievements of humankind is an item concerning the song "The Battle Hymn of the Republic." When you hear the song sung well, your blood boils and you feel like you want to go to war. The person who took that strident melody and transformed it into "Glory, glory hallelujah / Teacher hit me with a ruler" did a wonderful, jester-like thing. It is an accomplishment to take something heroic, passionate, and "high," produced by the king, and render it absurd, ridiculous, and "low." It is one reason we need jesters around. It is one reason we do not want them to lose their heads.

The divine plan requires that all four roles are played. It imagines that the roles are in balance. If there is no place in the intellectual court for one of the roles, or if there is a confusion of roles (for example, the jester becomes king), or if one role becomes too exaggerated, it can be a disaster for the intellectual life.

Kings can become megalomaniacs. Their reigning visions can become oppressive of alternative truths. The loyal opposition can lose its nerve and become more concerned with loyalty than opposition. Yea-saying may be encouraged or even cultivated by the king. A court full of jesters can be so discombobulating that everyone recoils in the backward direction of some old-fashioned literal truths. The secret society can become so fond of not having to answer tough questions that it stops having anything to do with the broader intellectual community. Worse yet, it may begin to think that its parochial principles are the principles of the broader intellectual community. Each of these exaggerations is a move in the direction of Puritanism, which is not good for the health of any community in which the brain is an erogenous zone and provocation is a virtue.

Sixth Commandment: There Are Only Two Things You Need to Know to Do Dermatology!

I have a brother-in-law who once did a medical residency in dermatology. He told me there are only two things you need to know to do dermatology: "If it is dry, make it wet. If it is wet, make it dry." Similarly, there are only two things you need to know to be successful in the liberal arts college of the University of Chicago: "If someone asserts it; deny it. If someone denies it, assert it."

So let's get to work and start having some fun. We expect nothing less of you than an eagerness to argue about the fundamentals of a liberal community. I have, in an unguarded way, made some bold assertions this evening, not the least of which is my suggestion that we are fundamentalists, too. I invite you to say, "That is something up with which I shall not put." I invite you to debate any or all of the legendary simplifications that I have dubbed commandments for saving the liberal soul. Replace them with other principles. Add to the list. Argue against lists. Argue against principles. Argue that the very idea of an "Aims of Education Address" is nothing more than an arbitrary imposition of values by some power elite bent on preserving its privileges. I invite you to do this later tonight at your houses and dorms. I hope you will do this over the next four years and for the rest of your life. On behalf of the faculty of the University of Chicago, I welcome you to this temple of liberalism. Honor it. Flourish in it. Defend it. May it live for a thousand and one years.

I have one last remark to make before we close. As you know, we have a new President at the University of Chicago, Hugo Sonnenschein. He comes to us from a great intellectual community, Princeton University. Allow me to end this address by expressing one of our many local conceits. Hannah Arendt (to whom I alluded earlier) once said during a lecture tour on the genteel campus of Princeton, "The idea of speaking here, of all places, about the concept of revolution has something ineffably comical about it." She preferred Hyde Park. The members of this faculty think they know why. Hanna Gray, our recent leader, concluded her presidency last June by describing the University of Chicago as "the only true American university." That is why you are here. That is why Hugo Sonnenschein is here. That is why we are all here. Welcome, Hugo Sonnenschein; welcome, class of '97; welcome, all new members of our community to the only true American university. May it live up to your expectations. May you help it live up to its reputation. May it live for a thousand and one years.

Conclusion: From Manywheres to the Civilizing Project, and Back

These are confusing and baffling times, especially when one tries to imagine the broad outlines of the new world order that is likely to replace the old Cold War scheme. What is the relationship, for example, between globalization (the linking of the world's economies), Westernization (the adoption of Western ideas, ideals, norms, institutions, and products) and economic growth? If you keep your ear to the ground these days, you can hear many prophecies or speculations about the shape of the New World order.

Prophesy #1. The West Is Best and Will Become Global (Or at Least It Should Try to Take Over the World). Western-like aspirations will be fired up or freed up by globalization and they will be the cause and the concomitant of economic growth. Western-like aspirations include a desire for liberal democracy, the decentralization of power, free enterprise, private property, individual rights, gender equality, and perhaps even a taste for Western products. With regard to globalization, Westernization, and economic growth, this prediction imagines causal effects in all directions. Basically this is the Western or Northern European "enlightenment" origin story universalized and projected into the future.

Prophesy #2: Others Will Have "A Piece of the Rock" and Hold on to Their Distinctive Culture Too. In the early 1970s I had a Sudanese student who did his Ph.D. on attitudes toward modernization among African students, using a beliefs and values questionnaire. He discovered that the materialism factor in his questionnaire was entirely unrelated to the individualism factor; it is possible to value material wealth without giving up the collectivist values of the tribe. The Saudi Arabians liked that message so much they hired him to teach in their universities. Perhaps that is why Sam Huntington's thesis (1996b) that the West is unique, but not universal, and that other civilizations do not need to become like us to benefit from the technologies of the modern world is so popular in the non-Western world. This prediction imagines globalization and economic growth without deep cultural penetration from the West. Cultures and civilizations are encouraged to remain diverse while everyone gets a piece of the economic pie.

Prophesy #3. A Liberal Ottoman-Like Empire; and the Complementary Citizens of the New World Order (Cosmopolitan Liberals and Local Nonliberals). I associate the first prophecy with Francis Fukuyama and the second with Sam Huntington. Here's a third augury. Imagine a world order that is liberal in the classical sense. Its leaders assume a stance of neutrality with regard to substantive cultural issues. They do not condition aid and protection on changes in local gender ideals, forms of authority, kinship structures, or coming-of-age ceremonies. They don't try to tell the members of different cultural groups that they have to live together or love each other or share the same emotional reactions, aesthetic ideals, and religious beliefs. They do not try to tell them how to run their private lives, or that they must have private lives. Imagine that in this world order various sanctioning mechanisms make it possible to enforce minimal rules of civility within ethnic enclaves and between cultural groups: exit visas are always available, and no aggression is permitted across territorial boundaries. Imagine that such a world system is set up to permit or encourage decentralized control over cultural issues and hence to promote local cultural efflorescence. Such an emergent New World Order might look like a postmodern Ottoman "millet system" on a global scale.

I imagine this system would be two-tiered and operate at two levels, global and local. I imagine its personnel would be of two complementary kinds. There would be the cosmopolitan liberals, who would be trained to appreciate value neutrality and cultural diversity and who would run the global institutions of the world system. And there would be the local nonliberals who would be dedicated to one form or another of "thick ethnicity" and inclined to separate themselves from others, thereby guaranteeing that there would be enough diversity remaining in the world for the cosmopolitan liberals to appreciate. The global elite (those who are cosmopolitan and liberal), would, of course, come from all nationalities. In the new universal cosmopolitan culture of the global tier of the world system, your ancestry and skin color would be far less important than your education, your values, and your travel plans. It is already the case in the postmodern cosmopolitan world that you do not have to grow up in the West to be Western any more than you have to grow up in the Southern world to adopt an indigenous Third World point of view. Finally I imagine that it would be possible in this New World Order for individuals to switch tiers or roles in both directions, moving from global liberalism to local nonliberalism or fundamentalism and back, within the course of a single life.

Speculations are speculations. Augury is a hazardous business. These are baffling times. One reason for the confusion is that the first prophesy, the Western or Northern European enlightenment story about the inevitability of the universal ascent of secularism, individualism, and science, has taken its lumps in recent years. Some serious doubts have been raised about its usefulness for predicting the direction of change in the early twenty-first century. Thirty or forty years ago many Western social scientists predicted that in the contemporary modernizing world, religion would go away to be replaced by science. They predicted that tribes would go away to be replaced by individuals. So far this has not happened, either globally or locally.

Multiculturalism is a fact of life. Religion thrives. The former second world, once an enforced secular empire, is now many little worlds. The development of a global world system and the emergence of local ethnic or cultural revival movements almost seem to go hand in hand these days, and at the limit, ethnically motivated political succession may even hold rewards for some cultural minority groups. The potential rewards include direct receipt of financial aid and military protection from various power centers and perhaps even a voice at the United Nations. Moreover, many of us now live in nation states composed, as Joseph Raz has put it, "of groups and communities with diverse practices and beliefs, including groups whose beliefs are inconsistent with each other." It seems likely that we will continue to do so, if for no other reason than the reality of global migration and the fact that community and divinity are essential goals or values and must be acknowledged for the sake of individual identity and human progress.

A second reason these are baffling times is that the recognition of the staying power and popularity of particularistic religious and cultural commitments has not necessarily been associated with attitudes of pluralistic tolerance or a willingness to "live and let live." Quite the contrary, recognition of the fact and durability of local identities has simply rekindled an evolutionary or developmental view of culture, reminiscent of the colonial "civilizing project" of the late nineteenth and early twentieth centuries. The ranking of cultures, civilizations, and religions from better to worse may have gone out of fashion in American anthropology long ago thanks to the efforts of Franz Boas and many others, but it is back, with a vengeance, and in some pretty fancy places. Indeed, as we enter the twenty-first century, the idea that "culture counts" or that "culture matters" is not only more popular than ever but is increasingly used to announce the superiority of particular ways of life. It is used to classify as backward, unenlightened, or insufferable the beliefs and practices of other groups, nations, or even whole civilizations. Consider, for example, events at two recent World Bank meetings, the first called Culture Counts (held in October, 1999) and the second on the topic of gender and justice in Africa (held in May, 2000).

Culture Counts was a large international gathering held in Florence, Italy. It included talks by Hillary Clinton, ministers of finance or culture or education from around the globe, and the President of the World Bank. But the highlight was the plenary academic session, which featured a keynote address by a prominent American economic historian. He reported on what he presumed to be the universal race among nations to get rich; and explained why cultural inheritance makes all the difference in whether a country is rich or poor. China was probably leading the race one thousand years ago, he supposed, but they inherited too many xenophobic beliefs from their ancestors and did not want to trade with outsiders. So the Chinese fell behind and did not get a ship to the Atlantic Ocean until well into the nineteenth century.

The keynote speaker then took the audience on an economic and cultural tour of the rest of the world. Culture counts everywhere, he said. In Latin America an attitude called machismo results in Latin men thinking they are little princes and not wanting to work. In Africa, the physical environment is not very good, but they fight all the time and they beat their wives. And then there is Southern Europe and Catholicism. The Catholic Church turned against Galileo and science. So Southern Europeans fell into ignorance and superstition. But now we have reached the year 2000. Look around! North Americans and Northern Europeans have won the race, and for good cultural reasons, the American exclaimed. Even before he could fully deliver his take-away message (get with the progressive program: westernize your culture, model yourself after us, or remain poor!), the Chinese delegate to the meeting had walked out of the room.

The second meeting, on gender and justice in Africa, was held at World Bank headquarters in Washington, D.C., with occasional satellite links to audiences in six African countries. A prominent Western liberal feminist, who believes that progressive social change requires that the sisters of the world unite in opposition to a loathsome and oppressive universal patriarchy, delivered the following message to a predominantly African female audience. Stop complaining about colonialism, she said. African traditions and customs were bad for women long before colonialism came along. She then invoked a sensational literary account of wife beating. As it turned out, the "sisters" in the audience were mainly united in opposition to what they perceived as the speaker's neocolonial attitudes and all-too-familiar and high-minded first world missionary zeal. They certainly had some complaints about their men. But they still viewed them as members of the family and generally felt at home with them in their traditions. And they actually thought African females were pretty powerful, in their own way.

But the meeting that was most revealing of the return of cultural developmental thinking was the one held in April of 1999 at the house of the American Academy in Cambridge, Massachusetts, sponsored by Harvard University's Academy for International and Area Studies, and organized by Lawrence Harrison and Samuel Huntington. A notable theme at that meeting was the general equation of progress and goodness with Protestant values. One of the organizers suggested that successful Protestant missionary efforts in Latin America might enhance economic growth, with the implication that the more Catholics who are converted to Northern European ways, the better. Others argued that Jews and overseas Chinese are good for the economy too, especially if they behave like Protestants—or at least subscribe to some version of the Protestant ethical law that only those who accumulate wealth have been chosen by God to be saved.

The most dominant theme of the meeting, however, was the emphasis on progressive cultural development, so as to make the world a better place. Hence there was a good deal of discussion of what might be called the imperial liberal civilizing project. The project is aimed at establishing that the West (or at least its northern-most sector) is best and at improving the rest of the world through exposure to Northern European and American values, beliefs, and customs. Perhaps it is a sign of the times that the conference publication (a book called *Culture Matters: How Values Shape Human Progress*) became a media event. The book was reviewed in the *Wall Street Journal* and *Time* Magazine and discussed in the *New York Times* and the *Atlantic Monthly*. For a short period of time, it was one of the top 800 best-selling books at Amazon.com, a stunning achievement for an edited academic volume.

I was invited to the Culture Matters conference to fill the role of a designated skeptic. And to some extent I played that part. But there were other, quite unanticipated, thoughts on my mind during those days at the American Academy. I found myself asking, is this how Franz Boas and other anthropological pluralists felt when debating with cultural evolutionary theorists in an earlier heyday of Western initiated globalization and empire building (roughly 1870–1914)? I found myself wondering, what happened to the pluralistic message of Anthropology 101? In other words, I came face to face with the utter failure of my own discipline of anthropology to accomplish its most basic mission, to raise the awareness of social scientists, policy analysts, and the public at large to the virtue in cultural variety and to the hazards of ethnocentrism. And I found myself acutely aware of the responsibility of anthropologists to once again develop and promote a conception of culture that might be useful in minimizing some of the risks associated with the problem of difference and with multicultural life in a global and migratory world.

It is entirely predictable that for an American anthropologist of my generation the events I just described should evoke a sense of déjà vu. Most American anthropologists who came of age in the postcolonial period learned about cultural development and the idea that the West is best in their history of anthropology books, in the chapter called "European Cultural Evolutionary Theories of the Nineteenth Century." Those theories were premised on the idea that all cultures or societies could be ranked or placed in stages, from low to high, from savage to civilized, from primitive to modern, from backward to advanced, culminating in the way of life of the English, the French, or the Germans. Then, as now, the staging or placement of cultures relied on a few supposedly highly correlated and supposedly objective indices of progress, development, or evolutionary value. The direction of advance was said to run from poor to rich, from magical to scientific, from illiterate to literate, from uneducated to educated, from simple to complex, from sickly to healthy, from authoritarian to democratic, from polygamous to

monogamous, from pagan to Christian, from oppressed to liberated. The basic claims were that our way of life is the most true,
good, beautiful, and efficient; and that to the very degree that the
beliefs, values, and practices of others differ from our own, they are
false, base, foul, or irrational.

Associated with late nineteenth-century cultural evolutionary
theories was an imperial liberal civilizing project, sometimes called
the white man's burden, although, then as now, it was understood
to be a white woman's burden too. The burden was the assumed
moral obligation of citizens from advanced, modern, or highly developed societies to enlighten, develop, and transform those who
live in backward, primitive, or dark age societies. Then as now, the
imperial liberal aim was to promote universal progress, which was
associated with Northern European sensibilities and English
(French, or German) conceptions of an orderly society. Nowadays
the reference point for defining progress is often the United States
(our wealth and free enterprise; our form of government; our notions of work, marriage, and family; our ideas about sexuality and
male/female relationships). But the basic project is pretty much the
same and, now as then, the popular press is full of sensationalized
stories about "barbaric practices" in foreign lands and of triumphal
accounts of Western cultural victories.

"Afghan women face the world!" was a recent headline. The implication was that our own local cultural standards for normal
modes of communication, social affiliation, and face-to-face contact provide the essential yardstick for measuring human progress
and defining what all men and women must want to do. The implication was that veiling in the Islamic world is a backward practice
and that it is widely experienced as oppressive. That implication
will certainly come as a surprise to many Islamic women, for whom
the head scarf or the veil conveys a sense of dignified modesty,

control, self-respect, civility, and a socially endorsed conception of proper sex identity, gender relationships, and expressive signaling. The burqa long preceded the Taliban and has not disappeared with the fall of Khandahar.

For much of the twentieth century, an introductory course in cultural anthropology, or at least its Platonic ideal, was meant to be an antidote to the "up-from-barbarism," "we're developed/you're not" message of precisely that sort of thinking. The aim of such a course was to enlarge the scope of our understanding of, appreciation of, and toleration for cultural differences. Its main message was this. Many things that we take for granted as natural, divinely given, logically necessary, and practically indispensable for life in an orderly, safe, and morally decent society are not natural, not divinely given, not logically necessary, and not practically indispensable for life in an orderly, safe, and morally decent society. They are products of a local history. They are ways of seeing and being in the world that lend meaning and value to our own form of life. But they are not the only ways to construct a rational, worthy, and practically efficient way of life. They are matters of opinion, not absolute truth. They are discretionary forms, not mandatory ones. Nature and reason leave plenty of room for cultural variety, and we should too.

This does not imply that anything goes. The message of a good Anthropology 101 course should not be confused with another: the self-refuting proposition (of the radical relativist) that one should never be judgmental or make claims about the superiority of the ideas, ideals, or practices of one society over others. One of the common (and by now boring) accusations against cultural anthropology is that it teaches that, just because something is different, it must be entitled to our respect. Or, that it teaches that nobody is base, vile, or irrational or holds false beliefs (except perhaps dead, white, Western males). Such accusations are as misguided as the views they critique. "Whatsoever is, is okay" may be an appealing message for those who believe all of God's creation is perfect, but it is not the proper message of Anthropology 101. A proper course is an invitation to be slow to judge others. It teaches the discipline of temporarily bracketing feelings of disgust, hate, or condescension toward others, so as better to be able to closely examine and determine the meaning and purpose of things that seem strange, alien, unfamiliar, or different. It cautions us against the ready assumption that our own commitments, tastes, and preferences must be the gold standard for evaluating the ways of "others." But it does not rule out judgment and critique. It just makes criticism less easy, more informed, less ethnocentric.

The pluralistic tolerance taught in Anthropology 101 is not opposed to the ideals of universalism. Normative theorists do not divide into only two types, those who believe that anything goes (the radical relativists) and those who believe that only one thing goes (the uniformitarians). I, for one, strongly believe in universalism, but the type of universalism in which I believe is universalism without the uniformity, which is what makes me a pluralist. In other words, there are universally binding values, just too many of them (for example, justice, beneficence, autonomy, sacrifice, liberty, loyalty, sanctity, and duty). I believe those objectively valuable ends of life are diverse, heterogeneous, irreducible to some common denominator such as "utility" or "pleasure," and inherently in conflict with each other. I believe that all the good things in life cannot be simultaneously maximized. I believe that when it comes to implementing true values, there are always trade-offs, which is why there are different traditions of values (for example, cultures) and why no one cultural tradition has ever been able to honor everything that is good.

One can be a pluralist and still grant that there are true and universally binding values and undeniable moral principles—for example, cruelty is evil, you should treat like cases alike and different cases differently, highly vulnerable members of a society are entitled to protection from harm. One of the claims of pluralism, however, is that values and principles are fully objective only to the extent they are kept quite abstract and devoid of content. A related claim is that no abstract value or principle, in and of itself, can provide definitive guidance in concrete cases of moral dispute. In other words, it is possible for morally decent and fully rational peoples to look at each other and at each other's practices and go yuck! (see Chapter 4).

There is plenty of mutual yucking going on in the world today. Circumcising and noncircumcising peoples, for example, almost always have a mutual yuck response to each other. The mutual yuck response is possible because objective values cannot in and of themselves determine whether it is right or wrong to arrange a marriage. Whether it is good or bad to sacrifice or butcher large mammals such as goats or sheep. Whether it is savory or unsavory to put your parents in an old age home. Whether it is vicious or virtuous to have a large family. Whether it is moral or immoral to abort a fetus. Whether it is commendable or contemptible to encourage girls as well as boys to enter into a Covenant with God (or to become full members of their society) by means of a ritual initiation involving genital modifications or circumcision. Morally decent and fully rational people can disagree about such things, even in the face of a plentitude of shared objective values. In such cases ethnocentrism amounts to the failure to recognize that basic truth.

Any course in anthropology aimed at countering ethnocentrism, may, of course, be discombobulating and unnerving, or produce highly controversial results. There would be little courage in the conviction that one should appreciate differences if such an attitude amounted to little more than a toleration or taste for each other's foods and festivities. So for the sake of illustration, let's consider a controversial case, in particular, the practice of polygamy. In the light of the renewal of cultural developmental thinking, polygamy is once again receiving attention as a putative barbaric practice, the kind of thing done by savages and those with a "traditional" (read "underdeveloped" or "not yet sufficiently modern") culture.

I say "once again" because one is reminded of the great nineteenth-century polygamy debate in the United States. Despite the fact that there is a good deal of precedent for polygamy in the bible, Mormons in the territory of Utah came under the gaze of that era's civilizing project and were forced out of their religiously based marriage customs (and imprisoned) by means of the law. In 1878 (*Reynolds v. United States,* 98 U.S. 145) the United States Supreme Court was asked to decide whether a law prohibiting polygamy was constitutionally permissible, because it might appear to place a burden on the free exercise of religion by Mormons. The court, in its wisdom, set out to define the limits on the coercive powers of the state, proclaiming that "Congress was deprived of all legislative power over mere opinion, but was left free to reach actions which were in violation of social duties or subversive of good order." That principle, of course, raises some obvious questions. Is a cultural preference for monogamy over polygamy more than a matter of opinion? Is polygamy subversive of social order? Are there transcendental values or social duties that demand that kinship and family life must be organized solely around (heterosexual?) monogamous family units?

Although no hard evidence was presented, the court answered those questions in cultural developmental terms. The Justices assumed that polygamy must be vicious and harmful to women and children and alien to the way of life of a civilized nation. They wrote, "Polygamy has always been odious among the northern and western nations of Europe, and, until the establishment of the Mormon Church, was almost exclusively a feature of the life of Asiatic and of African people." Whether they were right or wrong about the distribution of permissible polygamy among the cultures of the world, the judges were implying more than just "that's the way we [the descendents of Northern and Western Europeans] do it here, so you must too." They were aware that on a world scale there is little agreement among the many cultures of the world about the single best way to organize kinship, marriage, and family life. Yet the existence of cultural diversity did not lead them to view their own preference for monogamous marriages as a matter of opinion or local cultural taste. Why? In part because they ranked the northern and western nations of Europe high in the evolutionary hierarchy of cultures and assumed European cultures were superior at discovering moral truth.

What would Anthropology 101 have to say about the issue? How would it complicate our evaluation of the case? In fact, as anthropologists who study kinship now know, polygamy per se is not subversive of social order. Typically in polygamous societies the vast majority of marriages are monogamous, and the two forms of marriage have peacefully coexisted in almost every society in which polygamy has been socially acceptable. Many cultures of the world have found polygamy socially acceptable. In all such cultures there are healthy, happy, and socially dutiful people who have grown up or lived in polygamous households, including Mormon children prior to 1878. Indeed, the likelihood of being healthy, happy, and socially dutiful in life does not seem to turn on a family life issue of this type.

Polygamy may seem to be an exotic topic, but it is not just of historical or academic interest. In contemporary multicultural India, ever since independence from British rule, civil order has been enhanced (rather than disrupted) by allowing the large Muslim minority population the right to their own marriage laws, which are permissive of polygamous marriages (see Rudolph and Rudolph, 2002). Yet there is vocal opposition to this accommodation by liberal feminists and anti-Muslim Hindu fundamentalists (strange bedfellows indeed). In South Africa, where local ethnic group customs permissive of polygamy survived through the repressive years of the apartheid regime, there are ongoing imperial liberal attempts to "progressively" reform society by mandating monogamy, although there is resistance as well, in the name of the "right to culture" (see Chambers, 2000). Whether the contemporary leaders of Asia and Africa will now embrace the cultural preferences of the Northern and Western nations of Europe and react to the practices of their own ancestors as "odious" remains to be seen. It would be ironic indeed if the white man's burden to eradicate polygamy from the world not only returned but was embraced by the cosmopolitan African elite.

And what might a pluralistic Anthropology 101 course say about current developmental stories linking culture and economy, and why some nations are rich and others poor? Perhaps the message should be that we social scientists have not reached consensus on this question. It would be nice to have in hand a valid general causal explanation for the wealth and poverty of peoples, cultures or nations, but we do not. If by "causation" we mean what J.S. Mill meant by it—namely, all the necessary conditions that are jointly sufficient to produce an effect—I think we must admit that we do not know what causes economic growth. Sicily in the fifteenth century, Holland in the sixteenth century, Japan today—social scientists can pick a people, culture, or nation and tell a plausible story about some of the reasons for economic failure or success. But that is a far cry from a general causal theory. Try listing all the potential causal conditions for wealth production mentioned by David Landes (1998) in his monumental economic history of the world. Then ask yourself this question: Are any of those conditions sufficient to produce economic growth? The answer is no. Are any of those conditions even necessary?

Having guns did it here. Having Jews did it there. In this case it was immigration policy. In that case it was having access to quinine. In this case it was the freeing of serfs. In that case it was the availability of fossil fuel. In this case it was the weather. In that case it was willingness to trade with outsiders. In this case it was having good colonial masters. In that case is was high consumer demand. In this case it was gender equality. In that case it was luck. Singapore is not a liberal democracy, but it is rich. India is the world's most populous democracy, but it is poor. Sweden in the eighteenth century, on the other hand, was a sparsely populated democracy, and it was poor too. Peoples who are religiously orthodox and who do not believe in gender equality (for example, Hasidic Jews) can be rich. Fully secularized egalitarian societies such as the former communist countries in Eastern Europe may fail to thrive from an economic point of view. In 1950 Japan had "Confucian values" (which at the time did not seem Western), and that country was poorer than Brazil. In 1990 Japan still had the same Confucian values, which all of a sudden seemed very Protestant-like as Japan outstripped Brazil.

If I were a cynic, I would say that our most able economic historians excel at identifying some of the unnecessary conditions that might have been jointly sufficient to produce wealth in any particular special case. Less cynically, I think it is fair to say that, despite many impressive post-hoc historical accounts of the case-specific conditions that promoted growth, the general causes of economic success have not yet been identified, if by "causation" we mean what J.S. Mill meant when he defined the term.

Simple stories thus get qualified in Anthropology 101. Fossil fuels and good ports (noncultural environmental factors) have made some peoples rich, even where women prefer to be veiled and polygamous marriages are permitted. Nondemocratic countries (especially those with stable governments) are not necessarily poor, and stable governments are not necessarily democratic. Democratic governments are not necessarily stable, and even stable democracies are not necessarily rich. But they are more likely to be materially well off if they are in a favorable physical location or environment. Indeed, if you are going to bet your money on any theory, climate, natural resources, and physical ecology probably have far more to do with the production of wealth than do cultural beliefs, religion, or values; and those who get ahead first tend to stay ahead. It is a lot easier to get rich in the temperate locations of the world than in the tropics (see Sachs, 2000). Colonialism probably did not make peoples in the Third World poor—the gap between rich and poor grew in the postcolonial period. Culture did not make these peoples poor either; rather, noncultural environmental factors appear to be the big constraints.

And what about the Protestant ethic? Doesn't God bless individuals and ways of life in the sign of their prosperity, as the early Calvinists argued? The qualifications multiply. It is hard to know about the afterlife, but a non-Protestant 45-year-old Greek male (a Southern European) can expect to live longer than his Northern European Protestant English peer; and, within Europe at least, greater national wealth does not translate into greater national health. Moreover, having a much closer look at claims about Protestant conversion rates and wealth in the Southern world would be a good idea. The causal arrows may not run in the right direction. Protestant evangelical missionaries often discourage ancestor worship and thick ties of kinship; the creed provides a good excuse for refusing loans to relatives. What if those who get rich in Latin America convert to a Protestant faith only after they make their money (rather than the other way around)? Such hypotheses circulate among anthropologists. Let's have that closer look.

What about the gold standards that are used for measuring progress? How objective is the selection of yardsticks for ranking successful cultures? It may be an old argument, but it is still a relevant argument, to point out the subjective or discretionary side of cultural evolutionary rankings. As Franz Boas knew very well, there is lots of room to tell the progress story with different outcomes. The universe of goods and values is variegated and complex, not uniform and simple. For example, reproductive fitness or sheer quantity of life is the yardstick used by biologists for estimating the success of a population. By that standard China and India are on top. If spirituality and community are essential human goods, the Northern secular world has a way to go. Should the standard be the number of lonely people in a population? Or perhaps the number who die without suffering years of chronic pain (which may be negatively correlated with longevity)? If expected years of life (rather than population size) is the measure, when do we start counting? Should it be from birth (which excludes rates of abortion and miscarriage from the calculation and places a huge weight on infant mortality rates)? Should we start counting from the moment of conception (which figures prenatal mortality, including abortion rates—currently about 22% in the United States—in the life expectancy calculation)? Why not life expectancy at age 45 (a quality of life measure suitable for midlife adults)?

And then there is the really big question. Do we really know, other than by presumption, what people around the world "naturally" want? Is it to be rich, with all else in life viewed as a means to that end? Or perhaps to have sufficient resources to support some favored way of life and feel at home in it, even if that means living a shorter life, or a materially more modest life, or a life without miniskirts, beauty parlors, nightclubs, and MTV? Is there really a way to say which of those wants is universally superior?

Simple triumphal stories of progressive cultural development deserve to be carefully scrutinized, taken apart, qualified and, when and if they turn out to be overly simple, discarded. Why? In part because whoever is wealthiest and the most technologically advanced tends to think that their way of life is the best, the most natural, the god given, the surest means to salvation, or at least the fast lane to this-worldly well-being. In the sixteenth century Portuguese missionaries to China believed that their invention of clocks, of which they were very proud, was knock-down proof of the superiority of Catholicism over other world religions (Landes, 1998: 336–337). For all one knows, their mechanical timepieces may have been counted as an argument in favor of absolute monarchy. Dazzled by our contemporary inventions and toys (CNN, IBM, Big Mac, blue jeans, the birth control pill, the credit card) and at home in our own way of life, we are prone to similar illusions and the same type of conceits. This is what a course in Anthropology 101 is meant to do: teach students to beware of overly simple stories that end with the punch line "and therefore my way of life is the best."

Undoubtedly it was naïve of American anthropologists of the postcolonial period to imagine that the imperial liberal civilizing project was a peculiar ideological product of the late nineteenth century and had gone away. The intellectual roots of the project run deep. So deep that even in our contemporary skeptical anti-ideological postmodern world, which is highly suspicious of all grand and oversimplifying master narratives, it is the one story to which we are prone to return. Like the stories in the Bible, the story of the Enlightenment and the emergence of modern secular society in the West is a powerful origin tale. As the conventional story goes, the world woke up from the slumber of the "dark ages," became good, and finally got in touch with ways of discovering scientific and ethical truths about 300 years ago in Northern and Western Europe. As a result religion (superstition, fantasy, ignorance, subjectivity) gave way to science (fact, education, objectivity, reason). Parochialism and group allegiances gave way to humanism, cosmopolitanism, and individualism. Hierarchical structures and top-down command systems gave way to autonomous structures and the separation of church from state, politics from science, power from truth.

For those who are secular missionaries, the enlightenment story thus provides a charter for how to remake society and better the world in the image of the West. For those who are more theologically inclined, the idea that God blesses cultures in the sign of their prosperity serves the same function. With the end of the Cold War, the fall of communism, and the rise of global capitalism, the West is now in a better position to have its way. How long that will last, or whether it is a good thing, remains to be seen. Nevertheless, like it or not, the civilizing project is back. One now looks to the heirs of Franz Boas, and to pluralists of all kinds, to revive and develop a convincing counter-discourse about how to admire (and feel at home in) one's own way of life without implying that it is the only way of life that is valuable. Perhaps it will be counter-discourse explaining why human beings cannot live by ecumenism alone and why membership in some particular cultural tradition or system of meanings is an essential condition for personal identity and individual happiness. Perhaps it will be a counter-discourse explaining why cultural diversity and thick ethnicity both have their place in the natural and moral order of things and why mother nature does not want everyone to be alike. Perhaps it will explain why, when, and in what ways it is possible to be different, yet equal, at the same time.

Cultural psychology and the search for the view from many-wheres are parts of that discourse. The point of this quest is to teach us how to make critical judgments for the sake of identifying alternative conceptions of the world and ways of life that are deserving of tolerance (or even appreciation), and are morally and rationally defensible, even in the face of criticism from abroad. Their aim is to properly comprehend difference, and not only as a corrective to contemporary forms of ethnocentrism and cultural imperialism, although that is reason enough. Only time will tell whether intellectual history is repeating itself.

Notes

I. WHO SLEEPS BY WHOM REVISITED

1. Oriya family households are either joint or nucleated. When they are joint, two or more brothers co-reside, with their parents if the parents are still alive, and the brothers' wives and children all live together in a single patrilocal family home or compound. In our data, based on reports from children and adults, the co-sleeping network for a child almost never included that child's aunts, uncles, cousins, or father's father. Children did sometimes co-sleep with their father's mother. The father's father rarely co-slept with a child and most often slept alone, separated from his wife.

2. The first type of data was collected in 1983 (from Oriya informants) and in 1991 (from American informants). The second type of data was collected in 1991 from both Oriya and American informants. The third type of data was collected in Orissa, India, in 1983. (For a discussion of the moral basis of family and social life practices in the Oriya temple town of Bhubaneswar, see Mahapatra, 1981; Shweder, Mahapatra, and Miller 1987; Shweder et al., 1997; also see Chapter 5).

2. THE "BIG THREE" OF MORALITY

We gratefully acknowledge the support we received for research on moral reasoning and explanations of suffering from several

sources: The National Institute of Child Health and Human Development, the MacArthur Foundation Health and Behavior Research Network, the MacArthur Foundation Research Network on
Successful Midlife Development (MIDMAC), and a research grant
from Georgetown University to Nancy Much.

1. Lakoff and Johnson argue that the most significant, sublime, ordinary, and practical of human understandings are not based on the
processes of logical rationality operating on an objective world of
thing-categories, but rather on metaphors, which ultimately relate
back to our experience of our bodies and their ecological orienta-
tions to an animate and inanimate environment.

2. A second fifty-four-item coding scheme consisting of a wide range
of moral concepts from the moral psychology and moral philosophy literature, developed with the assistance of Sandra Dixon and
Deborah Pool, is available upon request.

3. CULTURAL PSYCHOLOGY OF EMOTIONS

1. For example, Bruner, 1990; Cole, 1988, 1990, 1996; D'Andrade, 1995;
Goddard, 1997; Howard, 1985; LeVine, 1990; Lutz, 1985a; Markus
and Kitayama, 1991, 1992; Markus, Kitayama, and Heiman, 1998;
Much, 1995; Peacock, 1984; Shweder, 1990a, 1991, 1999a,b; Shweder
et al., 1998; Shweder and Sullivan, 1990, 1993; Stigler, Shweder, and
Herdt, 1990; Wierzbicka, 1993, 1997; Yang, 1997.

4. "WHAT ABOUT FEMALE GENITAL MUTILATION?"

Many friends, colleagues, and experts on African initiation ceremonies have generously (and tolerantly) discussed this topic with
me or critiqued an earlier version of the chapter. Without in any
way holding them responsible for my perspective on this controversial issue, I wish to express my deepest gratitude to Fuambai
Ahmadu, Margaret Beck, Janice Boddy, David Chambers, Jane
Cohen, Elizabeth Dunn, Robert Edgerton, Arthur Eisenberg, Ylva
Hernlund, Albrecht Hofheinz, Sudhir Kakar, Jane Kaplan, Frank

Kessel, Corinne Kratz, Dennis Krieger, Maivân Lâm, Heather Lindkvist, Hazel Markus, Saba Mâhmood, Martha Minow, Carla Obermeyer, Anni Peller, Jane Rabe, Lawrence Sager, Lauren Shweder, Gerd Spittler, and Leti Volpp. This chapter was prepared while I was a Fellow at the Wissenschaftskolleg Zu Berlin (The Institute for Advanced Study in Berlin). An abbreviated version of this chapter appeared in the Fall 2000 issue of *Daedalus: Journal of the American Academy of Arts and Sciences* 129(4).

1. Susan Rich is an "anti-FGM" activist who developed "FGM eradication programs" in Africa for the Special Projects Fund of Population Action International. Stephanie Joyce is an independent consultant.

2. Carla Obermeyer is an anthropologist and epidemiologist in the Department of Population and International Health at Harvard University.

3. Olayinka Koso-Thomas is a gynecologist in Sierra Leone and an anti-FGM activist.

4. Susan Okin is a First World feminist and a political scientist at Stanford University who believes that "multiculturalism is bad for women".

5. Fuambai Ahmadu is a Kono woman from Sierra Leone. She grew up in the United States and is a Ph.D. candidate in anthropology at the London School of Economics. At age 22 she returned to Sierra Leone to be initiated into the "women's secret society" and to be circumcised according to the customs of her ethnic group.

6. Things are starting to change. Essays are beginning to appear that are more ethnographically informed, nondefensive, or skeptical of the current "anti-FGM" global discourse. Examples include Abusharaf, 2001; Ahmadu, 2000; Boddy, 1996; Coleman, 1998; Gilman, 1999; Gosselin, 2000, Gruenbaum, 2001; Johnson 2000, Kratz, 1994, 1999; Obermeyer, 1999; Obiora, 1997; Parker, 1995; Thomas, 2000. For a sample of views and representations concerning female initiation and circumcision, also see Abusharaf, 2000; Boddy, 1989; Cooper, 1999; El Dareer, 1982; Gruenbaum, 1988;

Gunning, 1992; Hernlund, 2000; Horowitz and Jackson, 1997; Kenyatta, 1938; Lane and Rubinstein, 1996; Meinardus, 1967; Slack, 1988; Walley, 1997; Williams and Sobieszyzyk, 1997.

7. The name of this group is variously spelled Gikuyu and Kikuyu. I have used Kikuyu throughout.

5. THE RETURN OF THE "WHITE MAN'S BURDEN"

1. For more on this temple and the community that serves it, see Mahapatra, 1981; Seymour, 1983, 1999; Shweder et al., 1990; Shweder, 1991; Shweder et al., 1997.

2. For a complete description of this sample, see Menon and Shweder, 1994.

3. Paul Cleary and his associates at the Harvard Medical School have collected comparable data on American women. In a large telephone survey, women were asked to assess their satisfaction on a ten-point scale.

4. An *anna* is a coin that is no longer in circulation. In pre-independence India, there were six *paisa* (or *pice*) to an *anna* and sixteen *annas* to a *rupee*.

5. We should, perhaps, clarify that our particular understanding is neither unusual nor peculiar to us. Today in India there is a burgeoning women's movement (see *India Today*, 30 September 1995) that disdains the label "feminism," distances itself from Western-inspired feminist movements, and does not identify gender equality at home or in the workplace as a significant goal. Instead, it seeks to identify potential sources of female power defined in Hindu terms and works to achieve female empowerment within that framework.

6. This is the tradition that worships the Sakti or Devi, the great goddess of Hinduism. Followers believe that the world is energized by her and that in her lies the ultimate meaning of life in this world.

7. For the Oriya Hindus of Old Town, *samsaro* stands for the family, for household life, the entire world of living beings as well as for

the never-ending cycle of rebirths and redeaths that characterizes all existence this side of release and liberation.

8. Not all Oriya Hindu women have sons, but traditionally, people in Old Town overcome this by adopting a relative's son, preferably one's own daughter's second or third son. The child is adopted formally into his maternal grandfather's lineage and all ritual ties to his biological father are severed. Dukhi, the old daughter-in-law quoted earlier, and her husband have done just that.

9. The Lingaraj temple bathing tank—literally, "ocean of droplets."

10. *Nirmaliya* is a solution made of water and desiccated *prasad,* which are leftovers of divine offerings from the Lingaraj temple.

11. According to Oriya Hindus of Old Town, the effects on the family of a man committing adultery are far less profound than if a woman does so, because men are considered to be marginal to the well-being of the family.

References

Abbott, S. 1992. Holding On and Pushing Away: Comparative Perspectives on an Eastern Kentucky Child-Rearing Practice. *Ethos* 1:33–65.

Abu-Lughod, L. 1985. Honor and the Sentiments of Loss in a Bedouin Society. *American Ethnologist* 12:245–261.

———. 1986. *Veiled Sentiments: Honor and Poetry in a Bedouin Society.* Berkeley, Calif.: University of California Press.

———. 1991. Writing against Culture. In R. Fox, ed., *Recapturing Anthropology: Working on the Present.* Santa Fe, N. Mex.: School for American Research Press.

Abusharaf, R. M. 2000. Rethinking Feminist Discourses on Infibulation: Responses from Sudanese Feminists. In B. Shell-Duncan and Y. Hernlund, eds., *Female "Circumcision" in Africa: Culture, Controversy and Change.* Boulder, Colo.: Lynne Rienner.

———. 2001. Virtuous Cuts: Female Genital Circumcision in an African Ontology. *differences: A Journal of Feminist Cultural Studies* 12:112–139.

Ahmadu, F. 2000. Rites and Wrongs: An Insider/Outsider Reflects on Power and Excision. In B. Shell-Duncan and Y. Hernlund, eds., *Female "Circumcision" in Africa: Culture, Change and Controversy,* pp. 283–312. Boulder, Colo.: Lynne Rienner.

Angel, R., and P. Guarnaccia. 1989. Mind, Body and Culture: Somatization among Hispanics. *Soc. Sci. Med.* 12(28):1229–1238.

Angel, R., and E. L. Idler. 1992. Somatization and Hypocondriasis:

Sociocultural Factors in Subjective Experience. *Research in Community and Mental Health* 7:71–93.

Angel, R., and P. Thoits. 1987. The Impact of Culture on the Cognitive Structure of Illness. *Culture, Medicine and Psychiatry* 11:465–494.

Appadurai, A. 1985. Gratitude as a Social Mode in South India. *Ethos* 13:236–245.

——. 1990. Topographies of the Self: Praise and Emotion in Hindu India. In C. Lutz and L. Abu-Lughod, eds., *Language and the Politics of Emotion*, pp. 92–112. New York: Cambridge University Press.

Asad, T. 1973. *Anthropology and the Colonial Encounter.* London: Ithaca Press.

Aunger, R. 1984. Sources of Variation in Ethnographic Interview Data: Food Avoidances in the Ituri Forest, Zaire. *Ethnology* 33:65–99.

Averill, J. 1980. A Constructivist View of Emotion. In R. Plutchik and H. Kellerman, eds., *Emotion: Theory, Research and Experience.* New York: Academic.

Babb, L. A. 1983. Destiny and Responsibility: Karma in Popular Hinduism. In C. F. Keyes and E. V. Daniel, eds., *Karma: An Anthropological Inquiry*, pp. 163–181. Berkeley, Calif.: University of California Press.

Barry, H., and L. M. Paxon. 1971. Infancy and Early Childhood: Cross-Cultural Codes 2. *Ethnology* 10:466–508.

Benedict, R. 1934. *Patterns of Culture.* Boston, Mass.: Houghton Mifflin.

Bennett, L. 1983. *Dangerous Wives and Sacred Sisters: Social and Symbolic Roles of High-Caste Women in Nepal.* New York: Columbia University Press.

Berlin, I. 1976. *Vico and Herder.* London: Hogarth Press.

Beyene, Y. 1999. Body Politics and Moral Advocacy: The Impact on African Families in the U.S. Oral presentation in the panel on "Revisiting Female Circumcision: Beyond Feminism and Current Discourse." Ninety-eighth annual meeting of the American Anthropological Association at Chicago, Illinois.

Bledsoe, C. 1990. No Success without Struggle: Social Mobility and Hardship for Foster Children in Sierra Leone. *Man* 25:70–88.

Bloom, A. 1987. *The Closing of the American Mind*. New York: Simon and Schuster.

Boddy, J. 1982. Womb As Oasis: The Symbolic Context of Pharaonic Circumcision in Rural Northern Sudan. *American Ethnologist*, 9:682–698.

———. 1989. *Wombs and Alien Spirits: Women, Men and the Zar Cult in Northern Sudan*. Madison, Wis.: University of Wisconsin Press.

———. 1996. Violence Embodied? Circumcision, Gender Politics, and Cultural Aesthetics. In R. E. Dobash and R. P. Dobash, eds., *Rethinking Violence against Women*. Thousand Oaks, Calif.: Sage Publications, pp. 77–110.

Bond, M. H., ed. 1988. *The Cross-Cultural Challenge to Social Psychology*. Newbury Park, Calif.: Sage.

Bond, M. H., K. Leung, and K. C. Wan. 1982. How Does Cultural Collectivism Operate? *Journal of Cross-Cultural Psychology* 13:186–200.

Boon, J. A. 1994. Circumscribing Circumcision/Uncircumcision. In S. B. Schwartz, ed., *Implicit Understandings*, pp. 556–585. Cambridge, England: Cambridge University Press.

Branigan, W., and D. Farah. 2000. Asylum Seeker Is Imposter, INS Says. *Washington Post*, 20 December.

Brazelton, T. B. 1990. Parent-Infant Cosleeping Revisited. *Ab Initio: An International Newsletter for Professionals Working with Infants and Their Families* 1:1 and 7.

Brenneis, D. 1990. Shared and Solitary Sentiments: The Discourse of Friendship, Play and Anger in Bhatgaon. In C. Lutz and L. Abu-Lughod, eds., *Language and the Politics of Emotion*, pp. 113–125. New York: Cambridge University Press.

Briggs, J. L. 1970. *Never in Anger: Portrait of an Eskimo Family*. Cambridge, Mass.: Harvard University Press.

Brown, J. K., and V. Kerns, eds. 1985. *In Her Prime: A New View of Middle-Aged Women*. South Hadley, Mass.: Bergin and Harvey.

Bruner, J. S. 1990. *Acts of Meaning*. Cambridge, Mass.: Harvard University Press.

Burton, R. V., and J. W. M. Whiting. 1961. The Absent Father and Cross-Sex Identity. *Merrill-Palmer Quarterly* 7:85–95.

Campbell, D. T. 1972. Herskovits, Cultural Relativism, and Metascience. In F. Herskovits, ed., *Cultural Relativism,* pp. v–xiii. New York: Random House.

Carstairs, G. M. 1967. *The Twice Born: A Study of a Community of High-Caste Hindus.* Bloomington, Ind.: Indiana University Press.

Caudill, W., and D. W. Plath. 1966. Who Sleeps by Whom? Parent-Child Involvement in Urban Japanese Families. *Psychiatry* 29:344–366.

Chambers, D. L. 2000. Civilizing the Natives: Marriage in Post-Apartheid South Africa. *Daedalus: Journal of the American Academy of Arts and Sciences* 129(4):101–124.

Clifford, J., and G. Markus. 1986. *Writing Culture: The Poetics and Politics of Ethnography.* Berkeley, Calif.: University of California Press.

Coburn, T. B. 1991. *Encountering the Goddess, a Translation of the Devi-Mahatmya and a Study of Its Interpretation.* Albany, N.Y.: State University of New York Press.

Cole, M. 1988. Cross-Cultural Research in the Sociohistorical Tradition. *Human Development* 31:137–157.

———. 1990. Cultural Psychology: A Once and Future Discipline? In J. J. Berman, ed., *Cross-Cultural Perspectives: Nebraska Symposium on Motivation 1989.* Lincoln, Nebr.: University of Nebraska Press.

———. 1996. *Cultural Psychology: A Once and Future Discipline.* Cambridge, Mass.: Harvard University Press.

Coleman, D. L. 1998. The Seattle Compromise: Multicultural Sensitivity and Americanization. *Duke Law Review* 47:717–783.

Collingwood, R. G. 1961. On the So-Called Idea of Causation. in H. Morris, ed., *Freedom and Responsibility: Readings in Philosophy and Law.* Stanford, Calif.: Stanford University Press.

Converse, P. E. 1986. Generalization and the Social Psychology of "Other Worlds." In D. W. Fiske and R. A. Shweder, eds., *Metatheory in Social Science: Pluralisms and Subjectivities.* Chicago, Ill.: University of Chicago Press.

Cooper, M. H. 1999. Women and Human Rights. *CQ Researcher* 9:353–376.

Cronbach, L. J. 1975. Beyond the Two Disciplines of Scientific Psychology. *American Psychologist* 30:116–137.

Culler, J. 1982. *On Deconstruction: Theory and Criticism after Structuralism.* Ithaca, N.Y.: Cornell University Press.

Daedalus: Journal of the American Academy of Arts and Sciences. 2000. Special issue on *The End of Tolerance: Engaging Cultural Differences.* 129(4).

Dahl, G. 1982. Notes on Critical Examinations of the Primal Scene Concept. *Journal of the American Psychoanalytic Association* 30:657–677.

D'Andrade, R. G. 1984. Cultural Meaning Systems. In R. A. Shweder and R. A. LeVine, eds., *Culture Theory: Essays on Mind, Self, and Emotion,* pp. 88–119. Cambridge, England: Cambridge University Press.

———. 1986. Three Scientific World Views and the Covering Law Model. In D. W. Fiske and R. A. Shweder, eds., *Metatheory in Social Science: Pluralisms and Subjectivities,* pp. 19–41. Chicago, Ill.: University of Chicago Press.

———. 1987. A Folk Model of the Mind. In N. Quinn and D. Holland, eds., *Cultural Models in Language and Thought.* Cambridge, England: Cambridge University Press.

———. 1993. Moral Models in Anthropology. *Current Anthropology* 36:399–408.

———. 1995. *The Development of Cognitive Anthropology.* New York: Cambridge University Press.

D'Andrade, R. G., and C. Strauss, eds. 1992. *Human Motives and Cultural Models.* New York: Cambridge University Press.

Daniel, S. B. 1983. The Tool Box Approach of the Tamil to the Issues of Moral Responsibility and Human Destiny. In C. F. Keyes and E. V Daniel, eds., *Karma: An Anthropological Inquiry,* pp. 27–62. Berkeley, Calif.: University of California Press.

Das, V. 1976. Masks and Faces: An Essay on Punjabi Kinship. *Contributions to Indian Sociology* 10:1–30.

Denzin, N. 1996. Epistemological Crisis in the Human Disciplines. In R. Jessor, A. Colby, and R. A. Shweder, eds., *Ethnography and Human Development: Context and Meaning in Social Inquiry.* Chicago, Ill.: University of Chicago Press.

Derne, S. 1993. Equality and Hierarchy between Adult Brothers: Culture and Sibling Relations in North Indian Urban Joint Families. In C. W. Nuckolls, ed., *Siblings in South Asia: Brothers and Sisters in Cultural Context.* New York: Guilford Press.

———. 1995. *Culture in Action: Family Life, Emotion, and Male Dominance in Banaras, India.* Albany, N.Y.: State University of New York Press.

Dhruvarajan, V. 1988. *Hindu Women and the Power of Ideology.* South Hadley, Mass.: Bergin and Garvey.

Dimock, E. C. 1974. *Literatures of India: An Introduction.* Chicago, Ill.: University of Chicago Press.

Dirie, M. A., and G. Lindmark. 1991. Female Circumcision in Somalia and Women's Motives. *Acta Obstetricia Gynecologica Scandanavia* 70:581–585.

Dugger, C. 1996. New Law Bans Genital Cutting in United States. *New York Times,* 12 November.

Dumont, L. 1970. *Homo Hierarchicus: An Essay on the Caste System.* Chicago, Ill.: University of Chicago Press.

Edelson, M. 1984. *Hypothesis and Evidence in Psychoanalysis.* Chicago, Ill.: University of Chicago Press.

Edgerton, R. B. 1989. *Mau Mau: An African Crucible.* New York: The Free Press.

Egan, T. 1994. An Ancient Ritual and a Mother's Asylum Plea. *New York Times,* 4 March.

Ekman, P. 1980. Biological and Cultural Contributions to Body and Facial Movement in the Expression of Emotions. In A. Rorty, ed., *Explaining Emotions,* pp. 73–101. Berkeley, Calif.: University of California Press.

Ekman, P. 1984. Expression and the Nature of Emotion. In K. Scherer and P. Ekman, eds., *Approaches to Emotion,* pp. 319–343. Hillsdale, N.J.: Erlbaum.

El Dareer, A. 1982. *Women, Why Do You Weep? Circumcision and Its Consequences.* London: Zed Press.

———. 1983. Epidemiology of Female Circumcision in the Sudan. *Tropical Doctor* 13:43.

Ellsworth, P. 1991. Some Implications of Cognitive Appraisal Theories of Emotion. *International Review of Studies of Emotion* 1:143–161.

Evans-Pritchard, E. E. 1937. *Witchcraft, Oracles and Magic Among the Azande.* Oxford, England: Clarendon Press.

Fish, S. 1980. *Is There a Textbook in This Class? On the Authority of Interpretive Communities.* Cambridge, Mass.: Harvard University Press.

Foucault, M. 1973. *The Order of Things: An Archeology of the Human Sciences.* New York: Vintage Books.

Fox, R., ed. 1991. *Recapturing Anthropology.* Santa Fe, N. Mex.: School of American Research.

Freeman, D. 1983. *Margaret Mead and Samoa: The Making and Unmaking of an Anthropological Myth.* Cambridge, Mass.: Harvard University Press.

French, H. F. 1997. Grafton Journal: The Ritual: Disfiguring, Hurtful, Wildly Festive, *New York Times,* 31 January.

Frijda, N. 1986. *The Emotions.* Cambridge: Cambridge University Press.

Fruzetti, L. M. 1982. *The Gift of a Virgin: Women, Marriage, and Ritual in Bengali Society.* New Brunswick, N.J.: Rutgers University Press.

Gaddini, R., and E. Gaddini. 1970. Transitional Objects and the Process of Individualization: A Study in Three Different Groups. *Journal of Child Psychiatry* 2:347–365.

Garvey, C. 1992. Talk in the Study of Socialization and Development. *Merrill-Palmer Quarterly* 38(1): 95–117.

Geertz, C. 1973. *The Interpretation of Cultures.* New York: Basic Books.

———. 1984. From the Native's Point of View. In R. Shweder and R. Levine, eds. *Culture Theory: Essays on Mind, Self and Emotion.* Cambridge, England: Cambridge University Press.

———. 2000. *Available Light: Anthropological Essays on Philosophical Topics.* Princeton, N.J.: Princeton University Press.

Geertz, H. 1959. The Vocabulary of Emotion: A Study of Javanese Socialization Processes. *Psychiatry* 22:225–236.

Gellner, E. 1985. *Relativism and the Social Sciences.* Cambridge, England: Cambridge University Press.

Gerber, E. R. 1985. Rage and Obligation: Samoan Emotions in Conflict.

In G. M. White and J. Kirkpatrick, eds., *Person, Self and Experience: Exploring Specific Ethnopsychologies*, pp. 121–167. Berkeley, Calif.: University of California Press.

Gilman, S. L. 1999. "Barbaric" Rituals. In J. Cohen, M. Howard, and M. Nussbaum, eds., *Is Multiculturalism Bad for Women?* Princeton, N.J.: Princeton University Press.

Gnoli, R. 1956. *The Aesthetic Experience According to Abhinavagupta.* Rome, Italy: Istituto Italiano per Il Medio ed Estremo Oriente.

Goddard, C. 1997. Contrastive Semantics and Cultural Psychology: "Surprise" in Malay and English. *Culture and Psychology* 2:153–181.

Gollaher, D. L. 2000. *Circumcision: A History of the World's Most Controversial Surgery.* New York: Basic Books.

Good, B. J., and A. M. Kleinman. 1984. Culture and Anxiety: Cross-Cultural Evidence for the Patterning of Anxiety Disorders. In A. H. Tuma and J. D. Maser, eds., *Anxiety and the Anxiety Disorders.* Hillsdale, N.J.: Erlbaum.

Goodnow, J., P. Miller, and F. Kessel, eds. 1995. *Cultural Practices as Contexts for Development.* New Directions for Child Development, Volume 67. San Francisco, Calif.: Jossey-Bass.

Gosselin, C. 2000. Handing Over the Knife: Numu Women and the Campaign against Excision in Mali. In B. Shell-Duncan and Y. Hernlund, eds., *Female "Circumcision" in Africa: Culture, Controversy and Change.* Boulder, Colo.: Lynne Rienner.

Greenfield, P. 1997. Culture As Process: Empirical Methodology for Cultural Psychology. In J. W. Berry, Y. H. Poortinga, and J. Pandey, eds. *Handbook of Cross-Cultural Psychology.* Vol. 1, *Theory and Method.* Boston, Mass.: Allyn and Bacon.

Greenfield, P., and R. Cocking. 1994. *Cross-Cultural Roots of Minority Child Development.* Hindsdale, N.J.: Erlbaum.

Greenwood, J. D. Unpublished. Durkheim, Weber, and the Demarkation of the Social. Available from John D. Greenwood, 29 Sheppard Ln., Stony Brook, N.Y. 11790.

Gruenbaum, E. 1988. Reproductive Ritual and Social Reproduction: Female Circumcision and the Subordination of Women in Sudan.

In N. O'Neill and J. O'Brian, eds. *Economy and Class in Sudan,* pp. 308–328. Avebory, England: Aldershot.

———. 1996. The Cultural Debate over Female Circumcision: The Sudanese Are Arguing This One Out for Themselves. *Medical Anthropology Quarterly* 10:455–475.

———. 2001. *The Female "Circumcision" Controversy: An Anthropological Perspective.* Philadelphia, Pa.: University of Pennsylvania Press.

Gunning, I. R. 1992. Arrogant Perception, World-Travelling and Multicultural Feminism: The Case of Female Genital Surgeries. *Columbia Human Rights Law Review* 23:189–248.

Haidt, J., and D. Keltner. 1999. Culture and Facial Expression: Open-Ended Methods Find More Faces and a Gradient of Recognition. *Cognition and Emotion* 13(3):225–266.

Haidt, J., S. Koller, and M. Dias. 1993. Affect, Culture, and Morality, or Is It Wrong to Eat Your Dog? *Journal of Personality and Social Psychology* 65:613–628.

Hammel, E. 1990. A Theory of Culture for Demography. *Population and Development Review* 16:455–485.

Hanna, J. L. 1991. *Issues in Supporting School Diversity: Academics, Social Relations and the Arts.* Washington, DC: Office of Educational Research and Improvement, United States Department of Education.

Harre, R. 1986. An Outline of the Social Constructionist Viewpoint. In R. Harre, ed., *The Social Construction of Emotions,* pp. 2–14. Oxford, England: Basil Blackwell.

———, ed. 1986. *The Social Construction of Emotions.* Oxford, England: Basil Blackwell.

Harrison, L. E. 1992. *Who Prospers? How Cultural Values Shape Economic and Political Success.* New York: Basic Books.

Harrison, L. E., and S. P. Huntington. 2000. *Culture Matters: How Values Shape Human Progress.* New York: Basic Books.

Hart, H. L. A., and A. M. Honore. 1956/1961. Causation in the law. In H. Morris, ed., *Freedom and Responsibility: Readings in Philosophy and Law,* pp. 572–583. Stanford, Calif.: Stanford University Press.

Haynes, D., and G. Prakash, eds. 1991. *Contesting Power: Resistance and Ev-*

eryday Social Relations in South Asia. Delhi, India: Oxford University Press.

Herdt, G. H. 1981. *Guardians of the Flute: Idioms of Masculinity.* New York: McGraw-Hill.

Hoffman, M. L. 1990. Empathy and Justice Motivation. *Motivation and Emotion* 4:151–172.

Hofstede, G. H. 1997. *Cultures and Organizations.* New York: McGraw-Hill.

Holland, D., and N. Quinn, eds. 1987. *Cultural Models in Language and Thought.* New York: Cambridge University Press.

Horowitz, C. R. and C. Jackson. 1997. Female "Circumcision": African Women Confront American Medicine. *Journal of General Internal Medicine* 12:491–499.

Horton, R., and R. Shweder. In press. Ethnic Pride, Psychological Well-Being and the Downside of Mainstreaming. In C. D. Ryff and R. C. Kessler, eds., *A Portrait of Midlife in the U.S.* Chicago: University of Chicago Press.

Hosken, F. 1993. *The Hosken Report: Genital and Sexual Mutilation of Females.* Lexington, Mass.: Women's International Network News.

Howard, A. 1985. Ethnopsychology and the Prospects for a Cultural Psychology. In G. M. White and J. Kirkpatrick, eds., *Person, Self and Experience: Exploring Specific Ethnopsychologies* pp. 401–420. Berkeley, Calif.: University of California Press.

Huntington, S. P. 1996a. *The Clash of Civilizations and the Remaking of the World Order.* New York: Simon and Shuster.

———. 1996b. The West Unique, Not Universal. *Foreign Affairs* 75:28–45.

Hymes, D., ed. 1972. *Reinventing Anthropology.* New York: Random House.

Inden, R. B., and R. W. Nichols. 1977. *Kinship in Bengali Culture.* Chicago, Ill.: University of Chicago Press.

Jacobson, D. 1982. Studying the Changing Roles of Women in Rural India. *Signs* 8(1):132–137.

Jahoda, G. 1991. *Crossroads between Culture and Mind: Continuities and Change in Theories of Human Nature.* Cambridge, Mass.: Harvard University Press.

Jain, D., and N. Bannerjee, eds. 1985. *Tyranny of the Household: Investigative Essays on Women's Work.* New Delhi, India: Shakti Books.

Jeffrey, P., R. Jeffrey, and A. Lyons, 1988. *Labour Pains and Labour Power.* London: Zed Books.

Jensen, L. A. 1995. Habits of the Heart Revisited: Autonomy, Community, Divinity in Adults' Moral Language. *Qualitative Sociology* 18:71–86.

Jessor, R., A. Colby, and R. A. Shweder. 1996. *Ethnography and Human Development: Context and Meaning in Social Inquiry.* Chicago, Ill.: University of Chicago Press.

Johnson, M. 1987. *The Body in the Mind.* Chicago, Ill.: University of Chicago Press.

———. 1993. *Moral Imagination: Implications of Cognitive Science for Ethics.* Chicago, Ill.: University of Chicago Press.

Johnson, M. 2000. Becoming a Muslim, Becoming a Person: Female "Circumcision," Religious Identity, and Personhood in Guinea-Bissau. In B. Shell-Duncan and Y. Hernlund, eds., *Female "Circumcision" in Africa: Culture, Controversy and Change.* Boulder, Colo.: Lynne Rienner.

Kagan, J. 1998. *Three Seductive Ideas.* Cambridge, Mass.: Harvard University Press.

Kakar, S. 1978. *The Inner World: A Psycho-analytic Study of Childhood and Society in India.* Delhi, India: Oxford University Press.

———. 1982. *Shamans, Mystics and Doctors: A Psychological Inquiry into India and Its Healing Traditions.* New York: Alfred A. Knopf.

———. 1990. Stories from Indian Psychoanalysis: Text and Context. In J. S. Stigler, R. A. Shweder, and G. Herdt, eds., *Cultural Psychology: Essays on Comparative Human Development.* New York: Cambridge University Press.

Kaplan, B. 1954. A Study of Rorschach Responses in Four Cultures. *Papers of the Peabody Museum of Archaeology and Ethnology,* Harvard University 42:2.

Kapp, K. W. 1963. *Hindu Culture, Economic Development and Economic Planning in India.* New York: Asia Publishing House.

Kardiner, A. 1939. *The Individual and His Society: The Psychodynamics of Primitive Social Organization.* New York: Columbia University Press.

———. 1945. *The Psychological Frontiers of Society.* New York: Columbia University Press.

Keesing, R. M. 1989. Exotic Readings of Cultural Texts, *Current Anthropology* 30:459–469.

Keith, A. B. 1924. *The Sanskrit Drama.* London: Oxford University Press.

Kenyatta, J. 1938. *Facing Mount Kenya: The Tribal Life of the Gikuyu.* London: Secker and Warburg.

Keyes, C. F. 1983. The study of popular ideas of karma. In C. F. Keyes and E. V. Daniel, eds., *Karma: An Anthropological Inquiry.* Berkeley, Calif.: University of California Press.

Keyes, C. F. and E. V. Daniel, eds. 1983. *Karma: An Anthropological Inquiry.* Berkeley, Calif.: University of California Press.

Kirsh, D. 1991. Today the Earwig, Tomorrow Man? *Artificial Intelligence* 47:161–184

Kitayama, S., and H. R. Markus. 1994. *Emotion and Culture: Empirical Studies of Mutual Influences.* Washington, DC: American Psychological Association.

Kleinman, A. 1986. *The Social Origins of Distress and Disease.* New Haven, Conn.: Yale University Press.

Kleinman, A., and B. Good. 1985. *Culture and Depression: Studies in the Anthropology and Cross-Cultural Psychiatry of Affect and Disorder.* Berkeley, Calif.: University of California Press.

Kluckhohn, C. 1944. *Navaho Witchcraft.* Boston, Mass.: Beacon Press.

Kluckhohn, C., H. A. Murray, and D. M. Schneider, 1953. *Personality: In Nature, Society, and Culture.* New York: Alfred A. Knopf.

Kondos, V. 1989. Subjection and Domicile: Some Problematic Issues Relating to High Caste Nepalese Women. In J. N. Gray and D. J. Mearns, eds., *Society from the Inside Out,* pp. 162–191. New Delhi, India: Sage Publications.

Koso-Thomas, O. 1987. *The Circumcision of Women: A Strategy for Eradication.* London: Zed Books.

Kratz, C. 1994. *Affecting Performance: Meaning, Movement, and Experience in*

Okiek Women's Initiation. Washington, DC: Smithsonian Institution Press.

——. 1999. Contexts, Controversies, Dilemmas: Teaching Circumcision. In M. Bastian and J. Parpart, eds., *Great Ideas for Teaching about Africa,* pp. 103–118. Boulder, Colo.: Lynne Rienner.

——. 2002. Circumcision Debates and Asylum Cases: Intersecting Arenas, Contested Values and Tangled Webs. In R. A. Shweder, M. Minow, and H. R. Markus, eds., *Engaging Cultural Differences: The Multicultural Challenge in Liberal Democracies.* New York: Russell Sage Foundation Press.

Kroeber, A. L. and C. Kluckhohn. 1952. *Culture: A Critical Review of Concepts and Definitions.* New York: Random House.

Kuhn, T. 1962. *The Structure of Scientific Revolutions.* Chicago, Ill.: University of Chicago Press.

Kuper, A. 1999. *Culture: The Anthropologists' Account.* Cambridge, Mass.: Harvard University Press.

Kurtz, S. 1991. Polysexualization: A New Approach to Oedipus in the Trobriands. *Ethos* 19:68–101.

——. 1992. *All the Mothers Are One: Hindu India and the Cultural Reshaping of Psychoanalysis.* New York: Columbia University Press

——. 1993. A Trobriand Complex. *Ethos* 21:79–103.

Lakoff, G. 1987. *Women, Fire and Dangerous Things: What Categories Reveal about the Mind.* Chicago, Ill.: University of Chicago Press.

Lakoff, G., and M. Johnson. 1980. The Metaphorical Structure of the Human Conceptual System. *Cognitive Science* 4:195–208.

——. 1986. *Metaphors We Live By.* Chicago, Ill.: University of Chicago Press.

Lâm, M. 1994. Feeling Foreign in Feminism. *Signs: Journal of Women in Culture and Society* 19(4):865–893.

Lamb, S. 1993. Growing in the Net of Maya. Ph.D. diss., Department of Anthropology, University of Chicago.

Landes, D. S. 1998. *The Wealth and Poverty of Nations: Why Some Are So Rich and Some Are So Poor.* New York: W. W. Norton.

Lane, S. D., and R. A. Rubinstein. 1996. Judging the Other: Responding to Traditional Female Genital Surgeries. *Hastings Center Report* 26:31–40.

Larsen, U., and S. Yan. 2000. Does Female Circumcision Affect Infertility and Fertility? A Study of the Central African Republic, Côte d'Ivoire and Tanzania. *Demography* 37:313–321.

Latour, B., and S. Woolgar. 1979. *Laboratory Life*. Princeton, N.J.: Princeton University Press.

Lazarus, R. S. 1991a. *Emotion and Adaptation*. New York: Oxford University Press.

———. 1991b. Progress on a Cognitive-Motivational-Relational Theory of Emotion. *American Psychologist* 46:819–834.

LeVine, R. A. 1984. Properties of Culture: An Ethnographic View. In R. A. Shweder and R. A. LeVine, eds., *Culture Theory: Essays on Mind, Self, and Emotion*, pp. 67–87. New York: Cambridge University Press.

———. 1990. Infant Environments in Psychoanalysis: A Cross-Cultural View. In J. Stigler, R. Shweder, and G. Herdt, eds., *Cultural Psychology: Essays on Comparative Human Development*, pp. 454–474. New York: Cambridge University Press.

LeVine, R. A., S. Dixon, S. LeVine, A. Richman, P. H. Leiderman, C. H. Keefer, and T. B. Brazelton. 1994. *Child Care and Culture: Lessons from Africa*. Cambridge, England: Cambridge University Press.

Levy, R. I. 1973. *Tahitians: Mind and Experience in the Society Islands*. Chicago, Ill.: University of Chicago Press.

———. 1984a. Emotion, Knowing and Culture. In R. A. Shweder and R. A. LeVine, eds., *Culture Theory: Essays on Mind, Self, and Emotion*, pp. 214–237. Cambridge, England: Cambridge University Press.

———. 1984b. The Emotions in Comparative Perspective. In K. R. Scherer and P. Ekman, eds., *Approaches to Emotion*, pp. 397–412. Hillsdale, N.J.: Erlbaum.

Lewis, M., M. Sullivan, and L. Michalson. 1982. The Cognitive-Emotional Fugue. *Annual Report: Research and Clinical Center for Child Development*. Sapporo, Japan: Hokkaido University. Also in C. E. Izard, J. Kagan, and R. Zajonc, eds. 1982. *Emotion, Cognition and Behavior*, pp. 264–288. New York: Cambridge University Press.

Lewis, M. 1989. Cultural Differences in Children's Knowledge of Emotional Scripts. In P. Harris and C. Saarni, eds., *Children's Understanding of Emotion*, pp. 350–375. New York: Cambridge University Press.

Liddle, J., and R. Joshi. 1986. *Daughters of Independence: Gender, Caste, and Class in India*. London: Zed Books.

Lightfoot-Klein, H. 1989. The Sexual and Marital Adjustment of Genitally Circumcised and Infibulated Females in the Sudan. *Journal of Sex Research* 26:375–392.

Lindkvist, H. L. 2000. Female "Circumcision" Comes to America: Cultural Aesthetics, Medical Management, and the Body Politic. Unpublished manuscript. Committee on Human Development, The University of Chicago, Chicago, Ill.

Litt, C. J. 1981. Children's Attachment to Transitional Objects: A Study of Two Pediatric Populations. *American Journal of Orthopsychiatry* 51:131–139.

Lovejoy, A. 1961. *Reflections on Human Nature*. Baltimore, Md.: Johns Hopkins University Press.

Lozoff, B., and G. Brittenham. 1979. Infant Care: Cache or Carry. *Journal of Pediatrics* 95:478–483.

Lozoff, B., A. W. Wolf, and N. S. Davis. 1984. Cosleeping in Urban Families with Young Children in the United States. *Pediatrics* 74:171–182.

Luhrmann, T. 1989. *Persuasions of the Witch's Craft*. Cambridge, Mass.: Harvard University Press.

Lutz, C. 1982. The Domain of Emotion Words on Ifaluk. *American Ethnologist* 9:113–128.

——. 1985a. Ethnopsychology Compared to What? Explaining Behavior and Consciousness among the Ifaluk. In J. White and J. Kirkpatrick, eds., *Person, Self and Experience: Exploring Pacific Ethnopsychologies*, pp. 35–79. Berkeley, Calif.: University of California Press

——. 1985b. Depression and the Translation of Emotional Worlds. In A. Kleinman and B. Good, eds., *Culture and Depression: Studies in the Anthropology and Cross-Cultural Psychiatry of Affect and Disorder*, pp. 63–100. Berkeley, Calif.: University of California Press.

——. 1988. *Unnatural Emotions: Everyday Sentiments on a Micronesian Atoll and Their Challenge to Western Theory.* Chicago, Ill.: University of Chicago Press

Lutz, C., and G. White. 1986. The Anthropology of Emotions. *Annual Review of Anthropology* 15:405–436.

Mahapatra, M. 1981. *Traditional Structure and Change in an Orissa Temple.* Calcutta, India: Punthi Pustak.

Mahapatra, M., N. C. Much, and R. A. Shweder. 1991. Sin and Suffering in a Sacred City: Oriya Ideas about Spiritual Debt and Moral Cause and Effect. Working paper.

Mandansky, D., and C. Edelbrock. 1990. Cosleeping in a Community Sample of 2- and 3-Year-Old Children. *Pediatrics* 86:197–203.

Markus, G. E., and M. J. Fischer. 1986. *Anthropology As Cultural Critique.* Chicago, Ill.: University of Chicago Press.

Markus, H. R., and S. Kitayama. 1991. Culture and the Self: Implications for Cognition, Emotion and Motivation. *Psychological Review* 98:224–53.

——. 1992. The What, Why and How of Cultural Psychology: A Review of Shweder's Thinking Through Cultures. *Psychological Inquiry* 3(3):357–364.

Markus, H. R., S. Kitayama, and R. Heiman. 1996. Culture and "Basic" Psychological Principles. In E. T. Higgins and A. W. Kruglanski, eds., *Social Psychology: Handbook of Basic Principles,* pp. 857–913. New York: Guilford Press.

Marriott, M. 1976. Hindu Transactions: Diversity without Dualism. In B. Kapferer, *Transaction and Meaning: Directions in Anthropology of Exchange and Symbolic Behavior,* pp. 109–142. Philadelphia, Pa.: Institute for the Study of Human Issues.

——. 1989. Constructing an Indian Ethnosociology. *Contributions to Indian Sociology* 23:1–39. Also available in M. Marriott, ed., *India through Hindu Categories.* Newbury Park, Calif.: Sage Publications.

Marsella, A. J. 1980. Depressive Experience and Disorder across Cultures: A Review of the Literature. In H. Triandis and J. Draguns, eds., *Handbook of Cross-Cultural Psychology,* Vol. 6, pp. 237–291. Boston, Mass.: Allyn and Bacon.

Masson, J. L., and M. V. Patwardhan. 1970. *Aesthetic Rapture: The Rasādhyāya of the Nātyaśāstra.* Poona, India: Deccan College.

Mead, M. 1928. *Coming of Age in Samoa: A Psychological Study of Primitive Youth for Western Civilization.* New York: Morrow Quill Paperbacks.

———. 1930. *Growing Up in New Guinea: A Comparative Study of Primitive Education.* New York: Morrow Quill Paperbacks.

———. 1932. An Investigation of the Thought of Primitive Children, with Special Reference to Animism. *Journal of the Royal Anthropological Institute* 62:173–190.

Meinardus, O. 1967. Mythological, Historical and Sociological Aspects of the Practice of Female Circumcision among the Egyptians. *Acta Ethnographica: Academiae Scientiarum Hungaricae* 16:387–397.

Menon, U. 1995. Receiving and Giving: Distributivity as the Source of Women's Well-Being. Ph.D. diss., University of Chicago, Committee on Human Development.

———. 2000. Does Feminism Have Universal Relevance? The Challenges Posed by Oriya Hindu Family Practices. *Daedalus: Journal of the American Academy of Arts and Sciences* 129:77–100. Special issue: "The End of Tolerance: Engaging Cultural Differences."

Menon, U., and R. A. Shweder. 1994. Kali's Tongue: Cultural Psychology and the Power of "Shame" in Orissa, India. In S. Kitayama and H. Markus, eds., *Emotion and Culture,* pp. 241–284. Washington, DC: American Psychological Association.

———. 1998. The Return of the "White Man's Burden": The Encounter between the Moral Discourse of Anthropology and the Domestic Life of Hindu Women. In R. A. Shweder, ed., *Welcome to Middle Age! (And Other Cultural Fictions),* pp. 139–188. Chicago, Ill.: University of Chicago Press.

Menon, U., and R. A. Shweder. In press. Dominating Kali: Hindu Family Values and Tantric Power. In J. Kripal and R. McDermott, eds., *Encountering Kali: Cultural Understanding at the Extremes.* Berkeley, Calif.: University of California Press.

Mesquita, B., and N. H. Frijda. 1992. Cultural Variations in Emotions: A Review. *Psychological Bulletin* 112:179–204.

Miller, J. G. 1997. Theoretical Issues in Cultural Psychology. *Handbook of*

Cross-Cultural Psychology. Vol. 1, *Theory and Method,* pp. 85–128. Boston, Mass.: Allyn and Bacon.

Miller, P., and L. Hoogstra. 1992. Language As Tool in the Socialization and Apprehension of Cultural Meanings. In T. Schwartz, G. M. White, and C. A. Lutz, eds., *The Social Life of Psyche: Debates and Directions in Psychological Anthropology.* Cambridge, England: Cambridge University Press.

Miller, P., J. Mintz, H. Fung, L. Hoogstra, and R. Potts. 1992. The Narrated Self: Young Children's Construction of Self in Relation to Others in Conversational Stories of Personal Experience. *Merrill-Palmer Quarterly* 38(1):45–67.

Miller, P., R. Potts, H. Fung, L. Hoogstra, and J. Mintz. 1990. Narrative Practices and the Social Construction of Self in Childhood. *American Ethnologist* 17:292–311.

Miller, P., and L. Sperry. 1987. The Socialization of Anger and Aggression. *Merrill-Palmer Quarterly* 33:1–31.

Minow, M. 1990. *Making All the Difference: Inclusion, Exclusion and American Law.* Ithaca, N.Y.: Cornell University Press.

Minturn, L. 1993. *Sita's Daughters: Coming Out of Purdah.* New York: Oxford University Press.

Morelli, G. A., B. Rogoff, D. Oppenheim, and D. Goldsmith. 1992. Cultural Variations in Infants' Sleeping Arrangements: Question of Independence. *Developmental Psychology* 28:604–613.

Morison, L., C. Scherf, G. Ekpo, K. Paine, B. West, R. Coleman, and G. Walraven. 2001. The long-term reproductive health consequences of female genital cutting in rural Gambia: a community-based survey. *Tropical Medicine and International Health* 6(8):643–653.

Much, N. C. 1992. The analysis of discourse as methodology for a semiotic psychology. *American Behavioral Scientist,* 36(1):52–72.

———. 1995. Cultural Psychology. In J. Smith, R. Harre, and L. van Langenhove, eds., *Rethinking Psychology.* London: Russell Sage Foundation Press.

Much, N. C., and R. Harre. 1994. How Psychologies "Secrete" Moralities. *New Ideas in Psychology* 12:291–321.

Much, N. C. and M. Mahapatra. 1993. *Karma As Theory and Experience: Symbolic Contexts and the Construction of Meaning.*

Mumford, S. R. 1989. *Himalayan Dialogue: Tibetan Lamas and Gurung Shamans in Nepal.* Madison, Wis.: University of Wisconsin Press.

Murdock, G. P. 1980. *Theories of Illness: A World Survey.* Pittsburgh, Pa.: University of Pittsburgh Press.

Myers, F. R. 1979a. Emotions and the Self: A Theory of Personhood and Political Order among Pintupi Aborigines. *Ethos* 7:343–370.

———. 1979b. The Logic and Meaning of Anger among Pintupi Aborigines. *Man* 23:589–610.

Myrdal, G. 1968 *Asian Drama: An Inquiry into the Poverty of Nations.* New York: Pantheon.

Nisbett, R. E., and D. Cohen. 1995. *The Culture of Honor: The Psychology of Violence in the South.* Boulder, Colo.: Westview Press.

Nisbett, R. E., K. Peng, I. Choi, and A. Norenzayan. 2001. Culture and Systems of Thought: Holistic vs. Analytic Cognition. *Psychological Review* 108(2):291–310.

Nisbett, R. E., and T. D. Wilson. 1977. Telling More Than We Can Know: Verbal Reports on Mental Processes. *Psychological Review* 84(3):231–259.

Obermeyer, C. M. 1999. Female Genital Surgeries: The Known, the Unknown, and the Unknowable. *Medical Anthropology Quarterly* 13:79–106.

Obeyesekere, G. 1980. The Rebirth Eschatology and Its Transformations: A Contribution to the Sociology of Early Buddhism. In W. D. O'Flaherty, ed., *Karma and Rebirth in Classical Indian Traditions.* Berkeley, Calif.: University of California Press.

———. 1981. *Medusa's Hair: An Essay on Personal Symbols and Religious Experience.* Chicago, Ill.: University of Chicago Press.

———. 1984. *The Cult of the Goddess Pattini.* Chicago, Ill.: University of Chicago Press.

———. 1990. *The Work of Culture: Symbolic Transformations in Psychoanalysis and Anthropology.* Chicago, Ill.: University of Chicago Press.

Obiora, L. A. 1997. Rethinking Polemics and Intransigence in the Campaign against Female Circumcision. *Case Western Reserve Law Review* 47:263–378.

Ochs, E. & Schieffelin, B. 1984. Language Acquisition and Socialization: Three Developmental Stories. In R. Shweder and R. LeVine, Eds., *Culture Theory: Essays on Mind, Self and Emotion* pp. 276–320. Cambridge, England: Cambridge University Press.

O'Flaherty, W. D. 1976. *The Origins of Evil in Hindu Mythology.* Berkeley, Calif.: University of California Press.

O'Flaherty, W. D., ed. 1980. *Karma and Rebirth in Classical Indian Traditions.* Berkeley, Calif.: University of California Press.

Okin, S. M. 1999. Is Multiculturalism Bad for Women? In J. Cohen, M. Howard, and M. Nussbaum, eds., *Is Multiculturalism Bad for Women?* Princeton, N.J.: Princeton University Press.

Olamijuto, S. K., K. T. Joiner, and G. A. Oyedeji. 1983. Female Child Circumcision in Ilesha, Nigeria. *Clinical Pediatrics* 22:580–581.

Ortner, S. 1974. Is Female to Male As Nature Is to Culture? In M. Rosaldo and L. Lamphere, eds., *Women, Culture and Society.* Stanford, Calif.: Stanford University Press.

Osgood, C., W. May, and M. Miron. 1975. *Cross-Cultural Universals of Affective Meaning.* Urbana, Ill.: University of Illinois Press.

Papanek, H., and G. Minault. 1982. *Separate Worlds: Studies of Purdah in South Asia.* New Delhi, India: Chanakya Publications.

Parish, S. 1991. The Sacred Mind: Newar Cultural Representations of Mental Life and the Production of Moral Consciousness. *Ethos* 19(3):313–351.

Park, L. 1992. Cross-Cultural Explanations of Illness: Murdock Revisited. Available from Lawrence Park, Committee on Human Development, University of Chicago, Chicago, Illinois 60637.

Parker, M. 1995. Rethinking Female Circumcision. *Africa* 65:506–524.

Peacock, J. L. 1984. Religion and Life History: An Exploration in Cultural Psychology. In E. M. Bruner, ed., *Text, Play and Story: The Construction and Reconstruction of Self and Society,* pp. 94–116. Washington, D.C.: American Ethnological Society.

Piaget, J. 1954. *The Construction of Reality in the Child.* New York: Basic Books.

——. 1967. *Six Psychological Studies*. New York: Random House.

——. 1970. *Structuralism*. New York: Basic Books.

Plutchik, R. 1980. *Emotion: A Psychoevolutionary Synthesis*. New York: Harper and Row.

Pollitt, K. 1999. Whose Culture? In J. Cohen, M. Howard, and M. Nussbaum, eds., *Is Multiculturalism Bad for Women?* Princeton, N.J.: Princeton University Press.

Popper, K. R., and J. C. Eccles. 1977. *The Self and Its Brain*. New York: Springer International.

Prentice, D., and D. Miller. 1999. *Cultural Divides: Understanding and Overcoming Group Conflict*. New York: Russell Sage Foundation Press.

Quine, W. V. O. 1953. Two Dogmas of Empiricism. In W. V. O. Quine, *From a Logical Point of View*, pp. 20–46. New York: Harper and Row.

——. 1969. *Ontological Relativity and Other Essays*. New York: Columbia University Press.

Rabinow, P. 1983. Humanism As Nihilism: The Bracketing of Truth and Consciousness in American Cultural Anthropology. In R. Bellah, P. Rabinow, and W. Sullivan, eds., *Social Science As Moral Inquiry*, pp. 33–51. New York: Columbia University Press.

Raheja, G. G., and A. G. Gold, 1991. *Listen to Heron's Words: Reimagining Gender and Kinship in North India*. Berkeley, Calif.: University of California Press.

Ramanujan, A. K. 1983. The Indian Oedipus. In L. Edmunds and A. Dundes, eds., *Oedipus: A Folklore Casebook*, pp. 234–261. New York: Garland Publishing.

——. 1990. Is There an Indian Way of Thinking? An Informal Essay. In M. Marriott, ed., *India through Hindu Categories*. New Delhi, India: Sage Publications.

Rawls, J. 1993. *Political Liberalism*. New York: Columbia University Press.

Redfield, R. 1941. *The Folk Culture of Yucatan*. Chicago, Ill.: University of Chicago Press.

Reyna, S. P. 1994. Literary Anthropology and the Case against Science. *Man* 29:555–581.

Rich, S., and S. Joyce, n.d. Eradicating Female Genital Mutilation: Lessons for Donors. Wallace Global Fund for a Sustainable Future. 1990 M Street NW, Suite 250, Washington, DC 20036.

Richter, F. M. 1986. Non-linear Behavior. In D. W. Fiske and R. A. Shweder, eds., *Metatheory in Social Science: Pluralisms and Subjectivities,* pp. 284–292. Chicago, Ill.: University of Chicago Press.

Roland, A. 1996. *Cultural Pluralism and Psychoanalysis: The North American and Asian Experience.* New York: Routledge.

Rogoff, B. 1990. *Apprenticeship in Thinking: Cognitive Development in Social Context.* New York: Oxford University Press.

Romney, A. K., S. Weller, and W. H. Batchelder. 1986. Culture As Consensus: A Theory of Culture and Informant Accuracy. *American Anthropologist* 88:313–338.

Rorty, A. 1980. *Explaining Emotions.* Berkeley, Calif.: University of California Press.

Rorty, R. 1991. *Philosophical Papers.* Cambridge, England: Cambridge University Press.

Rosaldo, M. Z. 1980. *Knowledge and Passion: Ilongot Notions of Self and Social Life.* Cambridge, England: Cambridge University Press.

——. 1983. The Shame of Headhunters and the Autonomy of Self. *Ethos* 11:135–51.

——. 1984. Toward an Anthropology of Self and Feeling. In R. A. Shweder and R. A. LeVine, eds., *Culture Theory: Essays on Mind, Self, and Emotion,* pp. 137–157. Cambridge, England: Cambridge University Press.

Rosaldo, R. 1989. *Culture and Truth: The Remaking of Social Analysis.* Boston, Mass.: Beacon Press.

Rosenau, P. 1992. *Post-Modernism and the Social Sciences.* Princeton, N.J.: Princeton University Press.

Rosenfeld, A. A., C. R. Smith, A. O'Reilly Wenegrat, W. Brewster, and D. K. Haavik, 1980. The Primal Scene: A Study of Prevalence. *American Journal of Psychiatry* 137:1426–1428.

Rosenfeld, A. A., A. O'Reilly Wenegrat, D. K. Haavik, B. Wenegrat, and C. R. Smith. 1982. Sleeping Patterns in Upper Middle-Class Families When the Child Awakens Ill or Frightened. *Archives of General Psychiatry* 39:943–947.

Rosenthal, A. M. 1995. The Possible Dream. *The New York Times* 13 June.

Roy, M. 1975. *Bengali Women.* Chicago, Ill.: University of Chicago Press.

Rozin, P., and C. Nemeroff. 1990. The Laws of Sympathetic Magic: A Psychological Analysis of Similarity and Contagion. In J. W. Stigler, R. A. Shweder, and G. Herdt, eds., *Cultural Psychology: Essays on Comparative Human Development.* New York: Cambridge University Press.

Rozin, P., J. Haidt, and C. McCauley. 2000. Disgust. In M. Lewis and J. Haviland, eds., *Handbook of Emotions,* 2nd ed., pp. 637–653. New York: Guilford Press.

Rudolph, L. I., and S. H. Rudolph. 2002. Living with Multi-Culturalism in India: Universalism and Particularism in Historical Context. In R. A. Shweder, M. Minow, and H. R. Markus, eds., *Engaging Cultural Differences: The Multicultural Challenge in Liberal Democracies.* New York: Russell Sage Foundation Press.

Russell, J. A. 1991. Culture and the Categorization of Emotions. *Psychological Bulletin* 110(3):426–450.

Sabini, J., and M. Silver. 1982. *Moralities of Everyday Life.* Oxford, England: Oxford University Press.

Sachs, J. 2000. Notes on a New Sociology of Economic Development. In L. Harrison and S. Huntington, eds., *Culture Matters: How Values Shape Human Progress.* New York: Basic Books.

Sager, L. 2000. The Free Exercise of Culture: Some Doubts and Distinctions. In R. A. Shweder, H. R. Markus, and M. Minow, eds., *The Free Exercise of Culture. Daedalus: Journal of the American Academy of Arts and Sciences* (Autumn 2000 issue).

Said, E. 1978. *Orientalism.* New York: Pantheon.

Sahlins, M. 1995. *How Natives Think, About Captain Cook, For Example.* Chicago, Ill.: University of Chicago Press.

Sahlins, M. 1999. Two or Three Things That I Know about Culture. *Journal of the Royal Anthropological Institute* 5:399–421.

Sangren, S. P. 1988. Rhetoric and the Authority of Ethnography.

Postmodernism and the Social Reproduction of Texts. *Current Anthropology* 29:405–435.

Sapir, E. 1963. *Selected Writings of Edward Sapir in Language, Culture and Personality.* D. Mandelbaum, ed. Berkeley, Calif.: University of California Press.

Sapir, E. 1986. Culture, Genuine and Spurious. In Sapir's *Selected Writings in Language, Culture and Personality.* Berkeley, Calif.: University of California Press.

Schechner, R. 1988. *Performance Theory.* London: Routledge.

Scheper-Hughes, N. 1990. Mother Love and Child Death in Northeastern Brazil. In J. Stigler, R. A. Shweder, and G. H. Herdt, eds., *Cultural Psychology: Essays on Comparative Human Development.* New York: Cambridge University Press.

———. 1995. The Primacy of the Ethical: Propositions for a Militant Anthropology. *Current Anthropology* 36:409–430.

Scherer, K. R., H. G. Walbott, and A. B. Summerfield, eds. 1986. *Experiencing Emotion: A Cross-Cultural Study,* pp. 173–190. Cambridge, England: Cambridge University Press.

Schieffelin, B., and E. Ochs, eds. 1986. *Language Socialization across Cultures.* New York and Cambridge: Cambridge University Press.

Schieffelin, E. L. 1976. *The Sorrow of the Lonely and the Burning of the Dancers.* New York: St. Martin's Press.

———. 1983. Anger and Shame in the Tropical Forest: On Affect As a Cultural System in Papua, New Guinea. *Ethos* 11:181–91.

———. 1985a. The Cultural Analysis of Depressive Affect: An Example from New Guinea. In A. Kleinman and B. Good, eds., *Culture and Depression: Studies in Anthropology and Psychiatry of Affect and Disorder,* pp. 101–133. Berkeley, Calif.: University of California Press.

———. 1985b. Anger, Grief and Shame: Toward a Kaluli Ethnopsychology. In G. M. White and J. Kirkpatrick, eds., *Person, Self and Experience: Exploring Specific Ethnopsychologies,* pp. 168–182. Berkeley, Calif.: University of California Press.

Segall, M. H., W. J. Lonner, and J. W. Berry. 1998. Cross-Cultural Psychology As a Scholarly Discipline. *American Psychologist* 53:1101–1110.

Seymour, S. 1983. Household Structure and Status and Expressions of Affect in India. *Ethos* 11:263–277.

———. 1999. *Women, Family and Child Care in India: A World in Transition.* New York: Cambridge University Press.

Shapiro, I., and W. Kymlicka. 1997. *Ethnicity and Group Rights.* New York: New York University Press. (Nomos, Volume 39).

Sharma, U. 1980. *Women, Work and Property in North-West India.* Honolulu, Hawaii: University of Hawaii Press.

Shaver, P., J. Schwartz, D. Kirson, and C. O'Connor. 1987. Emotion Knowledge: Further Exploration of a Prototype Approach. *Journal of Personality and Social Psychology* 52(6):1061–1086.

Shell-Duncan, B., and Y. Hernlund, eds. 2000a. *Female "Circumcision" in Africa: Culture, Change, and Controversy.* Boulder, Colo.: Lynn Rienner.

———. 2000b. Female "Circumcision" in Africa: Dimensions of the Problem and the Debates. In B. Shell-Duncan and Y. Hernlund, eds., *Female "Circumcision" in Africa: Culture, Change, and Controversy,* pp. 1–40. Boulder, Colo.: Lynn Rienner.

Shixie, L. 1989. Neurasthenia in China: Modern and Traditional Criteria for Its Diagnosis. *Culture, Medicine and Psychiatry* 13:163–86

Shore, B. 1996. *Culture in Mind: Cognition, Culture and the Problem of Meaning.* New York: Oxford University Press.

Shweder, R. A. 1982. On savages and other children. *American Anthropologist* 84:354–366.

———. 1984. Anthropology's romantic rebellion against the enlightenment: Or, there is more to thinking than reason and evidence. In R. A. Shweder and R. A. LeVine, eds., *Culture Theory: Essays on Mind, Self and Emotion.* New York: Cambridge University Press.

———. 1986. Storytelling among the Anthropologists. *New York Times Book Review,* 21 Sept., 1, 38–39.

———. 1988. Suffering in Style. Review of *Social Origins of Disease and Distress* by Arthur Kleinman. *Culture, Medicine and Psychiatry* 12:479–497.

———. 1990a. Cultural Psychology: What Is It? In J. Stigler, R. A. Shweder, and G. Herdt, eds., *Cultural Psychology: Essays on Comparative Human Development* pp. 1-43. New York: Cambridge University Press.

———. 1990b. In Defense of Moral Realism. *Child Development* 61:2060–2068.

———. 1991. *Thinking Through Cultures: Expeditions in Cultural Psychology.* Cambridge, Mass.: Harvard University Press.

———. 1993a. Everything You Ever Wanted To Know About Cognitive Appraisal Theory Without Being Conscious of It: A Review of Richard S. Lazarus' *Emotion and Culture. Psychological Inquiry* 4:322-326.

———. 1993b. The cultural psychology of the emotions. In M. Lewis and J. Haviland, eds., *Handbook of Emotions.* New York: Guilford Press.

———. 1993c. Fundamentalism for Highbrows. *University of Chicago Record* 28 (October 14): 2-5.

———. 1993d. "Why do men barbecue?" and Other Postmodern Ironies of Growing Up in the Decade of Ethnicity. *Daedalus* special issue "Children in America: Three to eleven" 122(1):279-308.

———. 1994a. You're Not Sick, You're Just in Love: Emotion As an Interpretive System. In P. Ekman and R. Davidson, eds., *The Nature of Emotions: Fundamental Questions* pp. 32-44. New York: Oxford University Press.

———. 1994b. Are Moral Intuitions Self-Evident Truths? Special Issues, Symposium on James Q. Wilson's *The Moral Sense. Criminal Justice Ethics* 13:24-31.

———. 1996a. True Ethnography: The Lore, the Law, and the Lure. In R. Jessor, A. Colby, and R. A. Shweder, eds., *Ethnography and Human Development: Context and Meaning in Social Inquiry.* Chicago, Ill.: University of Chicago Press.

———. 1996b. The View from Manywheres. *Anthropology Newsletter* 37(9):1.

———, ed. 1998. *Welcome to Middle Age! (And Other Cultural Fictions).* Chicago, Ill.: University of Chicago Press.

———. 1999a. Cultural Psychology. *MIT Encyclopedia of Cognitive Sciences.* Cambridge, Mass.: MIT Press.

———. 1999b. Why Cultural Psychology? *Ethos: Journal of the Society for Psychological Anthropology* 27:62-73.

———. 2000. From "Free Trade" to "West is Best." The University of Chicago Magazine, December, vol. 93, no. 2.

Shweder, R. A. and D. W. Fiske. 1986. Uneasy Social Science. In D. W. Fiske and R. A. Shweder, eds., *Metatheory in Social Science: Pluralisms and Subjectivities.* Chicago, Ill.: University of Chicago Press.

Shweder, R. A., J. Goodnow, G. Hatano, R. LeVine, H. Markus, and P. Miller. 1998. The Cultural Psychology of Development: One Mind, Many Mentalities. In W. Damon, ed., *Handbook of Child Psychology.* Vol. 1, *Theoretical Models of Human Development.* New York: John Wiley and Sons.

Shweder, R. A., and J. Haidt. 1993. The Future of Moral Psychology: Truth, Intuition and the Pluralist Way. *Psychological Science* 4:360–365.

———. 2000. The Cultural Psychology of the Emotions: Ancient and New. In M. Lewis and J. Haviland, eds., *The Handbook of Emotions.* 2nd ed. New York: Guilford Press.

Shweder, R. A., and R. A. LeVine. 1984. *Culture Theory: Essays on Mind, Self and Emotion.* New York: Cambridge University Press.

Shweder, R. A., M. Mahapatra, and J. G. Miller. 1987. Culture and Moral Development. In J. Kagan and S. Lamb, eds., *The Emergence of Morality in Young Children,* pp. 1–83. Chicago, Ill.: University of Chicago Press.

———. 1990. Culture and Moral Development. In J. S. Stigler, R. A. Shweder, and G. Herdt, eds., *Cultural Psychology: Essays on Comparative Human Development.* New York: Cambridge University Press.

Shweder, R. A., and J. G. Miller. 1985. The Social Construction of the Person: How Is It Possible? In K. G. Gergen and K. E. Davis, eds., *The Social Construction of the Person.* New York: Springer-Verlag. Reprinted in 1991 in R. A. Shweder, *Thinking Through Cultures.* Cambridge, Mass.: Harvard University Press.

Shweder, R. A. and N. C. Much. 1987. Determinations of Meaning: Discourse and Moral Socialization. In W. Kurtines and J. Gewirtz, eds., *Social Interaction and Socio-Moral Development,* pp. 197–244. New York: John Wiley and Sons.

Shweder, R. A., N. C. Much, M. Mahapatra, and L. Park. 1997. The "Big Three" of Morality (Autonomy, Community, Divinity), and the "Big Three" Explanations of Suffering. In A. Brandt and P. Rozin, eds., *Morality and Health,* pp. 119–169. New York: Routledge.

Shweder, R. A., and M. Sullivan. 1990. The Semiotic Subject of Cultural Psychology. In L. A. Pervin, ed., *Handbook of Personality: Theory and Research.* New York: Guilford Press.

——. 1993. Cultural Psychology: Who Needs It? *Annual Review of Psychology* 44:497–523.

Slack, A. T. 1988. Female Circumcision: A Critical Appraisal. *Human Rights Quarterly* 10:437–486.

Smedslund, J. 1991. The Pseudoempirical in Psychology and the Case for Psychologic *Psychological Inquiry* 2(4):325–338.

Solomon, R. C. 1976. *The Passions.* New York: Anchor/Doubleday.

——. 1984. Getting Angry: The Jamesian Theory of Emotion in Anthropology. In R. A. Shweder and R. A. LeVine, eds., *Culture Theory: Essays on Mind, Self and Emotion* pp. 238–254. Cambridge, England: Cambridge University Press.

Sperber, D. 1985. *On Anthropological Knowledge.* Cambridge, England: Cambridge University Press.

Spero, M. H. 1992. *Religious Objects as Psychological Structures: A Critical Integration of Object Relations Theory, Psychotherapy and Judaism.* Chicago, Ill.: University of Chicago Press.

Spiro, M. E. 1961. Social Systems, Personality and Functional Analysis. In B. Kaplan, ed., *Studying Personality Cross-Culturally.* New York: Harper and Row.

——. 1979. *Gender and Culture: Kibbutz Women Revisited.* Durham, N. C.: Duke University Press.

——. 1982. *Oedipus in the Trobriands.* Chicago, Ill.: University of Chicago Press.

——. 1986. Cultural Relativism and the Future of Anthropology. *Cultural Anthropology* 1:259–286.

——. 1987. *Culture and Human Nature: The Theoretical Papers of Melford Spiro.* Benjamin Kilbourne and L. L. Langness, eds. Chicago, Ill.: University of Chicago Press.

Stearns, C. Z. and P. N. Stearns, eds. 1988. *Emotion and Social Change: Toward a New Psychohistory.* New York: Holmes and Meier.

Stein, N. 2000. The Representation and Organization of Emotional Experience: Unfolding the Emotion Episode. In M. Lewis and J. Haviland-Jones, eds. *Handbook of Emotions,* 3rd ed. New York: Guilford Press.

Stein, N., and L. J. Levine. 1987. Thinking about Feelings: The Development and Organization of Emotional Knowledge. In R. E. Snow and M. J. Farr, eds., *Aptitude, Learning and Instruction.* Hillsdale, N.J.: Lawrence Erlbaum Associates.

Stigler, J. 1984. Mental Abacus: The Effect of Abacus Training on Chinese Children's Mental Calculation. *Cognitive Psychology* 16:145–176.

Stigler, J., L. Chalip, and K. Miller. 1986. Culture and Mathematics Learning. In E. Rothkopf, ed., *Review of Research in Education* 15:253–306.

Stigler, J., H. Nusbaum, and L. Chalip. 1988. Developmental Changes in Speed of Processing: Central Limiting Mechanisms on Shell Transfer. *Child Development* 59:1144–1153.

Stigler, J., R. A. Shweder, and G. Herdt, eds. 1990. *Cultural Psychology: Essays on Comparative Human Development.* Cambridge, England: Cambridge University Press.

Stolzenberg, N. M. 1997. A Tale of Two Villages (Or, Legal Realism Comes to Town). In I. Shapiro and W. Kymlicka, eds., *Ethnicity and Group Rights.* Nomos XXXIX. New York: New York University Press.

Strohman, R. C. 1993. Ancient Genomes, Wises Bodies, Unhealthy People: Limits of a Genetic Paradigm in Biology and Medicine. *Perspectives in Biology and Medicine* 37:112–145.

Swartz, M. J. 1988. Shame, Culture, and Status among the Swahili of Mombasa. *Ethos* 16:21–51.

Tamir, Y. 1996. Hands Off Clitoridectomy. *Boston Review* (October/November Issue), vol. 21.

Thomas, L. 2000. Ngaitana (I Will Circumcise Myself): Lessons from Colonial Campaigns to Ban Excision in Meru. In B. Shell-Duncan and Y. Hernlund, eds., *Female "Circumcision" in Africa: Culture, Controversy and Change.* Boulder, Colo.: Lynne Rienner.

Turiel, E. 1983. *The Development of Social Knowledge: Morality and Convention.* Cambridge, England: Cambridge University Press.

Veith, I. 1978. Psychiatric Foundations in the Far East. *Psychiatric Annals* 8(6):12–41.

Wadley, S. S. 1980. *The Powers of Tamil Women.* South Asia Series, no. 6. Syracuse, N.Y.: Syracuse University Press.

Wadley, S. S., and B. W. Derr. 1990. Eating Sins in Karimpur. In M. Marriott, ed., *India through Hindu Categories.* New Delhi, India: Sage.

Wadley, S. S. and D. Jacobson. 1986. *Women in India:* New Delhi, India: Manohar Publishers.

Walley, C. J. 1997. Searching for "Voices": Feminism, Anthropology, and the Global Debate over Female Genital Operations. *Cultural Anthropology* 12:405–438.

Weisner, T. S., M. Bausano, and M. Kornfein. 1983. Putting Family Ideals into Practice. *Ethos* 11:278–304.

Weisner, T., and H. Garnier. 1992. Nonconventional Family Lifestyles and School Achievement: A Twelve Year Longitudinal Study, *American Educational Research Journal* 29(3):605–632.

Werker, J. 1989. Becoming a Native Listener. *American Scientist* 77:54–59.

White, G. M., and J. Kirkpatrick. 1985. *Person, Self and Experience: Exploring Pacific Ethnopsychologies.* Berkeley, Calif.: University of California Press.

Whiting, J. W. M. 1964. Effects of Climate on Certain Cultural Practices. In W. H. Goodenough, ed., *Explorations in Cultural Anthropology.* New York: McGraw-Hill.

Whiting, J. W. M. 1981. Environmental Constraints on Infant Care Practices. In R. H. Munroe, R. L. Munroe, and B. B. Whiting, eds., *Handbook of Cross-Cultural Human Development.* New York: Garland.

Whiting, J. W. M., and I. Child. 1953. *Child Training and Personality.* New Haven, Conn.: Yale University Press.

Whorf, B. L. 1956. *Language, Thought and Reality.* Cambridge, Mass.: MIT Press.

Wierzbicka, A. 1986. Human Emotions: Universal or Culture-Specific? *American Anthropologist* 88:584–594.

———. 1989. Soul and Mind: Linguistic Evidence for Ethnopsychology and Cultural History. *American Anthropologist* 91(1):41–58.

———. 1990. Special Issue on the Semantics of the Emotions. *Australian Journal of Linguistics* 10(2).

———. 1991. *Cross-Cultural Pragmatics: The Semantics of Human Interaction.* New York: Mouton de Gruyer.

———. 1992a. Talk about Emotions: Semantics, Culture and Cognition. *Cognition and Emotion* 6(3–4):285–319.

———. 1992b. *Semantics, Culture and Cognition: Universal Human Concepts in Culture-Specific Configurations.* New York: Oxford University Press.

———. 1993. A Conceptual Basis for Cultural Psychology. *Ethos* 21:205–231.

———. 1997. *Understanding Cultures Through Their Key Words: English, Russian, Polish, German, Japanese.* New York: Oxford University Press.

———. 1999. *Emotions across Languages and Cultures: Diversity and Universals.* New York: Cambridge University Press.

Wikan, U. 1984. Shame and Honour: A Contestable Pair. *Man* 19:635–652.

———. 1989. Illness from Fright or Soul Loss: A North Balinese Culture-Bound Syndrome? *Culture, Medicine and Psychiatry* 13:25–50.

———. 1996. Culture, Power and Pain. Unpublished manuscript.

Williams, L., and T. Sobieszyzyk. 1997. Attitudes Surrounding the Continuation of Female Circumcision in the Sudan: Passing the Tradition to the Next Generation. *Journal of Marriage and the Family* 59:966–981.

Wilson, E. O. 1998. *Consilience: The Unity of Knowledge.* New York: Alfred A. Knopf.

———. 2000. How to Unify Knowledge. Keynote Address at the New York Academy of Science Conference on "The Unity of Knowledge: The Convergence of Natural and Human Science," 23 June.

Wilson, J. Q. 1993. *The Moral Sense.* New York: Free Press.

Wittgenstein, L. 1953. *Philosophical Investigations.* Oxford, England: Oxford University Press.

———. 1969. *On Certainty.* Oxford, England: Blackwell.

Yang, K. 1997. Indigenizing Westernized Chinese Psychology. In M. H.

Bond, ed., *Working at the Interface of Culture: Twenty Lives in Social Science*. London: Routledge.

Yatiswarananda, S. 1979. *Meditation and Spiritual Life*. Bangalore, India: Sri Ramakrishna Ashrama.

Zimmerman, F. 1979. Remarks on the Body in Ayervedic Medicine. *South Asian Digest of Regional Writing* 18:10–26.

Acknowledgments

Why Do Men Barbecue? Recipes for Cultural Psychology is a sequel to an earlier collection of essays titled *Thinking Through Cultures: Expeditions in Cultural Psychology* (Harvard University Press). During the decade since the publication of that book, I have been but one of many champions of the interdisciplinary study of cultural psychology. Yet I suspect I stand alone in being so fortunate as to have Lindsay Waters and Elizabeth Knoll as patient and encouraging editors, gently reminding me that this sequel is long overdue. Looking back over the rapid development of the discipline of cultural psychology during the 1990s, I would love to be able to convince myself that ten years was exactly the right amount of time to wait before selecting a new set of essays for publication. Self-deception aside, I am pleased that some of my previously published essays from the first half of the decade can now be joined with a selection of very recent work.

During the 1990s when many of these essays were written, I was a guest at three rare and remarkable institutions. In 1990–1991 I was a Visiting Scholar at the Russell Sage Foundation in New York (RSF), where I learned much about immigration and ethnicity in the United States and about New York City, and was free to pursue my own writing projects. In 1995–1996 I was a Fellow at the Center for Advanced Study in the Behavioral Sciences in Stanford, California (CASBS) and co-chair (with Hazel Markus and Paul Rozin) of a special working group on "Culture, Mind and Biology." In 1999–2000 I was a Fellow at the Wissenschaftskolleg zu Berlin (The Institute for Advanced Study in Berlin, or WIKO) where I worked on a project on "The Free Exercise of Culture" and broadened my knowledge of the social sciences and humanities in Europe. I am deeply grateful to each of those institutions and their brilliant leaders: Eric Wanner, RSF; Neil Smelser and Robert Scott, CASBS; and Wolf Lepenies, Jurgen Kocka, and Joachim Nettelbeck, WIKO. Thank you for your support of my scholarship and my writing habits. Thank you for being so tolerant during all those assumption-questioning lunch conversations and weekly seminar debates.

The 1990s were a good time for collaborative interdisciplinary research in the social sciences and I have been privileged to participate in several such collective endeavors. The Research Networks of the Health Program of the MacArthur Foundation, originated by Denis Prager and Bob Rose, are monuments in that regard. I wish to thank Bert Brim for assembling the sociologists, life-span psychologists, epidemiologists, and anthropologists who formed the membership of MIDMAC (The MacArthur Foundation Research Network on Successful Midlife Development), for including me on his research team, for broadening our intellectual horizons, and for teaching us how to live.

Of course, when one thinks of innovative interdisciplinary research planning in the social sciences, it is the Social Science Research Council (SSRC) in New York that immediately comes to mind. During the 1990s I have participated in two SSRC working groups. The first was the Working Group on Culture, Health and Human Development (initially co-chaired by Robert LeVine and Arthur Kleinman; later co-chaired by Veena Das and myself), which was supported by the MacArthur Foundation. The second is the Working Group on Ethnic Customs, Assimilation and American Law (which I co-chair with Martha Minow and Hazel Markus), which is supported by the Russell Sage Foundation. To all the participants in these interdisciplinary groups—scholars and friends from anthropology, psychology, law, sociology, political science and other disciplines—I owe a great intellectual debt. Many thanks to past and present SSRC presidents Ken Prewitt, Bert Brim, and Craig Calhoun for their support of these working groups. Special thanks to Frank Kessel, SSRC program director for both working groups, for many years of organizational nurturing and personal support.

The type of interdisciplinary work I do benefits immeasurably from the remarkable intellectual environment of the Committee on Human Development at the University of Chicago, where I have been a faculty member for twenty-nine years. The Committee on Human Development (HD) has been a Ph.D.-granting research program for over sixty years. In the late 1990s, with the support of Dean Richard Saller of the great Social Science Division of the University of Chicago, HD ascended to the status of a department in the University and began to recruit new faculty. The current mix of anthropologists, psychologists, sociologists, and biologists in the program helps explain why the field of cultural psychology is alive and well at Chicago. My love for this research and educational institution is surely apparent in my 1993 Aims of Education Address at the University of Chicago, the penultimate essay ("Fundamentalism for Highbrows") of this book.

Ancestor worship is a noble institution. So is admiration for friends, colleagues, and students. I have decided not to enumerate all the ancestral spirits, friends, colleagues, and students who have enriched my intellectual life in the 1990s, for there are so many and I would not want to leave anyone off the list. At the very least, however, I wish to acknowledge my gratitude to the co-authors of various essays in the collection: William Goldstein, Jonathan Haidt, Lene Balle-Jensen, Manamohan Mahapatra, Usha Menon, Nancy Much, and Lawrence Park. I also owe great thanks to Katia Mitova, Andrew Hostetler, and Heather Lindkvist, who have assisted me in innumerable ways in the preparation of this manuscript, and to my brilliant copyeditor Elizabeth Collins. Christine Thorsteinsson, the production editor at Harvard University Press, was not only efficient, creative, and professional but even made the process of copy reading seem like great fun. I offer this book to them all.

The original titles and publication sources of the essays in this volume are listed here. They are reprinted, with some editorial changes, with the permission of the publishers and co-authors.

Introduction. "Anti-Postculturalism (Or, The View from Manywheres)" is a composite account constructed out of several essays: (1) "Culture: Contemporary Views," reprinted from *International Encyclopedia of the Social and Behavioral Sciences*, pp. 3151–3158, © 2001 with permission from Elsevier Science; (2) "Cultural Psychology," reprinted from *International Encyclopedia of the Social and Behavioral Sciences*, pp. 3104–3110, © 2001 with permission from Elsevier Science; (3) "The Psychology of Practice and the Practice of the Three Psychologies," *Asian Journal of Social Psychology*, 3:207–222, © 2000 by Asian Association of Social Psychology. The introduction also incorporates a few paragraphs from "Why Do Men Barbecue? And Other Postmodern Ironies of Growing Up in the Decade of Ethnicity," *Daedalus*, 122(1): 279–308, © 1993 by the Russell Sage Foundation; "The View from Manywheres," Anthropology Newsletter, American Anthropological Association, December 1996; and "Globalization: From Free Trade to 'West is Best,'" *The University of Chicago® Magazine*, December, © 2000 by The University of Chicago® Magazine.

Chapter 1. "Who Sleeps by Whom Revisited: A Method for Extracting the Moral 'Goods' Implicit in Praxis." In *Cultural Practices as Context for Development*, edited by Jacqueline Goodnow, Peggy Miller, and Frank Kessel. © 1995 by Jossey-Bass.

Chapter 2. "The 'Big Three' of Morality (Autonomy, Community, and Divinity) and the 'Big Three' Explanations of Suffering." In *Morality and Health*, edited by Allan M. Brandt and Paul Rozin. © 1997 by Routledge, Inc.

Chapter 3. "The Cultural Psychology of Emotions: Ancient and New." In *Handbook of Emotions*, 2nd ed., edited by Michael Lewis and Jeannette Haviland-Jones. © 2000 by Guilford Press.

Chapter 4. "'What about Female Genital Mutilation?' And Why Understanding Culture Matters in the First Place." In *Engaging in Cultural*

Differences: The Multicultural Challenge in Liberal Democracies, edited
by Richard A. Shweder, Martha Minow, and Hazel Rose Markus.
© 2002 by the Russell Sage Foundation. Reprinted with permission. Russell Sage Foundation, 112 East 64th Street, New York, N.Y.
10021.

Chapter 5. Usha Menon and Richard A. Shweder, "The Return of the
'White Man's Burden': The Encounter between the Moral Dis-
course of Anthropology and the Domestic Life of Hindu Women."
In *Welcome to Middle Age! (And Other Cultural Fictions),* edited by
Richard A. Shweder. © 1998 by The University of Chicago Press.

Chapter 6. "Culture and Development in Our Post-Structural Age." In
Cultural Processes in Child Development, edited by A. S. Masten. (Volume 29 of Minnesota Symposium on Child Development.) © 1999
by Lawrence Erlbaum Associates.

Chapter 7. "A Polytheistic Conception of the Sciences and the Virtues of
Deep Variety." *Annals of the New York Academy of Sciences,* volume
935. © 2001 by the New York Academy of Sciences.

Chapter 8. "Fundamentalism for Highbrows: The Aims of Education Address at the University of Chicago." *The University of Chicago Record,*
October 14. © 1993 by The University of Chicago Record.

Conclusion. "From Manywheres to the Civilizing Project, and Back" is a
composite of the following essays: (1) "Moral Maps, 'First World'
Conceits and the New Evangelists," in *Culture Matters: Cultural Values and Human Progress,* edited by Lawrence Harrison and Samuel
Huntington, © 2000 by Basic Books, Inc.; (2) "On the Return of
the 'Civilizing Project'," *Daedalus,* 131(3):117–121, © 2002 American
Academy of Arts and Sciences.

Index

Abankwah, Adelaide, 211, 213
Abbott, S., 49–50
Abhivanagupta, 140–141
Accidents, 125
Accountability, 331
Adharmic acts, 120
Affective events, 155
African American families, sleeping arrangements, 49
African genital surgeries. *See* Female genital surgery
Ahmadu, Fuambai, 34–35, 169–171
Ainsworth, M., 42
American Academy of Pediatrics, 200
American folk culture, 102–103
American lies, 333
American women, life satisfaction, 220, 221
Amusement, 147, 148, 149
Ancestral spirit attack, 82
Anger, 146, 149, 161–162, 164
Anglo-American middle-class families, sleeping arrangements, 46, 47–53, 61–69

Animal phobias, 312–313
Animal souls, 104
Annas, 223–224
"Ann Landers" advice column, 51–52
Anthropology: challenges, 351–360; contemporary view of culture, 4, 9, 11–17; cultural analysis, 10; Piaget's theory and, 287–290; pluralism and, 6, 284; problem of difference, 19–20; tenets, 350. *See also* Cultural anthropology; Pluralism
"Anthropology 101," 347, 349–350, 353–354, 358
Anti-postculturalism, 1–3, 5, 6
Appalachian blue-collar families, sleeping arrangements, 49–50
Arendt, Hannah, 326–328, 339
Arrogance, 148
Artha, 122, 149
Astrophysical causal ontology of suffering, 78
Attachment, 165
Autonomy: analysis of moral discourse, 87–95; ethics of, 97, 98–99, 102, 103–105, 117–120, 133, 162, 163,

109; ethics of, 97–98, 102, 133, 162, 164, 165; feudal ethics metaphor, 106–113; personal health behaviors, 131–132; success factors, 357

Comprehensive liberalism, 196

Confucian values, 355

Confusionism, 300

Consciousness, 151

Consilience: polycentrism and, 294–300; relationship to knowledge, 300–302, 305–307; research, 291–293

Control over future events, 80

Converse, Philip, 307–309, 314

Cosmopolitan capitalist economy, 4, 21, 23

Courage, 327

Creative imagination, 16

Crisis literature: in the human sciences, 307–311; in the social sciences, 311–315

Cronbach, Lee, 312

Cross-cultural psychology, goals, 40–42

Cultural analysis, 10, 62, 290

Cultural anthropology: accusations against, 349–350; intellectual camps, 11–17, 20; sleeping arrangements, 45–46

Cultural developmentalism, 17–19

Cultural hybridity, 26

Cultural imperialism, 360. *See also* Liberalism

Cultural preferences, sleeping arrangements, 63–65

Cultural psychology: acts of meaning, 136; compared with other disciplines, 40–45; conception of culture, 135–136; defending, 360; of the emotions, 166–167; folk theories, 75; goals, 135; of morality, 35–40; others' mental states, 28–30; pluralism and, 26–28; research, 308; sleeping arrangements, 47, 55–57; views on suffering, 79–87; virtues, 44–45. *See also* Emotions; Folk psychology; Pluralism; Postmodern humanism

Cultural studies, 9

Cultural superiority, 4

Culture: common misattributions, 23–26; components of, 135–136; custom complex, 31–35; definitions, 7–8; economic issues, 354–355; Oriya moral themes, 96; psyche and, 26–28, 54–55; science and, 310; success factors, 357. *See also* Anthropology; Cultural anthropology; Morality; Western culture

Culture Counts meetings, 344–345

Culture theory: limitations, 18–19; types of, 38

Custom complex, 31–35

Customs, 96

D'Andrade, R. G., 10–11, 28, 314

Darwinian theory, 312–313

"Dear Abby" advice column, 52–53

Debate, 335, 338

"Deep" sound pattern, 315–317

Deliberate human action, 80–81

Desires, 110

Determinism, 8

Developmentalists, 20

Development economics, 18

Dharmas: goals, 122; individual *dharma,* 104, 105, 120; Oriya moral themes, 96, 239; perseverance and, 150; responsibility and, 115; sacred world metaphor, 109; of souls, 104, 105

Dhruvarajan, V., 231

Differential saliency, 100–103

Dignity. *See* Human dignity

Disciplinary matrices, 298–299

Discrimination, 120

Disgust, 147, 149, 150

Divinity: analysis of moral discourse, 87–95; attainment of, 150; discourses, 101; ethics of, 98, 102, 133, 162; sacred world metaphor, 109–113

Domesticity, 230–238

Dominance, 261

Dugger, Celia, 202

Durga, 159

Dusa, 151

Duty, 96, 106, 107, 163. *See also Dharmas;* Responsibility

Economic issues: causal explanations, 354–355; globalization, 20–23; public health issues, 123–133

Ecumenism, 359

Edgerton, Robert, 176, 187

Eichmann, Adolf, 326

Ekman, Paul, 144–145

El Dareer, Asma, 192–193

Eliot, T. S., 291, 314

Embarrassment, 136, 156, 164

Emotions: Hindu *lajja,* 156–162; "mutual yucking," 38; questions to define, 137–138; of the "Rasadhyaya," 138–153; reaction to loss, 29; research, 134–135; Sanskrit texts, 138–153; social and moral context, 162–166; suffering and, 129–130; symbolic structure of, 153–156

Emotion scripts, 154

Empathy, 143

Empowerment, 124, 136

Enlightenment story, 2, 359. *See also* French Enlightenment

Epigenetic complexity, 297

Epiphanes, Antiochus, 204

Equality Now, 213

Essentialism, 8

Ethics: Hindu worldview, 101; Oriya moral themes code, 96–100, 103–107; sacred world metaphor, 109–113. *See also* Culture; Morality

Ethnocentrism, 6, 351–352, 360

Ethnographic representation, 4, 13, 23, 84, 230–238. *See also* Cultural psychology

Ethnography of difference, 4, 5, 7, 15–16, 23

Ethnonationalism, 21

Evans-Pritchard, E. E., 24–25

Evil, 123

Fairness, 96

Family life: cultural developmentalism, 18; divinity and, 109; gender issues, 1–3, 5;

moral obligations, 106–107; polygamy, 352–354. *See also* Sleeping arrangements

Fear, 146, 149

Federal Prohibition of Female Genital Mutilation Act, 202

Feeling-tone associations, 315–317

Female genital mutilation. *See* Female genital surgery

Female genital surgery: African genital surgeries, 33–35, 210–214; cultural perspectives, 184–189; epistemic concerns, 214–216; ethnic considerations, 198–210; Federal Prohibition of Female Genital Mutilation Act, 202; historical perspectives, 189–198; legal issues, 201–204, 211–212; moral pluralism and, 177–184; research, 168–177

Feminism: identity politics, 12; views on genital alterations, 170–177. *See also* Family life; Oriya Hindu women; Women's movement

Feudal ethics, 75, 106–113

FGM. *See* Female genital surgery

First World, 4, 17–19, 23, 173–174, 189, 191–195, 199

Folk psychology: American folk culture, 102–103; causation theories, 75, 79–82; classification of emotions, 150; views on karma, 114, 116; voluntary actions and, 303

Free trade, 22

Frege, Gottlob, 311

French Enlightenment, 279–280, 323

Freud, Sigmund, 149, 191

Friendship, 330

Frijda, N., 154

Fukuyama, Francis, 341

Functionalism, 8

Fundamentalism for highbrows. *See* Liberal arts education

Gandhi, Mahatma, 328

Geertz, Clifford, 10, 28, 31, 292, 295–296, 298–300

Gender and justice in Africa, 345

Gender issues: African genital surgeries, 33–35; cultural developmentalism, 18; cultural psychology and, 27–28; custom complex, 32–33; postmodern humanism and, 2–3, 5; raising children, 1. *See also* Family life; Female genital surgery; Feminism; Oriya Hindu women

Gene-environment interactions, 296

Genetic reductionism, 297–298

Genome project, 297

Gilman, Sander, 205

Globalization: anti-cultural critics, 4; economic issues, 20–23; female genital surgery and, 172; of Western culture, 340

God-essence, 104

Goodnow, J., 31

Grammar, 336

Greenfield, P., 31

Greou, Hawa, 202

Guilt, 130

Guinier, Lani, 331

Lingaraj temple, 219
Logic, 288
Longevity, 357
Lonner, W. J., 40–41
Loyal opposition, 335, 337–338
Loyalty, 108–109, 163
Lucy, J., 31
Luhrmann, T., 31
Luo males, 212

Maasen, Sabine, 302–303
Machismo, 344–345
Mahisasura, 159
Male circumcision, 190–191, 203–204, 211–212
Markus, H., 31
Marriage, 352–354
Marriott, McKim, 147
Mead, Margaret, 1
Meadow, Bill, 329
Medical issues. *See* Public health
"Medicalized" life practices, 131
Medical Research Council Study, reproductive health consequences of female circumcision, 186–187
Meinardus, O., 189
Menon, Usha, 219–220, 270
Mental development: Piaget's theory, 276–280; poststructural themes, 280–283
Mental states, 151–152. *See also* Emotions
Merit, 96, 121
Mesquita, B., 154
Metaphysical ontology, 113–114
Mill, J. S., 79, 354–355, 356
Miller, J., 31

Miller, P., 31
Mind/body interaction, 301–307, 315–317
Modernism, 2, 323
Modesty, 136, 156
Moi, Daniel Arap, 183
Moksha, 122, 150
Monumentalism, 8
Moral causal ontology of suffering, 79
Moral emotions, 163
Moral imagination, 100–103, 105, 121–122
Morality: analysis of moral discourse, 87–95; cultural psychology of, 35–40; discourses, 100–103; karma and, 113–122; Oriya moral themes code, 95; personal effort of discrimination and judgment, 120; sleeping arrangements, 51–53, 56–60. *See also* Autonomy; Culture; Divinity; Ethics
Moral judgment, 29
Moral Majoritarians, 333
Moral pluralism, 177–184
Moral transgressions, 82–84
Mormons, 352, 353
Multiculturalism: identity politics, 12; in postmodern society, 26, 45, 343
Multiplicity, 100–103
Murdock, George Peter, 82
Muslims, marriage laws, 354
Mutual "yuck" response, 39, 177–184, 351
Mystical-aesthetic experiences, 111–112
Mythology, 116–120

Nagel, Thomas, 6
National character studies, 42–44
National Conference of Christians and Jews, 327
Nationalism, 8
Natural law, 109
Natural sciences, 294–296
Nātyaśāstra, 134, 138–153, 167
Neocolonialism, 345
Neopositivism, 14–15
Neo-Puritanism, 131
Neutrality, 341–342
New World Order, 342
Nihilism, 320
Nisbett, R., 31
Normality, 80
North American cultural anthropology, 9–11, 345
Northern European enlightenment, 342–344, 345
Northern World, 4

Obermeyer, Carla M., 168–169, 172–173, 186–188, 189, 192, 208
Objectivity, visual metaphor, 6
Obligations: ethical, 107; Hindu obligation structures, 105; Oriya moral themes, 96; sacred world metaphor, 111; transgression of, 122. *See also Dharmas;* Responsibility
Okiek women, 175
Okin, Susan Moller, 196–197
Old New Dealers, 333
Open-mindedness, 319–320, 324, 326, 333–334
Organic matter, 109

Organ pathology, 83
Orientalism, 8
Oriya Hindu women: *annas,* 223–224; cultural world, 220, 223–224, 238–242; daily routines, 218–219, 243–257, 274–275; domesticity, 230–238; family life, 257–260; joint living arrangements, 222; moral meanings of service, 243–257; phases of life, 225–230; *prauda,* 217–218; well-being, 242–243, 260–273
Oriya moral themes code, 95, 239, 241–243
Oriya sleeping arrangements, 46, 51, 56–57, 61–72
Ortner, S., 272
Osgood, Charles, 300–301

Pain. *See* Suffering
Parent-child relationships, 106–107, 114–115. *See also* Family life; Sleeping arrangements
Parish, Steven, 151, 157
Patriarchal domination, 12, 160, 184–185
Penis envy, 191
Perseverance, 147, 148, 149, 150, 165
Personal health behaviors, 131–132
Personal hygiene, 121
Personal identity, 106
Personal integrity, 132
Pharaonic circumcision, 179–180
Physiological impairment, 83
Piaget, Jean, 276–280, 283–284, 287–290
Plath, D. W., 53–55

Pluralism: anti-postcultural issues, 6–7; cultural developmentalism and, 20; female genital surgery and, 177–184; mental development and, 282–283; psyche and, 26–28; romantic discipline, 15–17; in sciences, 314–315; tolerance, 350–351. *See also* Cultural psychology

Poisoning, 82

Political correctness, 333

Political economy, 21

Political liberalism, 196

Pollitt, K., 196

Pollution, 96

Polycentrism, 294–300

Polygamy, 352–354

Popper, Karl, 310

Porter, Cole, 320

Positivism, 8, 323, 333

Postcolonial period, 356

Postmodern humanism: gender issues, 2–3, 5; intellectual roles, 335–338; language issues, 323; in liberal arts education, 318–319; pluralism and, 7. *See also* Cultural psychology; Liberalism; Pluralism; Western culture

Postmodernism, 2, 13–14, 323–324, 333, 335, 359

Postmodern liberalism. *See* Liberalism

Prauda, 217–218, 230, 242, 243–257

Premodernism, 323

Pride, 163

Primordialism, 8

Prinz, Wolfgang, 302–303

Problem of difference, 19–20

Prosperity, 356–357, 359

Protestant ethic, 356–357

Provocation, 332

Psyche, 26–28, 54–55

Psychiatry, 111–112

Psychic pluralism, 30–31

Psychic unity, 135

Psychological causal ontology of suffering, 77–78

Psychological pluralism, 26–28

Psychology: relationship to divinity, 111–112; theories, 298–299. *See also* Cultural psychology

Public health, 123–133

Puritanism, 330–338

Purity, 96

Quality of life, 22

Queens, 335, 337–338

"Queep" sound pattern, 315–317

Racism, 8

Radical skepticism, 6

Raga, 162

Ramanujan, A. K., 272

"Random catastrophe" explanation, 126–127

Rasa: components of, 152–153; facial expressions of, 144–145; of Hindu aesthetic experience, 140–142

"Rasādhyāya," 134, 138–153, 167

Rationalism, 282–283

Rawls, John, 195

Raz, Joseph, 25, 343

Redfield, Robert, 10, 28

Regret, 130

Social order, 96
Social sciences: discourses, 100; types of, 8
Sociopolitical causal ontology of suffering, 77
Somatic events, 153, 155
Sonnenschein, Hugo, 339
Sorcerers, 86
Sorrow, 146, 149. *See also* Suffering
Souls: feudal ethics and, 106, 107; individual *dharma*, 104, 105; Oriya moral themes, 96; sacred world metaphor, 110
Sound patterns, 315–317
Southern Europe, 345
Southern world, 342, 357
Soviet Union, 328
Spero, M. H., 111–112, 122
Spirituality, 96, 105, 121, 357
Stereotyping, 8, 16
Sthayi-bhava, 152
Stress, 78–79, 85
Strohman, Richard, 297
Structural adjustment process, 21–22
Subjectivism, 320
Sudan Demographic and Health Survey, 179
Suffering: causal ontology, 76–82; depersonalization of, 128; explanations of, 74–76, 86–87; karmic causes, 119–120; responsibility for, 127; theodicy and, 124. *See also* Autonomy; Community; Divinity
Suka, 162
Superstitions, 75

Theodicy, 123–133
Third World, 328, 342
Thought, modes of, 29
Tibetan community, views on suffering, 85–86
Tolerance, 350–351
Tradition, 96, 109, 330
Transcendence, 96, 104
Trustworthiness, 96
Truthfulness, 96

"Underdeveloped world," 328
Unification metaphysics, 291–293
Uniformity, 135
United States: discourse on suffering, 128–133; ethics of autonomy, 102–103; public health issues, 133; views on female genital surgery, 198–210
Unity, 295–296, 298
Universalism: others' mental states, 20; pluralistic emphasis, 38, 135; without uniformity, 350–351
Universal knowledge, 323
Universally binding rational standard, 284–285
University of Chicago. *See* Liberal arts education

Veiling, 348–349
Victimization, 125, 128–129
"View from nowhere in particular," 6
Villains, 320
Virtue, 96, 330–338

Voluntary action, 302–307
Vonnegut, Kurt, 319–320